Sites of memory, sites of mourning

Jay Winter's powerful new study of the 'collective remembrance' of the Great War offers a major reassessment of one of the critical episodes in the cultural history of the twentieth century. Using a great variety of literary, artistic, and architectural evidence, Dr Winter looks anew at the culture of commemoration, and the ways in which communities endeavoured to find collective solace after 1918. Taking issue with the prevailing 'modernist' interpretation of the European reaction to the appalling events of 1914–18, Dr Winter instead argues that what characterized that reaction was, rather, the attempt to interpret the Great War within traditional frames of reference. Tensions arose, inevitably. *Sites of memory, sites of mourning* is a profound and moving book of seminal importance for the attempt to understand the course of European history during the first half of the twentieth century.

Canto is a paperback imprint
which offers a broad range of
titles, both classic and more recent,
representing some of the best and most
enjoyable of Cambridge publishing.

Sites of memory, sites of mourning

The Great War in European cultural history

JAY WINTER

Pembroke College, Cambridge

CAMBRIDGE
UNIVERSITY PRESS

PUBLISHED BY THE PRESS SYNDICATE OF THE UNIVERSITY OF CAMBRIDGE
The Pitt Building, Trumpington Street, Cambridge, United Kingdom

CAMBRIDGE UNIVERSITY PRESS
The Edinburgh Building, Cambridge CB2 2RU, UK
40 West 20th Street, New York, NY 10011–4211, USA
477 Williamstown Road, Port Melbourne, VIC 3207, Australia
Ruiz de Alarcón 13, 28014 Madrid, Spain
Dock House, The Waterfront, Cape Town 8001, South Africa

http://www.cambridge.org

First published 1995
First paperback edition 1996
Canto edition 1998
Sixth printing 2005

Printed in the United Kingdom at the University Press, Cambridge

A catalogue record for this book is available from the British Library

Library of Congress Cataloguing in Publication data
Winter, Jay
Sites of memory, sites of mourning: the Great War in European
cultural history / Jay Winter.
    p.   cm.
ISBN 0 521 49682 9 (hardback)
1. World War, 1914–1918. 2. Europe – Civilisation – 20th century.
3. Europe – Intellectual life – 20th century. 4. Memory. I. Title.
D523.W58   1995
940.4′2 – dc20   94-44386 CIP

ISBN 0 521 49682 9 hardback
ISBN 0 521 63988 3 paperback

Cover illustration: *The Menin Road*, 1919, by
Paul Nash (1889–1946). Imperial War Museum,
London / Bridgeman Art Gallery, London.

Contents

Illustrations

Acknowledgements

The list of those without whose help this book would have been poorer is much longer than I can acknowledge here. Special thanks are due, though, to many people who have put aside their own concerns to read and reread drafts of this book. Particularly helpful were comments on the text as a whole provided by Stéphane Audoin-Rouzeau, Joanna Bourke, Elisabeth Domansky, Hilary Gaskin, Diana Goodrich, Ira Katznelson, Ken Inglis, George Mosse, Emmanuel Sivan, Barry Supple, and Marie Wood.

For comments on specific points or areas of expertise beyond me, I am grateful for the help of: Susanna Barrow, Annette Becker, Barbara Bodenhorn, Jillian Davidson, Adrian Gregory, Caroline Humphrey, Samuel Hynes, Martin Jay, Alex King, Reinhard Kosseleck, Tom Laqueur, David Lloyd, Sarah O'Brien-Twohig, Antoine Prost, and Maria Tippett. A special note of gratitude goes to Fritz Stern, teacher and friend, with whom I have been fortunate enough to walk these paths for nearly three decades.

The assistance of librarians and archivists has been both rewarding and full of friendship. Marie Wood made the Australian War Memorial a home away from home, and Irina Rens drew me into the riches of the Bibliothek für Zeitgeschichte with kindness and sympathy. Cécile Coutin at the Bibliothèque de documentation internationale contemporaine (now at the Bibliothèque de l'Arsenal), Ilena Danielson at the Hoover Institution, and Nigel Steel at the Imperial War Museum went out of their way to be helpful. If there is a war between historians and archivists, I have been blissfully ignorant of it.

The company of the Master and Fellows of Pembroke College and colleagues in the Faculty of History has been a great support; they have been liberal in providing space for thought, tolerance for its expression, and an academic home for visiting scholars working in this field. Many of the final stages of writing this book took place in the splendid setting of the Villa Serbelloni at Bellagio, and in Canberra at the Australian National University. Hospitality is an art form; some of the finest practitioners of the art have helped me finish this book. Thanks are due to them all.

My students at Cambridge have helped me in ways most do not know. They patiently and critically listened to the ideas that grew in the course of writing this book, and threw cold water more than once on overheated and ill-considered interpretations. Periods as visiting professor at the University of California at Berkeley and at Yale University provided congenial communities for the discussion of the issues in this book. Over the years librarians at the Cambridge University Library and the Pembroke College Library have borne with my requests and queries with exemplary patience.

To my colleagues at the Historial de la grande guerre at Péronne, Somme, goes a more general acknowledgement. We have been lucky enough to create our own 'site of memory', and the effort, so rewarding in and of itself, also demonstrated what collective work and commitment can mean in historical scholarship. They will know in what ways this book could not have been written without them.

For permission to reproduce copyright material held in archives I am grateful to the Archives nationales, the Bibliothèque Nationale, the Archives départementales des Vosges, the British Library, Imagérie d'Epinal, the Royal Institute of British Architects, the Australian War Memorial, and the Mortlock Library of South Australia. For permission to cite from family papers deposited in the Imperial War Museum, I am grateful to Miss Joyce Badrocke (Wakeman papers); Mr David Lloyd (Lloyd papers); Mr Len Wade (Claydon papers), and to the Trustees of the Imperial War Museum. Richard Davis has agreed kindly to permit use of material originally published in the book he jointly edited with R.J. Helmstadter, *Religion and irreligion in Victorian society* (London, Routledge, 1992).

Abbreviations

ADV	Archives départementales des Vosges
AFC	*L'art funéraire et commémoratif*
AIF	Australian Imperial Force
AN	Archives nationales
ARAC	Association Républicaine des Anciens Combattants
AWM	Australian War Memorial
BDIC	Bibliothèque de documentation internationale contemporaine
BEF	British Expeditionary Force
BN	Bibliothèque Nationale
CIAMAC	International Conference of Associations of War Wounded and War Veterans
IWM	Imperial War Museum
RCPA	Red Cross papers, Adelaide
RCPC	Red Cross papers, Canberra
WP	Wakeman papers, Imperial War Museum

Introduction

The history of the Great War is a subject of perennial fascination. In some ways the end of the twentieth century appears disturbingly close to its beginnings. We have witnessed recently the collapse of elements of the European state system and the ideological and geo-political divide which grew out of the 1914–18 conflict. The end of the 'Cold War' has brought us back not to 1939 or 1945, but in a sense to 1914. Ethnic and nationalist splits that seemed past history are painfully present today.

In other ways the chequered recent history of European integration makes even clearer the need to recall the bloody history of European disintegration. If we want to understand and ultimately to put behind us the cataclysmic record of European history in this century, we must revisit the war that set in motion these enduring centrifugal and centripetal forces, propelling us away from and towards a unified Europe.

In some respects, this historical terrain is very familiar. Whole libraries exist on the military, economic, and diplomatic history of the period. Less attention has been paid, though, to the process whereby Europeans tried to find ways to comprehend and then to transcend the catastrophes of the war. The many sites of memory and sites of mourning, both public and private, created in the wake of the conflict have never been analysed in a comparative framework. It is to these sites that we turn in this book.

Remembrance is part of the landscape. Anyone who walks through northern France or Flanders will find traces of the terrible, almost unimaginable, human losses of the war, and of efforts to commemorate the fallen. War memorials dot the countryside, in cities, towns, and villages, in market squares, churchyards, schools, and obscure corners of hillsides and fields. Scattered throughout the region are larger sites of memory: the cemeteries of Verdun, the Marne, Passchendaele, and the Somme.

Contemporaries knew these names and the terrible events that happened there all too well. The history of bereavement was universal history during and immediately after the Great War in France, Britain, and Germany. In the military service of these three countries alone, more than 4 million men died, or roughly one in six of those who served. This figure represents nearly half the total death toll in the then bloodiest war in history.[1] Among the major combatants, it is not an exaggeration to suggest that every family was in mourning: most for a relative – a father, a son, a brother, a husband – others for a friend, a colleague, a lover, a companion.

Transcendence was a privilege, not a commonplace experience. To remember the anxiety of 1,500 days of war necessarily entailed how to forget; in the interwar years those who couldn't obliterate the nightmares were locked in mental asylums throughout Europe. Most people were luckier. They knew both remembering and forgetting, and by living through both, they had at least the chance to transcend the terrible losses of war. This book is about aspects of that process.

In the years following the war, in the face of the army of the dead, the effort to commemorate went beyond the conventional shibboleths of patriotism. Yes, these millions died for their country, but to say so was merely to begin, not to conclude, the search for the 'meaning' of the unprecedented slaughter of the Great War. Even to pose that question was bound to be appallingly difficult; full of ambivalence and confusion, charged with tentativeness and more than a fragment of futility. But that search went on in all the major combatant countries from the first months of the war.

The 'traditional' and the 'modern'

Current interpretations of the cultural history of the Great War focus on two basic components of that process of understanding. The first is encapsulated in the term 'modern memory'.[2] It describes the creation of a new language of truth-telling about war in poetry, prose, and the visual arts. 'Modernism',[3] thus defined, was a cultural phenomenon, the work of elites whose legacy has touched millions. It had sources in the pre-war period, but flowered during and after the 1914–18 conflict. As Samuel Hynes has argued, the war turned back the clock on cultural experimentation at home. But at the same time, soldier-writers brought the 'aesthetics of direct experience' to bear on imagining the war in a way far removed from the 'lies' or 'Big Words' of the older generation which sent them to fight and die in France and Flanders. Their vision paralleled that of the non-combatant modernists – Eliot, Pound, Joyce – whose break with literary tradition seemed so valid after the upheaval of the war.[4]

The second way of understanding the war entails what many modernists rejected: patriotic certainties, 'high diction'[5] incorporating euphemisms about battle, 'glory', and the 'hallowed dead', in sum, the sentimentality and lies of wartime propaganda. Some modernists, notably the Italian futurists, struck nationalist poses during the war; most were more ambivalent about the war. But the power of patriotic appeals derived from the fact that they were distilled from a set of what may be called 'traditional values' – classical, romantic, or religious images and ideas widely disseminated in both elite and popular culture before and during the war. It is this set of values and the languages in which they were expressed which I call the 'traditional' approach to imagining war.[6]

Of course, both the 'modernist' and the 'traditional' forms of imagining the war were evident long before the Armistice. Furthermore, the distinction was at times more rhetorical than real. Modernists didn't obliterate traditions; they stretched, explored, and reconfigured them in ways that alarmed conventional artists, writers, and the public at large. Frequently that shock to the cautious was part of the programme of modernist art and literature,[7] but it is important to bear in mind the continuing affinities between avant-garde artists and mainstream styles and modes of thought.[8]

This book attempts to go beyond the cultural history of the Great War as a phase in the onward ascent of modernism. This now fashionable and widely accepted interpretation will not stand scrutiny, primarily for two reasons. First, the rupture of 1914–18 was much less complete than previous scholars have suggested. The overlap of languages and approaches between the old and the new, the 'traditional' and the 'modern', the conservative and the iconoclastic, was apparent both during and after the war. The ongoing dialogue and exchange among artists and their public, between those who self-consciously returned to nineteenth-century forms and themes and those who sought to supersede them, makes the history of modernism much more complicated than a simple, linear divide between 'old' and 'new' might suggest.

Secondly, though, the identification of the 'modern' positively with abstraction, symbolic representation, and an architectural exploration of the logical foundations of art, and negatively through its opposition to figurative, representational, 'illusionist', naturalistic, romantic, or descriptive styles in painting and sculpture,[9] is so much a part of cultural history, that it is almost impious to question it. But question it we must. What is at issue is both whether such a distinction is accurate and whether it contributes to an understanding of the cultural consequences of the Great War. On both counts, I dissent from the 'modernist' school.

Equally sacrosanct is the view that there was a 'modernist' moment in literary history, beginning in the 1860s, maturing before 1914, but coming of age after the Great War.[10] 'Modernism', one literary scholar tells us, 'is part of the historical process by which the arts have dissociated themselves from nineteenth-century assumptions, which had come in the course of time to seem like dead conventions.' In this process, the war of 1914–18 had both a crystallizing and a hastening effect.[11] A second literary historian has added: 'The Great War created one world by freeing us from that old one.'[12] A third view is that the war 'uncovered' the 'decay' of Edwardian values,[13] and helped provoke a rejection of what had gone before, 'two gross of broken statues', 'a few thousand battered books', the cultural artefacts of what Pound called 'an old bitch gone in the teeth', 'a botched civilization'.[14]

The iconoclastic element in 'modernism', 'a rage against prevalent traditions',[15] is taken frequently as its chief defining feature. Artist and audience are separated at times by an almost unbridgeable gulf. Gone is the comfort of conventional art and literature, for example, the safe, sentimental narrative of Dickens' prose or the warm embrace of the yellows and greens in Monet's water lilies. In its place are the harsher disciplines and forms of Joyce and Picasso, and the paradoxical, esoteric, fractured images of a host of their contemporaries.[16] They offered, in the words of T.S. Eliot, 'something stricter' than conventional art, as a means 'of controlling, of ordering, of giving a shape and a significance to the immense panorama of futility and anarchy which is contemporary history'. Eliot wrote this essay in 1923, a year after the publication of James Joyce's *Ulysses*. In that work, Stephen Dedalus 'complains that history is a nightmare from which he is trying to awake'.[17] In the same spirit, two critics writing in the 1970s argued that 'Modernism is our art; it is the one art that responds to the scenario of our chaos' defined in many ways, but marked indelibly by 'the destruction of civilization and reason in the First World War'.[18] Once again, this book offers a dissenting point of view on these widely held convictions about the location of the 1914–18 war within European cultural history.

That some aspects of twentieth-century art and literature are revolutionary goes without saying. It seems equally inoffensive to identify modernism as both an 'aesthetic project' – an exploration of the foundations of art – and a 'cultural force' – a critical and powerful commentary on contemporary events.[19] What is more difficult to accept is that 'modernism' – more a temperament than a set of fixed beliefs – left behind as neatly and surgically as some scholars suggest the host of images and conventions derived from eighteenth and nineteenth-century religious, romantic, or classical traditions.[20] Furthermore, those outside the 'modernist' canon, whose work I shall explore in later chapters – Kipling, Lutyens, Käthe Kollwitz – were hardly as banal and barren of innovation as this argument has it. Lutyens' Cenotaph was described by one champion of modernism as 'derivative popular modern architectural sculpture. Not being an original work it has no intrinsic value.'[21]

It is the very teleology of this position – the search for precursors or exponents of what later critics have admired or rejected – which makes the 'modernist' hypothesis about the cultural history of the early twentieth century just as misleading as other tendentious interpretations of recent or not so recent history. To array the past in such a way is to invite distortion by losing a sense of its messiness, its non-linearity, its vigorous and stubbornly visible incompatibilities.

The history of the Great War and its aftermath is full of them, and one purpose of this book is to go beyond the so-called modernist/traditionalist divide to a more sophisticated appreciation of the way Europeans imagined the war and its terrible consequences. I do so by concentrating primarily on aspects of one particular theme in the cultural history of the war: the theme of mourning and its private and public expression.

Tradition and the mediation of bereavement

The Great War brought the search for an appropriate language of loss to the centre of cultural and political life.[22] In this search, older motifs took on new meanings and new forms. Some derived them from classical strophes. Others explicitly elaborated religious motifs, or explored romantic forms. This vigorous mining of eighteenth and nineteenth-century images and metaphors to accommodate expressions of mourning is one central reason why it is unacceptable to see the Great War as the moment when 'modern memory' replaced something else, something timeworn and discredited, which (following contemporaries) I have called 'tradition'.

It is the fundamental argument of this book that the enduring appeal of many traditional motifs – defined as an eclectic set of classical, romantic, or religious images and ideas – is directly related to the universality of bereavement in the Europe of the Great War and its aftermath. The strength of what may be termed 'traditional' forms in social and cultural life, in art, poetry, and ritual, lay in their power to mediate bereavement. The cutting edge of 'modern memory', its multi-faceted sense of dislocation, paradox, and the ironic, could express anger and despair, and did so in enduring ways; it was melancholic, but it could not heal.[23] Traditional modes of seeing the war, while at times less challenging intellectually or philosophically, provided a way of remembering which enabled the bereaved to live with their losses, and perhaps to leave them behind.

Facets of the cultural history of mourning

Catastrophe and consolation

There is no alternative to starting with the palpable shock of the catastrophe of the war. I begin with a scene from the 1919 Abel Gance film *J'accuse*, in which the dead arise and return home to see if their sacrifice has been in vain. This terrifying metaphor had an all too material reality. The question of finding the dead, gathering their remains in cemeteries or bringing them home, was posed in all combatant countries and answered in very different ways. Some of those answers are addressed in chapters 2–4, where we follow those in mourning from the shock of discovery, through the painful effort to understand what had happened, to the acceptance of their loss.

I begin with the families that suffered the losses, and with the multiple forms of associational life which had as their focus the commemoration of the dead and assistance to those they had left behind. I then consider the history of spiritualism – a reaching out of the living towards the dead, and metaphorically of the dead towards the living – which spread rapidly in this period. Then I turn to the history of war memorials, both during the war and in its aftermath, both at home and in military cemeteries.

Almost all towns and villages in the major European combatant countries were, in another sense, communities of the bereaved. Primary mourners – those directly related to the men who died in the war – numbered in the tens of millions. The construction, dedication, and repeated pilgrimages to war memorials in the interwar years provided a ritual expression of their bereavement, and that of their local communities. The grief of widows, orphans, parents, friends was 'seen' at the annual commemorative ceremonies, and, to a degree we will never know, their loss was shared by their neighbours and friends. Community here had a very local character, some of whose rich variety I discuss in chapter 4.

There is considerable evidence of the power of traditional modes of commemoration within communities, from small groups of men and women in family circles, to séances, to those gathered in more conventional forms of religious worship, to universities, ex-servicemen's associations, widows' organizations, to communities unveiling war memorials, and finally, to the 'imagined community' of the nation itself.[24] How to accept the shock of the war, how to remember the 'Lost Generation', were questions with disturbing communal and political repercussions; and in this part of the book I examine ways in which different groups of people tried to answer them.

The history of mourning discloses much about social solidarities in the wake of the war. Yes, in some ways, the Great War brought brutality into the centre of social life. But brutalization was not the only or even the dominant response in many quarters. Compassion was there too, and deserves to be recognized as an essential component in the process of recovery from the war.[25]

Cultural codes and languages of mourning

In the second part of the book, I explore a number of ways in which the search for a language of mourning went on during and after the Great War. The evidence presented deals primarily with Britain, France, and Germany. Chapter 5 locates the cinematic visions of war, with which the book started, in an older tradition of popular religious art. I examine film as a language of aesthetic redemption, and present what was, for the time, a very modern, cinematic way of 'seeing' the dead. Here the most 'modern' techniques are used to present ancient motifs and images about sacrifice, death, and resurrection.

Gance's film is a remarkable mixture of two visions of war: the first is full of conventional romanticism; the second supersedes it by imagining the Apocalypse. I find in this film two facets of the romantic temperament confronting the problem of mourning the dead of the Great War. In the fifth and sixth chapters I trace these responses, initially, through the self-conscious naiveté of the French graphic art tradition of *l'imagerie d'Epinal* and similar modes of expression drawing on popular piety and religion; and then, through the apocalyptic visions of artists who reflected on the war and who, in very different ways, resurrected the dead.

I then approach the problem of the search for appropriate languages of mourning from other perspectives: those of war literature, in fiction, plays, and poetry. Here too 'seeing' the war meant more a return to older patterns and themes than the creation of new ones. Among the most powerful was the reformulation of the sacred, as an exploration of apocalyptic themes in prose, or as a poetic language of communication about and with the dead.

Aspects of cultural history: the Great War in the twentieth century

My primary aim here is to explore the complex impact of the 1914–18 war on European cultural history by focusing on one and only one central theme: the form and content of mourning for the dead of the Great War. I make no claim to present a *tour d'horizon* of the effect of the Great War on systems of representation of gender, social groups, or nations.[26] It would also be misleading to assert that I have presented a comprehensive history of mourning practices in Britain, France, and Germany. Such a task is beyond the scope of this inquiry.[27]

Instead I take the reader on a journey past a number of 'sites of memory'. The physical, emotional, and artistic artefacts we pass testify to the catastrophic character of the Great War and to the multifaceted effort of the survivors to understand what had happened both to their lives and to those who had died in the war. These facets of cultural history are no more than that: they are neither representative nor exhaustive; instead they are meant to suggest the dimensions of the disaster and the search for a language within which to try to find some meaning in it. My claim is that many were still able to do so after the Great War; the task was infinitely harder after 1945.

I have reformulated the question to what extent was the Great War a moment of discontinuity in cultural history, by reference to the history of bereavement. My emphasis is on the enduring character of what I have termed 'traditional' languages of mourning. But I recognize as equally true that the 1914–18 war was, if not the end of one phase of European cultural history, at least the beginning of the end. In contrast to the post-1918 period, the rupture of language and imagery which followed the Second World War was profound and enduring.

Continuities and discontinuities: 1939 and 1914

This book has focused on continuities in the cultural history of three combatant countries in the period surrounding the Great War: Britain, France, and Germany. But even in these three cases, by no means all 'traditional' languages survived the 1914–18 war and its aftermath intact. Slowly but surely, expressions of patriotism, or inhumanly idealized images of combat, suffering, and death as 'glory', began to fade away. It is true that, because of the 1914–18 conflict and popular understanding of its costs and uncertain outcome, the outbreak of war in 1939 was not greeted with patriotic bravado. Partly this was a result of the newsreels of the 1930s, and the knowledge, drawn from the Spanish Civil War, they spread about air raids and civilian casualties. But as Samuel Hynes has shown, by the 1930s the 'Big Words' – duty, honour, country – had a hollow ring for many people who had never read the war poets. The Dean of Durham, Hensley Henson, noted that clerical patriotism had to be muted in 1939; the patriotic lexicon of 1914 could no longer be used in the same way as before. Romantic notions about war did indeed take a battering during the 1914–18 war, and some wartime and postwar literature helped to discredit them further.

Nevertheless, in 1939 war could still be justified. What had changed in Western European culture was that the days of its glorification were over.[28] Whatever was true in Nazi Germany, Fascist Italy, and (after June 1941) the Soviet Union, the rest of European society greeted war as the abomination that it was.

The men and women who went to war in 1939 knew more about the cruelties of modern warfare than did the generation of 1914. They enlisted or supported the men in uniform without much patriotic fanfare, in part because they felt they had no other choice. But when the time came to mourn fallen soldiers, many of the survivors tried to use the sombre languages and forms which derived from the memory of the Great War. After 1945 the names of the fallen were added to communal war memorials, and in Britain it is the poetry of the 1914–18 war which is still intoned to recall the 'Lost Generation' of both world conflicts.

1945 and after

There is a sense in which the dead of the two world wars formed one community of the fallen. But in time both the political character of the Second World War and some of its horrific consequences made it impossible for many survivors to return to the languages of mourning which grew out of the 1914–18 war when they tried to express their sense of loss after 1945.

The sources of this rupture are not hard to find. Many of the commemorative forms created after 1918 were intended to warn; when the warning was not heard, when the Nazis forced war upon reluctant Western European democracies in 1939, that message of hope, of using the witness of those who had suffered during the war to prevent its recurrence, was bound to fade away.[29]

Warfare too had changed. In the 1939–45 conflict, more than half of the approximately 50 million people who died directly as a result of hostilities were civilians; and the ways millions of innocent people perished were new. The nuclear bombardment of Hiroshima and Nagasaki was new. So was the extermination of the Jews of Europe, an act with affinities to earlier mass atrocities, but which transcended them in method, character, and scale. Both of these catastrophes raised the possibility that the limits of language had been reached; perhaps there was no way adequately to express the hideousness and scale of the cruelties of the 1939–45 war.[30]

Those doubts were present both during and after the Great War, but a host of writers, sculptors, poets, and others stilled them – at least for a time – to create some enduring works of art and monuments to those who died in war. After Hiroshima and Auschwitz, the earlier commemorative effort simply could not be duplicated. As Julia Kristeva has observed, the Second World War undermined the very symbols through which meaning – any meaning – could be attached to the 'cataclysm' of war.[31]

The Second World War helped to put an end to the rich set of traditional languages of commemoration and mourning which flourished after the Great War. Before 1939, before the Death Camps, and the thermonuclear cloud, most men and women were still able to reach back into their 'traditional' cultural heritage to express amazement and anger, bewilderment and compassion, in the face of war and the losses it brought in its wake. If this book has drawn attention to their achievement, so human and so sad, then in part it will have realized its aim.

Towards a comparative cultural history of the Great War

A few words may be useful at this point to indicate the principles of selection and presentation of evidence used in this book. Cultural history suffers from two different problems. The first is that it tends towards eclecticism. Instances are chosen at random to indicate features of cultural life, without any attempt to establish significance or affinities. The second is too narrow a focus on canonical texts, the works of 'high culture' which, in an older Germanic tradition, are said to describe the 'spirit' of the age.

This study tries to avoid the scattered approach of eclecticism and the too-restrictive approach of *Geistesgeschichte* through an exploration of the comparative method. In other words, each chapter examines a theme in cultural history, based on evidence drawn whenever possible from all three countries' histories. Evidence has been selected to highlight comparative points, either with respect to national peculiarities or to cultural convergences. Where relevant, the history of non-European combatant countries forms part of the story.

The comparative approach is the only way to break out of cultural history limited by national perspectives. The rise of Hitler and a set of methodological problems stated by Max Weber at the turn of the century still dominate the agenda of German cultural history. In France, what might be described as the civic culture of the Third Republic is the focus of much important research. Here the study of *Les lieux de mémoire*, a seven-volume library of cultural history edited by Pierre Nora, is entirely restricted to French evidence.[32] Incidents and artefacts are analysed with respect and affection in the search for some ineffable quality called 'Frenchness'. A certain antiquarian and reverential tone dominates this work, which abjures any attempt at systematic analysis or even assortment of the cornucopia of images and texts so lavishly presented. Much of this work is original; some brilliant; and in the *Annales* tradition, Pierre Nora and his colleagues have helped to expand further the range of evidence which historians must consult. I have gained much from this extraordinary project, but my 'sites of memory' are other than Nora's. First, they are international; secondly, they are comparative; thirdly, they are there for their value in answering specific historical questions related to the cultural consequences of the 1914–18 war. That is why my 'sites of memory' are also 'sites of mourning'.

Note too that this book makes no pretence as to the exhaustiveness of the material presented on this vast subject. We cannot visit *the* sites of memory in several lifetimes. Instead this journey through the cultural history of Europe in the early twentieth century stops at places which tell us about the common history of mourning, which is inextricably linked with the common history of war.

National styles have limited the usefulness of much Anglo-American research as well. Many of the pioneering studies on modernism in literature are based primarily on British sources or on North American literary theory. The work of Northrop Frye, for example, has been profoundly important in this field.[33] The problem remains, though, that interpretations of 'modern memory' – as global a term as one can find – are rarely examined in a comparative perspective. Once this is done, the distorting effects of a narrowly national approach become apparent.

The exploration of mourning and remembrance during and after the Great War discloses striking convergences in the experience of loss and the search for meaning in all combatant countries. For this reason, this book ends with some thoughts on a sketch by Paul Klee, entitled *Angelus Novus*. The drawing grew out of a caricature of Kaiser Wilhelm II as the 'iron eater'. But Klee's search for the meaning of history did not end with this national stereotype. Instead, he transformed the image into the angel of history, a transcendental figure whose gaze embraces us all.[34] The *Angelus Novus* evokes our admiration for Klee's genius. Perhaps his angel can also encourage us to accept his challenge: the challenge to leave behind national boundaries and to keep searching beyond them.

Part I
Catastrophe and consolation

1
Homecomings: the return of the dead

The army of the dead

Let us begin with one of the most powerful and haunting visions of the Great War. It is the final sequence of Abel Gance's film *J'accuse*, made in 1918–19. The hero, Jean Diaz, a wounded soldier-poet, begins to lose his mind. He escapes from hospital, and reaches his village. There he summons the villagers and tells them of a dream. The dream as we see it starts in a battlefield graveyard with wooden crosses all askew. A huge black cloud rises behind it and, magically, ghostlike figures emerge from the ground. They are wrapped in tattered bandages, some limping, some blind walking with upraised arms, some stumbling like Frankenstein's monster. They leave the battlefield and walk down the rural lanes of France to their villages. Their aim is to see if their sacrifices had been in vain. What they find is the pettiness of civilian life, the advantage being taken of soldiers' businesses, the infidelity of their wives. The sight of the fallen so terrifies the townspeople that they immediately mend their ways, and the dead return to their graves, their mission fulfilled. After recounting this dream, the poet, now totally mad, accuses the sun above of standing idly by and watching the war go on. Then he dies.[1]

This sequence of the dead rising from their graves is one of the great scenes of the early cinema. Its force is made even more poignant when we realize that most of the men we see on the screen were actual French soldiers lent to Gance by the French army to play in this film. Gance's assistant in this film was the poet Blaise Cendrars, a Swiss-born veteran of the French Foreign Legion who lost his right arm fighting with the Legion's 'Moroccan Division' in Champagne in September 1915.[2] He can be seen clearly, the bandages around his stump unravelling, leaning on the shoulder of Jean Diaz, played by Severin Mars. Cendrars survived, but many of the soldiers in earlier scenes of Gance's film had returned to the front in the last months of the war and had been killed. Gance himself noted that some of those playing the dead in his film soon became the dead. Representation and reality had become one.[3]

1. Before the Dead arise, in a scene from the film *J'accuse* (1919)

2. The Return of the Dead, in a scene from the film *J'accuse* (1919). Cendrars is in the centre, leaning on Severin Mars.

This terrifying and profoundly moving moment, when on film the dead came home to judge the living, is unlike any other in the history of wartime propaganda. At the very end of the 1914–18 conflict, Gance's film brought to the cinema a vision of war in which the dead were the central figures. This is what turned it from a celebration of patriotic certainties into the exploration of eternal themes of love, death, and redemption.

Gance returned to the theme of the resurrection of the dead of the Great War in his second version of *J'accuse*, made in 1937. This time the hero, once more called Jean Diaz, is the sole survivor of his unit, the 'Death Patrol', sent out near Mort-Homme at Verdun on a pointless mission on the last day of the war in 1918. Only his moans save him from being buried with his comrades, who died for nothing. In effect, Diaz rises from the dead to be their spokesman, their emissary to those who don't know what war is.

Diaz is a scientist who works in a glass factory. To prevent another war, he invents an impenetrable form of armour, 'steel glass' so powerful that it would make war impossible. He keeps it as his secret weapon against war, but alas, it is stolen by a venal ex-serviceman and pillar of the *anciens combattants*, and put into the military arsenals of the day. The only way the hero can stop the outbreak of war is to go back to Verdun and raise the dead of the Great War from their graves. In a scene of epic grandeur, he gathers up the storm clouds at the vast military cemetery at Douaumont, and recalls the dead of all armies from their eternal sleep: 'My twelve million friends killed in the war, I call you.' They rise and terrify the populations of Europe into forming a world government and putting an end to war for ever. But before this happens, evil and fear still fester. Diaz's Christlike mission ends, as it must, in his death, burned at the stake – appropriately at the foot of a war memorial – by the ignorant masses who failed to see that war must never happen again. This last sacrifice, preceding the final triumph of peace, took place at Douaumont, near Verdun, where the hero had fought and had nearly died two decades before.

Gance's apocalyptic reveries are celebrated moments in the history of the cinema. His images of the return of the fallen were far from unique, though very few who worked in film so powerfully captured the almost unendurable sense of mass death in war which pervaded European society from 1914. That cloud of grief, and its expression in European culture, are the subject of this book.

I want to sketch some of the ways in which Europeans imagined the postwar world as composed of survivors perched on a mountain of corpses. How to relate to the fact of mass death, how to transcend its brutal separations and cruelties, were universal dilemmas. How artists, politicians, soldiers, and ordinary people understood them, imagined them, dreamed about them, feared them, tells us much about the cultural consequences of the Great War.

Death of a poet

To start with Gance's *J'accuse* is to bring to the fore the theme of the return of the dead, a return longed for, dreamed of, dreaded, and both physically and symbolically realized in many parts of Europe after the Great War. The context of the film and the powerful notions it evoked are, therefore, much broader than may be apparent at first sight. As in the work of many other artists, Gance's power derived from his ability to express sentiments about the tragedy of the war shared by millions of his contemporaries.

The filmic art of Abel Gance touched on a theme, the return of the dead, which transformed melodrama into myth. I am primarily interested in the way that myth emerged during the Great War, and the subsequent forms in which it was expressed. But the events surrounding the making of *J'accuse* in 1918 also shed light on other key issues in the cultural history of the war. Among them is the often cited impact of war on the emergence of 'modernism', however defined.

It is my contention that the war gave a new lease of life to a number of traditional languages expressed both conventionally and in unusual and modern forms. One such form was cinema, the most modern vehicle for the delivery to mass audiences of timeless messages.

The false antithesis of the 'moderns' and the 'ancients' was a theme well known to contemporary experimental avant-garde artists. Among them was the poet Guillaume Apollinaire. He is in *J'accuse*, amongst the dead, though not by name. Born Wilhelm de Kostrowitsky, of mixed Italian and Polish Catholic ancestry, Apollinaire (as he became known) was one of the great avant-garde poets of the pre-war years. He introduced Braque to Picasso in 1907, and spent years announcing the virtues of cubism. He was a young rebel, but not the enemy of tradition. A volunteer in 1914, and rewarded later with French citizenship, he was wounded in the head in 1916. In the poem 'La jolie rousse' ('the pretty redhead'), written after Apollinaire was wounded, he asks his elders for forgiveness for the sins of the young rebels. They are not the enemies of tradition, but exuberant spirits who 'want to bequeath to you vast and strange domains'. He asks not for the downfall of the old, but for its renewal, and above all for pity. He begs those of an older generation to take

> Pity on us who are always fighting on the frontiers
> Of limitlessness and the future
> Pity our mistakes pity our sins[4]

Pity is a word appropriate to the circumstances of Apollinaire's death. After surviving combat, a head wound, trepanning, and military

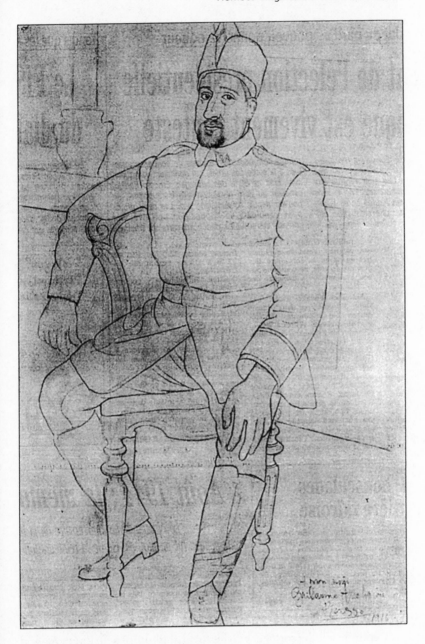

3. *Portrait of Apollinaire*, by Picasso (1916)

medicine, Apollinaire was struck down in the last days of the war by the 'Spanish flu'. Blaise Cendrars tells of the poet's death. Cendrars was then in the midst of filming *J'accuse* with Gance in Nice. He went north to Paris to arrange for film clips and other items for the set. There he bumped into Apollinaire on Sunday 3 November 1918. They lunched at Montparnasse and spoke of 'the subject of the day, the epidemic of Spanish flu which had more victims than did the war'. Five days later, Cendrars passed the *concierge* of Apollinaire's building, who told him that his tenant had caught the flu. Cendrars bounded up the stairs, and was met by Apollinaire's wife Jacqueline. She too was ill, but not as bad as her husband, who was 'all black' and still. Cendrars rushed to get a doctor, who said it was too late to help Apollinaire. The following evening, Saturday 9 November, he died.[5]

According to Cendrars, the burial was held on Wednesday 13 November. He has left an unforgettable account of it, one which touches the themes of *J'accuse* in unanticipated ways. Cendrars told an interviewer in 1950 that he was still disturbed by memories of the burial of Apollinaire. For Cendrars, Apollinaire inhabited not the kingdom of the dead, but the kingdom of the shadows.[6] Why? Because 'I had such an experience at the burial that after 32 years I still have trouble believing that he is dead.' What had happened?

The final absolution having been given, the casket of Apollinaire left the church of St Thomas Aquinas, draped in a flag, Guillaume's lieutenant's helmet on the tricolor, among the flowers and wreaths. A guard of honour, a squad of soldiers, arms at their sides, led the slow convoy, the family behind the carriage, his mother, his wife, in their mourning veils, poor Jacqueline, who had escaped the epidemic which had taken Guillaume, but who was still weak, the intimate friends of Apollinaire, Prince Jaztrebzoff, Serge, his sister, Baron d'Oettingen, Max Jacob, Picasso, all the other friends of Guillaume, including Pierre-Albert Birot and his wife who had given everything to stage *The Breasts of Tiresias* in the Maubel Theatre, all of literary Paris, Paris of the arts, the press. But as it reached the corner of Saint-Germain, the cortège was besieged by a crowd of noisy celebrants of the Armistice, men and women with arms waving, singing, dancing, kissing, shouting deliriously the famous refrain of the end of the war:
No, you don't have to go, Guillaume
No you don't have to go . . .
That was too much. And behind me, I heard the old glories of the end of symbolism, all the 'immortal' poets forgotten today, chattering, discussing the future of poetry, what young poets will do after the death of Apollinaire and rejoicing, as if they had come to celebrate victory in the battle of the Ancients and the Moderns. That was awful and I felt anger, indignation come over me.[7]

Cendrars left the cortège with his lover and future wife Raymone and the soldier-artist Fernand Léger. They had a warm drink to protect themselves against the flu. Then they took a taxi to the cemetery of Père

Lachaise in northeast Paris, only to find that the funeral was over, and Apollinaire's friends were leaving. They asked directions to the grave, and started searching among the headstones. They stumbled into two fresh graves, to the annoyance of the gravediggers. At times they seemed to be in Elsinore, not Paris. They asked the way, but though the gravediggers were decent men, they were of little help:

'You understand, with the flu, with the war, they don't tell us the names of the dead we put in the ground. There are too many.' . . . But I said, he was a Lieutenant, Lieutenant Guillaume Apollinaire or Kostrowitsky. We have to fire a salvo over his tomb! – 'My dear sir', the head of the gravedigging team answered me, 'there were two salvoes. There were two lieutenants. We don't know which one you are looking for. Look for yourselves.'[8]

They saw a grave with a bit of frozen earth nearby exactly in the shape of Apollinaire's head, with grass for hair around the scar where he had been trepanned. 'The psychisme was so intense, that one did not believe one's eyes.'

We were stunned . . . We left the cemetery, where already a thick glacial mist was enveloping the tombs and the cemetery, and said; 'It was he. We saw him. Apollinaire isn't dead. Soon he will appear. Don't forget what I tell you.'[9]

This surrealistic scene took place near the grave of Allan Kardec, the founder of French spiritualism. Cendrars and the other mourners passed the motto on Kardec's grave. It says: 'To be born, to die, to be born again and to progress without end. That is the law.'

'It was fantastic', Cendrars said. 'Paris celebrating. Apollinaire lost. I was full of melancholy. It was absurd.' He returned to the question which obsessed him: 'Under what mask will Guillaume return to the great celebration in Paris?'[10]

Eight days later, Cendrars returned to Nice to complete the work he had begun on Gance's *J'accuse*. He recruited a number of wounded soldiers, known as *les gueules cassées* (the smashed faces) to play the dead in the fourth part of the film, the section on 'The return of the dead'. Then Cendrars joined the dead himself. This is how Cendrars described his work in the final stages of the film:

in *J'accuse*, I did everything: troubleshooter, props, electrician, costume and stage designer, producer, cameraman, assistant director, chauffeur, accountant, cashier and in the scene 'The dead return', I became a Maccabee, covered in horses' blood because I had to lose my arm a second time in the interests of the scene. You know the song:
When Jean Renaud went to war
Holding his guts in his hand . . .
That was cinema![11]

The personal impressions Cendrars brought to *J'accuse* were inscribed in a new and revised scenario of the film. In 1922, Gance re-edited it, and incorporated a powerful image, which went straight to the heart of Cendrars' experience. Gance added a scene which had not happened before the Armistice. On 14 July 1919, a victory parade traversed the Champs Elysées in Paris. Foch, Joffre, Pétain, Clemenceau were there. But leading the way, and changing the entire tone of the occasion were the *mutilés de guerre*. What had started as a victory celebration turned into a sombre moment of mass mourning.[12]

Three years later, Gance took film footage of this event and added another element to it. While the living soldiers defiled through the Arc de Triomphe, the army of the dead marched *above* it, in every sense *au dessus de la mêlée*. Apollinaire had come back, together with a million other men. What Cendrars had seen in Père Lachaise cemetery, what countless men and women had imagined in these immediate postwar years, Gance captured in cinematic form. It is an image to which I shall return.

Homecomings

Gance's film characterized a broad cultural response to the disaster of the Great War. The return of the dead was treated through allegory, metaphor, and allusion. I will sketch some of these figurative approaches in later chapters, but first I want to emphasize that there was a matter-of-fact dimension to this issue, of which everyone touched by the war was aware. The problem was where and how to bury the dead of the war.

The incident surrounding the burial of Guillaume Apollinaire captures the moment. The mix of despair and delirium in the celebration of victory suggests something of the manic, melancholic nature of the Armistice of 1918. Cendrars' sense that a fresh grave somehow resembled Apollinaire's profile, that he wasn't really dead, indicates the power of denial, the retention of hope in a loved one's survival, even if only in metaphoric form. So many others had no known grave that the possibility did indeed exist that they were still alive.[13] But for most people, such hope faded rapidly, and all that was left was finding and honouring the grave of a loved one. Here too Cendrars' difficulty in finding Apollinaire once in Père Lachaise cemetery paralleled the problems millions had in locating their dead and in making the pilgrimage to their graves.[14]

The cultural history of the Great War was not only a matter of representations; real bodies were there in every theatre of military operations. Real friends and families in their millions mourned their loss, and wanted to give them a final, dignified resting place. That task was fraught with difficulty. How it was achieved tells us much about patterns of mourning and remembrance in the aftermath of the war.

By 1918 there were thousands of *ad hoc* cemeteries in northern France and Flanders (and elsewhere), and the remains of millions of dead soldiers, both identified and unknown, were scattered over vast tracts of land. In 1915 the French government agreed to finance the creation of an archipelago of military cemeteries, and to enlarge existing cemeteries at state expense for the burial of soldiers.[15] Initially the French government agreed to look after the burial of Allied soldiers too, but in 1916 the British decided to separate their commemorative work from the French. Initially as the Prince of Wales' Committee for the Maintenance of Military Tombs,[16] later as the Imperial (now Commonwealth) War Graves Commission, a separate organization was formed to deal with the creation of cemeteries to house British, Imperial, and Dominion war dead. With some exceptions, none was to return home.[17]

The creation of cemeteries for French war dead was a more complicated matter. Civilian graves were used, and civilian authorities sought compensation for loss of space.[18] The final disposition of the war dead was undecided. They were buried in separate cemeteries, in civilian cemeteries in the 'Zone Rouge' or former combat zone, or – if they had died in hospital behind the lines – in their native villages. Not surprisingly, no decision was taken about policy on war cemeteries before the end of the war; consequently all three types of site were used, with disturbing results.

The sheer chaos of the devastated areas led many bereaved people to call for governments to let them bring their dead home, back to their villages where they could be interred in local cemeteries. This argument was voiced early in the war, but with little success. On 17 October 1914, the Mayor of Mantauban in the Tarn et Garonne, near Bordeaux, forwarded the request of a father in his town who wanted to bring his son's body home. The request was refused. A ship construction merchant from Dunkerque wrote to the Minister of the Interior on 14 February 1915 to ask for permission to exhume his dead son from a common grave in the civilian cemetery at Esternay, near where he had died. His body was clearly identified; thus the bereaved father asked to rebury him in a separate grave until the end of the war. At that time, he would bring his son home, all at his own expense. Permission was denied. At the same time, a bereaved father and mother asked to rebury their son, whose grave they had identified, so that they could conduct a funeral before the body had become 'impossible to identify'. The plea to hear 'la prière d'un père et d'une mère désolés', was refused by the Ministry.[19]

Such bureaucratic obstacles were circumvented by less scrupulous people. The Mayor of Florent on the Marne wrote to his prefect about the secret exhumation of the body of a soldier of the 47th Infantry Regiment. The Mayor of Bouchy-le-Repos reported another case of grave-robbing. The Mayor of Compalay told the Prefect of Seine et Marne of the arrival in July 1919 of one widow Terrouet with the body of her son, who had died in September 1918. She had been helped by a 'Parisian entrepreneur' named Tanguy, who provided transport, exhumation, helped verify identification, placed the body in a coffin, and conducted the bereaved woman and the body of her son back to her village. All for a fee of 2.50 francs per kilometre and a handling charge. Such 'entrepreneurial flair' was recognized as widespread and unscrupulous.[20]

It was a futile hope that such private enterprise would come to an end at the Armistice. Still, an attempt to bring order to the situation was made soon after the cessation of hostilities. On 24 November 1918, a Commission on Military Cemeteries was created, under the Presidency of General Castelnau, a bereaved father himself. The Commission's charge was to regroup isolated burials, and to create and maintain designated military cemeteries. While this process was under way, for a period of three years, no private exhumations and reburials were to be allowed.[21]

This decision did not end the matter. It simply intensified a long and at times acrimonious debate about the appropriate resting place for the fallen of the Great War. The spokesman for the view that the fallen should remain on the Western Front was Castelnau, Joffre's right-hand man at the outbreak of the war and later commander of the Armies of the East. An anti-Dreyfusard, he was one of the most prominent Catholic traditionalists in the army. He had lost three sons in the war. His view, and that of many other staff officers, was that the dead should rest where they had fallen.[22] They had died for that land. It was sanctified by their sacrifice. Some hoped that the eventual return of greenery would create sacred forests, places of pilgrimage for the whole world.[23] 'Don't separate those whom death has united', wrote another advocate of the status quo in 1920.[24]

These views were held by a minority. Over the next year, hundreds of people, prominent and obscure, from all over France joined in a campaign to bring the dead back home. One reason was to avoid a three-year wait while cemeteries were being built. To tarry, some argued, was to assure misidentification of the dead. On a more emotional level, others decried 'the cruelty of the erection of a new barrier between families and the bodies which belong to them'. After all, 'their sacrifice was made only to reinforce the family ties that bind them to us'.[25]

In May 1919, these contradictory views were exchanged at a meeting of the Conseil d'Etat. On the one side stood those in favour of letting the dead rest where they had fallen. In De Morey's words:

I think my son must rest among those with whom he fought; he led his men in battle and I want him to remain among his comrades; that the battle will continue for him, that he be on the frontier and there inspire future generations, in case of a new attack to defend his Country . . . I am convinced that, facing this army of sleeping heroes on the field of battle, the Country will be very profoundly moved.

In cemeteries already built, like Saint-Menehould, one sees the army that saved France; there, under the earth, and each year we will come to render homage where homage is due. Won't this be better, infinitely more beautiful than to scatter the bodies of our heroes in communal cemeteries, where, after one generation, military tombs will not be maintained?

He told his colleagues of a letter from Lady Cecil, who wrote to him that her British son, killed in 1915, 'should remain with his men, asleep in the soil of France, which will become dearer to me because my child is buried there'.[26]

On the other side of the argument also stood bereaved and distinguished men. Louis Barthou, President of the Conseil d'Etat and soon to be Minister of War under Briand in 1920,[27] said: 'I have been told I could have retrieved the body of my son; others have done so' for a fee. But he had refused. He objected to waiting for three years after the end of the war; his son had died in 1914. Why wait seven years before he could properly be laid to rest?[28]

Castelnau and his colleagues won the day. In June 1919, the Ministry of War forbade all exhumations in the Zone of Military Operations.[29] In September 1919, the Ministry of the Interior wrote to all prefects ordering the stamping out of the clandestine traffic in bodies.[30]

As one might have predicted, such edicts carried little weight with families whose sadness led them to seek comfort even in illegal ways. A change in the government's line was urged from many angles. The journal L'art funéraire et commémoratif and its editor Lucien Marie took a leading part in this effort. It may be said ungenerously that memorial artists had a vested interest in bringing the dead home, and indeed alongside appeals to the government to let the dead return were advertisements for the latest tasteful designs for funereal statuary and sculpture. But the views aired in this journal were echoed throughout the country. 'Our sons, no, no, we don't want to leave them there', wrote one obscure father in July 1919,

Though they are dead, we want to remove them from those accursed places in the battlefields. They did their duty. Now we must do ours for them: to let them rest in peace in the cemetery of their ancestors. To abandon them there, is to condemn them to eternal torment.

The war today is over. The living are going home. Let's let the dead return to their villages, to those villages which were in their last thoughts at the tragic moment of their deaths.[31]

Others called for 'the demobilization of the dead'[32] for religious reasons. French war cemeteries were civic memorials, sanctified by a state which only a decade earlier had formally severed its ties with the Catholic church. For many Catholics, to bring the dead home was to return them to the parish church. In the pages of *L'art funéraire et commémoratif*, Lucien Marie even went so far as to suggest that the reluctance of the Ministry of War to accede to their demands was because some of the responsible officials were Jews. As we all know, he intoned, the Jews were 'the most materialist people on earth, and also the people with the least developed cult of the dead'.[33]

It would be a mistake, though, to locate this agitation solely on the extreme right. Very respectable centrist groups and individuals subscribed to it as well. 'Return to families the remains of our heroes', wrote the editor of *Souvenir et fraternité*, the journal of the National Union of the Families of the Dead of the Great War.[34] He had the support of the Union of Fathers and Mothers of those who Died for their Country, an association of eminent Parisian politicians, scholars, and other public figures, whose meetings were held regularly at the Panthéon from 1915.[35]

Bereaved people had the right to a free annual visit to the war cemeteries of the north of France. But those who lived in the south and southwest could not easily undertake such pilgrimages. It made sense, they felt, to bring the remains of the fallen back to the bereaved, so that they, the ordinary people of France, could put the dead to rest, and provide them with a funeral ceremony which many had been denied by the butchery at the front.

What may finally have swayed the authorities was that the return of the dead continued to take place illegally. Parents with means were still making private arrangements with gravediggers, who for a fee were willing to bring their sons home again. This form of private enterprise infuriated the army, which had to deal with both bribery and churned-up cemeteries, as well as the anger of poor parents, irate at the crassness and privilege of wealth.[36]

On 28 September 1920, the French government finally gave in. It promulgated a decree establishing the right of families to claim the bodies of their loved ones, and to transmit them home, at state expense.[37] It took over a year to organize the bureaucracy, the procedure, and necessary transport,[38] but, starting in the summer of 1922, about 300,000 of the dead of the Great War actually went home. Since roughly 700,000 of over 1 million fallen French soldiers had been identified, this figure represented about 40 per cent of those whose families had the right to request their return.[39]

It didn't all go smoothly. There was a dispute as to who had the right to claim the body: parents or widows. The parents' association argued that the filial tie was the only one that could not be broken, and hence they had precedence. The widows' organization thought otherwise. The parents won. There were substantial difficulties in providing irrefutable proof of the identities of the fallen, a theme recently recreated in the film of Bertrand Tavernier, *La vie et rien d'autre*, where two women separately seek to find alive or claim the remains of the man they both loved. There were the real logistical problems of reaching the devastated areas, finding the appropriate grave, filling out the right forms, finding and paying for the right trains, and so on.[40] The anguish of disinterring the dead in the chaos of the battlefields, of distinguishing the remains of one man from another,[41] of fighting off the 'jackals' ready to offer their help at exorbitant prices, accompanied this *rite de passage*.

But the operation was concluded, more or less successfully, by the beginning of 1923, to the great relief of the French military. As the man responsible for overseeing the military cemeteries of the north of France, General Ferre, put it:

1922 was a baneful year for our cities of the dead due to numerous exhumations which, practically without precautions, upset the soil of military burial places, broke some funerary emblems, destroyed trees and shrubs and surroundings. Thanks to the devotion and perseverance of our committees, we have just about escaped from the chaos and the damage has been repaired. Exhumations at state expense are over; there are no more transports of bodies (with a few exceptions); the situation has stabilized, and it is time to give these cemeteries their final crosses and steles.[42]

War cemeteries are scattered over a vast area, in Eastern Europe, Africa, the Middle East. But since most of the casualties suffered by the major combatants were incurred on the Western Front, it is in France and Flanders that the problem of creating war cemeteries was most acute. For different reasons, the decision to let the dead rest where they had fallen was taken by all participants. Having lost the war, the Germans were in no position to return to the areas they had occupied and exhume the remains of their fallen soldiers.[43] The Americans were committed to the return of their dead soldiers, but the British ruled it out on grounds of expense and equality. So many men had no known grave that granting the privilege of bringing back only identified bodies would discriminate against about half the population.[44]

Instead, symbolic gestures of the return of the fallen were made in many countries. In 1920, unknown soldiers were interred in Westminster Abbey in London,[45] and under the Arc de Triomphe in Paris.[46] In the following year, the same ceremony took place in the United States, Italy, Belgium, and Portugal. Most other countries followed suit, or, as in the cases of Canada, Australia and New Zealand, accepted the tomb in the Motherland to represent their own unknown soldiers.[47] On 11 November

1993, the Australians broke ranks, and brought home one of their unknown soldiers who had been buried in a Commonwealth War Graves Commission cemetery. After a full military funeral, he was laid to rest in the 'Hall of Memory' of the Australian War Memorial in Canberra.[48]

The German approach to this question was bound to entail greater difficulty and ambiguity. A number of projects were formulated, but they lacked the power to focus attention on one sacred site. The absence of any consensus on the meaning of the war, the origins of the defeat, and the place of the military within German political culture ensured that the idea of burying an unknown soldier in Berlin or Tannenberg or Munich had a divisive as much as a unifying effect. Monumental art in Germany remains contested material to this day.[49] As the distinguished German scholar Reinhard Kosseleck put it in an article in the *Frankfurter Allgemeine Zeitung*, who is to say that the unknown soldier of the Great War hadn't shot the unknown war resister?[50] Among the 'winners', these problems also existed, but they could be absorbed in a consensus as to the value of commemorating the fallen who gave their lives for victory.

Commemoration was a universal preoccupation after the 1914–18 war. The need to bring the dead home, to put the dead to rest, symbolically or physically, was pervasive. All I aim to do here is to suggest the significance of an issue which was both allegorical and real. Those who tried to reunite the living and the dead, to retrieve their bodies and to give them a secure and identifiable resting place, faced staggering problems. There was the scale and chaos of the battlefields at the end of the war; there was as well terrible uncertainty as to the survival of thousands of men who simply had vanished in combat. Before commemoration came discovery, a theme to which I turn now.

2
Communities in mourning

Grief is a state of mind; bereavement a condition. Both are mediated by mourning, a set of acts and gestures through which survivors express grief and pass through stages of bereavement.[1] Many of these moments are lived within families supported by social networks.

Families were torn apart by war. Nothing could have reversed completely this tide of separation and loss. But after 1914 there was as well a gathering together, as people related by blood or by experience tried to draw strength from each other during and after the war. The bonds thus formed were powerful and in many cases durable. The process of their formation and expression is at the heart of this chapter.

In all countries touched by the war, there was a progression of mutual help, a pathway along which many groups and individuals sought to provide knowledge, then consolation, then commemoration. These elements were always there, though the language in which they were expressed varied considerably.

First I approach the initial stages of bereavement in terms of discovery: of how relatives and friends heard the awful news about casualties, and what some of them were able to do about it. Some were near the front lines. Moreover, the sheer scale of the conflict made it difficult, if not impossible, to discover the whereabouts of individual soldiers, whether alive or dead, missing or at base camps, on leave or in transit. Mistakes proliferated. Even when people were informed accurately that a man had been wounded, there was almost always a void of silence about what he had suffered and what were his chances of recovery. Into these silent spaces, fears and rumours flooded. The same silences attended the terse official messages about men who died in uniform.

As we shall see, some people were able to penetrate the maze and go to the bedside of a wounded man. Most were unable to do so. Instead, many different groups were formed to try to act on behalf of those who could not reach their loved ones, and to replace bureaucratic formulae by further information or by simple statements of fact. Some groups were officially sanctioned; most were private bodies of people committed

29

to offering to those in mourning or unsure about the fate of their loved ones the only solace that they believed could help: the truth, or that part of it which could be confirmed.

Out of this effort to burn away the wartime fog of confusion, misinformation, and stylized official language, a set of organizations worked to find out what had happened to individual soldiers and thereby to link families at home with the men at the front and in captivity. The search for the fate of soldiers, and the effort to comfort the bereaved, created a kind of kinship bond between families in wartime and those who set about helping them. Everyone in mourning for a soldier was a victim of war, and to see the ways they were helped (and the ways they helped each other) enables us to appreciate the importance of kinship – familial or socially defined – in the process of coming to terms with bereavement in wartime.

From 1914 on, kinship bonds widened, through a process of informal or figurative 'adoption'. For a time, Red Cross volunteers, searchers, and officials *joined* the families of men at war. They stood as proxies for parents, wives, brothers, and sisters, and expressed in a hundred ways what Meyer Fortes had described as the essence of kinship: a kind of 'amity' or 'artificial brotherhood' based on a 'set of normative premises' of 'prescriptive altruism', a 'bond of moral obligation to help and support one another', 'an ethic of generosity' parallel to early notions of 'Christian charity'.[2]

Consolation was a second objective of this broadened experience of kinship during and after the war. Helping people through the early days of their loss prepared the way for other forms of material assistance. The Protestant voluntary tradition came into its own in this effort, but Jewish and Catholic groups also worked to ease the plight of widows, orphans, and aged parents who had lost their sons in the war. Men who had suffered mutilation or illness during the war needed long-term help, and joined the wider population of victims of war who created and were served by such organizations. As in their search for information about individual soldiers in wartime, these groups tried to compensate for the shortcomings of central authorities, too mean or preoccupied to provide adequately for those whose circumstances were reduced by the war.

From consolation and support, it was a short step to commemoration. The bonds shared by those in mourning, by widows, ex-servicemen, the disabled, the young and the old alike, were expressed openly in ceremonies of collective memory. On Armistice Day and on other important dates in the calendar, groups and associations drew attention to the victims, both living and dead. Such efforts marked indelibly much of interwar communal life. In this chapter I attend to some of these phenomena. In the next two chapters, I shall investigate two facets of postwar mourning and commemoration. The first is the phenomenon of spiritualism; the second is the complex history of war memorials.

Discoveries

For families with someone in the army, waiting was an onerous and unavoidable reality. 'Every day, every hour, . . . they probe the unknown', wrote one Frenchman of parents during the war. The mother with her vacant stare, the father pacing up and down, trying to convince himself that their son will be all right, were there in all combatant countries.[3] 'Such distress, to know nothing, to be alone . . . like a beast', were the despairing words of one woman who learned later that her husband would not return.[4]

When their wait was over, and the bad news came, it took many forms. In France the mayor received from the military authorities notification of the deaths in uniform of local residents. It was his duty to pass on the message to the family. On his way from the *mairie*, he or his deputy was watched from classrooms and alleyways by people young and old, glad to be passed by, apprehensive for those whom he sought.[5] In Britain, the message came by letter to the families of men in the ranks, by telegram to officers' families. Some messages arrived by telephone. Further afield, cables, sometimes supplemented by phone calls, were the rule. In Australia, clergymen delivered the news.

Delays in passing on the news of death on active service were inevitable. Some were lengthy. The family of the poet Wilfred Owen learned of his death one week after he was killed, as it happened, on Armistice Day. Their other son, Harold, was in the Royal Navy, on a ship off Africa. At sea, there was no way for him to learn what had happened until his mail caught up with him around Christmas, six weeks later. Yet Harold Owen says that he knew before the family letter arrived, following a 'vision' of Wilfred in his cabin one evening at sea, in December 1918.[6]

Those less telepathic had to await official notification. The problem was, though, that up to half of the men killed had no known grave; many people could go on doubting that their loved ones were indeed dead. When we consider as well how far flung were the families of those serving in the Great War, we begin to appreciate how scarce a commodity was verified evidence of life and death among millions of civilians all over the world.

Near the front lines

People who lived near the theatres of military operations had an option closed to those further afield. If notified in time, they could try to find their wounded and attend to them in hospital. The history of one British family able to be with their son before he died is a story of their good fortune. Less lucky were those so far away that they had no chance to say goodbye or to engage in any material rite of passage on the spot. Knowing where people lived is critical to understanding the different ways families and those around them confronted the loss of their loved ones.

When he joined the army in 1917, Malcolm Wakeman was an 18-year-old Mancunian, the son of a modestly prosperous building-materials merchant. He had been an apprentice clerk at two Manchester banks and one insurance company, training to join his father's business. His course in wireless telegraphy in the Manchester Technical School came to an abrupt end when he was conscripted.[7] He joined the Royal Air Force and was commissioned as a flight observer in a two-man plane.

Wakeman was posted to France on 14 July 1918. He was an ordinary young man, without much imagination and full of schoolboy notions. He wrote to his family about the adventures of flying, and entertained them with a story of a crash-landing, after which he and his pilot were picked up, brought to an officers' mess 'where we had a jolly good dinner and a top pole [sic] lunch'. He commented on how his plane caught some anti-aircraft fire, and how his co-pilot had to stand on the wing with his foot in a hole to stop petrol leaking. He was keen that his mother send him caramels and boiled sugar sweets.[8] His last letter, written on 1 October 1918, announced that 'things are going absolutely OK'.[9]

The next day Wednesday, 2 October, his plane was shot down on patrol near the German lines in the Ypres sector. The family in Manchester received this cable from the War Ministry four days later, at 1.30 p.m. on Sunday 6 October: 'Regret to inform you that 2/Lt M.W. Wakeman Royal Air Force reported missing on October the Second Letter follows. Secretary Air Ministry.' Around 8.30 the same day a second cable arrived: 'Your son wounded head [sic] Doing well evacuated base OC 53rd Squadron.'[10]

The Wakemans decided to travel to France immediately. They took the night train to London, then travelled by boat train to France. They reached the base hospital near Calais on Monday evening, and saw their son for an hour.[11] The doctors thought his head wounds were not life-threatening, and he had no other injuries. Remarkably, his plane had not exploded on crash-landing, though it was still carrying a full bomb load. Wakeman's co-pilot, Lieutenant Basil Pierce, had been killed, and the injured man asked his parents to inform Pierce's mother. This they agreed to do, since, like the Wakemans, Mrs Pierce had received initial notification only that her son was missing in action.[12] Reassured as to the prospects of Malcolm's recovery, Mr Wakeman decided to return to England on Wednesday 9 October. Mrs Wakeman remained with her son.[13]

On Thursday 10 October an X-ray revealed that a bullet was lodged in Malcolm Wakeman's skull. The wound was inoperable, but they still hoped for a slow recovery.[14] One week later, at 2 a.m. on 18 October, Mrs Wakeman was asked by telephone to come to the hospital, about two miles from her hostel. Since no car was available, she had to walk through the rain with a Royal Army Medical Corps orderly to reach her son. She got to his bedside at around 4 a.m. He had died about one hour before.[15] Later that day she cabled the news to her husband.[16] The military doctor asked her for permission to perform a post-mortem to provide some clues to help similarly wounded men in the future. She agreed, and saw the site of her son's grave. She then returned to England on Saturday 19 October, before her son's funeral.[17]

The funeral was held two days later, on Monday 21 October. Malcolm Wakeman was buried alongside an American officer. About 100 American servicemen saluted the two men. The chaplain who conducted the service, and who had attended Malcolm, added a personal note to the Wakemans. 'Everything was done with all reverence . . . I was so touched by the calm devout spirit of your son – & I felt his loss more than that of any other whom I laid to rest out here, in sure and certain hope of the resurrection.'[18]

On her return home, Mrs Wakeman was bedridden for a time. Her husband presented a more stoical front, and proceeded to try to tie up his son's affairs. This entailed an entirely unanticipated set of bureaucratic wrangles with the army. First came the matter of retrieving his son's effects. This took two months and three letters to achieve. Then came the correction of the date of death: the army had it as 20 October; the Wakemans knew better. This too was done after a delay.[19]

These minor irritations were bad enough for a bereaved couple. But what annoyed Wakeman most was that his request was denied for reimbursement of the fare of £8 12s. 8d. he had paid to be with his son before he died. The Air Ministry was prepared to reimburse those too poor to pay, provided they went in advance to their local police station. They thought Wakeman was not in this category. The bereaved father exploded. He was not a 'convict' required to report to the police station; he had had no time to comply with such rules before catching the night train to London. Furthermore, he was

surprised at the Air Ministry trying to treat anyone in such a shabby & what I may say rather brutal manner . . . The sum I paid out was a big item for a man of modest resources & I should like to state that I am not one of those fortunate individuals who are highly paid for doing a little work in many of the Government Offices, and I have not gone about for the last few years with my eyes closed. I am engaged in business & unfortunately my trade has suffered very much during the war through lack of labour and my sales have amounted to only about half of the pre-war figure.

How can these people 'lay down one law for the poor and another law for those people who are careful and try to pay their way & who are not "Rich" nor are spongers on the public service for office'? Threats to write to prominent figures followed. Two months later, he won the argument.[20]

Such callousness on the part of public servants did not deflect Wakeman from his belief that his son's death had been in a good cause. In the weeks and months following his son's death, he conducted a long correspondence with the mother of the co-pilot of his son's plane, and with other bereaved parents. 'There is such a bond of emotion between us', wrote Mrs Pierce, a bond felt by many other friends who had lost their sons in the war.[21] The family mourned together, and tried to help others in the same situation. Wakeman sent a two-franc piece to the orderly who had conducted his wife to the hospital on the rainy night his son had died.[22] He also sent serviette rings to the hospital, to mark the dedication of the sisters who attended his son. They too were part of the community of kindness helping those in mourning during and after the war. One nurse replied: 'Tradition says that "Time is a great healer." If so Time will have her hands full for the next few years. This awful war has broken more than one heart and crippled more than one man.'[23]

For Wakeman, the symbol of that extended family in mourning was the Royal Family. He treasured the royal cable expressing the grief of the King and Queen, and in language more direct than he used to any of his neighbours and relatives, he opened his heart to his monarch. He told of the action in which his son was killed, quoted from his son's last letter, and enclosed his son's photograph. 'You will see how serious and keen he looks.' Speaking perhaps as one father to another, he continued:

To myself & wife it is a real pleasure to have our Sovereign's telegram – *our* loss is great, he was our only Son – I have now no Son to succeed to my important chemical business, nor even to carry on the name of Wakeman.

This one story, repeated millions of times, tells us something of the initial stages of grief experienced by those in mourning for fallen soldiers during and after the war. The Wakemans were fortunate. They could act; they could try to help; and once their son had died, they tried to help others. Some bureaucratic problems were inevitable in wartime, but most people realized that if they were to find solace, the state or the army was not where they would find it. It was from their families, their friends, their neighbours, sometimes their churches, that hope came. Together they formed a wide circle of those who knew the sorrow of war, and worked both then and in later years to lessen its bitterness.

The language that some used in speaking to the bereaved was euphemistic and elevated. But others, especially comrades in arms, took a different path. When they wrote to parents or widows, at times they told the truth, unvarnished and direct. A.S. Lloyd was a British soldier killed on 8 August 1916. From the front, his friend Julian Yeatman described Lloyd's fatal injuries to Lloyd's mother:

If I have wearied you with so many words at a time of stress, I am very sorry, but it is only fair that the parents of soldiers, the real sufferers from the war, should have some of these things which go to compensate.[24]

In distant lands: supplementing the story

What of the millions who lived too far from the front to have undertaken the Wakemans' journey? How did they react to the same bad news? There is abundant evidence of alternative ways in which families tried to help, or to confirm or supplement the official story.

One distant case reveals the basic elements of this search for details, a multi-national effort to find some shreds of evidence about the men who had fallen. Here we can see the emergence of support groups dedicated to helping families grieve by telling them what had happened. Among the furthest removed from the main theatres of military operations were Australian families. Over 330,000 Australians served in the Australian Imperial Force. Of these, approximately 60,000 were killed or died on active service, a casualty rate at or above that suffered by the British, French, or German armies.[25] The fate of these men 12,000 miles from home at Gallipoli and in France was communicated to their families by clergymen,[26] who were notified by official cable, at an interval of about 10 to 14 days after the event. At times the delay was longer still. But, as elsewhere, the terse language of the army's formal regret was just the beginning of the quest for the 'truth' about the men at the front. The truth they wanted was more detailed and in most cases less anodyne or strictly formal than the standard messages expressing official regret and noble thoughts.

The bereaved received two kinds of additional information. The first was a letter from an officer in the dead man's unit. This was slightly less stylized than the official communiqué. It was handwritten, but it usually contained three stock messages: the man in question was loved by his comrades; he was a good soldier; and he died painlessly.[27]

Whatever balm these words provided, most people knew that they were not wholly true and always incomplete. Bereaved parents, wives, siblings, children wanted to know more. Many yearned to share the last moments of their man; to know what he knew; and at least for a moment, to attempt to feel what he felt. This kind of identification with the fallen required a more human and to a degree more brutal disclosure of information than the state or the army provided.

Fellow soldiers and voluntary organizations often spoke a different language, and communicated a surprisingly vivid and disturbing set of images of combat and death to people in mourning during the Great War. For this reason, we must discount or qualify the argument that civilians did not know how awful trench warfare was.[28] They were *told* about it by those who were there, often in the immediate aftermath of learning that their father, husband, brother, son, friend, colleague had died at war.

Perhaps half of the men who died in action were unidentified or unidentifiable. Thousands simply disappeared. Even when remains were gathered together, the chaos and danger of the battlefield precluded the orderly recovery of bodies and identification tags. On Gallipoli, the site of a nine-month Allied landing in 1915, burial parties worked at night, in the dark. For much of the period the heat was so intense that bodies quickly putrefied and stank. Burial parties simply dumped the bodies into collective graves without retrieving identification tags. So tens of thousands of families were notified by cables indicating that their men were missing, presumed dead.[29]

That presumption left a huge gap of conjecture. What if the man were a prisoner of war? What if he were lost and wandering around the battlefield? What if he were wounded and in need of care? The families of missing men were put in an excruciatingly difficult position: aware that something dreadful had happened, but not able to identify how bad it was.

To help discover the truth, voluntary organizations were set up in many countries. Their natural model was the Red Cross, the accepted intermediary between combatants with special responsibility for prisoners of war.[30] We can follow these expressions of the 'amity' of wartime 'adoptive kinship' in a number of cases. Particularly active were the Australian Red Cross Information Bureaux, set up in 1915 in Melbourne, Sydney, and Adelaide, with offices in Cairo, Paris, and London. Their agents were the eyes and ears of the families at home, scouring the hospitals, base depots, war fronts, and prisoner-of-war camps for news of casualties and evidence of their survival or death.

We are very fortunate in that the voluminous records of one part of this organization have been preserved. This is the primary reason why it is useful at this point to concentrate on the Australian case. But it was not unique; the Red Cross had offices serving every combatant nation. What we see here is the outline of a story which could be (and should be) told from the point of view of civilians on both sides of the conflict.

Those who worked for the Red Cross came from many parts of

4. An Australian Red Cross hospital

Australian society. James (later Sir James) A. Murdoch was a prosperous retail trader in men's wear in Melbourne. In October 1915 he volunteered to serve with the Australian branch of the British Red Cross. He administered depots in Boulogne and Rouen before becoming Chief Commissioner of the Australian Red Cross in 1917.[31] He was surrounded by an array of soldiers and civilians whose job it was to cater for the needs of Australian soldiers and their families at home. The most energetic of them all was Vera Deakin, daughter of the pre-war Prime Minister Alfred Deakin. She volunteered for Red Cross work in September 1915, and opened an inquiry office of the Red Cross in Cairo the day after she and her companion, Winifred Johnson, set foot in Egypt. The next year she moved to London and served as secretary of the central inquiry office in Victoria, just behind Buckingham Palace.[32]

Deakin returned to Australia in 1919, after three years of ceaseless work in London trying to get at the truth about the fate of Australian soldiers. From 1 to 21 November 1916, for example, her office received 1,402 inquiries, and sent 1,036 cables to Australia, supported by 1,358 reports.[33] In 1917 the work load increased as casualties mounted. In that year, Deakin and her co-workers dealt with approximately 4,000 inquiries per month. Her searchers sent in over 32,000 reports on missing soldiers. They travelled throughout Britain and scoured the

Western Front. They handled 4,500 reports from officers, matrons, chaplains, and other soldiers.[34] They engaged in a substantial correspondence with the International Red Cross, and through them, with German authorities responsible for prisoner-of-war camps. They quarrelled with officers worried that censorship regulations were violated by direct communications between the Red Cross and the men in the ranks who could say whether or not a friend had been killed. Deakin testily replied that 'the greater part of our work deals with unofficial information received direct from the men and naturally not within the scope of a battalion orderly room'.[35] They wrangled with overworked medical officers, exasperated that tired nurses were troubled by Red Cross inquiries.[36] Deakin was steadfast. Her office would

continue to ask for details concerning the last hours, deaths and burials of Australians, as we have had so many instances of sisters' or chaplains' letters to the next of kin having gone astray, either owing to submarines or incorrect or old addresses.[37]

They had the delicate task of deflecting problematic cases. One mother suspected foul play when her son died in a Turkish prisoner-of-war hospital forty-eight hours after contracting the 'Spanish flu'; in fact, none was involved.[38] Another mother wrote about the whereabouts of her son, who had sent her a mysterious card in September 1917. The card read:

I am a prisoner in Germany; wounded; first night I ran away to France, got hit, taken to Bruges. Do not know the name of place. Will meet you some day. Feeling weak. Trying to escape with a mate of mine. He is going to send this letter if possible. Fancy Christmas Day.

In fact he had been absent without leave since August.[39]

Most of their work was more serious. The real difficulty was to reconcile contradictory evidence concerning those missing in action. The wife of Corporal C.T. Owen wrote to Deakin from South Australia in September 1916. She had received a cable telling her that her husband had been wounded. A second cable arrived with the news that he had been wounded and was missing. The Red Cross investigated. Three soldiers reported three different stories: one said Owen had been killed at Pozières on the Somme; a second was sure he had been wounded but was in hospital in England; a third said he was a prisoner of war. To make matters worse, Mrs Owen tracked down the soldier who testified to her husband's death. Back in Australia, he denied ever having said it. In this case, there was no resolution. Owen was one of thousands whose body was never found. He had vanished without trace.[40]

Where final answers were established, and verified information was gathered, Deakin cabled the results to Australia, where they were forwarded to state headquarters. Red Cross workers on the spot then wrote to families, including verbatim, uncensored, and at times contradictory reports on the missing.

In the regional offices, the same diligent voluntary system provided the essential link between front and home front. In Adelaide, for example, in October 1915 a prominent solicitor, Sir Josiah Symon, appealed to the legal profession of the city to come forward and put their investigative experience at the disposal of the Red Cross. Their job was to link up with agents in every hospital in Egypt, Malta, or any other place where Australian soldiers were in treatment. They prepared lists of local men in military hospitals, provided families of those dying in hospitals with this information, and searched for news of the missing and of others 'for whom further inquiry is necessary'. Sir Josiah told his colleagues that:

The object aimed [sic] is to assist in relieving the anxiety and suspense of the relatives and friends of our men at the front by collecting and communicating to those interested information as to their whereabouts and welfare, supplementing as much as possible the information which the Defence Department obtains, and receiving and dealing with specific enquiries whenever and as far as possible.[41]

The local enquiry office opened in January 1916, and provided a meeting point for anxious relatives and friends for the rest of the war.

Missing, presumed dead

They investigated three classes of cases: men who had vanished, presumed dead; wounded men; and prisoners of war. In the case of the missing, inquiries continued to be made throughout the war and occasionally well after the Armistice. Two ordinary cases illustrate this point. Private J.A. Briggs disappeared at Pozières, near Mouquet Farm, on or around 10 August 1916. He was listed as missing on 28 September 1916. The Red Cross searchers found a soldier in Briggs' platoon who said he had been killed. His name was therefore added to the list of missing, presumed killed, and the change was communicated to Briggs' father in Western Australia on 3 January 1917. But the presumption still left room for doubt. Inquiries continued. The Red Cross wrote to one member of Briggs' unit for information to 'enable us to satisfy his relations that no error had been made'. The man confirmed that he had seen Briggs 'cut in two by a shell' near Mouquet Farm, while helping a wounded man out of the line. Then the Red Cross found Sergeant C.J. Drake, who had also served with Briggs. Drake was in a German prisoner-of-war camp in Soltau. He wrote to the Red Cross in November 1917 about Briggs:

He was my best pal and I have tried everywhere to find out all I can about him . . . I do not think there is any chance of the poor boy turning up but if I happen to hear anything of him in this country I will let you know at once.[42]

Briggs' body was never found, but his fate was determined beyond reasonable doubt.

Similar efforts were made by the Red Cross on behalf of the family of two brothers killed on the same day, also in the Pozières sector of the Somme. Four days after Private Briggs had vanished, on 14 August 1916, both Private Stephen Charles Allen and Private Robert Beattie Allen, serving in the 13th Battalion of the AIF disappeared. A few weeks earlier, Stephen Allen had sent his mother a poppy growing in his dugout. In the files of the Australian War Memorial, the poppy is still there, pressed into the letter.[43] By mid-August, there was no trace of either man. In March 1917, the commanding officer in the Allens' unit, Captain J. Wills, wrote to Mrs Allen that there was a faint possibility that her boys were alive and in a prisoner-of-war camp.[44] The Red Cross investigated. They found Will Hale, a man wounded in the same operation that cost the Allen brothers their lives. Hale had also served there with his own brother, who had been wounded as well. This is what he told the Red Cross, and repeated in a letter of June 1917 to the Allens' sister:

I seen a good lot of your Brothers from the time I met them, and was not more than five yards off when the shell caught us. Your two poor Brothers were between my Brother and I. When the shell exploded I knew by the screams that someone had caught it. I could not get through for some time, as I was half silly through the shock. However when I could get through, my brother was seriously wounded, and your to [sic] Brothers were laying there, they had been shifted, because when I was returning to the front line again I could not see them. My brother is having a rough time he is still in Hospital, he cannot walk but gets about on crutches as best he can. I expect he will be home in a few months time. I am pretty well again my hand is not much good to me at the present but I have hopes that in time it will come alright.[45]

In August 1917, another soldier in the 13th Battalion wrote to Mrs Allen that 'Bob was blown up by a shell.'[46] Formal certificates of death were issued on 25 September 1917, more than a year after the men had vanished, but still inquiries continued.[47]

We can see here most of the elements of adoptive or informal kinship ties: the extension of the family searching for evidence about the disappeared brother; the essential liaison role of the Red Cross in that effort; and the painstaking work of finding reliable evidence of the fate of the men long after official death certificates were issued. This band of men and women kept hope alive as long as they could. But when they found evidence that pointed towards the unavoidable conclusion that the men had been killed, that evidence was transmitted verbatim to the families affected.

This openness can be confirmed by examining the case records of the

South Australia branch of the Red Cross. Corporal K.C. Moore of the 52nd Battalion of the AIF was lost near Bullecourt on 11 April 1917. In October, Moore's brother was told by the Red Cross that there was no trace of him. It was possible he was a prisoner of war. But, the Red Cross went on, three of Moore's fellow soldiers reported that he had been killed on 11 April. One said Moore 'by mistake had walked into the German trenches'. The family were given the full text of the reports; the testimony slips correspond exactly to the text of the letter sent to the family. The Red Cross added:

We regret that the foregoing reports are contradictory and that no definite tidings have been obtained. However we thought you would be anxious to have every particular which comes to hand. Our Commissioners will continue this inquiry and immediately we obtain any further tidings whatever, we will again communicate with you as we understand a little of your great anxiety.

Still the confusion went on. On 21 November, another soldier told the Red Cross that Moore had been taken prisoner, but the weight of evidence was solidly against the family's hope that he had survived. The formal death notice was delivered in early 1918, but searches continued among prisoner-of-war files in Germany after the Armistice. Nothing ever turned up. This too was communicated to the family.[48]

This straightforwardness was not exceptional. F.L. Donnelly was killed on 8 August 1918. The family received the report of the man who had carried him from the field 'after he had been hit in the back by an explosive bullet. He died on the way out on the stretcher.'[49] The family of Corporal L. Marks was told that three distinct witnesses confirmed that his head was blown off by a shell, and that he had been killed 'instantaneously'.[50]

However harsh the imagery, it conveyed reality and finality. Unluckier were the parents of the missing, whose fate was uncertain. Here too the truth was not obscured by lofty language or delicate euphemisms. Private J.R. Skinner was lost at Lone Pine at Gallipoli on 6 August 1915. His sergeant, T. Pestell, gave this account to the Red Cross, which then passed it on to Skinner's family. Pestell himself had been shot through the neck and was unconscious. He woke to find Skinner next to him, shot in the right breast; 'a gaping wound showed there . . . His case was a very bad one, his eyes were protruding almost as if in death.'[51] Two days later Pte D. James also disappeared at Gallipoli. One comrade told the Red Cross that he fell away from the Turkish lines. 'It was terrible, the men were falling like rabbits. Many were calling out for Mothers and Sisters.' James' body was never found.[52]

Occasionally, the Red Cross went out of its way to help the bereaved to learn of the final days of fallen soldiers whose graves were known. This was most likely in the case of prominent soldiers in well-documented encounters. Lieutenant Colonel Ernest Brown was killed on Gallipoli in the August 1915 charge at Lone Pine. The progression from official language to fuller information is evident in the correspondence Brown's widow received. First came the cable to the local clergyman, the Revd Newmark, instructing him, a week after Brown's death, to 'convey deep regrets and sympathy of the Commonwealth government'.[53] Then, the following week came the condolences of one of the officers in Brown's unit, the 3rd Battalion. 'After all', Major Gallagher wrote, 'it is a glorious thing to die for one's country and loved ones: that is really what we are fighting for.'[54] Four weeks later came a factual report from another man serving at Gallipoli. He told the widow:

It appears that he was first injured in the head by a shot which affected his mind, and shortly after he was killed outright in leading a charge of his men: I give you these details from a reliable source, which you can depend on.[55]

Other accounts, with additional details, followed.[56]

This case was unusual, in that it involved a high-ranking officer in a highly publicized encounter, out of which legends quickly grew.[57] The fact that the dead man was a professional soldier also separated his story from that of the volunteers who fell around him. This lay behind Major Gallagher's noble rhetoric. But even here, in this special case, we observe the two important parts of the work of the Red Cross. It served as a conduit for information on all victims of war, and it helped the local community to support those in mourning.

Other casualties: the wounded and prisoners of war
Locating the sick and the wounded was a second facet of the work of the Red Cross. Families receiving notification of casualties were rarely told initially the nature and seriousness of the injury or where the soldier was being treated. Once he was located they had a chance of finding out how bad the situation was.

Again, those in close proximity to the front had difficulty in locating their men, but people further afield were in an impossible situation. The Red Cross tried to act on their behalf.

A 'poor washerwoman' in South Australia was 'heartbroken' to learn that her son, Private P.W. Kyloh, was wounded in action in 1915. Friends (presumably her employers) wrote to the Red Cross on her behalf, and paid the costs of the inquiry. She was lucky. Red Cross searchers found her son in a British hospital. He had a serious back wound.[58] Other parents sought similar information time and again during the war. As soon as possible, the Red Cross passed on the news that soldiers were recovering in hospital.[59] At times, this information happily superseded erroneous notifications of death in action.[60]

After the dead and the wounded, prisoners of war formed the third group under the scrutiny of the Red Cross. Here the institution fulfilled its traditional intermediary role. First, it informed the families of prisoners of their safety, health, and whereabouts. One of Vera Deakin's co-workers, Miss M.E. Chomley, ran the prisoners' desk of the Australian Red Cross office in London. In May 1917 she found an Australian soldier, Private E.H. Dowd, in the list of prisoners of war in Minden camp. She wrote to Dowd that she had informed his wife, and hoped thereby 'to relieve her anxiety'. A year later he was still in captivity. His wife wrote to Chomley that Dowd 'is suffering very much from nervous breakdown and I fear is in a very bad state of health'. The best the Red Cross could do was to ensure that regular parcels arrived, with an assortment of tea, sugar, milk, raisins, jam, cigarettes, soap, cornflour, beef, sausages, cheese, and lentils. Shoes were provided too, but getting the right size was a hit-and-miss operation.[61] The Red Cross pressed the Germans to exchange this wounded prisoner, but he was released only after the Armistice.[62]

The Red Cross also pressed Turkish authorities to release wounded prisoners of war. Private T.H. Dowell was a wounded Australian held in a Constantinople hospital. His leg and knee were mangled at Lone Pine in 1915. Two years later he was still in captivity. He wrote to Miss Chomley in March 1917:

Is it possible for you to do anything to help the exchange along? There are some of us here who greatly need good doctors to attend to us. My own wound has broken out again after six months at the camp. And there are two other Australians here who are just as bad.[63]

Chomley passed on the request, but nothing happened. They despaired. Dowell wrote to his sister that 'another year in this country would just about see me off'.[64] The only thing that Miss Chomley could do was to try to keep his spirits up by ensuring that parcels arrived and that friends wrote to him. She chided one former prisoner friend of Dowell: 'I dare say you remember what it feels like to be cut off from the world and your friends.'[65] She tried to celebrate Anzac Day – commemorating the Australian landing at Gallipoli on 25 August 1915 – with Dowell by letter in 1918.[66] She also kept Dowell's family informed about his condition.

Dowell made it. He was released after the Armistice and sailed to Australia on 15 November 1918, profoundly grateful to those who remembered him and pressed his case for freedom.[67] All prisoners of war were painfully aware that thousands of others had been less fortunate. They died in camps and were buried in Germany or the Middle East. Here too the Red Cross served as their surrogate family, ensuring (in so far as they could) that they were buried with dignity and that their families were notified as soon as possible.[68] Given the numbers involved and the chaos of the last months of the war and the first months of peace, it was inevitable that some families waited for years in hope, and in vain, with their hopes dashed long after the Armistice. Private C.P. Down died in Germany in a prisoner-of-war camp on 23 March 1917. The Red Cross received documentation of his date and place of burial only in October 1919. Then and only then did his family in Australia receive notification of their son's death.[69]

In each of these cases, we can see how voluntary workers helped families to cope with the anxieties of war. I have chosen one particular case, that of the Australian Red Cross, but it can stand for the support networks which sprang up in every combatant country. Nothing was easy in this work, but the most straightforward tasks entailed helping the wounded or imprisoned either materially or in terms of keeping in touch with their families. Secondly, the Red Cross opened channels through which the families of men thousands of miles from home could seek information and receive it, even when it was painful. Not to know was worse than finding the truth. This was also at the heart of the hardest job of all: to shrink the massive lists of men missing, presumed dead, by finding those who had seen what had happened. Only with such confirmation could families escape from the shadows of uncertainty. To help them do so was one face of humanity in war.

Consolation and support

The meaning of 'adoptive kinship' as 'Christian charity' in the original sense of the words,[70] is evident in the work of groups and individuals in helping those whose lives were damaged by the war: the disabled, widows, and orphans. What could be done for these people was limited. For some the state of medical science and the character of the injury made recovery either very long term or impossible. But even those who could return to a full productive life faced massive material problems of reintegration and retraining. While state support was given to these victims of war, it was almost always inadequate to cover the hidden (and not so hidden) costs of rehabilitation. The army of the disabled was too large; the limits on state expenditure were too restrictive. Some groups were organized to defend their interests and wring from the state a level of adequate or decent treatment initially denied to them. Most had to rely on their own resources, on their families, and on their 'adoptive kin' for a hand on the road to recovery. What those who helped could do was strictly limited, but that fact should not obscure the humanity of what they did.

Mutilés de guerre

In every year between the wars, men died of wounds or disease contracted on active service. Mourning began, for many, after years of caring for ex-servicemen. Most of this repetitive and entirely unglamorous service happened within families; virtually all of it went unrecorded. Sometimes the disabled were cared for by friends. Charles Berg was an Australian soldier who enlisted at the age of nineteen. He saw service at Gallipoli and in France, and was wounded in the spine by shrapnel. His mother died shortly after he returned home. For seventeen years he was cared for by a neighbouring couple, Mr and Mrs J. Semple, who did what they could 'with unremitting kindness' to help a man who, throughout his life, 'hardly knew what it was to be free from pain'.[71] This was not an isolated case. In 1940, a Lambeth woman, Elizabeth Grace, answered an inquiry about an Australian man who had died in England as a result of war injuries:

Robert Rae came to us during the war with a friend of ours from Australia. He spent all his sick leave with us and after the war was over made his home with us.

My husband and I treated him as one of the family as he had a wounded arm and weak lungs and was advised not to go back to Australia till he was stronger.

He passed away in Colindale Hospital with lung troubles through the effects of gas on Jan. 17, 1924.[72]

Care of this kind cannot be valorized. It went on unrewarded and in many cases unnoticed in millions of households after the war. All of these families needed material assistance; rarely did they receive what they needed. The history of the struggle for adequate war pensions has been told elsewhere.[73] For our purposes, what emerges from this story is the strength of the bonds forged among the wounded and disabled themselves.

These ties emerged during the war. In 1916 a French association of the disabled started to publish a newspaper with the following title: the *Journal des mutilés, réformés et victimes de guerre*. It broadcast the existence of a host of local groups, under the sponsorship of mayors or prefects. Out of this activity came a large national organization. The first congress of war wounded met at the Grand Palais in Paris on 11 November 1917. Delegates named by 125 societies representing 125,000 disabled men were there.[74] In the years that followed, a myriad of societies sprang up in towns, villages, and cities to voice the demands and aspirations of these men and the millions of others who joined them. One of the most poignant of such groups was the association of disfigured men, those with face wounds so terrible that they bought their own property for collective holidays and rest.[75]

Most of these groups were local in character, and many represented small-town, *petit-bourgeois* aspirations to escape from political or class conflict through the perpetuation of the camaraderie of the trenches, the spirit of social solidarity they knew in the army.[76] These groups were inclusive: they spoke for all victims of war, not just old soldiers. This is reflected in the baroque name of one of the largest French organizations: the Union Fédérale des associations françaises des mutilés, réformés. anciens combattants de la grande guerre, de leurs veuves, orphelins, ascendants. The president of this organization, Gaston Vidal, a teacher, journalist, and officer, wounded several times, winner of the Croix de guerre with nine citations, was a man who loved his country and hated war. No jingoism here, just the vision of a man who believed, as he told a Marseilles audience in May 1919, that 'the voice of the dead speaks for all the widows, the parents, the orphans they left behind'.[77] 'What affects widows, affects us all', he wrote in June 1919.[78]

Many activists in this movement had no illusions as to the evanescence of adequate public support for their cause. One wounded man spoke out at a meeting of war wounded in Nancy as early as April 1916. He said, 'Today we are welcome, but after the war no one will speak of us and work will be hard to find.'[79]

This unknown soldier's words were prophetic. It is true that the victory parade on Bastille Day 1919 was led by the *mutilés de guerre*.[80] But over time, the honour due to the wounded and the infirm became more rhetorical than real. The nations remembered; but words could not feed the victims or their families. For their survival, they could look only to themselves and the groups of 'fictive kin' which rallied around them. This was as true of German or Austrian veterans as it was of the British, the French, or any of the vast army of officially recognized *mutilés de guerre*, estimated by the International Labour Organization as numbering 10 million men in 1923. This is probably an underestimate.[81]

Widows and orphans

Perhaps 3 million of the 9 million men killed in the war left widows behind. If British figures are an indication of the approximate size of their young families, each widow had two small children to look after. Six million children were deprived of their fathers by the Great War.[82] How did they mourn and what became of them?

In most cases we shall never know. What was mourning like for Flora Kennedy-Smith, an Australian woman twice widowed by the war: first in 1916, through the death of her first husband in France; then in 1933, when her second husband passed away, a victim of his war wounds?[83] What could have lifted the spirits of Elsie Bennett, whose father enlisted after a furious row with his wife, who shamed him into joining up? Bennett was killed in 1917 at the age of thirty-seven. His wife was never forgiven by the family for his death. In Elsie Bennett's school, a Thanksgiving service was organized on Armistice Day. When the National Anthem was played, Elsie refused to stand up. The headmaster asked why. 'All the other little boys' and girls' Daddies would be coming home now; but her Daddy would never come home again.' She was caned for disobedience.[84]

We must not overestimate the appeal of fictive kinship for victims of war. Callousness and compassion were both in evidence in the postwar years. But even when kindness replaced such brutality, most people could do nothing to shield widows and orphans from the harshness of their fate.

Before the war, widowhood meant poverty for the mass of the population.[85] War widows were in an even more unfavourable situation. After 1914, millions of women faced a bleak financial future as a result of the death of their husbands on military service, despite the provision of state widows' pensions in all combatant countries. These entitlements followed the provision of wartime separation allowances, money payments to wives made by the state as the surrogate wage-earning husband.[86]

It is true that war pensions extended significantly the notion of welfare as a right rather than a privilege. This was of particular importance in the long-term history of pensions, especially in France and Britain.[87] In the short term, though, money payments in the form of widows' pensions rarely reached average wage levels. In addition, such transfer payments were reduced drastically in real terms by rampant price inflation.[88] In 1916, the widow of a private soldier killed in the German army received 33.30 marks per month. The *average* monthly wage for a skilled worker on the eve of the war was between 120 and 150 marks.[89] Though inflation, especially after 1916, was more savage in Germany than on the Allied side, war widowhood almost always meant deprivation or poverty.

The scale of the problem was so vast that no one dreamt it could be remedied through state action alone. In Germany, for example, in 1920, there were approximately 525,000 war widows and over 1 million war orphans.[90] According to one survey of war widows in Darmstadt at the end of the 1920s, whatever level of public assistance they received, the income of most of these women was lower than they would have had if their husbands had lived *and* remained employed. The unemployment crisis in Berlin in the early 1920s[91] and in all of Germany later in the decade made such comparisons highly academic, but the inference to be drawn was clear. The state was in no position to prevent widows and children from suffering distress after the war.

In many ways the 'victors' were no better off. Pension levels never approximated to wage levels. Furthermore, distress came in many forms, all of them bleak. Private Albert Claydon was a British soldier killed in 1918. His widow Kate, with two young daughters to raise alone, suffered a nervous breakdown shortly after the war. She died in an Epsom mental hospital in 1974.[92] In such cases, it is impossible to separate the impact of war from longer-term instabilities. But even emotionally robust widows faced daunting problems in trying to rebuild their lives.

The gap between what the state could or would provide and what war widows and their families needed to survive was covered irregularly and partially by a host of voluntary institutions during and after the war. In Britain, the Soldiers' and Sailors' Families Association carried on very much in the spirit of Victorian philanthropy.[93] In Germany, the bewilderingly complex system of welfare provision was administered largely by municipal authorities and charitable organizations at the local level.[94] In France, a host of charities, many Catholic, did what they could.

On 15 March 1917, an assembly of fourteen French organizations in aid of war orphans was convened in Paris. In this period, 'orphan' usually meant a child whose father had died. Speakers drew attention to these children's plight, which was treated with greater urgency, according to Françoise Thébaud, than that of their mothers.[95] In fact, since the vast majority of children whose fathers died on active service were very young,[96] there was no way to separate the problems of widows and orphans during and after the war.

To try to compensate in part for official parsimony and to perpetuate the wartime community of shared sacrifice, many other groups emerged to help widows and children in the spirit of 'fictive kinship'. This may be described succinctly with reference to one of the most enduring of them. 'Legacy' was (and is) an association of Australian veterans, dedicated to perpetuating the spirit of mutual assistance fostered by the men who had volunteered for the first AIF. General Sir John Gellibrand was instrumental in setting up a 'Remembrance Club' in Hobart, Tasmania, in March 1923. The club was dedicated to 'reviving the old comradeship and esprit de corps of the A.I.F.' and to render 'mutual assistance' to members in business and other matters.[97] A few months later in Melbourne a 'Legacy Club' was founded by discharged former soldiers. A former sapper, Frank Doolan, was acting secretary, and devoted himself to promoting the cause of helping war orphans.[98] By 1925 a consensus had emerged that these groups, and others like them, should dedicate themselves to looking after the children of dead comrades, something many had already been doing. As the official historian of the AIF, C.E.W. Bean, put it, they knew that

a field of great importance was the care, guidance and encouragement of the families of those comrades who, through death, were themselves no longer there to give those benefits . . . In a great many cases someone was needed to act virtually as guardian and sponsor, with the thought, help and advice that our dead comrade would have given.[99]

5. Australian women waiting for returning soldiers

In 1926 a national association had emerged. The Melbourne branch formed a Boys' Club, with 'a membership of 175 boys, all sons of deceased soldiers'. It helped to sponsor a cafeteria for daughters of dead soldiers attending the East Sydney Technical College, and organized 'motor picnics' for 150 wives and children of fallen comrades.[100] Orphans were placed in apprenticeships. A 'big-brother movement' took charge of English war orphans coming to Australia.[101] By the 1930s, Legacy helped young people to find jobs in a very inclement economic climate.[102]

By assisting these children, ex-soldiers both eased the burden war widows faced and helped to rebuild family life. These former soldiers self-consciously tried to repay the debt they owed to their fallen comrades. But the damage inflicted by the war was so deep that such manifestations of 'fictive kinship', while admirable, could not eliminate the problems faced by millions of families.

Consider the case of two war widows. Their husbands succumbed years after the Armistice to war-related infirmities. They thus became widows after many years of caring for disabled men. For two decades, Mrs Rebecca Hinds, a Tasmanian woman, looked after her disabled husband Joseph, who finally died of his wounds in Sydney in April

49

1941. With no savings, and with a bare £2 2s 0d a week as war pension, she was unable to keep up payments on her home. When asked by the Australian War Memorial to verify her husband's particulars, so that his name could be accurately inscribed on his country's roll of honour, she mused:

I have filled in the enclosed form as you requested. But at the same time I am not in favour of all this kind of thing, as we wives and mothers do not need them to remind us of those we have lost.

I think it would be more fitting to put the money to better use for those that are living and finding it hard to live these days . . . Why worry over the dead, I'm sure they would not wish it, if they only knew how we who are left are treated.

They gave their lives 'tis true and I often wonder what for?[103]

Mrs Hinds' case may have been extreme; there is no record of Legacy or similar groups coming to the rescue. In any event, she was not alone in facing adversity after the death of a war invalid she had spent much of her life nursing. Violet Selma Aiken's husband, Harry, served in the Australian army. He died in England in 1928. His wife wrote that he was

a long sufferer from his war injuries . . . and was nursed the last 18 months night & day in our little home here by myself after he had been in many hospitals & sanitoriums in France and United Kingdom.

I am proud to be his widow but regret that because I live in the mother country I have since 1932 had my 9/- a week stopped from my war widow's pension. I am told it is the exchange rate that is the cause of this. It is a struggle to live in these times.

. . . I appreciate my husband's name being erected on the 'Hall of Memory' immensely but what about those left behind?[104]

What indeed? These letters hint at the grim world of uncertainty and precariousness faced by most war widows without independent means. They also highlight the link, and occasional clash, between the lofty phrases enjoining everyone to remember the dead and the harsher official treatment of their survivors. Local charity and benevolence healed some of these wounds; others remained unattended.

Commemoration

So far I have presented aspects of the work of men and women in several countries in helping soldiers and their families through the chaotic days of the war and the difficult period of adjustment to postwar life. I have used the notion of 'fictive kinship' to describe such efforts at truth-telling and solidarity. A third area in which such bonds are evident is in wartime and postwar commemoration. In the fourth chapter, I shall

6. French children tending Australian war graves at Villers-Bretonneux, France, 1919

discuss these issues as they informed the construction, dedication, and meaning of war memorials. Here I offer some preliminary remarks on the ways commemoration and mourning were inextricably entwined.

War memorials are collective symbols. They speak to and for communities of men and women. Commemoration also happened on a much more intimate level, through the preservation in households of possessions, photographs, personal signatures of the dead. That is why it mattered so much to parents to retrieve the kit of their sons after notification of their deaths.[105]

Comrades in arms at times wrote to widows and parents, frequently offering condolences and memories in equal part. One British soldier engaged in a long correspondence with the widow of his officer, Alan Lloyd. A year after Lloyd's death, Gunner Manning sent Mrs Lloyd the following poem about her husband:

In Memoriam

A year has passed since that sad day
When God called my dear friend away
God took him home
It was his will
Forget him. No I never will.

51

O how I miss you dear friend
I often wish that you were here
When trials come and friends are few
Dear friend O how I long for you.

Mrs Lloyd sent parcels to her dead husband's unit, and followed the fortunes of these men after the war. Manning told her of his troubles. One of his brothers had been killed; another was a prisoner of war in Germany; a third, bedridden, 'with no hope of recovery'. He would 'never go down mine again'; and seemed resigned to an arranged marriage. He hoped to open a pub in Manchester.[106] There is the whiff of class difference about this correspondence, but it reveals also the notion that mourning for the same man created a strong bond between the two.

Those who went on pilgrimages to war cemeteries and sacred sites – Verdun, Ypres, Langemark – also developed affinities with parents, widows, sons, and daughters like themselves, who were there to remember the dead. Mr and Mrs Wakeman returned to their son's grave in France in 1923. They took advantage of the services of the 'St Barnabas Hostels', simple hostelries not very different from the ones they had stayed in five years before. This organization was founded in 1919, after it was apparent that help was needed for the 'many Pilgrims miles from their hotels, vaguely wandering about in search of cemeteries and with no sign-posts to guide them thereto'.[107] Instead of charging as much as £35, as one London travel bureau did for a visit to Loos, the price of St Barnabas tours was at first £14 and then by 1923, only £4. The Wakemans, like other pilgrims, were met at Calais by a St Barnabas 'lady worker'. The organization noted that 'the tact and sympathy of these unselfish women has soothed many a Sorrowing Pilgrim, and brought a glimmer of peaceful sunshine into many a desolate and lonely heart'. They were then conducted by car to the cemetery, and were taken back to a small hotel in time for their return to England the following day. Similar journeys could be made to the cemeteries of the Somme and Ypres and, from 1924, facilities were available to conduct pilgrims to Gallipoli, Palestine, and Italy. A fund for those who could not pay even this modest fee enabled 2,000 'poor relations' to visit their sons in 1923 alone.[108]

The history of the pilgrimage movement is a subject worthy of a book in itself.[109] For our purposes, what matters most is the way it drew upon and added to the kinship bonds already forged by war victims and their families. Those who made the journey, for many both physically and emotionally difficult, did so in the company of others like them, who knew what it meant to mourn fallen soldiers. Kipling's short story 'The Gardener' (see chapter 3) speaks of this community of people in mourning. So does Abel Gance's film *J'accuse*, set in 1937 among the countless graves at Douaumont. So too does Käthe Kollwitz's timeless war memorial, which I shall examine in the fourth chapter. In this community, men were not privileged over women. Indeed, the imagery of mothers on pilgrimage tending the graves of their sons is at least as present and certainly as powerful as that of General Plumer, in 1927, telling each set of parents, visiting the Menin Gate in Ypres, 'He is not missing. He is here.'[110]

One final example may point to the union of such people in an even wider community of suffering and solace. As Annette Becker has shown, after the war one Parisian parish priest, Abbé Alfred Keller, dedicated himself to creating a manifestation of Catholic compassion for 'humanity in distress'. He sponsored a housing project for poor families, each of which 'adopted' a dead soldier of the Great War. They were unrelated formally, but the dead man's name and dates of birth and death were over the door of each apartment. In the courtyard is a chapel decorated by murals painted by Desvallières. The murals portray the soldier's war as the way of the Cross.[111] This 'Cité de souvenir', dedicated in 1934, still stands in a quiet street in the 14th *arrondissement* of Paris. Over the gate is the following inscription: 'To honour the dead by an act of life and so that large families can adopt them (*une descendance adoptive*).'[112] Here dwell the living and the dead, children born after the war, and young men who never had the chance to know the fullness of family life. This instance of fictive kinship in a Catholic form illustrates my central theme: the powerful, perhaps essential, tendency of ordinary people, of many faiths and of none, to face together the emptiness, the nothingness of loss in war.

3
Spiritualism and the 'Lost Generation'

Introduction

The Great War, the most 'modern' of wars, triggered an avalanche of the 'unmodern'. One salient instance of this apparent contradiction is the wartime growth in spiritualism. Here was one of the most disturbing and powerful means by which the living 'saw' the dead of the Great War, and used their 'return' to help survivors cope with their loss and their trauma.

In this context, the study of religious beliefs and practices is of real significance. This chapter examines one facet of this issue. We have valuable studies of religious institutions and religious dissent during the war.[1] But a subject until recently largely unexplored is the effect of the war on the religious imagination, broadly defined, both within and outside the confines of the traditional churches.[2] Here it may be useful to highlight the history of the somewhat unconventional, but by no means insignificant, community of European spiritualists, whose number grew during the war and because of the war, and whose beliefs and practices carried much of the Victorian temperament into the war period and beyond. Continuity, not transformation; reiteration, not alteration, are the key features of the wartime and postwar history of what may be described as the spiritualist communion.

Spiritualism may be defined in two ways. First, secular spiritualism encompasses the views of those who explore the supposed existence of human personality after death and the possibility of communication with the dead. It makes little difference whether or not such people believe in God; their quest is psychical and psychological, not theological. Secondly, religious spiritualism describes the attitudes of people who see apocalyptic, divine, angelic, or saintly presences in daily life, and do so at the margins of or outside the confines of the traditional churches. The best way to understand spiritualism is as a family of men and women who were prepared to go beyond conventional materialism or theology and did so in societies, séances, and a host of publications.

Spiritualism was indeed a house of many mansions, including many who simply wanted to converse with the dead. This last category, of course, grew rapidly after 1914. Nevertheless, we should not restrict the spiritualist communion to those bereaved during and because of the war. Most either continued their pre-war search for psychical experiences or embarked on spiritual quests of a kind they had undertaken time and time again in the pre-war period.

Some spiritualists were unbalanced; others were charlatans. Most were honest true believers. Their activities were controversial and occasionally bizarre, but the social and intellectual prominence of leading spiritualists, as well as the widespread belief in the paranormal among soldiers made it difficult to brush them aside simply as crackpots.[3]

This chapter presents some of their wartime history. First, I examine spiritualism on the home front, through the work of those who popularized spiritualism in this period, as well as those who rejected their belief in communication with the dead. Secondly, I explore the uncanny world of combat, recreated in the stories of those who were there, as soldiers, chaplains, nurses, or writers. Thirdly, I discuss aspects of the spiritualist dimension of the commemoration of the fallen in the postwar years.

The Victorian spiritualist quest

The spiritualist movement both in Britain and on the Continent was socially and politically more a radical than a conservative phenomenon. Many Victorian spiritualists were freethinkers who rejected mainstream religious practice and belief. But the cold certainties of positivism, the search for laws of behaviour and development left many radicals untouched or dissatisfied.[4] One impulse was to turn to spiritualism as a means of reconciling science, deism, and socialism. This utopian project took many forms, from an exploration of autokinesis (moving objects) to automatic writing to séances. These manifestations were treated as serious scientific matters by a variety of eminent writers, scholars, and public figures, both in Britain and on the Continent. Among them were Hugo, Ruskin, Tennyson, as well as Faraday, Flammarion, Alfred Russel Wallace, and William Crookes.

Women played an important role in the spiritualist community. It is, therefore, not surprising that spiritualists were advocates of feminism and that the Roman Catholic Church repeatedly anathematized the movement and especially the women within it.[5] The opposition of the Roman Catholic Church had a strong scriptural basis. Leviticus 20: 6 and Deuteronomy 18:10–12 left no doubt about the sin of attempting communion with the dead. In 1864, spiritualist writings were placed on the Index of proscribed writings. The movement was denounced by the Holy See in 1898 (and in 1917) and, to identify the enemy still more precisely, Pope Pius IX himself condemned the twin evils of spiritualism and socialism.[6]

Many spiritualists did indeed combine a subversive outlook on social questions with a taste for the unexplained and the occult.[7] Some were poets of the paranormal; some meditated on the after-life; others were fascinated by contemporary psychological research. The work of Charcot on hypnotism and trances helped to popularize the paranormal, as, in later years, did Freud's theory of the unconscious.

In the early twentieth century those who entertained at least a suspension of disbelief about spiritualism did so for many different reasons. Some tried to translate traditional theology or the poetry of ancient metaphors about human survival into the language of experimental science. They pointed to magnetism, electricity, and radio waves as constituting unseen yet real phenomena of distant communication. Thought waves or other forms of human feeling or expression conceivably did the same. These speculations were the stuff of which experiments could be and were made.[8]

The spiritualist approach was as remote as could be from the mental environment of fundamentalist Christianity. Observation, not Scripture, was the source of wisdom. Numerous societies and journals spoke to and for those whose minds were open to the possibility that spiritualist phenomena were worthy of investigation. Dozens of periodicals and reviews discussed the latest findings and exchanged information and advertisements. The *Revue spirite* had been founded by Allan Kardec in 1858. It was subtitled *Journal d'études psychologiques et spiritisme expérimental*, and catered for all those who believed that 'science and religion are two sides of human intelligence'.[9] In addition to learned articles, readers could consult advertisements for the sale of spiritualist equipment. Mediums' tables sold for 10 francs in 1914; crystal balls sold for 10–40 francs, according to their size and purity. Mediums and healers placed notices in the *Revue spirite*. Sylvain Albert, of 20 avenue Secrétan, in the 14th *arrondissement* in Paris, announced that he held séances from 2 to 4 p.m. daily, but not on Sundays or holidays. Others appealed for this-worldly philanthropy, in the form of gifts for the needy.[10] The Institut Métaphysique was headed by Charles Richet, Nobel prize winning physiologist, and his colleague Dr Gustave Geley. They edited the *Annales des sciences psychiques*, with an even more ornate and all-inclusive sub-title. It was, its editors affirmed, a *Publication mensuelle illustrée consacrée aux recherches expérimentales et critiques sur les phénomènes de télépathie, lucidité, prémonition, médiumnité, etc.* as well as being the *Organe de la société universelle d'études psychiques*. Provincial spiritualist societies and monthlies flourished throughout France.[11]

The spiritualist press in Britain was similarly prolific.[12] For the less scientifically inclined, there was the *Light* and the *Occult Review*. For the more rigorous, the centre of much spiritualist activity and discussion was the Society for Psychical Research, founded in 1882. Its membership was far from undistinguished. Sir Oliver Lodge, Professor of Physics at Liverpool and later Principal of Birmingham University, was president of the Society between 1901 and 1903. He was succeeded by the physicist Sir William Barrett and by Charles Richet himself. A few years later Henri Bergson presided over the society.[13] Other eminent scholars who openly explored psychical phenomena before the war were William McDougall, the Oxford and (after the war) Harvard psychologist, the Oxford classicist Gilbert Murray, the Harvard philosopher William James, and Lord Rayleigh, Cavendish Professor of Physics at Cambridge and Nobel Prize-winner in 1914.

On the Continent, spiritualism found many champions and drew many prominent people to it, at least for a time. The Italian criminologist Lombroso took part in séances. As a young man, and before he had become Kaiser, Wilhelm II dabbled in spiritualism with his friend Prince Eulenberg.[14] J.C.F. Zollner, Professor of Astronomy at the University of Leipzig, was a prominent spiritualist, and attended séances with other university colleagues. The Russian court was a hotbed of the occult, and Russian scientists joined the movement too. P. Wagner, Professor of Zoology at the University of St Petersburg and his colleague A.M. Butlerov, Professor of Chemistry at the same university, published studies in spiritualism.[15]

Thomas Mann provided a masterly literary account of pre-war spiritualism and its attraction for the European bourgeoisie. See, for example, the long and ironical treatment of a series of séances in *The Magic Mountain* (1924), in which the central character, Hans Castorp, a very ordinary man, tries to get in touch with the cousin who had invited him to the mountains in the first place. Spiritualism is the last of Castorp's experiences in the sanatorium, before he descends to the plain below, and the war – 'the shock that fired the mine beneath the magic mountain' – in which he 'vanishes out of our sight'.[16]

Mann's treatment of the phenomenon was certainly ironic, but it would still be wrong to locate all spiritualist views on the lunatic fringe. Yes, there were sharks who swam in these troubled waters, and who fed off the gullible and the weak. But in appreciating the sources of the spiritualist revival during and after the Great War, we must accept that many individuals, both obscure and prominent, earnestly believed in the paranormal or in communication with the dead, and did so because they had taken psychical phenomena seriously before the war.

Wartime spiritualism: the Home Front

David Cannadine has called spiritualism the 'private denial of death'.[17] But the spiritualist movement was anything but private, and spoke with renewed confidence after the Great War. During and after the

Great War, interest in the paranormal and the after-life naturally deepened. It was inevitably and inextricably tied up with the need to communicate with the fallen. One French observer reversed the point. 'After a murderous war', he wrote, 'who would doubt that the dead would try to communicate again?'[18] This became a key feature of the wartime and postwar appeal of spiritualism. It provided a means through which the dead led the way. They helped both to lift the burden of grief borne by their families and to spread the 'truth' of spirit communication.

Just as in the Victorian and Edwardian period, the cause of spiritualism was promoted by well-known public figures. The continuities from earlier years, as well as the personally traumatic effect of the Great War, appear clearly in the indefatigable efforts of many eminent people.

Let us first consider the case of Sir Arthur Conan Doyle. The creator of Sherlock Holmes was too old to fight, but he lost his son, Kingsley, his brother, and his brother-in-law in the war. The first to fall was his wife's brother Malcolm Leckie, who was killed at Mons in 1914. Conan Doyle's son, a medical officer in the 1st Hampshire Regiment, was wounded while serving on the Somme and died of pneumonia in London in 1918. Conan Doyle's brother Innes, adjutant general in the 24th Division, also died in the last months of the war.[19] In addition, a bridesmaid at Conan Doyle's second wedding, Lily Loder-Symonds, who had been a nanny to the family, lost three brothers in 1915. She was able to bring back messages from her dead brothers and from her mistress' brother. Apparently her voice was fundamental in finally dispelling the lingering scepticism Conan Doyle had had since the days of his medical education about the possibility of communication with the dead.[20]

During the war Conan Doyle became interested in spirit photography,[21] and attended séances during which he was able to reach his son. Through a 'Mrs B.', Kingsley asked his parents for forgiveness and offered them consolation. Whatever had happened in the war, 'in any case he would not have stayed in England, as he had intended to go abroad in the medical services'.[22]

Conan Doyle and his wife attended a more unusual séance at Portsmouth in September 1919. On this occasion the medium, Evan Powell, a Welsh spiritualist from Merthyr Tydfil, spoke through his 'control', a Red Indian spirit named Black Hawk. The message was the same: Kingsley asked for forgiveness and said he was happy. Conan Doyle's brother Innes also appeared to the couple in a séance, in which the spirit regretted not the fact of his death, but rather that he had died before seeing the Allied victory at the end of the war.[23]

Conan Doyle's fame as the creator of the ultimate rationalist, Sherlock Holmes, as well as his writings and public appearances, ensured that other parents in mourning would consult him. He told an audience in Southsea in 1918 that thirteen mothers had written to him about their communication with their fallen sons.[24] The fictive kinship of the victims of the war, the living as well as the dead, impelled him to action.

Given his enhanced convictions, and the evident need for help among so many people who had lost loved ones in the war, Conan Doyle entered into full-time evangelism. It is evident that the war did not create these beliefs; it clarified them and enabled him to use them to try to create a new synthesis between Darwinian evolution and humanistic Christianity. Writing in the third person of his own wartime experience, Conan Doyle reflected that

the sight of a world which was distraught with sorrow, and which was eagerly asking for help and knowledge, did certainly affect his mind and cause him to understand that these psychic studies, which he had so long pursued, were of immense practical importance and could no longer be regarded as a mere intellectual hobby or fascinating pursuit of a novel research. Evidence of the presence of the dead appeared in his own household, and the relief afforded by posthumous messages taught him how great a solace it would be to a tortured world if it could share in the knowledge which had become clear to himself.[25]

In 1918 he wrote *The new revelation*, a title bound to offend conventional religious sensibilities. The book arose out of lectures delivered to the London Spiritualist Alliance. In the book's preface he cited the prediction of 'a celebrated Psychic', Mrs Piper, that 'there will be a terrible war in different parts of the world' which would 'cleanse and purify' it before the truth of spiritualism would be revealed for all to see. The meaning of the war was therefore 'essentially religious, not political'. It was a cataclysm set in motion to 'reform . . . the decadent Christianity of to-day' and to reinforce it 'by the facts of spirit communion and the clear knowledge of what lies beyond the exit-door of death'.[26] As he told the spiritualist newspaper *Two Worlds*, he could not accept the doctrine of original sin, nor the vision of redemption for sin through the blood sacrifice of Christ. But he did accept the truths of Christianity, which were in his view entirely compatible with spiritualism. He never doubted that Christianity could be revived, so long as it ceased to be 'a mummy wrapped up in ecclesiastical bindings'.[27] Indeed, he even went so far as to describe Christ as a man who had deep 'knowledge of psychical matters' and the early Christians as 'spiritualists'.[28]

In 1919 Conan Doyle embarked on full and successful lecture tours of the United States and Australia, and continued to speak to packed international meetings about his experience of psychical phenomena.[29] In 1923 he helped to found a spiritualist church in London, the outcome, as Sir Oliver Lodge disapprovingly put it, of decades of 'missionary activity'.[30]

7. Captain Will Longstaff beside his picture *The Immortal Shrine*, depicting the spirits of soldiers who lost their lives in the war, marching past the Cenotaph in London (*Sydney Morning Herald*, 3 November 1928)

8. Will Longstaff, *The Menin Gate at Midnight* (Australian War Memorial 9807)

In 1928 he got involved in a debate about whether the Australian artist Will Longstaff's painting of *The Menin Gate at Midnight* was a spiritualist work. Longstaff had worked as a war artist on the Western front, and had been temporarily blinded by mustard gas. In the postwar decade he worked in England. On 24 July 1927 Longstaff attended the unveiling of the Menin Gate memorial to the missing of the Ypres salient. That night, he had a reverie about British soldiers rising from the ground, passing out of Ypres and into eternity. This dream inspired the painting, which shows shadowy figures marching forward just outside the town and beyond the moonlit memorial. The painting was purchased by Lord Woolavington, and went on tour in Australia in 1928–9.[31] There it was viewed by large crowds, who filed past as sombre music was played.[32] Conan Doyle insisted that Longstaff's paintings were produced under 'psychic influences'. Longstaff admitted attending séances, but claimed that he wasn't a spiritualist. 'I do not paint ghosts', he insisted. 'I show the mere trappings of a soldier – the rifle, the equipment, the tin hat – never a face or figure. This is the only way in which I can symbolize the dead.' Unlike Conan Doyle, his interest was in mood and metaphor, not in parapsychology.[33]

Conan Doyle highlighted the visionary and emotional attraction of spiritualism. Oliver Lodge represented its scientific and rational appeal. His work as a physicist brought him a knighthood and international recognition as the man whose work had helped to create the electrical ignition spark for the internal combustion engine.[34] He was a pillar of the Society for Psychical Research, publishing in its journal learned articles both on spiritualist phenomena and on the physics of wireless telegraphy.[35] Before the war, he had had wide experience of telepathy, trying always to see it as an experiment in paranormal psychology. The same Mrs Piper who had prophesied the disaster of the war to Conan Doyle was introduced to Lodge by the Harvard scholar William James.

Lodge's youngest son, Raymond, was a 26-year-old engineer serving in the Ypres salient. He was killed on 14 September 1915. A few days after his father had received the tragic news, he picked up a scrap of paper on which his wife had written these words: 'To ease the pain and to try to get in touch.' The bereaved couple attended a séance led by a celebrated medium, Mrs Osborne Leonard, who spoke in the voice of a young Indian girl called Feda. She normally had several sittings a day, but after 1914, 'declined all those who came to her only out of commercial or fortune-telling motives' in order 'to help those who are disturbed by the war'. Among those convinced of Mrs Leonard's uncanny powers to reach the dead was the radical journalist Robert Blatchford, editor of the *Clarion*.[36]

In the following weeks the Lodge family – father, mother, and at least two of the eleven children – continued the sessions and built up a detailed picture of Raymond's life in what they called 'Summerland'. Raymond's guide and comforter, indeed his surrogate father, was Sir Oliver's friend and fellow spiritualist intellectual, F.H.S. Myers, a Fellow of Trinity College, Cambridge, who had died in 1902. The details of the supernatural odyssey were published in a book entitled *Raymond*, which went through a dozen printings between 1916 and 1919 and was republished in abridged form as *Raymond revisited* in 1922.[37]

The interest in and controversy surrounding this book tell us much about the spiritualist revival during the war. *Raymond* is both a personal memorial and a scientific exposition. It is divided into three parts. The first is a memoir in the form of Raymond Lodge's letters home from the front. The second is entitled the 'Supernatural Portion' and describes the means through which Raymond communicated with his family. The emphasis is on a sober recounting of 'the evidence . . . for the persistent existence of one of the multitude of youths who have sacrificed their lives at the call of their Country when endangered by an aggressor of calculated ruthlessness'.[38] The third part considers the philosophical implications of psychical phenomena, and makes out a case for the compatibility of spiritualism with a belief in the divinity of Christ.

The vivid description of Raymond himself helped to give this book its power. Once we read his letters it becomes easier to imagine what Lodge and millions of others dreamed of: the continued development and growth of those whose lives were brutally cut short. But the book demonstrates another powerful source of the spiritualist appeal. It shows the dead themselves attempting to reach the living in order both to help them cope with the pain of bereavement and to help establish the truth of the spiritualist message. War service, in this context, carried on in the after-life as well. Indeed, in the words of one writer in the *Occult Review*, which published testimonies of those who spoke to dead soldiers, the fallen were 'helping to form a Britain or Empire beyond the grave, a better Britain or Empire than exists now on the material plane'.[39]

Raymond was a best-seller during the war, but it was not uncritically received. Even some allies were sceptical of the strength of its findings. Charles Richet did not believe that the case of Raymond had proved the existence of survival after death.[40] Neither did Dr Charles Mercier, who lectured on insanity to medical students in London teaching hospitals. He considered *Raymond* to be debased science. In his view Lodge was simply the 'high priest of telepathy', who uncritically accepted as evidence the flimsiest material provided by unscrupulous mediums, profiting from the wartime 'epidemic of the occult'.[41]

Equally scathing in their criticism of spiritualism were some prominent Anglicans, both lay and clergy. Viscount Halifax, the author of popular volumes of ghost stories, spoke about *Raymond* at St Martin in the Fields in February 1917. He condemned its defence of spiritualism as a snare and a delusion, leading some to disappointment and despair, others to 'ruin', 'madness', or 'diabolical possession'. To claim communication with the dead is to attempt 'to draw a curtain which He has not withdrawn', and to do so without reference to sin or judgment or the

Gospel. 'Such books as those of Sir Oliver', Halifax intoned, 'are the Nemesis which comes from our neglect of the dead.'[42]

The Anglican Bishop of Worcester invited Conan Doyle to speak on spiritualism in the cathedral in October 1919. In response, Canon James Wilson presented a Christian case against spiritualism. Its errors, Canon Wilson said, were many. It assumed that human personality existed after death; for this, no evidence had ever been presented. While the Canon was prepared to recognize psychotherapy, hypnosis, and telepathy as emanations of the subconscious, psychic communication with the dead was pure speculation or worse.[43]

J.N. Figgis, the political philosopher and theologian of the Community of the Resurrection at Mirfield, repeated the denunciation. Spiritualism, he claimed, had increased 'by leaps and bounds' during the war, because those 'crying for light' had been turned away by the church, and had been succoured instead by 'practitioners in the occult who could assure them that all was not lost'. Spiritualism was therefore 'a Nemesis on the Church for its neglect' of those in search of the departed. What could be done in this area, Figgis noted, was limited by Anglican hostility to 'noxious' Catholic practices of praying for the dead. Somewhat obstinately, he asserted that the answer to 'all exaggerated spiritualism is the doctrine of angels'.[44] By this he meant that the belief in the supernatural world could be tolerated if it was constrained by a belief that the human and divine orders were separate. Within this theology, angels could exist and appear; dead spirits could not.

In France, such disputes were part of the longer battle of the Roman Catholic Church against heretical enthusiasms. Many Catholics of conventional temperament, especially in the church hierarchy or in the Society of Jesus, viewed with regret the rash of Marian cults which spread throughout Central and Western Europe in the two generations before the Great War.[45] Such enthusiasms were uncontrolled; some were uncontrollable. Many were dominated by women, and provided a conduit linking the pagan and the Christian which threatened to flood the faithful with elements of folklore vivid enough and attractive enough to displace or eclipse both Christianity and the church. As usual, the practice of parish priests confronted with such phenomena diverged from the blanket denunciation of the church authorities. The range of wartime miracles attested to by priests, nuns, and true believers, was so vast as to suggest that unconventional things did happen in wartime. But on balance, the subtle difference in French – absent in English – between *spiritisme* (spiritualism) and *spiritualisme* (spirituality) defined the distinction between the profane and the sacred as propounded by the Roman Catholic Church.

The boundary between suspect spiritualism and orthodox spirituality was explored by one Catholic writer during the war. In a series of articles in the Catholic review *Frères d'armes*, Yves Villeneuve recounted the inspiring story of a devout woman who was a *marraine de guerre*, a civilian 'godmother' sending letters, packets, and encouragement to soldiers during the war. This woman believed that she could do much more as a *marraine de guerre* for dead soldiers in Purgatory. They were the abandoned ones; they too were stuck in no-man's land; they too needed support and the prayers of the faithful.[46] Notice the differences from the spiritualist position. First, the act of worship advocated in *Frères d'armes* for the souls of the fallen was perfectly consistent with church teaching. Secondly, the prayers of the living were directed towards helping the dead, and not, as in spiritualist séances, the other way around; and thirdly, and perhaps most significantly, the material gap between the living and the dead was not crossed. For orthodox Catholics, the boundaries held; for spiritualists, they were there to be crossed.

Spiritualism at the Front

Superstitions, the uncanny and spiritualism at the Front

Whatever doctrine taught, soldiers believed in the supernatural. Many had little difficulty in accepting the incongruous and the uncanny as part of everyday life. As one Catholic scholar noted, the range of psychic phenomena produced at the front was vast. Some were laughable. But to laugh at them would be a mistake. 'They are manifestations of obscure and profound needs in the popular soul, intimate yearnings which seek their way and which, without wise orientation, will lose their way.'[47]

Soldiers of whatever faith, it appears, had their own 'doctrine of angels'. *Raymond* was read by British soldiers at the Front, and provoked a mixed reaction among Anglican and Non-conformist clergymen in uniform. Some chaplains discussed the book sympathetically, as presenting a challenge to Anglicans to accept that some could arrive at Christian beliefs in unconventional ways.[48] Others were hostile. F.W. Worsley considered it 'a wee bit unhealthy'.[49] G.K.A. Studdard Kennedy wrote that it could never 'take the place of the lively hope which comes of faith in a communication with God'.[50]

The problem for chaplains was that wartime spiritualism was in vogue as much among serving men as among the families they had left behind. As one chaplain told David Cairns, the Aberdeen theologian, 'The British soldier has certainly got religion; I am not so sure, however, that he has got Christianity.'[51] To Geoffrey Gordon, soldiers' prayers – 'petitions from the trenches' – were liberally mixed with 'large numbers of idle and sometimes degrading superstitions which men hold side by side with a vague belief in God'. Spiritualism was a form of superstition and had to be combated, he argued. 'The superstitious man must either be a polytheist or a devil-worshipper, or, more probably, just a fool.'[52] The statement shows why so many soldiers simply ignored what the chaplains had to say.

Soldiers' spiritualism

What Gordon missed was that the experience of the trenches could not easily be explained in conventional theological (or indeed in any other rational) terms. For this reason a host of spiritualist images, stories, and legends proliferated during the conflict among frontline troops. Some tales were about the dead; others about magical forces affecting the living. The sense of the uncanny, of the overdetermined nature of survival in combat can be found in many memoirs and letters written by serving men. Many maintained and occasionally celebrated the robust paradox of a belief in their personal invulnerability and also in the power of fate in determining whether a sniper's bullet or shell had 'their name' written on it. The presence of pagan or pre-rational modes of thought under the appalling stress of combat should surprise no one. Such responses are common enough today; why should we assume that soldiers of the Great War were any different from us?

A Swiss anthropological study addressed the rituals, superstitions, signs, prophecies, legends, and remedies of soldiers in combat. When applied to French and Italian soldiers, this approach yielded a host of strategies for coping with the stress and danger of war. Italian soldiers were particularly ingenious. Some carried three cards, with Caspar, Melchior, and Balthasar written on them; each card was carried in a separate pocket. Soldiers from the Abruzzi carried a small sack of their native soil or dust from a chapel of pilgrimage. British and French soldiers had their mascots, their amulets, and their rituals. So did Wilhelm II, who reportedly wore an amulet of prayers, given to his father by the Emperor Frederick, and inscribed thus: 'With me in Schleswig-Holstein in 1870; in 1870–71 during the religious service at Versailles; at the moment of the reestablishment of the Empire, 18 January 1871.'[53] As one commentator noted, 'L'extraordinaire appelle l'extraordinaire.'[54]

The overlap between folklore and conventional religious modes of expression was considerable. The popular art of all combatants included images of saints or Jesus on the field of battle, and a brisk business in religious bric-a-brac grew during the conflict.[55] Soldiers' spiritualism in the British army did not reach the levels of popularity it apparently enjoyed among French, Italian, or Russian soldiers. Partly this was a reflection of the pagan elements within Catholic and Orthodox imagery, of the flowering of pre-war Marian cults, and of the tastes of a rural population much larger on the Continent than in Britain. For similarities to Continental Catholic spiritualism, one must go across the Irish Sea. There we can find to this day images and objects similar to those produced widely during the 1914–18 war.[56]

In 1917 the cult of Fatima was born, after a sighting of the Virgin Mary in Portugal. Such veneration of the Virgin was a feature of popular piety in the period surrounding the war, and soldiers shared in its imagery, and its fervour. Some 'adopted' St Thérèse of Lisieux, 'the little sister of Jesus' as their protector; others returned to Joan of Arc, whatever the nationality of her executioners.[57]

Religious almanacs provided dozens of tales of miracles on the battlefield. The almanac of the French society of the 'Trois Ave Marias' is but one example. In 1917 it reported one German soldier's belief that the German army had Paris at its mercy in 1914, until the Virgin blocked their way. In the same issue, a secularist teacher who cried 'There is no God. If He exists, He should break the gun in my hand', was immediately killed by a stray bullet, and so on.[58] In such Catholic circles, the hallowed dead were visible through the miracles which faith alone could explain.

Among those without strong ties to the established churches, spiritualism in various forms proliferated. Substantial evidence of spiritualism in the ranks of the French army was published as a result of a remarkable enquiry conducted by Charles Richet during the war. He published in the *Bulletin des armées de la République* on 10 January 1917 an appeal to soldiers to report evidence of 'prophetic dreams, presentiments, telepathy, troubling metaphysical occurrences'. He cautioned them to beware of mistaking false images for true ones, and to pay attention to evidence – notes, comments to friends – which established that the psychic message was received before its external confirmation.[59]

The several hundred responses, Richet noted, came from 'ordinary soldiers, officers, doctors – the ignorant and the intellectual'. Many reported premonitions of death among soldiers not visibly in immediate danger. Ernest Bergeron of the 5th Engineers told of a comrade who, certain of his approaching death, said farewell to his comrades. His death was similar to that of a Captain V., who approached a chaplain, said his time had come, turned to walk in a safe area, but was mistakenly shot by a sentry. Others anticipated wounds or accidents themselves, or uncannily, family members far from the front knew of their misfortunes.[60]

Less rigorous, but parallel, reports emerged in Britain at the same time. One spiritualist writer, Carrington Hereward, produced dozens of 'cases' of spiritualist life in the trenches in his book *Psychic phenomena and the war*. Among them were soldiers' visions of their dead comrades back in the trenches.[61] Hereward also reported cases of dead soldiers who sent messages of hope and consolation to their grieving loved ones. These spirits tried to lift any 'inordinate grief' among the bereaved. Not only was such lingering sadness unnecessary, but it tended to 'mar the happiness of our friends in the Beyond'.[62]

It is evident that soldiers' tales were important in deepening popular spiritualism, in that they added the prestige of the soldier and the weight of his experience to those who lived within or on the fringes of the spiritualist community. On Easter Sunday 31 March 1918, a meeting of spiritualists took place at the grave of Allan Kardec in the Père Lachaise cemetery in Paris. As one observer noted, fallen soldiers joined the ceremony. A huge crowd of them came 'to sustain and inspire us'.[63] This is admittedly an extreme case, but it merely hints at the proliferation of reports of spiritualist phenomena recorded during the war by or about soldiers. It is not that most soldiers were avowed spiritualists. It is rather that the bizarre and unnatural world in which they fought was the perfect environment for the spread of tales of the supernatural.

Legends divine and demonic

As Eric Leed has noted, given the noise and disorientation of battle, myths and stories tend to quieten and reorder the world.[64] This occurred from the earliest days of the conflict, when the shock of war was greatest and the imminence of Allied defeat was hard to deny. When the British army suffered heavy casualties trying to slow the German advance in Belgium in 1914, stories began to circulate about supernatural phenomena on the field of battle.

The most celebrated of these tales concerns the appearance of angelic figures over British soldiers at Mons. The popular writer Arthur Machen claimed he made it up while day-dreaming during a sermon on a Sunday early in the war. He recalled Kipling's tale of a ghostly Indian regiment, added his own 'medievalism that is always there' and produced an army of Agincourt Bowmen to help defend the British army at Mons. The story appeared in the *Evening News* on 29 September 1914, and then took on a life of its own.[65] But this admission of authorship was fiercely contested by others who were convinced that soldiers really did see angelic figures on the battlefield. Harold Begbie recounted the evidence of British nurses who had heard wounded soldiers speak of having seen 'strange lights' at Mons or phantom cavalrymen. Others recalled strange figures tending the wounded, whose gentleness was as remarkable as the fact that they vanished as soon as others started to seek them out. Perhaps, Begbie suggested, Machen had received a telepathic message from a wounded soldier who wanted the word to go forth that the forces of Good were arrayed against the forces of Evil.[66]

The emotional mood of the first months of the war created the perfect atmosphere for such eschatological images, which were incorporated into sermons and religious publications in 1915.[67] The same minds which conjured up angels had little difficulty in seeing demonic forces at work on the other side. Supernatural tales mixed abundantly with shock and fear were rich sources of the proliferation of atrocity stories during the first two years of the war.

The mix of the angelic and demonic in direct accounts of the war may be illustrated by the memoirs of an English nurse, Phyllis Campbell, who had studied music in Germany before the war, and had been trapped in France when it began. She saw cartloads of Belgian refugees passing by, filled with what she said were civilian victims of German atrocities: women whipped or whose breasts had been cut off, children without hands and feet. During this terrible 'Week of Terror and Faith' she also saw the other side of the supernatural struggle. 'The wounded were in a curious state of exaltation', she wrote. They said that the Germans were 'devils – that's why St George is fighting for us'. Others described a 'golden cloud', a 'luminous mist', protecting the British and French. 'Is it strange', Campbell noted, 'that the torment of these has dragged at the feet of the Ruler of the Universe till he sent aid?' 'I have seen no visions', she admitted. 'But in my heart I believe that the Captains of God are leading the Allies to victory.'[68]

The supernatural made another appearance in the language of soldiers who used the metaphor of the trenches as hell on earth. Ford Madox Ford offered these words after peering down on the landscape of the Battle of the Somme:

in the territory beneath the eye, or hidden by folds in the ground, there must have been – on the two sides – a million men, moving one against the other and impelled by an invisible moral force into a Hell of fear that surely cannot have had a parallel in this world.[69]

Henri Barbusse spoke the same language when, in his trench novel *Under fire*, published in 1916 and translated into English in 1917, he spoke of the hell of trench warfare. This anticipates Ezra Pound's now-clichéd litany of soldiers walking 'eye-deep in hell / believing in old men's lies' and was repeated in a more mundane fashion both in soldiers' letters and in journalists' prose and photographic captions. To a degree the frequency of its use helped turn 'hell' into something more than a metaphor, since it provided a set of very old images to describe the indescribable features of the war on the Western Front.

The otherworldly landscape, the bizarre mixture of putrefaction and ammunition, the presence of the dead among the living, literally holding up trench walls from Ypres to Verdun, suggested that the demonic and satanic realms were indeed here on earth. Once this language had a foothold in everyday parlance, it became easy for ordinary men to imagine that hell was not some other place, some exotic torture chamber under the trap doors leading to the nightmare worlds of Hieronymus Bosch or Roger van der Weyden. To all too many Englishmen and women, Hell was indeed just across the Channel.

The legend of the return of the dead

Apocalyptic legends marked the first two years of the war. As the casualty lists lengthened and the war dragged on, the realm of the supernatural was dominated more by ghostly apparitions than by divine or demonic ones. Again this is hardly surprising, since the problem of coping with a war of annihilation through legends and tales had been eclipsed by the problem of mass bereavement in a war seemingly without end. Here too we inhabit the perimeter of pagan beliefs, for conventional Christian modes of burying the dead and commemorating them were simply irrelevant in this war. The dead were literally everywhere on the Western Front, and their invasion of the dreams and thoughts of the living was an inevitable outcome of trench warfare. Lieutenant George Goddard of the Royal Garrison Artillery spoke for many soldiers when he wrote: 'In a world of Death one would expect to penetrate the veil when it hangs so constantly before one!'[70] Both during and after the war, tales of the return of the fallen were common, and produced a form of popular literature linking front and home front in a kind of spiritualist embrace.[71]

To Léon Denis of the *Revue Spirite*, the dead formed their own army 'to assist soldiers in the epic struggle'.[72] Even after the Armistice, the fallen are still at their posts. To one spiritualist poet, the dead also marched past to celebrate the victory.[73] As we have noted in chapter 1, it is precisely this image that the French film-maker Abel Gance used in his classic romantic epic of the war, *J'accuse*. On the day of the celebration of victory, on 14 July 1919, the living march through the Arc de Triomphe; the dead march above it.[74]

Spiritualism and escape

There is one instance of wartime 'spiritualist' behaviour which is so unusual, and yet so indicative of the chords the subject touched during the war, that it deserves separate discussion. Two prisoners of war, Lieutenants E.H. Jones of the Indian Army and C.W. Hill of the Royal Flying Corps, were incarcerated in the prison camp at Yozgad in Turkish Anatolia, where many of the survivors of the British garrison at

Kut-el-amara were held. Jones had been captured in Sinai; Hill was shot down in the same sector, also in 1916.[75] Their camp was in a village 'cleansed' of Armenians by Turkish troops convinced that Armenian wealth had been stashed in the area by the inhabitants before they were murdered. Jones and Hill concocted the story that they were spiritualist mediums, able to lead the camp commandant, his cook, and his aide – a Turkish Jew, Moïse Eshkenazi – to this cache of wealth. The prisoners did so by convincing the Turks that the two men were in the hands of a spirit of unlimited power. They first established their spiritualist credentials with the camp hierarchy, using Moïse (whom they called the 'pimple') as their interlocutor, and then, unbeknownst to all but one of their fellow prisoners, conjured up an identity as madmen: Jones as a raving lunatic convinced that the English were his enemies, out to poison him; Hill as a religious melancholic, who only read the Bible and sulked in silence. This enabled them to guide the camp commandant and his assistants on a wild-goose chase for buried treasure and to convince them first to isolate the two 'mediums' in separate accommodation, and then to send them to hospital for treatment of the insane in Constantinople. They left Yozgad in April 1918, and managed to convince a host of Turkish physicians and soldiers in the Turkish capital that they were indeed out of their minds. The purpose was to be sent back to England. Their 'performance' entailed severe hardship, and Hill contracted dysentery which almost killed him in Constantinople.

In the spring of 1918, when they put on this astonishing performance, exposed by no one, it was impossible to know that the war was reaching its decisive phase. The war, they thought, could last for years. By the time the Turkish medical authorities arranged their dispatch back to England, the war was in its final weeks. When repatriated to Egypt, they met fellow prisoners who had been freed a mere two weeks after Jones and Hill.

What makes the story even more remarkable, though, is the way it came about. We have noted that soldiers on the Western Front read Oliver Lodge's *Raymond*. Astonishingly, the book also reached British prisoners of war in Turkey at the end of February 1918. Jones read it and thought it was dangerous nonsense. But he had the brilliant idea of using it to effect an 'escape' from the camp, a use of spiritualism Lodge would never have imagined. 'The pimple' also read *Raymond*, and translated it into Turkish for the benefit of the camp commandant. Thus the book served as a blueprint for one of the more remarkable frauds of the war.[76]

Jones' hostility to spiritualism was caustic and complete. In the preface to his account of his escapades, he wrote:

If this book saves one widow from lightly trusting the exponents of a creed that is crass and vulgar and in truth nothing better than a confused materialism, or one bereaved mother from preferring the unwholesome excitement of the seance and the trivial babble of a hired trickster to the healing power of moral and religious reflexion on the truths that give to human life its stability and worth – then the misery and sufferings through which we passed in our struggle for freedom will indeed have had a most ample reward.[77]

Jones knew all the tricks of the 'professional medium' to whom a wife or mother in mourning

represents so much bread and butter. Assuredly these bereaved ladies should be invited to attempt to communicate with their dead husbands and their dead sons! The more the merrier, and there is no time like the present. We have a million souls just 'gone over' in the full flush of manhood. The fodder of last year's cannon is the splendid manure for the psychic harvest of the years to come. Carry on! Spread the glad tidings! Our glorious dead are all waiting to move tables and push glasses, and scrawl with planchettes, and speak through trumpets, and throw mediums into ugly trances – at a guinea a time. There they are 'on the other side', long ranks of them, fresh from the supreme sacrifice.[78]

Jones used *Raymond* as a script. He had Moïse, the 'pimple', adopt the stance of Sir Oliver Lodge, a man of science able to transcribe the psychic events Jones conjured up.[79] Without the assistance of this gullible Turkish Jew, treated with contempt (and a touch of anti-Semitism) by Jones, the fraud would never have succeeded. They convinced Moïse not only that they were in touch with the 'Beyond', but that the Jewish people were the only hope for the future of humanity, and that he, Moïse, would be their leader.[80] 'I'd like to get him an introduction to Sir Oliver Lodge', Hill remarked to Jones at one point in their escapade.[81]

Jones and Hill had to pass the scrutiny of some very sophisticated Turkish physicians, one of whom, Mazhar Osman Bey, was both an authority on mental illness and a man of such shrewdness that the 'lunatics' feared detection. They fooled him too, despite the fact he was the author of a pamphlet in Turkish, presented to Jones, entitled *Against spiritualism*. Osman Bey challenged Jones to 'write a reply to his pamphlet from the spiritualist point of view'. Jones' dry comment on the whole episode is encapsulated in the phrase: 'Perhaps this book will do instead.'[82]

Spiritualism and commemorative art

The link between the spiritualist world and the experience of the Great War is evident in the commemorative art and ritual of the postwar period. This was perhaps more prominent in France and Germany than in Britain. Different romantic and religious traditions informed British developments, but they shared with French and German art the same tendency to envision the dead as part of the landscape or the lives of postwar society. German romanticism drew heavily on classical images, and especially on motifs of heroic masculinity.[83] British romanticism emphasized the pastoral, perhaps best exemplified in the English country-garden ambience chosen for the thousands of small British cemeteries scattered throughout France and Flanders and looked after to this day by the Commonwealth War Graves Commission (see chapter 4).

The man who chose the Biblical phrase which dominates the approach to these cemeteries was Rudyard Kipling.[84] 'Their name liveth for evermore' had a particular meaning for Kipling, the poet of Empire. His 18-year-old son was severely wounded in the face, and then was lost, presumed killed, at Loos in September 1915. Kipling's poem 'En-Dor' brings out the mood of bereavement and the spiritualist temptation which he, like so many other grieving men and women, had felt during and after the war.

> The road to En-Dor is easy to tread
>> For mother or yearning Wife.
> There, it is sure, we shall meet our Dead
>> As they were even in life.
> Earth has not dreamed of the blessings in store
> For desolate hearts on the road to En-Dor.

The reference is to the Book of Samuel, in which Saul asks the witch of En-Dor to call up the ghost of Samuel. This is a terrible sin for Saul, who thus violated Jewish law, which treated witches as pariahs and their practices as anathema. For this sin (and others), Saul dies in battle. The Biblical reference to spiritualism and to the fate of Saul gives a sombre ending to Kipling's poem:

> Oh, the road to En-Dor is the oldest road
>> And the craziest road of all!
> Straight it runs to the Witch's abode,
>> As it did in the days of Saul,
> And nothing has changed of the sorrow in store
> For such as go down on the road to En-Dor!

We have already noted the use of this poem by E.H. Jones, the escape artist of Yozgad. He entitled his memoirs *The road to En-dor* and placed this stanza of the poem on the title page. Kipling's view of spiritualism, though, was more complex than that of Jones and many other enemies of the practice.

Kipling explored the spiritualist world with the same ambivalence in a number of his short stories. A positive and gentle spiritualism may be found in 'The gardener'. Here he tells the story of Helen Turrell, a woman who (we are told) had selflessly raised her brother's illegitimate child, who is killed in the war. Helen travels to his grave in France. After an unpleasant encounter with a half-deranged Englishwoman secretly visiting the grave of her illicit lover, Helen goes to the vast cemetery where her 'nephew' is buried. Unable to find the grave, she is helped by a man she 'supposes' to be a gardener, who 'with infinite compassion' shows her the spot where her 'son' lies. Whether or not the dead soldier is her nephew or her son, the Christ figure guides her to the grave.

More negative and less Christian in its treatment of spiritualism is Kipling's story 'A Madonna of the trenches'. This is a tale of a soldier, Clem Strangwick, who went mad after the war because he had witnessed a few years earlier a ghostly trench encounter. Serving in the same unit was a friend of his family, Sergeant Godsoe, who one night sees an apparition of his Aunt Armine, to whom Godsoe was engaged. In the trenches, the lovers reach out for each other, but he stops, saying, 'No, don't tempt me, Bella. We've all Eternity ahead of us.' He invites her into a dugout, wedges the door shut, and is found dead the next day. Strangwick goes completely mad when he receives a telegram saying that his Aunt Armine had just died. All this is told in a spiritualist or Masonic Lodge, full of people who seek some kind of spiritualist truth, and 'go down the road to En-Dor'.[85]

Kipling's tales drew on wartime legends[86] and tell, in a highly ambiguous manner, of the spiritualist way of remembering the dead after the war. Other writers did so too. Poetry conjured up the dead in metaphors common to all languages. In later years, the publication of soldiers' writings, both fiction and autobiography created a new genre of 'War literature'. Much of this prose was in itself a kind of war memorial, a ritual entombment of and separation from those who had fallen by those who had survived.[87] In both ephemeral and more enduring works by ex-soldiers, the presence of the dead, both as metaphor and myth, was acknowledged. This literature recreated the uncanny world of the soldiers and brought home, as Kipling had done, their mixed language of irony, humour, and superstition. If the war created 'modern memory' as Paul Fussell has claimed, it was a traditional, even archaic, kind of memory that came out of the conflict.[88]

One good example of the persistence of older forms of commemoration within the spiritualist communion is the phenomenon of psychic photography. As I will show in chapter 6, this business antedated the war,[89] but had a special market during and after it. Mrs Ada Emma Deane was an Islington charwoman, whose brother, a chemist, set her up in a lucrative profession. She offered the credulous visions of the dead on Armistice Day, hovering above the living. One such photograph was taken from the wall of Richmond Terrace in Whitehall during the two-minute silence of 1922. The brand-new plate was given to her by

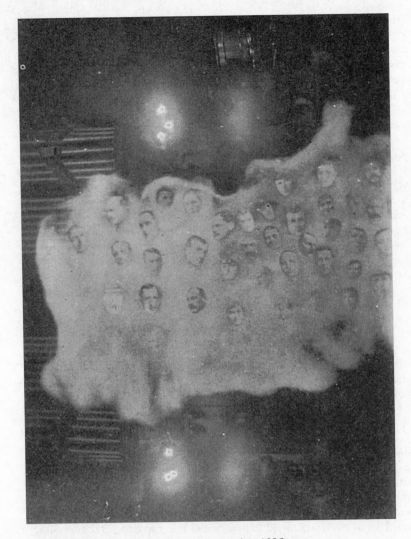

9. Spirit photography, Woolwich, 11 November 1926

Mrs E.W. Stead, whose late husband had been a well-known journalist and a radical spiritualist. He went down with the *Titanic*. The plate was exposed throughout the two-minute silence, then developed in the dark-room of 5 Smith Square, a half-mile away, in the presence of Mrs Stead. The inchoate mass floating above the heads of the mourners was flecked

10. A spirit photograph taken by Mrs Deane during the two-minute silence, Remembrance Day, Whitehall, 1922 (before the ghosts of the dead appear)

11. A spirit photograph taken by Mrs Deane, Remembrance Day, Whitehall, 1922 (with the ghosts of the dead)

by faces, presumably of the dead.[90] Other similar photographs taken by Mrs Deane show other extra-terrestrial presentations on Armistice Day. One is at Woolwich Town Hall, where the dead, oddly, are at right angles to the living.

Before we sneer at these (and other) photographs as of the Elmer Gantry variety, it is important to note how widespread was the interest in psychic photography, and how many people of different social positions, levels of education, and political beliefs were prepared, at least for a moment or two, to suspend disbelief about it. One such moment was the extended period of bereavement during and after the Great War.

Artists of very different outlooks used images of the dead of the Great War rising from their graves. I have noted Will Longstaff's *Menin Gate at Midnight* above, and in chapter 6 I will try to show how Stanley Spencer's *Resurrection of the Soldiers* at Burghclere shares the imaginative space in which spiritualism flourished. Neither Longstaff nor Spencer shared the faith, but both described the dead as both in this world and beyond it. Here was the essential premise on which the spiritualist search rested.

Conclusion

The period of the 1914–18 war was the apogee of spiritualism in Europe. By the 1930s its appeal had waned, especially among scientists, and it had relatively few prominent adherents during and after the Second World War.[91] In private practice, spiritualism still flourishes, but as a subject of public debate it has become marginal or merely exotic. The reasons for this change go beyond the purpose of this book. Our intention here is simply to suggest the powerfully conservative effects of the Great War on one aspect of European cultural history. The upheaval of war led not to a rejection or recasting of attitudes about spiritualism, but to the deepening of well-established Victorian sentiments and conjectures concerning the nature of the spiritual world.

Some of these practices and beliefs were superstitious. Others entered the realm of the uncanny, the paranormal, the necromantic or the mystical. All shared a tendency to slide from metaphors about remembering those who have died to the metaphysics of life after death. The 1914–18 conflict certainly did not create these modes of thought, but neither did the war discredit or destroy them. Millions needed all the help they could get. Should we really be surprised that the magical and mythical realm flared up at a time of mass death and destruction?

However 'modern' the Great War was, its immediate repercussion was to deepen and not transform older languages of loss and consolation. As we shall see in chapter 6, Stanley Spencer was certainly not the only artist who explored the spiritualist realm in the aftermath of the war. André Breton was obsessed by automatic writing, a sure sign that the history of spiritualism and the history of surrealism overlapped substantially.[92] The Romanian-born surrealist painter Victor Brauner acted as a medium.[93] Max Beckmann was fascinated by the Kabbala and other esoteric texts,[94] as is the contemporary German artist Anselm Kiefer.[95] With respect to spiritualism, these artists were closer to the mainstream of their culture than some of them were prepared to admit.

It is one of my central arguments that the enduring appeal of spiritualism, alongside many other traditional motifs, was related directly to the universality of bereavement in the Europe of the Great War and its aftermath. When the survivors of the Great War were able to transcend their losses, when after many years they left the war behind, then the force of the spiritualist revival waned. The search for the sacred did not cease; it simply took other forms. After the Second World War, spiritualism, in its original sense of communication with the dead, faded into the margins of cultural history, where it has remained to this day.

4

War memorials and the mourning process

The search for the 'meaning' of the Great War began as soon as the war itself. For some people that search goes on to this day. Visible evidence of that quest may be found in towns and villages throughout Europe. There are war memorials in virtually all of them: sculptures, plaques, or other objects that recall the 1914–18 war and the sacrifices it entailed.

Whom or what do they commemorate? Precisely what about the Great War do they ask us to remember? There is no single answer to these questions. Different cultural norms and religious traditions yield different meanings. First, the visible or stated subject of commemoration varied as between national communities. In France, a visitor to any major town or village will encounter a *monument aux morts*. This funereal term locates French war memorials within a tradition of suffering and sacrifice. In Britain and other Anglo-Saxon countries, and in Germany and Austria, the visitor will soon find his way to the local war memorial or *Kriegerdenkmal*. Here the specific subject of remembrance is at times fixed less precisely; the suggestion is that war memorials invite us to recall more than the central facts of loss of life and bereavement in the Great War.

But central facts they remain. While ambiguities of iconography and ritual are undeniably present in war memorials, and while they embody and proclaim a host of commemorative messages about war, they do not obliterate the simple truth that people die in war, and in the Great War their number was legion. That message may be direct; it may be indirect or muted; it may be drowned in sentimentality or lies, but between the lines of noble rhetoric, through the mass of figurative or sculptural detail, the harsh history of life and death in wartime is frozen in public monuments throughout Europe and beyond.

Decades after the Great War, what we now see obscurely, or with a hurried glance, was once visible and arresting to all. In this chapter, I concentrate on war memorials as foci of the rituals, rhetoric, and ceremonies of bereavement. This aspect of their significance has not attracted particular attention from scholars in this field. Most have been drawn to war memorials as carriers of political ideas, from Republicanism[1] to nationalism,[2] imperialism,[3] fascism,[4] Stalinism,[5] or the multiple justifications of the call to arms.[6] There is as well a flourishing interest in these objects as public sculpture, and art and architectural historians have contributed much to our understanding of their character and form.[7]

From the Acropolis to the Arc de Triomphe, war memorials have been central to the history of European architecture and public sculpture. They have been important symbols of national pride. But however powerful the aesthetic or political message they carried or attracted, these monuments had another meaning for the generation that passed through the trauma of the war. That meaning was as much existential as artistic or political, as much concerned with the facts of individual loss and bereavement as with art forms or with collective representations, national aspirations, and destinies.

War memorials were places where people grieved, both individually and collectively. The ways they did so have never been fully documented. For anyone living in Europe, these 'documents' are part of the landscape. To find them one must simply look around. The still visible signs of this moment of collective bereavement are the objects, both useful and decorative, both mundane and sacred, placed in market squares, crossroads, churchyards, and on or near public buildings after 1914. Some were built during the war, mostly in the decade following the Armistice. They have a life history, and like other monuments have both shed meanings and taken on new significance in subsequent years.

This chapter tells one part of their life history and the life history of those who built them and visited them, and of some whom they helped to cope with loss. To understand war memorials is to see more clearly how communities mourned together during and after the Great War.

War memorials inhabit three distinctive spaces and periods: first, scattered over the home front before 1918; second, in postwar churches and civic sites in the decade following the Armistice; and third, in war cemeteries. The first category includes many objects of commemoration which drew on heroic images of war. The second had ecumenical and conventional patriotic elements, emphasizing at once the universality of loss and the special features of national political and aesthetic traditions. These local war memorials arose out of the postwar search for a language in which to reaffirm the values of the community for which soldiers had laid down their lives. The third embodies a more enduring achievement and a more universal language, drawing on particular traditions but, on occasion, transcending them.

The Home Front, commemoration and citizenship in wartime

Preserving the nation at war

After August 1914, commemoration was an act of citizenship. To remember was to affirm community, to assert its moral character, and to exclude from it those values, groups, or individuals that placed it under threat. This form of collective affirmation in wartime identified individuals and their families with the community at large, understood both in terms of a localized landscape and a broader and more vaguely defined national entity under siege or threat.

The first event commemorated was the call to arms. Mass armies were mobilized in all the major combatant nations without any significant opposition or obstruction, and monuments were built early in the war to celebrate this unprecedented response to the call to arms. Where the prompting of notables stopped, and popular initiatives began is very difficult to determine. Proud citizens of a working-class district in the East End of London marked the voluntary enlistment of 65 men in a street of 40 houses in one cul-de-sac by setting up what they called a 'street shrine'.[8] The religious echo was one they chose, possibly reflecting the strength of Irish Catholicism in the area, but also blending well with general views of the war as a conflict of the children of light against the children of darkness.[9] According to the Bishop of London, the Anglican rector of South Hackney helped to create the shrines, which were visited by the Queen in 1917.[10] In Australia and New Zealand, celebrating the act of volunteering was also central to commemoration. The lists engraved in stone during the war of those who had joined up helped to encourage further enlistment; later lists formed a permanent and immediate chastisement of those who chose not to go.[11]

As soon became apparent, the war the men of 1914 engaged to fight was nothing like the war that developed after the Battle of the Marne. Henceforth, the focus of commemoration shifted away from the moment of mobilization to the stupendous character of the conflict itself. One form of such commemoration was the collection and preservation for posterity of the ephemera of war. This was by and large a civilian operation, although many soldiers were collectors as well. It was also a patriotic act, and led (unintentionally at times) to the creation of what remain to this day the most important public repositories of artefacts and documents about the war.

In Britain, an officially sponsored Imperial War Museum was formed in 1917, ironically enough on the grounds of the former 'Bedlam' lunatic asylum.[12] It houses many military objects and records, as well as an invaluable collection of photographs, manuscripts, books, and works of art. In France, the initiative was private. What is now known as the Bibliothèque de documentation internationale contemporaine started as the repository of wartime records, collected by the Leblanc family in their apartment in avenue de Malakoff, but intended from the start as a state museum. In the trench journal *Tacatacteufteuf*, soldiers on leave were encouraged to visit the collection, which ultimately was indeed passed on to the City of Paris, and then the University of Paris, in one of whose outlying campuses it remains to this day.[13] The Australians established a 'War Museum' (now the Australian War Memorial) in October 1917. Soldiers were invited to submit objects for display. As Ken Inglis has written, one 'Digger' replied forthrightly:

> The GOC recently made a request for articles to be sent to the Australian War Museum, especially those illustrating the terrible weapons that have been used against the troops in the war. Why not get all the Military Police photographed for the Museum?[14]

A more austere parallel is the private initiative of a German industrialist, Richard Franck, which led to the creation of the Kriegsbibliothek (now the Bibliothek für Zeitgeschichte) in Stuttgart.[15] The Director of the Historical Museum in Frankfurt was responsible for yet another German collection of documentation and ephemera related to the Great War.[16] On a smaller scale, the Cambridge University Library, spurred on by the University Librarian, gathered together a war collection of printed books and other documents.[17] Similar efforts produced war collections in the New York Public Library.

Most of these acts of preservation were intrinsically valuable. They were the work of civilians, many too old to fight, or with sons in uniform, and determined to preserve the dignity and honour of their country's war effort. By their very nature, they both glorified the war effort and contained, at least initially, little about the appalling character and costs of trench warfare.

This was in part a function of censorship. But it also reflected some features of the mystification of warfare, especially in the press, whose 'eye-wash' struck many soldiers as absurd or dangerous.[18] Commemorating the war in this ill-informed and blatantly non-combatant manner took on the air of propaganda, as indeed some intended it to do. Like most propaganda, it did not dwell on the sadder facets of the war: the maimed, the deformed, the dead, the widows, the orphans, and the bereaved.

After the war, the character of such collections was criticized powerfully by the pacifist activist Ernst Friedrich, who set up an Anti-war Museum in Berlin in 1924. Its collection of documents and gruesome photographs showed everything the patriotic collections omitted. In displays of savage images of the mayhem caused by war, Friedrich pointed out graphically the dangerous selectivity of the patriotic collectors of wartime memorabilia, documents and books.[19] It is important to note that even though Friedrich's monument to the victims of war was more unsparing and (in a sense) more truthful than the pro-war collections, both arose out of prior political commitments. Commemoration was a political act; it could not be neutral, and war memorials carried political messages from the earliest days of the war.

War memorials and popular culture

The mobilization of popular culture on behalf of the nation's war effort occurred in all combatant countries, and was bound to mark commemorative forms. Each nation developed its own language of commemoration, but some features were universal. One was the tendency to locate the men of 1914–18 in the long history of martial virtue. There is hardly any difference between the treatment of Marlborough at Blenheim, Nelson in Trafalgar Square and, a century later, Hindenburg in Berlin, except that Hindenburg was immortalized in gigantic form while the war was still going on. The victor of Tannenberg became a towering figure, whose lofty achievements were symbolized by a three-storey model placed prominently in the Tiergarten in the heart of Berlin.

The celebration of military or naval commanders was one way in which to glorify national military traditions. In some countries, though, a more egalitarian language was used to proclaim the virtues of the martial spirit. In Australia and New Zealand, generals and admirals did not bear this symbolic weight; the common soldier or sailor was the link with the past.[20] In France, both elevated and obscure soldiers celebrated the Gallic military tradition.

What cities did on a grand scale, individual households could replicate in a more domestic manner, thanks to the emergence of the thriving industry of wartime kitsch. Commemorative images were marketed on a mass scale in the Great War. Iron Hindenburgs were available in many materials and sizes.[21] As I note in chapter 5, the French martial tradition was sold in poster form through the thriving 'industry of *imagerie d'Epinal.*

Whether on the level of national celebration or domestic ornamentation, each nation adopted its own distinctive commemorative forms. One excellent example is the German phenomenon of 'iron-nail memorials'.[22] These objects decorated sculptures, plaques, and domestic items like tables, and have (to my knowledge) no equivalent in France or Britain. We can learn much about them from an instruction book prepared by two public-spirited Germans early in the war. They were made of 'Ready-for-use materials' and were ideal 'for patriotic undertakings and

12. The Iron Hindenburg

ceremonies in schools, youth groups and associations'. These objects were described both as 'war landmarks' and as war memorials, but the distinction between the two was rarely clear. In each case, the figure or image to be celebrated or sanctified was outlined or described by a series of nails. The iron cross was the most popular choice for such objects, requiring according to the handbook between 160 and 200 nails per cross.[23] Among the images they displayed were iron crosses embellished by the Imperial initial or the date, but other nail memorials picture the turret or outline of a U-boat, Teutonic floral designs, swords, and mosaic designs for table tops.

Austrian examples of this form of patriotic art may also be found,[24] but it would be a mistake to assume a common Catholic origin. Indeed, Crucifixion images and motifs were probably more prevalent in Protestant than in Catholic art, especially in Germany, where Marian and other saintly iconography proliferated. Furthermore, the culture of popular nationalism in Imperial Germany was essentially Protestant. Sedan Day was to some extent an anti-Catholic festival, and the ambiguous place of Catholics within the state was not resolved before 1914. Iron-cross nail memorials fit in much more closely with Protestant celebrations of the Prussian military genius and the grandeur of the *Kaiserreich*.[25]

Ceremonies at which these iron-nail memorials were created or displayed enabled patriots of whatever faith to show their commitment to the cause. Some paid for the privilege of nailing by contributing to a war charity or benevolent organization. Others introduced schoolchildren to the nobility of sacrifice in war by the declamation of lofty poetry. We can get some idea of the deliberate medievalism of this practice by citing one of these poems:

> From whistle of lead, the bloody wound
> A warrior falling
> A red cross on the white ground
> A trusted arm;
> Leaning and leading in the heat of battle
> A red cross arm
> A good bed is made
> Warm and comfortable . . .[26]

And so on into a misty, medieval past remote from the ugliness of industrialized war.

A 24-part ceremony surrounding such poetic affirmations was outlined for school or other civic use. It was replete with the choreography of uplifting allegorical Teutonic plays, songs, and noble poetry. Items 22–4 were the following: 'Deutschland über alles', a Pledge of Truth and Faith in Victory, and a round of 'A mighty fortress is our God', Luther's hymn. The imagery of cleansing through the shedding of blood is repeatedly invoked, further suggesting the militarized Christianity of the memorial itself.[27] It is not at all surprising that such iron-nail memorials, and the ceremonies surrounding them, soon framed the lists of the fallen.[28]

This is indeed the commemorative art of Tannenberg, not Verdun, and we can almost see the idealized form of Hindenburg, presiding in spirit over these ceremonies, just as he had done after his victory. Here is his own version of it, written just after the war:

In our new Headquarters at Allenstein I entered the church, close by the old castle of the Teutonic Knights, while divine services were being held. As the clergyman uttered his closing words all those present, young soldiers as well as elderly 'Landsturm', sank to their knees under the overwhelming impression of their experiences. It was a worthy curtain to their heroic achievement.[29]

Some of the central themes of commemoration are visible in these early wartime rituals and the legends surrounding them. The need to reaffirm the nobility of the warrior by an appeal to 'ancient' tradition, the tendency to highlight soldiers' sacrifice and civilian debt, and the consequent unending duty of dedication to some noble communal task: all are expressed here in a romanticized form which described a war which changed rapidly after August 1914. So rapidly indeed that these rituals and the verse they inspired, were bound, as Sassoon put it, 'to mock the corpses' of whatever nationality 'round Bapaume'.

War memorials after 1918: metaphor and allegory in public space

The phenomenon of 'nail memorials' is just one example of the initial phase of commemorative art, in which the glorification of sacrifice was expressed in a deliberately archaic language, the cadences of knights and valour, of quests and spiritualized combat. The problem with this language was that it was too unreal, too uplifting, too patriotic, and insufficiently sensitive to the desolation of loss. For this reason, other forms of commemorative art emerged, both during and after the war. These objects and rituals expressed sadness rather than exhilaration, and addressed directly the experience of bereavement.

These two motifs – war as *both* noble and uplifting *and* tragic and unendurably sad – are present in virtually all postwar war memorials; they differ in the balance struck between them. That balance was never fixed; no enduring formula emerged to express it, though traditional religious images were used repeatedly to do so.

Both religious and lay communities devoted themselves to the task of commemoration after 1918. The resulting monumental art provided a focus for ceremonies of public mourning beginning in the decade following the Armistice, and continuing to this day. The languages, imagery, and icons adopted varied considerably according to artistic convention, religious practice, and political conviction. They also reflected more mundane considerations, such as the ability of the community to pay for monuments. Consequently, some plans were scrapped and others had to be scaled down or redesigned to suit the means of the donors. Despite powerful currents of feeling about the need to express the indebtedness of the living to the fallen and the near-universality of loss in many parts of Europe, commemoration was and remained a business, in which sculptors, artists, bureaucrats, church-men, and ordinary people had to strike an agreement and carry it out.

The business of commemoration

As Bertrand Tavernier showed in his recent film *La vie et rien d'autre*, the mix of the profane and the sacred is vividly evident in the chequered history of public commemoration after the Great War. His account of the mixed cast of characters surrounding postwar commemorative work is remarkably close to reality.

The first group of actors consisted of public officials. These were either elected or self-appointed notables who took upon themselves the time-consuming and frequently fractious task of drawing up plans, interviewing artists, arranging subventions, overseeing acquisition of a site, and the final construction or emplacement of the memorial. 'Quality control' was a worry for both artists and their patrons; self-appointed groups offered their services to communities seeking to distinguish between appropriate and inappropriate commemorative art.[30]

Some people had personal reasons for investing so much time in the business of commemoration: they had lost a son, or a brother, or another loved one. Others did it in the same way as they approached urban renewal or traffic problems. Even allowing for English understatement, the proceedings of the local committee which oversaw the construction of the Cambridge War Memorial, at a prominent intersection near the railway station, resemble discussions about many other town or university affairs. To such perennial committeemen, the construction of a war memorial was just one more task to overcome.[31]

Some individuals devoted themselves to this work with unusual energy and dedication. Consider the case of the war memorial in Mulhouse in the east of France. Over 2,000 men from this city had died on active service in the war. One man was primarily responsible for the construction of the town war memorial. Max Dollfus, *délégué générale* of the organization Souvenir Français, became vice-president of the Comité d'initiative pour le Monument aux Morts. The mayor was titular head of the committee, but Dollfus did the work. He spent five years on the project. After initial discussions about what to do in 1919–20, during which no consensus emerged, two commissions were convened, a *commission financière* and a *commission artistique*. Dollfus chaired both. A site was chosen on a prominent boulevard, and an estimated budget of

TRUMPINGTON
WAR MEMORIAL

Ceremony of Unveiling and Dedication

SUNDAY, 11TH DECEMBER, 1921

13. Poster advertising the inauguration of the war memorial, Trumpington, Cambridgeshire, 11 December 1921

250,000 francs was prepared, for the costs of the monument and a garden in which it would be set. The artistic committee invited eighteen artists to submit designs. Of these, seven produced models in October 1922. The choice was in the hands of a jury composed of both local people and outside specialists, including the director of the Office of

14. The War Memorial at March, Cambridgeshire, after Remembrance Day

Fine Arts in Strasburg, and the president of the Société des amis du Louvre. They chose three projects as worthy of prizes, of 5,000, 4,000, and 1,000 francs each. The first and third were both given to the same team, which had submitted two designs to the committee. They were both the work of the prominent Catholic sculptor Maxime Réal del

Sarte, who was awarded the job of constructing the memorial, in conjunction with a firm of architects in Mulhouse. To obtain the services of Maxime Réal del Sarte was a major achievement for the city. He was a celebrated artist, an *ancien combattant* who had lost an arm in combat at Les Eparges, and who went on to design over fifty war memorials.[32] His plan for Mulhouse was suitably impressive. It included two statues of deliverance and peace, two *chimères* (mythical beasts), an obelisk, and a floral garden with reflecting pools.

The original estimate of costs was increased to 300,000 francs, to be divided between professional payments, works, materials, and other purchases. The *conseil municipal* set aside 50,000 francs for the project, and looked to private donations for the rest. The final cost was 309,000 francs. The deficit was made up through the indefatigable efforts of individual fundraisers. Approximately 260,000 francs were raised from 8,563 donors. One woman, Mme Henriette Deiber, whose son was killed in 1918, knocked on 630 doors in a working-class quarter, and over 3,000 schoolchildren from 31 schools collected about 8,000 francs.

Five years after the project had been approved, the monument was ready for assembly, and the landscaping was finished. The statues weighed 7,500 kilograms each, and the surrounding construction and *chimères* required two blocks of 10,500 kilograms each. It was completed in June 1927 and officially inaugurated in that month.[33]

The Mulhouse memorial was characteristic of many other commemorative projects. One public-spirited individual, who happened to be the brother of the president of the Chamber of Commerce, spent years in committee-work and negotiation to see it through. In small towns, it was usually the mayor.[34] He had to navigate through artistic, political, and financial troubles, the solutions to which required the help of many local people, great and obscure.

Money was never irrelevant to the task at hand, nor were the interests of local contractors and artisans. Local committees attached late-fee penalties to the agreement with sculptors, who were often well-known local craftsmen. Unlike a man of the standing of Réal del Sarte, they could be instructed explicitly as to the requirements of the community. The small town of Belvaincourt in the Vosges insisted on a guarantee that the statue would be unpainted. The village of Bult opted for granite from the Vosges for a *poilu*, sculpted 'on the model of 1871', 'painted and bronzed', and precisely 1.80 metres high. Public funds were also supplemented by private subscriptions.[35] In some projects, the costs were shared by the municipality, the department, the state, and local inhabitants. In some communities people gave generously; in others, they did not.[36]

Financial problems were not always resolved through public donations. The Cambridge War Memorial had to be scaled down when funds ran out. An eight-foot-high returning soldier became a six-foot-high statue. The design intended to make the figure's stride abnormally long, to emphasize its athleticism; the smaller version did not increase this distortion, but visually reinforced it.[37] The reasons for this effect are pecuniary, not artistic, and this in a town where some of the richest private institutions in the country were based. Most were engaged in their own, private acts of commemoration, which limited their contribution to other public projects.[38]

However sacred the task of commemoration, it still touched all the chords of local loyalties, petty intrigues, favouritism, apathy, and indifference. It also was about contracts, payments, and profits. In all major combatant countries there were firms like Swanser & Son of Kingsway, London, who advertised regularly as makers of 'Memorials, bronze, brass, duralumin'.[39] Their appeal serves to remind us that the business of commemoration was always that: a business, shaped by the character of the community which undertook it.[40]

Metaphor and religious expressions of mourning in commemorative art

Some war memorials were essentially religious in character; others, primarily secular. It is important, though, not to exaggerate the difference. In Germany many memorials with specific religious reference were placed not only in churchyards and cemeteries but also in public thoroughfares. The separation of church and state in France, and the character and history of Anglican iconophobia made it more difficult to adopt such flexibility in reference to explicitly religious imagery, but exceptions occurred in these countries too. It is preferable to speak of religious expressions in commemorative art as a whole, rather than to limit the discussion to those located within the precincts of parish churches or their superior institutions.

Furthermore, as I suggested in chapter 3, the pagan perimeter of Christianity was inhabited by a host of spiritualists, many of whom believed that their practices were compatible with traditional religious teachings. Their quasi-religious approaches to communicating with the dead should also be considered when approaching the varied terrain of commemoration after the Great War.

With these caveats in mind, it may be useful to suggest that religious commemorative art had certain features found less prominently in secular forms. Not surprisingly, artists and sculptors drew on the rich traditions of late-nineteenth-century funerary art.[41] Among the choices available for religious commemorative sculpture, the Pietà was perhaps best suited to express the sadness of the millions who had lost their sons. It also fitted on rectangular surfaces of a funerary kind, and drew the viewers' gaze to the fallen body held in the Madonna's arms.

We can see this form of religious art throughout Europe, and especially in Germany. Consider a few examples. In 1927, the sculptor Otto Hitzberger carved a wood Pietà as a war memorial for the Laurentiuskirche in the Moabit district of Berlin.[42] The same motif was used by Ruth Schaumann for her 1929 stone casting of a Pietà sponsored by the German Catholic Women's League, and placed in the crypt of the Frauenfriedenskirche in Frankfurt. The inscription is specifically female: 'In praise of our husbands, sons, brothers, fathers, R.I.P.'[43] Here the metaphor was direct: there is no image of a soldier, only the unstated metaphor of the equivalence of his death with the Passion of Christ.

Variations abound. They included the Pietà form, but with mother and fallen soldier, as in the town of Brotterode, by Hans Dammann,[44] and in Karl Haussmann's sandstone sculpture (1929) in the old cemetery in Grötzingen.[45] There is the parallel motif of the comrade and fallen soldier (the work of Hermann Neppel in 1923), placed in the market square of Backnang,[46] and the more classical design by Friedrich Bagdons (also 1923) in the entrance to the cemetery at Freudenstadt, incorporating an unclothed seated woman staring out over a prone and unclothed dead man identified as a soldier only by his helmet.[47]

Other scenes from the New Testament were used in similar ways in other German war memorial art. In 1922 Georg Busch designed an altarpiece for the Chapel of the Nails in Bamberg Cathedral. His work is in painted lime wood, and depicts the two Marys and St John grieving over the body of Christ.[48] At Euskirchen, a plaque was placed in the town *Gymnasium*. It was designed by Albert Figel in 1922, and lists teachers and students killed in the war. The image is of a dead soldier attended by three angels, with the archangel Michael on the right and St Barbara on the left.[49] At Frauenzell, the war memorial shows a statue of Jesus cradling a dying soldier, still holding a hand grenade.[50]

Clearly the range of Christian reference was infinitely malleable and easily identified. Many examples of such art are visible in stained-glass windows in churches throughout Europe. Here the rule of horizontality does not apply. In glass, at least, religious motifs point upwards. In the Pas-de-Calais, 235 churches had been destroyed or severely damaged during the war. The stained glass incorporated in these resurrected churches shows the same ingenuity at adapting Christian metaphors and sacred stories to contemporary history. The flight from Egypt paralleled the flow of refugees away from the north of France early in the war.[51] Joan of Arc makes an appearance here, as at the church of Saint-Martin at Graincourt-Lès-Havrincourt,[52] and there are many neighbouring churches, as at Eglise Notre-Dame at Bertincourt, with scenes of Mary interceding with Christ for the soul of a dead soldier,[53] or (at Ecourt-Saint-Quentin) of angels accompanying the souls of the fallen to heaven.[54] Stained glass in Britain was used to similar effect, with images of tanks and aircraft adding to the traditional lexicon of warfare in art.[55] The stained-glass windows at Brampton in Cambridgeshire show a soldier receiving the Sacrament at the front, and other scenes equating the Passion with the war. In one window a soldier's gaze at a wayside crucifix leads us to the same message.[56] In Germany, similar adaptations appeared. One example is the stained-glass window in Kemnath Cathedral, showing a Benedictine monk holding a cross and kneeling next to the coffin of a dead soldier.[57]

None of this iconography is surprising or particularly original. Those in mourning who turned to the churches for aid in their sorrow were bound to dwell on traditional devotional art and sculpture. In Britain and (not surprisingly) in Ireland, Celtic crosses were particularly popular.[58] As Catherine Moriarty has shown, wayside crucifixes and crosses appeared in many parts of England,[59] as indeed they did in British war cemeteries, where Reginald Blomfield's Cross of Sacrifice, a bronze sword on a stone cross, was placed.[60]

The Cross of Sacrifice was an abstract, chivalric, form. In some war art, though, crucifixion was more closely related to the fate of individual soldiers. The best-known example is Derwent Wood's 'Canada's Golgotha', a commemoration of an alleged German atrocity, showing a crucified Canadian soldier, surrounded by a group of mocking German soldiers. The diplomatic furore produced by this bronze sculpture resulted in its removal from displays of official Canadian war art. Whatever the morality of its suppression, the realism of this sculpture was far removed from the healing intentions of most commemorative art which referred to Christian iconography for consolation, not accusation.[61]

One important vehicle for the propagation of Christian messages of consolation was photography. Here the suffering of Christ could be suggested in the mutilation of his image in wayside crosses or churches. The Saarburger Cross, an image of Christ with outstretched arms, magically liberated from the Cross, obliterated presumably by bombardment in the first months of the war, was especially popular. It sold well as a wartime postcard. Other illustrations showed churches and religious objects torn by war, in the same way (it was suggested) as were the bodies of soldiers. These images were widely distributed before and after 1918.[62]

In many ways, therefore, both 'high' and 'popular' culture (rarely divided clearly in any case) found in traditional images and techniques the inspiration for much of their work. In Germany, older art forms were rediscovered. The removal from Colmar in Alsace to Munich of the Isenheim Altarpiece 'for restoration' or 'safekeeping' in 1917 led to a renewed interest in Grünewald's art. According to one scholar, he provided a language to express the anguish many felt about the 'crucifixion' of Germany during and after the war.[63] The sources of

Rouault's remarkable series of engravings, *Miserere*, explicitly located in the artist's meditations on the 1914–18 war, may similarly have been late medieval.[64]

Both popular craftsmen and avant-garde artists experimented with religious forms and icons in the aftermath of the war. The German sculptor Ernst Barlach created a remarkable aerial, suspended sculpture of an angel in the Gustrow Memorial, removed by the Nazis from Magdeburg Cathedral.[65] Otto Dix and Max Beckmann both chose the triptych as the framework for their extraordinary paintings on the war. Dix's may have been a direct comment on Grünewald's crucifixion. His interest in the old masters is evident both in his war art and in his overall painting technique.[66] One context of the work of Dix, Beckmann, and a host of other artists is the efflorescence of religious commemorative art after the Armistice.

None of it reached the nadir of despair perhaps most powerfully evoked in the masterpiece of Hans Holbein, *Christ in the Tomb*, painted in 1521, to which I will refer in chapter 6. Here there is no vertical line, no attendant mourners, no hope at all. Even Grünewald's masterpiece, with its pock-marked and hideously tortured Christ, places the crucifixion in a cycle of hope. Not so Holbein. Dostoyevsky's Prince Mishkin captures its chilling effect when he tells us that 'some people may lose their faith by looking at that picture!'[67] That is what those seeking sustenance from religious art after the Great War least wanted. Consequently, the rudiments of hope, of aesthetic redemption of the suffering of the war, of resurrection, of transcendence are never far from commemorative art of religious inspiration.

Bereavement, political messages and civic war memorials

Hope is a central theme in secular commemoration of the Great War. It is expressed in a multitude of ways, some banal, some profound. But there is another level on which to understand the wave of construction of these monuments after the Great War. They were built as places where people could mourn. And be seen to mourn. Their ritual significance has often been obscured by their political symbolism which, now that the moment of mourning has long passed, is all that we can see. At the time, communal commemorative art provided first and foremost a framework for and legitimation of individual and family grief.

Other interpretations of war memorials stress their political character. George Mosse refers to them as places where the nation worshipped itself. They are conservative expressions of the 'cult of the fallen', successfully exploited by Fascists in Italy and Germany.[68] Patricia Dogliani has pointed out the significance in Italian commemorative art of messages about the Risorgimento.[69] A study of American war memorials is appropriately entitled *War memorials as political landscape*.[70]

These, and many other works, have enriched our understanding of the character of civic commemoration. But we must beware of mistaking the part for the whole. War memorials had a specific purpose; lack of attention to this can lead to misunderstanding their meaning. One scholar, adopting a Foucaultian framework, has interpreted war memorials as exercises in 'biopolitics'. His argument takes this form. In the construction of war memorials, death is deconstructed: its horror, its undeniable individuality, its trauma, and the ignominy often associated with it, are buried. Then it is reinvested with meaning, as an abstraction, a collective sacrifice remote from individual extinction. 'A nos morts' is a disembodied message – there is no one speaking. Similarly, the dead are no longer individual people. They appear solely as names, inscribed on the war memorial. Their sacrifice thereby takes on the form of an expression of a general will, a collective spirit embodied in the state. In these memorials, the state affirms its right to call on its citizens to kill and to die. The only way to see their force is to place them in the context of 'une véritable économie de pouvoir'.[71]

Such are the fruits of this kind of semiological analysis. The strength of this approach is that it identifies war memorials as sites of symbolic exchange, where the living admit a degree of indebtedness to the fallen which can never be fully discharged. What this interpretation lacks, though, is an historical sense of the meaning ascribed to war memorials at the time they were constructed. That meaning was highly personal. It used collective expression, in stone and in ceremony, to help individual people – mothers, fathers, wives, sons, daughters, and comrades-in-arms – to accept the brutal facts of death in war.

One expression of the sombre, existential purpose of war memorials set in civic space is their relative freedom from expressions of anger and triumph. There are clear national differences here, reflecting the distinction between victors and vanquished. But even in the victorious powers, the faces of noble soldiers sculpted in stone in hundreds of village squares only occasionally express exhilaration. Fatigue, and a reflective acceptance of duty and fate, are etched into their features. They have been through the fire, and rarely proclaim its virtues.

When anger appears, it is located less in soldiers than in the bereaved. One good example is the war memorial at Péronne, on the Somme, where a mother stands, clenched fist outstretched in rage, over the prone body of her son. However, as Annette Becker has shown, the sculptor Paul Auban simply refashioned a pre-war memorial to the victims of shipwreck by putting a uniform on the dead man.[72] The evils of war, like the cruel twists of natural disasters, are hardly moments for political celebration; the elemental fact is that they leave armies of the dead and the bereaved in their wake.

Prost was the first to draw attention to what he called the 'monument funéraire', both patriotic and pacifist, in French commemorative art of the Great War.[73] More recently Annette Becker has discussed sensitively many other instances of the iconography of bereavement in war memorials. Old people, women, children: they are there in the memorials themselves. A mother with a Breton headdress, alongside a father, cap in hand, stand near a cross in the war memorial at Plozevet. At Gentioux, in the Département of Creuse, a child points to the inscription 'Maudite soit la guerre'. The sculptress Emilie Rodez engraved the same message in the monument at Equeurdreville, near Cherbourg, recalling the children of the village who died in the war. This monument is unusual in that it shows mother and children as victims, rather than primarily as mourners. More characteristically, at Suippe, in the Marne, a woman brings in the harvest alone, sadly gazing at all that is left of her husband, his helmet. At Compiègne, in one of Réal del Sarte's monuments, a mother and child grieve together.[74]

The Compiègne memorial reveals another level of meaning. The child in this statue looks to his mother with a questioning face. What are we to assume she is enjoined to tell him? Surely that his dead father died for a just cause. But there is little in war memorials to suggest that they are there to instil in the young a belief in the virtues of *their* return to the battlefield.

Citizenship is affirmed in war memorial art, but it is expressed in terms of a sacrifice which must never be allowed to happen again. The Abraham and Isaac myth, the Akedah, is the clear reference. As in Genesis, the message is the end of human sacrifice, not its eternal perpetuation.

Almost all commemorative monuments also express a sense of indebtedness. The living can go about their lives in freedom because of the selflessness and dedication of the man who fell. But it is only now, decades later, that anyone could see this message as repetitive, or enjoining a repetition. To do so ignores the sheer magnitude of the war effort, the pain of loss, the exhaustion of the populations who endured it, and the reluctance of many Europeans to contemplate the need to fight yet another war against Germany, until forced to do so by the Nazis.

This is not to suggest that most war memorials were pacifist. A few were; the overwhelming majority were not. But the attitude to the war they represent reflects their local character and their sensitivity to the needs of the bereaved, whose identities were in no sense a mystery to those who attended the annual ceremony, or who stopped for a moment's reflection or just passed by. The names inscribed were of the men who had died, to be sure. They were also the names of families in mourning, and pointed out who needed help in the aftermath of the war.

The form of many war memorials and the ceremonies surrounding them reinforce the view that their initial and primary purpose was to help the bereaved recover from their loss. In many war memorials there is a fence, doorway, or border clearly marking the distinction between an area adjacent to the monument, a space set apart from the rush of daily life. In some larger memorials, the border described the space set aside for mourners, either family members, veterans, or officials, speaking for the community, who were present during annual commemorative ceremonies. But this point must not be pressed too far, since there was a more practical reason why war memorials were enclosed: to protect the monument from accidental damage through contact with passers-by, or even from the attentions of grazing animals. In these village sculptures, there was no space for individuals to stand between the memorial and the fence. They, and everybody else, stood alongside it when they remembered the dead.[75]

These ceremonies took many forms, but they usually involved a procession to the war memorial, either on 11 November or on other similarly hallowed days relating to great battles like the Somme. The order of the procession showed the character of the ceremony. In Royston in Hertfordshire, the war memorial was inaugurated in March 1922. The monument was visited in turn by the Anglican vicar and Congregational minister, followed by 'a large number of relatives of the fallen men carrying wreaths', 150 ex-servicemen from the town, the local Voluntary Aid Detachment of nurses, and then civic groups, including the fire brigade, the urban district council, the girl guides, and the boy scouts. The chairman of the memorial committee spoke first, recalling the Biblical story of King David, who mourned the loss of his son, but who nonetheless returned to his tasks. He noted 'if we live true and useful lives', then our turn will come to meet the fallen 'on the Eternal shore'.[76] The memorial itself is unusual, in shadowing the Tommy in stone with ghostly white stone figures in relief, representing the men of Royston who had gone to wars past.[77]

In Macclesfield, the procession was led by all the local worthies, the Mayor, the Town Clerk, the Town Council, the Board of Guardians, the War Memorial Committee, the Higher Education Committee, the headmaster of the local grammar school. We see the full battery of the Protestant voluntary tradition, the same tradition that had created the Pals' battalions of volunteers, many of whose names were inscribed on the memorial itself. They made way at the memorial for a soldier, Private George Taylor, blinded in the war, and (as the local newspaper report noted) 'being particularly pitiful as he leaned on the shoulder of a comrade who led the way'. Those bereaved looked up at the memorial, which showed a soldier gassed, and a grieving woman, 'a wife, mother, sister and sweetheart, who suffered in silent agony, and without complaint. She stands in the attitude of sad but stoic sorrow, holding in her hand a wreath of remembrance.'[78]

In Dartford, the war memorial was unveiled by a lady, her 'voice, broken with emotion, but bravely struggling to express a calmness she is far from feeling'. Her words were followed by a stirring speech by the mayor asking the living 'to reap the harvest, so prodigal in the sowing, before the forces of evil once more capture the citadel of human intelligence and set men warring against their fellows'.[79]

In both places, we can see clearly the two essential components of these ceremonies: the public recognition, and mediation through ritual, of bereavement; and the appeal to the living to remember the dead by dedicating themselves to good works among their fellow men and women. Grief and indebtedness, sadness and personal commitment are the pillars of local commemoration.

British ceremonies parallel the structure of ritual surrounding war memorials in interwar France, described so eloquently by Antoine Prost.[80] The local processions of mourners, the local dignitaries and veterans were all there. So were the town schoolchildren. What they heard was not a recounting of the names of glorious generals, or a celebration of the grandeur of victory, but a simple list of the names of the fallen. They heard old soldiers speak in the name of the living and the dead; they heard of the horrors of war and of the need to act for peace as the first duty of citizenship. Equality in death meant a dedication to promote equality in life; the appeal was for an extension of the camaraderie of arms into civilian life, in order to temper the petty local quarrels that faded into insignificance when set against the terrible sacrifices of the war.[81] The rhetorical emphases in French ceremonies and the prominence of veterans reflect the specific features of the tradition of the nation in arms.[82] But it was natural that ex-soldiers should feel a special responsibility to their fallen comrades, a responsibility expressed through care of their often makeshift graves on the battlefield, and care to mark their sacrifice in later years. The wartime pledge not to forget the tombs of the fallen, stated openly in French trench journals,[83] was honoured in later years in front of village war memorials.

There are important differences in national forms of commemoration. Utilitarian war memorials were preferred in many parts of Britain, a reflection of Protestant traditions remote from French political culture.[84] Some English communities carried on the old Puritan war against graven images, preferring obelisks to crosses. Obelisks abound in France, too, in part because they were cheaper to build than figurative art. Images of chivalry were preferred in some British memorials, though they are not entirely absent in French war art. Gertrude Alice Meredith Williams put a Crusader knight on horseback among Great War infantrymen in her design for the Paisley War Memorial. Even though he survived the war, the myth of Lawrence of Arabia is intrinsically tied up with the war. His gravestone shows the same search for the medieval. Eric Kennington carved an effigy of Lawrence, berobed, and with legs crossed, Crusader-style, for his grave in Dorset.[85] A similar monument was built for André Thome, a 'soldier of the right' who fell near Douaumont at Verdun. New Zealand memorials commemorated the dead; most Australian memorials list all who served, not just those who fell. This distinction arises in part from the fact that New Zealand had conscription, but Australia did not.[86] In addition, the uniformity of ritual in France was missing in Britain, where administration never became the work of art perfected by French bureaucrats.

Particularities abound, especially on the regional level.[87] But the absence of hatred, or triumph, or worship of the military *per se* is evident not only on both sides of the English Channel, but also in Antipodean memorials. In their place, we find abundant evidence of commemorative ceremonies as moments of collective bereavement, during which the special place of those who lost their loved ones, their comrades in arms, friends, or family members, was recognized and solemnized.[88] War memorials marked the spot where communities were reunited, where the dead were symbolically brought home, and where the separations of war, both temporary and eternal, were expressed, ritualized, and in time, accepted.

That act was located specifically in time and place. Once the moment of initial bereavement had passed, once the widows had remarried, once the orphans had grown up and moved away, once the mission of veterans to ensure that the scourge of war would not return had faded or collapsed, then the meaning of war memorials was bound to change.

They could have had no fixed meaning, immutable over time. Like many other public objects, they manifest what physicists, in an entirely different context, call a 'half-life', a trajectory of decomposition, a passage from the active to the inert. Their initial charge was related to the needs of a huge population of bereaved people. Their grief was expressed in many ways, but in time, for the majority, the wounds began to close, and life went on. When that happened, after years or decades, then the objects invested with meaning related to loss of life in wartime become something else. Other meanings derived from other needs or events may be attached to them, or no meaning at all. The public experience of fête and civic ritual has also tended to fade away,[89] so that now, seventy-five years after the Armistice, war memorials have become the artefacts of a vanished age, remnants of the unlucky generation that had to endure the carnage of the Great War.

War cemeteries, abstraction and the search for transcendence

So far I have examined the passage from wartime celebration to postwar commemoration in religious and secular space. There was one other site of memory important for collective bereavement in the aftermath of the

Great War. War cemeteries were civil in character, as befitted the fact that men of all beliefs and of no belief fell in the war. These cemeteries were the repository of remarkable commemorative art, and some of it reaches a level of abstraction and universality unattainable in other memorials. Four examples are at Verdun, at the Cenotaph in London, at Thiepval on the Somme, and in Vladslo in Belgium.

The Trench of the Bayonets

The mix of traditional forms – pagan as well as Christian – with abstract motifs appears clearly in the war memorials located in military cemeteries. Consider the case of the monument near Verdun at what has become known as the Trench of the Bayonets. The story of this trench was bathed in myth. The facts are undisputed. The 3rd company of the 137th French Infantry Regiment was wiped out on 12 June 1916, in a ravine between Thiaumont and Douaumont. After this engagement, the trench they had occupied was found to have been completely filled in. Protruding from the earth at regular intervals were a number of bayonets, beneath which were the remains of the men of this unit. Legend had it that they had stayed at their posts until buried alive; common sense suggests that they were buried by bombardment, and that their graves were marked by the German soldiers who, briefly, had occupied this sector.[90]

The Trench of the Bayonets, like the Battle of Verdun, became the stuff of myth, therefore, during the war itself.[91] A French army commission was sent to Douaumont in 1917 to verify the incident. They found an aviator who had flown over the battlefield on 12 June, and who told of seeing ground shift suddenly, thus accounting for the cave-in of the trench. What better, more moving, symbol could there be of the indomitable will of the French army not to be broken at Verdun? The Commission decided that the site must be preserved.

To realize this objective, an American banker, George F. Rand, donated 500,000 francs. He had visited Verdun in December 1919, and had been deeply moved by the site and worried about its desecration. He noted that while the men buried there are mute, 'their appeal to the world is eloquent'. Urgent action was needed, since 'already bayonets were stolen and gashes made in the guns and pieces taken away as souvenirs'.[92] Immediately after conferring with Clemenceau and confirming the gift, Rand was killed in a plane crash. The monument therefore had a double meaning: to remember the giver as well as the event he wished to commemorate.[93]

The form of the memorial was minimalist. The architect-in-chief of the Meuse and Marne, André Ventre, summed up the idea behind his

15. The Trench of Bayonets at Verdun, as illustrated in the *Guide Michelin* to Verdun of 1926

design in the following terms:

It is evident that nothing could typify the tragedy and heroism of the bayonet trench better than the trench itself. With its rugged, broken outlines and in its narrow space in which are entombed the erect forms of nearly one hundred soldiers, the trench is enclosed with an impressiveness no monument could ever equal.

My design comprises a steel and concrete covering over the position, protecting the protruding rifle barrels and bayonets from the rain and snow and providing also a suitable tomb for the dead soldiers who, of course, remain interred in the trench. The structure will be heavily reinforced with steel and everything possible to ensure durability will be done. I guarantee the monument to last for at least 500 years.[94]

The monument was inaugurated in December 1920 by a host of dignitaries: the President of the Republic, Millerand, Generals Joffre, Foch, and Pétain. Rand's surviving son and American dignitaries were also there. As one contemporary observer put it, the sacred character of the monument was entailed by its design:

The Trench of the Bayonets will be everlastingly protected against the attacks of time or the cyclical pillage of the tourists. It will also be saved from the invasion of vegetable growths that would destroy its aspect and will remain under the dome of stone which shelters it, the symbol of all the trenches of the French front where the same magnificent drama of anonymous sacrifice has taken place.[95]

In its 'utmost severity' and its avoidance of 'Anything cheap or approaching the fantastic', the monument to the Trench of the Bayonets sidestepped the dangers of 'sacrilege'. Instead it took on the character of a Roman memorial. The emerging bayonets were likened to the slaves supporting Roman generals who, according to Herodotus, heard voices saying to them: 'Look behind you; they make you what you are.'[96]

The need to preserve the sacred from the twin dangers of 'destruction and commercialization' is a repeated theme in the creation of war memorials after the Armistice. The Trench of the Bayonets is unusual, though, in its austere avoidance of allegory, figurative art, or ornamentation. The hope is to approach the timeless by avoiding contemporary icons. The preference for the traditional is explicit. As one observer put it, the Trench of the Bayonets resembles the 'eternal monuments of Brittany, of that primitive age when man fought against the savage beast and the chaotic forces of nature'. The reference to Breton forms was entirely appropriate; the 137th Infantry was composed of men from Brittany and the Vendée, two of the most traditionally Catholic and conservative regions of France.[97]

This monument is both unique and characteristic of many others built in the immediate postwar years. The fact that it was a joint Franco-American venture set it apart from most other commemorative projects. But in its character and iconography, it was like many others. Both Rand and the architect Ventre understood that the sites of memory needed preservation to stop the voyeur or the tourist from degrading them. But what form was appropriate to the necessary act of preservation?

Their answer was original. They concluded that the most fitting memorial was the site itself, unembellished, unchanged. That is why they simply covered it with a concrete shell. Safe from the elements and the public, the men whose sacrifice symbolized millions of others', could rest in peace, undisturbed by art. The Trench of the Bayonets is a war memorial of a special kind: a tomb frozen in time and preserved not *by*, but *from* art.

Such minimalist sensibilities drew attention to the unmistakable fact that the site of memory was a tomb. But there is one irony which must be recognized. The location chosen for commemoration was flat; the place where the bayonets were found was a series of shell craters some 30 metres away. The memorial is, therefore, on an *imaginary* site of heroism. It is at best adjacent to the place where the men of the 137th regiment died.[98] Thus from the very outset the attempt to preserve the site of memory 'as it really was' entailed the creation of myth. Given the nightmarish quality of the landscape created by ten months of combat, it is hardly surprising that no one knew the precise location of the Trench of the Bayonets. What mattered was to preserve a site as modestly and austerely as possible, and this they did.

In the architecture which appeared both elsewhere at Douaumont and throughout the vast military cemeteries of the Western Front, artistic forms approached and sometimes replicated the simplicity of the Trench of the Bayonets. Many drew on pagan and Christian motifs to announce and (where possible) preserve the sacredness of the site.

Lutyens and elemental commemoration

A striking minimalism is evident in two of the most important British war memorials, the Cenotaph in Whitehall and the Memorial to the Missing at Thiepval on the Somme. Both are the work of Sir Edwin Lutyens, and show the specific features of abstract funerary art, so different from wartime patriotic commemorative forms and from postwar exercises in civic or religious art.

The Cenotaph
The story of the creation of the Cenotaph in Whitehall in the heart of London has been told many times.[99] But some features of this extraordinary moment of British commemoration are worth noticing here as they specify the distinctive features of what Lutyens himself referred to as the 'elemental mode' of commemorative art.

16. The Cenotaph, shortly after the unveiling ceremony, 11 November 1920

It was elemental in form and substance. Lutyens was a geometrician, who saw in mathematical relationships a language to express both architectural ideas and religious beliefs of an unconventional kind. He was a pantheist who moved in theosophist circles, through his wife's commitment to the movement and their friendship with some prominent spiritualists, Oliver Lodge, Arthur Balfour, and above all Annie Besant, president of the Theosophical Society and life-long champion of the cause of India. Lutyens' theosophy was ecumenical rather than occult, and his work in India as architect of New Delhi deepened his knowledge of and commitment to express what he took to be universal truths.[100] 'All religions have some truth in them', he wrote to his wife Emily in 1914, 'and all should be held in reverence.'[101]

Those universal truths were expressed in his two great projects in commemoration of war. The Cenotaph was initially meant to be the temporary centrepiece for a march past of the victorious armies and their leaders in London on 19 July 1919, along the lines of a similar parade in Paris five days earlier. The catafalque erected for the event in Paris was hastily removed when Clemenceau and other leaders objected to its 'Germanic' monumentality.[102] The object designed by Lutyens for the London march, in contrast, was so powerfully evocative

103

of the mood of collective bereavement that, later that year, it was transformed by popular demand into a permanent, indeed, *the* permanent British war memorial, fixed to the place in Whitehall it had been meant to occupy only temporarily.[103] An abstract architectural form had somehow managed to transform a victory parade, a moment of high politics, into a time when millions could contemplate the timeless, the eternal, the inexorable reality of death in war.

A cenotaph is, literally, an empty tomb, and by announcing its presence as the tomb of no one, this one became the tomb of all who had died in the war. In the heart of London, in Whitehall, in the middle of the street adjacent to the Houses of Parliament – the seat of government – Westminster Abbey, and Horse Guards Parade, it brought the dead of the 1914–18 war into history. It did so without the slightest mark of Christian or contemporary patriotic or romantic symbolism, a feat which did not endear Lutyens or his work to traditional Christians.[104]

There is a mathematical precision to the work which is entirely invisible to most viewers. It was unabashedly ancient, recalling Greek forms, with their curved surfaces creating the illusion of linearity, or entasis. As Lutyens himself noted of the Cenotaph:

all its horizontal surfaces and planes are spherical, parts of parallel spheres 1801 ft. 8 in. in diameter; and all its vertical lines converge upwards to a point some 1801 ft. 8 in. above the centre of these spheres.[105]

Lutyens the geometer took the form of Greek commemorative architecture but stripped it of any hint of celebration.

Lutyens' Cenotaph is a work of genius largely because of its simplicity. It says so much because it says so little. It is a form on which anyone could inscribe his or her own thoughts, reveries, sadnesses. It became a place of pilgrimage,[106] and managed to transform the commemorative landscape by making all of 'official' London into an imagined cemetery.

How far we have come from the patriotic mode of commemoration, from the collection of artefacts of victory, from the trophies distributed among Allied communities, or the evidence of heroism under arms. Lutyens' Cenotaph leapt over the mundane into myth, and by doing so provided a focus for collective mourning of a kind unknown before or since in Britain.

There is an interesting recent analogy to the phenomenal appeal of the Cenotaph, which helps account for its strength. Maya Lin's Vietnam Veterans Memorial of 1982 is like the Cenotaph in many ways. She also brought the American dead of the Vietnam war back into American history, by placing the memorial between the Lincoln memorial and the Washington monument. She also eliminated all hint of a celebration or affirmation of patriotism, the nobility of arms, or the dignity of dying for a just cause. All we see are names, and our own reflection. Just as in the case of the Cenotaph, the Vietnam memorial has become a point of pilgrimage, drawing people to it as none of the more figurative and clichéd monuments has done.[107] Both monuments go beyond the political, and beyond conventional architectural forms, to express existential truths too often obscured in the rhetorical and aesthetic fog of war and its aftermath.

Thiepval

Though Lutyens drew on classical forms, he tended to reduce them to simpler and simpler outline or notation. This process has no better expression than in the Monument to the Missing of the Battle of the Somme at Thiepval. The hill dominated the battlefield. The terrifying and murderous task of taking it and the surrounding terrain was one of the most appalling chapters in the history of the war. Total casualties on both sides exceeded 1 million men; perhaps 600,000 died among the British and French forces. Of the British and Allied losses, the bodies of approximately 73,000 of these men were never found. It is their names which are inscribed on the internal walls of Lutyens' memorial.

Lutyens again chose geometry to express the inexpressible nature of war and its human costs. He took the form of the triumphal arch, and multiplied it. Four such arches describe the base of the memorial; their height is two and a half times their width, and they are superseded by a series of larger arches placed at right angles to the base. The ratio of the dimensions of the larger to the smaller arches is also precisely $2\frac{1}{2}$ to 1. The progression extends upward, from smaller arch, and therefore smaller area of emptiness to larger arch, and larger area of emptiness, to still larger arch in the centre of the monument, to nothing at all. We arrive at the vanishing point well above the ground, just as was the case with the Cenotaph. Just as in the case of the Cenotaph, Lutyens brilliantly managed to create an embodiment of nothingness, an abstract space unique among memorials of the Great War.

In the centre of the monument is a simple sarcophagus, from which one sees two small cemeteries of French and British soldiers, whose names are 'known to God', as the British inscription reads. All around are the other, smaller monuments to phases or encounters in the Battle of the Somme. The Thiepval monument is in the red brick characteristic of the region, and, depending on the angle of vision, it is either massive (when the open archways are hidden) or spacious (when the archways are confronted head-on).

One prominent recent interpreter, the architectural historian Vincent Scully, has described the face of Thiepval as 'a silent scream', a cry of protest against the unimaginable suffering of the Battle of the Somme. This is probably mistaken, though a good indication of the extent to

17. The Monument to the Missing at Thiepval (Somme)

which great art attracts different meanings in different generations. It is difficult to accept Scully's view that Thiepval was meant to be 'an enormous monster' with 'demonic eyes', or a 'horrific mask'.[108] We of the late twentieth century see these things in the monument, but Lutyens did not put them there. He was a conventional patriot, whose wartime swings of mood followed closely the trajectory of the fortunes of the British army.[109] Pacifism was simply not in his bones.

Not that Lutyens romanticized the battlefields or the cemeteries covering them. On the contrary. He wrote to his wife in July 1917 from France, and told her about the shock of seeing the detritus of warfare and some of the awful wrecked terrain of the Western Front.

The 'cemeteries' – the dotted graves – are the most pathetic things, specially when one thinks of how things are run and problems treated at home.

What humanity can endure, suffer, is beyond belief . . .

The graveyards, haphazard from the needs of much to do and little time for thought. And then a ribbon of isolated graves like a milky way across miles of country where men were tucked in where they fell. Ribbons of little crosses each touching each across a cemetery, set in a wilderness of annuals and where one sort of flower is grown the effect is charming, easy and oh so pathetic. One thinks for the moment no other monument is needed. Evanescent but for the moment is almost perfect and how misleading to surmise in this emotion and how some love to sermonise. But the only monument can be one in which the endeavour is sincere to make such monument permanent – a solid ball of bronze![110]

Here we see in embryo the two facets of Lutyens' commemorative art: the minimalist and the geometric, either nothing or a ball of bronze to commemorate loss of a kind and on a scale unfathomable perhaps even to those who went through the battle.

The same impulse is behind his design of a 'Great Stone of Remembrance', a white altar, placed in British military cemeteries, alongside Blomfield's Cross of Sacrifice.[111] Once again Lutyens's choice was ecumenical and abstract, not Christian. He sought out pictures of the Great Stone Elephant at the Ming tombs in China, and aimed to use such imagery to escape what he took to be the narrow parochialism of Christian symbolism.[112] It is not at all surprising that his approach was not to the taste of all Christians, or that the British government found a way to incorporate both his approach to commemoration and that of more conventional architects like Blomfield and Sir Herbert Baker, his rival and colleague with whom he had worked in Delhi before the war.[113]

Lutyens designed over ninety war memorials, both private and public, and many of his public commissions bore the same distinctive marks of mathematical abstraction in preference to figurative or allegorical forms. His design for a memorial at St Quentin, which was never realized, as much as his completed plans for memorials at Etaples, Arras, Gezaincourt, Hersin, and Barlin in the Pas-de-Calais all show the same mind at work.[114] It was not at all a mind closed to conventional imagery, especially when an individual was commemorated. Witness the mounted cavalry officer, by Alfred Munnings, on a plinth designed by Lutyens in commemoration of Edward Horner in the Church of St Andrew, Mells, Somerset. Lutyens also accompanied Horner's mother when the two of them placed a tablet in the parish church for Raymond Asquith, the Prime Minister's son and her son-in-law.[115] Here too the subject was the loss of one man. But so many individuals had died that, for Lutyens, a different language was required to express the meaning of the 'lost generation'. While inspecting sites for the war memorial at Mells, Lutyens simply noted of the people accompanying him: 'All their young men are killed.'[116] In this setting he went beyond Christian symbols of sacrifice, and explored what he called more 'elemental' (or universal) responses to the terrible loss of life in war.

His monument to the missing at Thiepval is not a cry against war, but an extraordinary statement in abstract language about mass death and the impossibility of triumphalism. In Thiepval Lutyens diminished the arch of triumph of Roman or French art, and indeed of his own imperial designs in New Delhi, executed on the eve of the war, literally to the vanishing point. Whether or not his calculations had it in mind, it is a singular fact that the most imposing view of this monument is from the air, where it presents a majestic form, light and eternal, invisible to those of us who come to Thiepval, as the soldiers did in 1916, on foot.

Käthe Kollwitz and Vladslo

Lutyens was present at the dedication of his war memorial at Thiepval on 2 August 1932.[117] A few days before, another war memorial had been erected at the Roggevelde German war cemetery, near Vladslo in Flemish Belgium. It is the work of Käthe Kollwitz. Her sculpture is of two parents mourning their son, killed in October 1914. There is no monument to the grief of those who lost their sons in the war more moving than this simple stone sculpture of two parents, on their knees, before their son's grave.

There is no signature of the artist, no indication of individual proprietorship, no location in time or space. Only sadness, the universal sadness, of two aged people, surrounded by the dead, 'like a flock' of lost children. The image is Käthe Kollwitz's own.[118] The story of her struggle to commemorate her son Peter's death in war testifies both to her humanity and to her achievement in creating a timeless memorial, a work of art of extraordinary power and feeling. Through the monument to her son Peter, she brought commemorative art to a level beyond that of most of her contemporaries.

Käthe Kollwitz was forty-seven when the Great War broke out. She was a prominent Berlin artist, whose lithographs *A weavers' rebellion* (1898) and *Peasants' war* (1908) established her as a master printmaker and visual poet *par excellence* of the suffering of the masses. She was the granddaughter of a Königsberg pastor, and his message of duty and calling informed all her work. Her husband was a physician, whose practice was in the drab Prenzlauer Berg district of Berlin, and whose patients brought before her eyes the evidence of deprivation, degradation, illness, and tragedy which she transformed into art.[119] Her aim was to avoid formalism and overelaboration, and to use drawing and printmaking to simplify and render immediately accessible the humanity of her subjects. Her drawings of working-class life, past and present, all exhibit her belief in the need to keep 'everything to a more and more abbreviated form . . . so that all that is essential is strongly emphasized and all that is unessential denied'.[120]

Peter Kollwitz volunteered early in the war, and was killed, on 30 October 1914, aged eighteen, in Flanders, not far from Langemarck, a name henceforth synonymous with the self-sacrificing idealism of German youth.[121] 'Your pretty shawl will no longer be able to warm our boy', was the touching way she broke the news to a close friend.[122] To another friend she admitted, 'There is in our lives a wound which will never heal. Nor should it.'[123]

By December 1914, she had formed the idea of creating a memorial to her son, with his body outstretched, 'the father at the head, the mother at the feet' to commemorate 'the sacrifice of all the young volunteers'. She initially thought of placing it 'on the heights of Schildhorn' near Berlin.[124] As time went on, she attempted various other designs, with Peter above the parents,[125] with the parents 'kneeling, as they carry their dead son',[126] with Peter's body wrapped in a blanket.[127] Then she wrestled with the possibility that 'a relief of the parents might be set upon his grave', or near the entrance to the war cemetery where Peter was buried.[128] The relief became a sculpture in the round by November 1917, with the parents kneeling before their son's grave, 'leaning against one another. Her head very low on his shoulder.'[129]

Dissatisfied with all these designs, Käthe Kollwitz put the project aside temporarily in 1919. Her commitment to see it through when it was right was unequivocal. 'I will come back, I shall do this work for you, for you and the others', she noted in her diary in June 1919.[130] Five years later, she kept her word. Her idea was still to sculpt two parents, kneeling before their son's grave, perhaps at the gate of the cemetery, 'blocklike figures, Egyptian in size, between which the visitors would pass'.[131] In October 1925, she began work on the parents. In June 1926 Käthe and Karl Kollwitz visited the German war cemetery at Roggevelde. This is what she saw:

The cemetery is close to the highway . . . The entrance is nothing but an opening in the hedge that surrounds the entire field. It was blocked by barbed wire . . . What an impression: cross upon cross . . . on most of the graves there were low, yellow wooden crosses. A small metal plaque in the center gives the name and number. So we found our grave . . . We cut three tiny roses from a flowering wild briar and placed them on the ground beside the cross. All that is left of him lies there in a row-grave . . .

We considered where my figures might be placed . . . What we both thought best was to have the figures just across from the entrance, along the hedge . . . Then the kneeling figures would have the whole cemetery before them . . . Fortunately no decorative figures have been placed in the cemetery, none at all. The general effect is of simple planes and solitude . . . Everything is quiet, but the larks sing gladly.[132]

The project occupied her throughout the following years, and she was at last able to complete it in April 1931. 'In the fall – Peter, – I shall bring it to you', she noted in her diary.[133] Her work was exhibited in the National Gallery in Berlin and then transported to Belgium, where it was placed, not near the entrance, but adjacent to her son's grave.[134] There it rests to this day.

Käthe Kollwitz's war memorial was an offering to a son who had offered his life for his country. She could not complete it until eighteen years after his death. This alone should tell us something about the process of bereavement described so movingly in her diary and in her work. On 31 December 1914, she noted in her diary:

My Peter, I intend to try to be faithful . . . What does that mean? To love my country in my own way as you loved it in your way. And to make this love work. To look at the young people and be faithful to them. Besides that I shall do my work, the same work, my child, which you were denied. I want to honor God in my work, too, which means I want to be honest, true and sincere . . . When I try to be like that, dear Peter, I ask you then to be around me, help me, show yourself to me. I know you are there, but I see you only vaguely, as if you were shrouded in mist. Stay with me . . .

She spent hours sitting in his room.[135] In October 1916, she wrote in her diary that 'I can feel Peter's being. He consoles me, he helps me in my work.' She rejected the idea of spirits returning, but was drawn to the 'possibility of establishing a connection here, in this life of the sense, between the physically alive person and the essence of someone physically dead'. Call it 'theosophy or spiritism or mysticism', if you will, she noted, but the truth was there nonetheless. 'I have felt you, my boy – Oh, many, many times.'[136] Even after the pain of loss began to fade, she still spoke to her dead son, especially when working on his memorial.[137] Kollwitz continued to be haunted by dreams of her son, and felt his presence in the same way that other bereaved parents did throughout the world.[138]

What gives Kollwitz's mourning an added dimension was her sense of guilt, of remorse over the responsibility the older generation had for the slaughter of the young. This feeling arose from her initial reaction to Peter's decision to volunteer. Her attitude was apprehensive but positive. Her vision was internationalist and hostile to the philistine arrogance of official Germany. But, as she said time and again, she believed in a higher duty than mere personal self-interest, and had felt before 1914 that 'back of the individual life . . . stood the Fatherland'.[139] She knew that her son had volunteered with a 'pure heart', filled with patriotism,[140] 'love for an idea, a commandment',[141] but still she had wept bitterly at his departure.[142]

To find, as she did later in the war, that his idealism was misplaced, that his sacrifice was for nothing, was terribly painful for many reasons. First, it created a distance between her and her son. 'Is it a break of faith with you, Peter', she wrote in October 1916, 'if I can now see only madness in the war?'[143] He had died believing; how could his mother

DiE LEBENDEN DEM TOTEN . ERiNNERUNG AN DEN 15.JANUAR 191⁹

18. *Gedenkblatt für Karl Liebknecht* by Käthe Kollwitz, 15 January 1919

not honour that belief? But to feel that the war was an exercise in futility led to the even more damaging admission that her son and his whole generation had been 'betrayed'. This recognition was agonizing, but she did not flinch from giving it artistic form.[144] This is one reason why it took so long for her to complete the monument, and why she and her husband are on their knees before their son's grave. They are there to beg his forgiveness, to ask him to accept their failure to find a better way, their failure to prevent the madness of war from cutting his life short.

Käthe Kollwitz also wrote in her diary of the 'need to kneel down and let him pour through, through me. Feel myself altogether one with him.'[145] This form of prayer was deeply important to her, and showed that despite the depths of her grief, she never abandoned the outlines of her Christian humanist faith. Before the war, she had produced two remarkable etchings entitled *From many wounds you bleed, O people* and *The downtrodden*. Both are in triptych form,[146] and both show a body remarkably similar to Holbein's *Christ in the Tomb*. In 1903 she produced an etching entitled *Woman with dead child – Pietà*,[147] and became renowned for her images of mothers and children. One of her most powerful etchings is a starkly primitive woman holding a dead child, modelled for her in 1903 uncannily by her son Peter.[148] The Christian Lamentation motif found perhaps its most celebrated form in her work entitled

19. *Der Leichnam Christi im Grabe*, 1521, Hans Holbein the Younger

Memorial print for Karl Liebknecht, which dwells more on the mourning workers than on their murdered leader. Here we can see the influence of the Christian sculpture of Ernst Barlach, whose war memorial sculpture in Gustrow Cathedral she admired in later years.[149] Her *Mary and Elizabeth* (1928) is derived from contemplating a devotional painting attributed to Konrad Witz and hung in the art gallery of Berlin-Dahlem.[150] As we shall see in chapter 6, a return to the German Renaissance was not unique in the postwar period.

What does separate the Kollwitz memorial from so many others, either of religious or secular inspiration, is its sheer simplicity, and its power to escape from the notation of a particular school of art or ideology. Her memorial to her son Peter has a timelessness derived from her gift for taking an older religious frame of reference and remoulding it to suit a modern catastrophe.

I saw Käthe Kollwitz's memorial to her son in a light drizzle, not at all foreign to the region of Belgium. What it produced was extraordinary: a hunched-over figure in granite, with drops of water falling from her face.

At Roggevelde, on their knees, Käthe and Karl Kollwitz suggest a family which includes us all; and that may be precisely what she had in mind. The most intimate here is also the most universal. The placing of her memorial in the German war cemetery where her son's body lay was a family reunion, a foretaste of what her broad religious faith suggested would happen at some future date. The sense of completeness, of healing, of transcendence is transparently present in her moving account of her last visit to the memorial. She was alone with her husband:

we went from the figures to Peter's grave, and everything was alive and *wholly* felt. I stood before the woman, looked at her – my own face – and I wept and stroked her cheeks. Karl stood close behind me – I did not even realize it. I heard him whisper, 'Yes, yes.' How close we were to one another then![151]

Conclusion

Touching war memorials, and in particular, touching the names of those who died, is an important part of the rituals of separation which surrounded them. Many photographs of the period show mourners reaching out in this way,[152] thus testifying that whatever the aesthetic and political meanings which they may bear, they are also sites of mourning, and of gestures which go beyond the limitations of place and time.

Freud's essay of 1917 on 'Mourning and melancholia' provides a way of understanding these gestures.[153] For some people the burden of bereavement is bearable; for others, it is crushing. The latter Freud

20. *Die Eltern*, by Käthe Kollwitz, Roggevelde German war cemetery, Vladslo, Belgium

termed 'melancholic'. They are trapped in a forest of loss, unable to focus on what had been torn from their lives. Their loss is palpable, but also generalized. In contrast, the non-melancholic mourner tests the reality of loss and ultimately disengages from the departed. The melancholic cannot do this, unless some mediating element can help isolate the loss, and establish its limits. Then the individual knows what is gone, and what has survived. Is it fanciful to suggest that rituals at war memorials, and in particular the reading of the names of the fallen, and the touching of those statues or those names, were means of avoiding crushing melancholia, of passing through mourning, of separating from the dead and beginning to live again? Ritual here is a means of forgetting, as much as of commemoration, and war memorials, with their material representation of names and losses, are there to help in the necessary art of forgetting.

This *rite de passage* was expressed in many different languages. Most of them were traditional, drawing on ancient motifs and tropes from religious, pagan, and secular sources. Art placed in cemeteries tended to a greater degree of abstraction than did that located in village squares or within the perimeter of churches, but even in the work of Lutyens or Käthe Kollwitz the humanist tradition is still robustly intact.

This point raises one of the most widely debated issues of the cultural history of the early twentieth century: the clash between 'traditional' and 'modernist' approaches to twentieth-century art. When we contemplate war memorials erected before the 1960s, the evidence is overwhelmingly on one side. There are numerous instances of the stubborn survival in the aftermath of the Great War of older forms in commemorative art. What may be termed 'traditionalism' in wartime and postwar religious and secular commemoration entails everything the modernists rejected: romanticism, old values, sentimentality, in sum, late-Victorian and Edwardian clichés about duty, masculinity, honour. Of course, both the 'modernist' and the 'traditional' forms of imagining the war were in evidence long before the Armistice, and they were never as distinctive as apologists on both sides suggested. But even when we add the towering examples of commemoration in war cemeteries to the catalogue of civilian art, religious or secular, the strength of traditional modes of expressing the debt of the living to the dead must be acknowledged.

That strength, I argue, lay in the power of traditional languages, rituals, and forms to mediate bereavement. Irony's cutting edge – the savage wit of Dada or surrealism, for example – could express anger and despair, and did so in enduring ways; but it could not heal. Traditional modes of seeing the war, while at times less profound, provided a way of remembering which enabled the bereaved to live with their losses, and perhaps to leave them behind.[154] This is the central reason why most commemorative art until the Second World War harks back to earlier conventions, rather than forward to pure abstraction.

We confront here questions which may be posed and answered more appropriately by poets than by historians. How healing occurs, and what quietens embitterment and alleviates despair can never be fully known. But not to ask the question, not to try to place the history of war memorials within the history of bereavement, a history we all share in our private lives, is both to impoverish the study of history and to evade our responsibility as historians. For we must attend to the faces and feelings of those who were bereft, and who made the pilgrimages to these sites of memory, large and small, in order to begin to understand how men and women tried to cope with one of the signal catastrophes of our century.

Part II
Cultural codes and languages of mourning

5
Mythologies of war: films, popular religion, and the business of the sacred

This book opened with the apocalyptic imagery of the return of the dead in Abel Gance's *J'accuse*. In 1919, using the most advanced mode of communication of the time, one film-maker reached back into the reservoir of romantic ideas about war, and fashioned a *mélange* of the new and the old, a collage of the strikingly original and the profoundly banal. In the following chapters I explore some ways in which the catastrophic losses of the Great War stimulated reflections of many kinds about war and the sacred. Here I discuss the link between films, the graphic arts, and popular piety. *J'accuse* was only one of many works of art which appropriated religious images both before and during the war to create a revived form of popular romanticism, which both dwelled on mass death and attempted to strip it of some of its most disturbing features. In later chapters, I shall turn to images of the Apocalypse in contemporary art and literature and to the reconfiguration of the sacred in war poetry. Here the focus is on works aimed at a mass audience.

The sacred and the secular: nineteenth-century popular piety

To appreciate the emotional appeal and allusions of this romantic epic, we must turn to the history of popular piety from the middle of the nine-teenth century. Virtually everywhere in nineteenth-century Europe, popular religious imagery was produced, bought, and sold. A flourishing industry of such art dated back to the seventeenth century, but grew rapidly when printing techniques became simpler and products cheaper.[1]

The business of catering for this market was highly developed in many parts of Europe, but it was elaborated perhaps more fully in France than anywhere else. Strikingly similar ventures and products can be found elsewhere in Europe for the simple reason that the demand for them was international – and growing. There was a religious revival in the nineteenth century, a facet of the social history of Europe neglected until recently in scholarly circles.[2] It was not exclusively

Catholic, though it took on a particular force within popular Catholicism. Of central importance in this movement was the mobilization of women. They were the market for popular religious art. For a few centimes, they bought medals, trinkets, and especially posters, readily displayed on cupboards, doors, or walls. Children had their own fare, moral tales or games, but because of the dominant trade in religious art, even these innocent images were called 'Saints'.[3]

Women were the major consumers. A burgeoning taste for popular piety among predominantly rural women in mid-nineteenth-century Europe lay behind the spread of cheap religious art, an indication of wider trends in religious history. The number of women in religious orders grew. So did their domination of parish congregations.[4] Some scholars go so far as to suggest that, as a popular institution, the Roman Catholic Church was 'feminized in the course of the nineteenth century'.[5] Popular art followed in the wake of these developments.

This increasing fervour came at a difficult time for the clergy. Disrupted by the French Revolution and the revolutionary wars, the French Catholic church had trouble recruiting clergy in the 1820s.[6] What one scholar has called a 'vacuum of clerical power' on the local level helped change the balance of religious life, especially in the French countryside.[7] Never far from pagan elements, popular Christianity in many areas took its own course in the mid-nineteenth century, so that by the time the Roman Catholic Church recovered its institutional strength in the middle of the century, greater church attendance was consistent with a set of processions, rituals, festivals, and magical beliefs deeply alarming to many orthodox Catholics.[8] At a time of periodic and devastating epidemics, the cult of saints and the healing powers they offered to the many women to whom peasants turned in desperation far outstripped the appeal of modern medicine.[9]

Christianity, as it was lived in everyday life, was consistent with diametrically opposite political convictions. Some used the Gospels to preach miracle, mystery, and authority, and the virtues of a head bowed to the established order. Others saw in Jesus a common man like themselves, suffering poverty and injustice. The Christian socialist Alphonse Constant published a visionary work in 1844, *La mère de Dieu, épopée religieuse et humanitaire*, the utopian socialist contents of which infuriated conservative clergy.[10] Popular literature and imagery – for instance the *Bible des Noëls*, a version of the Nativity and Christian tales sung by itinerant merchants, passing thereby into local custom – catered for both radical and reactionary interpretations, and for those entirely indifferent to politics.[11] Quarrels with the local clergy were frequent, but they led not to unbelief, but rather to unconventional ideas and their elaboration in legends, folk beliefs, magical tales, songs, and ceremony.[12]

The most powerful manifestations of the new cult of piety were visions, and especially visions of the Virgin Mary. From the 1830s onwards, sightings of the Virgin became *causes célèbres* within Catholic communities.[13] Greeted with disbelief, indifference, or hostility, those claiming to have seen the Virgin caused a stir which is still remembered.[14] First in Paris in 1830, then in La Salette in the Isère in 1846, at Lourdes in the Pyrénées in 1858 and at the northern town of Pontmain in 1871, women and especially children brought the supernatural into everyday life; and the everyday into the supernatural. For surrounding these incidents there arose a vast pilgrimage movement, active to this day.[15] According to one scholar, the town of Lourdes attracts twice as many pilgrims as Mecca.[16]

The vision at Pontmain took place during the Franco-Prussian war. According to local accounts, in a region of northern France near Laval, threatened by the Prussian army, five peasant children saw the Virgin on a clear winter's night. The Virgin wore a blue robe, a black veil, a gold crown, and she carried a Crucifix. The colour imagery was fitting for wartime: blue for the monarchy, black for mourning, gold for triumph. Her message was one of hope: 'But pray, my children. God will answer you soon. My Son is letting himself be touched by compassion.' Priests, nuns, and the faithful gathered in the woods in a spirit of renewed hope. The village was spared invasion, and all the local men in uniform returned home alive.[17] Army chaplains, as well as General Charette, commander of the Légion de l'ouest, signed a statement affirming their belief that a miracle had taken place; Mary herself had deflected the Prussian army.[18]

In the past, the Roman Catholic Church had treated similar incidents with a mixture of condescending indulgence and paternal alarm. But this time, after a national disaster, a more benign approach emerged to this and other contemporary Marian apparitions. It was still true, on the one hand, that the Pontmain vision and its aftermath were evidence of uncontrolled religiosity, tinged with pagan elements considered dangerous by the clergy unless directed into appropriate channels. On the other hand, it was an opportunity to gather the faithful at a time of turmoil. The history of visions is therefore twofold: a move by obscure and ordinary Catholics away from conventional, controlled expressions of faith; and a subsequent and chequered history of their appropriation, their 'domestication' by the church itself.[19]

Unlike earlier zealots, nineteenth-century visionaries were almost always children or young women, mostly from poor and troubled families.[20] To a degree the church had lost touch with these people, and the appearance of the Virgin constituted for them a potential indictment of an indifferent or remote clergy. One year after Pope Pius IX had proclaimed his doctrine of infallibility, a group of obscure children had found their own way to the divine, and the divine had found a way to them. It is not surprising, therefore, that visions were extremely important to the church in its efforts to consolidate its power at a time of political and economic instability.[21]

In 1873, over 3 million pilgrims visited French shrines.[22] National organizations grew to propagate the Marian cult. Their appeal may be seen in the rising number of pilgrims in the later decades of the nineteenth century and in the early twentieth century. A huge popular literature emerged to assist and reflect the work of their activities.[23]

Five years after the apparition at Pontmain, on the other side of the Rhine, another visionary incident occurred. In July 1876, in the woods surrounding the tiny Saarland farming village of Marpingen, five young girls, aged six to eight, gathering berries, had a vision of the Virgin. She reappeared in the days that followed, and quickly a cult formed around the spot. Miners flocked to the site. The possibility that Marpingen would become the 'German Lourdes' comforted many devout people. But it was a matter of concern to the Prussian bureaucrats responsible for public order. In an extraordinary series of blunders and mishaps, spies appeared in the village, the army was dispatched, the girls were interrogated time and again in the hope that they would admit that they had made up the incident, and a number of locals were brought to court in an attempt to show that their motives in broadcasting the news of the sighting of the Virgin were pecuniary. They were acquitted.[24]

The special and peculiar features of the German state mark off this incident from those across the Rhine. But what is remarkable is less the evidence of clumsy and totally ineffective state repression than the fact that such an event should have caused echoes throughout the *Kaiserreich*. The episode at Marpingen showed clearly that the phenomenon of popular piety had ramifications for guardians of public order in regimes whose legitimacy was at best uncertain and at worst under siege.[25] Political messages were mixed with millenarian images; to extricate the secular from the sacred was a hopeless task.[26]

Images d'Epinal and the business of the sacred

Popular piety, then, was a lucrative and growing business in late nineteenth and early twentieth century Europe. The elision between the secular and the sacred was not only a matter of ideas and images. It was also a matter of cultural production. A powerful instance is one upon which Gance himself drew, *imagerie d'Epinal*. From these posters, sold throughout Europe, we can glimpse some of the sources of popular images of war in the nineteenth century, notions which were given renewed life during the Great War.

Images d'Epinal were traditional forms of French folk art. In the sixteenth century, craftsmen in Nancy and in Epinal in Lorraine were licensed to produce what we today call posters. First in woodcut form, then in lithograph, this provincial industry grew rapidly in the nineteenth century. By 1836, forty engravers were employed by the firm of Pellerin.[27] Six years later, they sent to middlemen and merchants about 875,000 prints a year. One estimate places the total output of *imagerie d'Epinal* at 17 million before 1870.[28]

Eighteenth-century religious images were both decorative and instructive. Simple portraits of the Holy Family were sold alongside 'The hours of the Passion', including a long text in small print recounting the Stations of the Cross and appropriate prayers for each. The Wandering Jew was a perennial favourite: 'I travel the world for the fiftieth time', with only the Last Judgment as the end of his travails. 'With extreme sadness, I am en route, from the day of the Crucifixion, I travel day and night.'[29]

After the defeat of 1815, the Pellerin firm in Epinal prospered by producing a stream of posters with traditional motifs: scenes from saints' lives, other religious themes, and drawings of military life. Fifteen years later, in the wake of the revolution of 1830 and before the imposition of harsh censorship in 1835, the Pellerin firm diversified its output. Less emphasis was placed on religious images, and more was devoted to Napoleonic graphic art. In place of some traditional 'saints' came the iconography of classicism, freemasonry, and Republicanism. The Pellerin firm's most famous craftsman, François Georgin, studied the imperial art of David and Gros, and adapted it for a popular, predominantly rural, audience.[30] The imperial trappings vanished, and instead Napoleon emerged as both a military genius and a man of the people.

Martial themes were traditionally popular in the east of France, and struck a chord in the Restoration decade. This art appealed to patriots outraged at the terms of the Peace of 1815, as well as to the tens of thousands of ageing, but still robust, *anciens combattants* and their families, ready to purchase nostalgia for a few sous. Rural almanacs also catered for this public, and reproduced anecdotes about Napoleon and the days of glory. Other merchants cashed in on the market for 'Napoleona' by displaying statues and other household items decorated in unmistakably Napoleonic terms.

These posters were sold throughout France by pedlars and designated dealers, and helped to foster the quasi-religious aura which came to surround the name of Napoleon in some provincial milieux. In 1842, an image of Napoleon surrounded by flowers and female saints playing the harp made the point. Dozens of *images d'Epinal* spoke to the same market. 'Gloire nationale: Napoléon' was typical, showing an eagle on top of a bower with the imperial portrait and any one of several great victories. Then there was Napoleon and the mother of the grenadier.

21. *Apothéose de Napoléon*

This told a tale of an encounter in 1804 when Napoleon gave an 82-year-old woman petitioner a pension from his own pocket.

The funeral cortège of Napoleon was a popular print. The caption was unambiguous:

After having astonished the world over 20 years, he who 17 armies could not defeat, yielding to conspiratorial elements, betrayed by the treason of his allies, and by the disloyalty of those on whom were heaped honours and dignity, Napoleon ceased to live at Sainte-Hélène and the Sovereigns of Europe ceased to tremble . . . There he lies, the Conqueror of Kings, the Dominator of Nations, the Man who filled the Universe with his name and with the glory of the French people.[31]

The best illustration of the mixture of religious and secular romanticism in this form of popular culture can still be seen. In 1847, a statue of Napoleon was placed near the village of Fixin in Burgundy. The statue showed Napoleon recumbent, covered by a blanket, and poised Lazarus-like, ready to emerge from his grave. The pilgrims to this shrine were addressed by one *ancien combattant*, Noisot, who declared that 'Napoleon is about to rise from the dead – his spirit is that of democracy which illuminates and catches fire in all those souls who swarm to witness his resurrection.'[32]

In the later nineteenth century, after the loss of Alsace and Lorraine in 1871, the output of the Pellerin firm took on a more right-wing and Catholic character. But its market was still primarily rural households and families looking for traditional secular and sacred images. The Parisian scene was not neglected. Street scenes and popular entertainers were represented. So were the 'Cris de Paris', an alphabet of occupations and trades.

The stock list of the company indicates an impressive range of wares, and an impressive range of markets open to these products. The 'Special catalogue of images' was distributed to agents and merchants all over Europe, from Algiers to Constantinople. It is impossible to state the balance of sales within France itself, but a rough estimate is that 70 per cent of the firm's trade was domestic.

Songsheets show how these items were traditionally sold by *colporteurs*. Some had a direct political content. One flysheet presented the words to 'La Terre Nationale', a song intended for those interested in responding to or shouting down the 'Internationale'. The same mind lay behind 'La Catholique', intended to answer 'La Carmagnole'. The words can give only a bare sense of the ways it was sung:

> For 1900 years and more, France and the French have been
> for Jesus
> For 1900 years and more, France and the French have been
> for the Cross

> Bold against the clique without country and without God
> For the Catholic faith
> Frenchmen arise! because God wills it!
> Sing 'La Catholique'!
> Long live France and God![33]

Political publicity was not restricted to the right. The company did its best in 1902 for 'the League of French Women', which represented provincial women of moderate views. The Pellerin firm provided them with 500,000 posters.[34] But it also supported candidates to the 1902 legislative assembly and urged citizens 'not to vote at any price for Jews or Free-Masons' or for 'Dreyfusard candidates, defenders of a Jewish traitor justly convicted *twice* by the War Council'. It produced caricatures against taxes,[35] and for the re-election of the liberal administration of the City of Brussels.[36] Companies and groups were charged 100 francs for publicity for their own designs. The lottery of decorative arts, offering a prize of 1/2 million for one franc, was one such customer.[37]

Commercial publicity was a fairly new form of business for the company, pointing to its future in advertising and phonograph records.[38] But most of the Pellerin trade was directed to domestic clients, serviced by an army of agents and tradesmen throughout Europe and North Africa. The October 1910 'Special catalogue of images' sent to Athens is preserved in the firm's archives.[39] It shows a vast range of secular and sacred items for sale. Customers could choose among alphabets, and proverbial, legendary, familial, natural, travel, theatrical, military, or patriotic images. These conventional scenes constituted the bulk of the stocklist. There were posters, games, cutouts, kites, and medallions for sale. The balance of trade was non-religious, though it was possible to obtain numerous 'pious subjects', including scenes of the Virgin at La Salette, Lourdes, and Pontmain.

A merchant in Athens ordered 80 'sujets diverses', 10 portraits, 50 battles, 5 scenes of the 1870 war, 10 military instructions, 10 country scenes, 10 alphabets, and 250 patriotic games. An agent in Algiers wanted 400 images, 200 'récréations', and 300 amusements; another agent in the same city wanted 500 constructions, of which 100 had to be about war.[40] Merchants and middlemen simply checked off the items they wanted on the stocklist, and these were despatched direct from Epinal.

How big was the operation before the Great War? The business records of the company indicate *net* receipts of roughly 1,200,000 francs in 1913. Posters cost roughly 8 centimes per 1,000 to produce: 3 centimes to the middleman; 5 for the firm. The rough per-unit cost of their average product was 0.008 centimes. Market prices varied, but since posters sold for roughly 2 centimes each, then 1,000 would bring in 2,000 centimes or 20 francs. Of this income, 60 per cent went directly to the firm. Thus for an outlay of 8 centimes per 1,000, the firm made 12 francs, or a profit of 1,500 per cent. Allowing for operating costs, salaries, and the maintenance of stock and equipment, a net income of over 1.2 million francs indicates sales in the region of 3.6 million items per year.[41]

The firm was prosperous. Its product was world famous, to the point that the term *image d'Epinal* stood not for particular merchandise, but for a genre of naive and sentimental expression. The firm was one of the few whose name became synonymous both with a category of domestic consumption and a way of looking at the world.

That set of notions was the source of much romantic imagery produced after the outbreak of war in 1914. Its range was vast and its audience in the millions. We will never know the effect such objects had on children and others who sought them, but their vitality may be judged by their robust strength in the popular market. For unmistakable signs of what 'tradition' meant to ordinary people on the eve of the Great War, *imagerie d'Epinal* was on display all over France, the European continent and beyond.

Images d'Epinal and mythologies of war

After 1914, this art form, derived from religious sources, but transformed into patriotic art, emerged as a language of popular sentiment. 'Still another effect of the war'; wrote the critic Clément Janin in the *Gazette des Beaux Arts* in 1917, 'the renaissance of the *image d'Epinal*!'[42] The Pellerin firm's do not indicate pre-war retardation in sales or production; their iconography simply became more noticeable, since it fitted in so well with more general propaganda themes. Consequently, *images d'Epinal* did indeed form a remarkable part in the history of the graphic arts produced in France during the Great War. They bore the message of war enthusiasm in a direct and unadulterated way. Their very naivety and self-consciously childlike style had a dual effect: to mythologize the war and to announce the virtues of escape from a reality at times too harsh to bear. In effect *images d'Epinal* helped to create an imaginary war, a war which hardly corresponded to the reality of the conflict and was not intended to do so. Time and again the mythical war was refought in this corner of the visual arts, as it was refought in posters, illustrations, and eventually in film.

Images d'Epinal came to form an important part of the unofficial propaganda effort of France. Ironically enough, the Pellerin factory itself was closed in wartime, partly because of its proximity to the front, partly because of mass mobilization. Three years later, when it reopened, it issued a new sales catalogue, full of wartime images.[43]

One in particular drew from older sources in new form. The story of

Lieutenant Péricard, who called the dead to rise from their trenches and stop the invader, was told time and again during the war. I shall investigate a number of versions of this legend in chapter 8 with reference to war poetry. Suffice it to say here that the firm of Pellerin was quick to exploit this nineteenth-century trope of the return of the dead from the field of battle. One of their more popular posters captured the moment of the 'miracle', alongside other acts of superhuman bravery on the part of children and soldiers alike.[44]

The market for such images grew rapidly during the war. And not surprisingly, whatever the fate of Epinal, by late 1914, the popular printing houses of Paris were more than able to fill the gap. What had once been provincial culture now became a national asset and a national campaign.

Too much has been written about state-directed propaganda in wartime, and not enough about the source of most popular images – the private sector.[45] Alongside the officially sponsored war-loan posters and exhibitions of war art, commercial printing firms grew rapidly in wartime. The attractiveness of the messages they disseminated was reflected in their sales. Some posters were produced in small runs; others were sold by the hundreds of thousands. They offered a respectable language which civilians used in all kinds of mundane circumstances. Birthdays, saints' days, anniversaries, and the normal gift-giving days of the Christian calendar in wartime called for purchases of an inexpensive piece of patriotic art. *Images d'Epinal* met this demand perfectly. They were relatively cheap, and had a more enduring quality than did the other two most important forms of popular art as communication – the commercial advertisement[46] and the picture postcard.[47]

It is against this background that we should set the re-emergence of *images d'Epinal* during the 1914–18 war. As I have noted, *imagistes* like Georgin used masonic and anti-clerical as well as radical and egalitarian motifs in their posters. Nonetheless, the most important feature of their work was its indisputable Frenchness. After 1914, *images d'Epinal*, as a familiar and adaptable art form, easily came to embody a popular iconography of the French nation at war.

What had been a repository of radical and Republican values was revived and appropriated by those whose sympathies were not necessarily of the Republican left. Artists of many political persuasions produced these images. Their aim was to bring home to the civilian population at war the enduring features of eternal France. As Jean Cocteau put it, 'There were no politics at the time, no political Left or Right, there was only a Left and Right in art, and what we were full of was the patriotism of art.'[48]

One purpose of this art was to create a myth: the myth of war enthusiasm, a story about the early days of the war. The battles of 1914 form probably the worst bloodbath in French history. Over 400,000 men were killed in four months, a density of sacrifice unmatched at any other time during the war. We now know that ordinary people greeted the war with stupefaction and fear, not bravado and song.[49] But in *imagerie d'Epinal*, a romantic and utterly unrealistic account of these days became the stuff of legend. To accept a compromise peace, to waver in determination to see the war through, to give in after years of struggle, in January 1917 or January 1918, was to betray the trust of those who – according to the myth – had gone to war bravely, unquestioningly, with the simplicity of children and the conviction of saints. The moment of their mobilization and their pure enthusiasm for the cause were frozen in art, the art of *l'images d'Epinal*.

Images d'Epinal expressed this myth and other patriotic messages in a number of ways. One was by placing the war in the long-term perspective of French history in general and of the French martial spirit in particular. Thus, in Guy Arnoux's poster, the sleeping sentry in the trenches is rescued from dishonour by none other than Napoleon himself, who stands guard over the exhausted and neglectful soldier. Here we return squarely and emphatically to the origins of this genre. Another of the same kind is entitled 'Old-timers to the Rescue', and aligns the men of battles past with the front-line soldiers of 1914. Again we see the mark of the Pellerin prints celebrating the martial virtues of the Grand Army and its glorious victories a century before.

A constant preoccupation of this kind of art is the need to place within a wider historical sweep a war which threatened to destroy all that was familiar. This is precisely why *images d'Epinal* were so popular; they spoke of a common past in terms which made sense of the present crisis. A good example of this genre is a popular drawing of 1915 by Raoul Dufy. It is entitled *The end of the war* and is a collage of past and present with a message for everyone. Surrounding the Gallic cock, trampling on the German eagle, are easily identifiable sketches of Joan of Arc, Rheims Cathedral set ablaze by German shelling in 1914, the execution of civilians, and General Joffre himself. Dufy's artistic reference was clear to all. As Cocteau noted of another Dufy wartime sketch, 'Voilà de l'excellente tradition d'Epinal tricolore . . .'[50]

'Papa' Joffre was a reassuring figure in much of this popular art work. Hardly a man of the people, nonetheless he came to symbolize a grandfatherly solidity and reassuring calm during the war. How far we have come from the little corporal of François Georgin; here is one clear instance of the adaptation of traditional art to suit the demands of the moment.

A poster entitled *The victory of the Marne* shows a spirited female figure striding forward to battle, with her dress high on her legs, and row upon row of French soldiers below and in the background, following the lead of Joffre, their general. The allegorical woman suggests both winged victory and Marianne: classicism and Republicanism are thus united in wartime art. Again, there is the reassuring figure of Joffre leading two children, wearing the traditional dress of Alsace and Lorraine, back to their national family.

The second preoccupation of this form of propaganda was the unity of the nation at war. Here we can see how artists appealed to civilians who wanted and needed to believe that they too were contributing to the war. One *image d'Epinal* shows two *marraines* doing their bit, one by darning socks, the other by writing letters to a soldier, who will soon receive the parcel on the table. Another depicts a community of soldier, priest, employer in blue, and worker in white and announces the true character of the 'union sacrée'. The introduction of the priest is another good example of ecumenism in this wartime art form, and of the variance from the iconography of the Pellerin prints of the 1830s. One of the most beautiful of all *images d'Epinal* is of a theatre party, in which an elegant actress enthrals the ranks of soldiers before her. This could have been a reference to the appearance of Sarah Bernhardt before French troops in 1916,[51] as well as a reiteration of the ties that bound front and home front during the war.

The third major emphasis in this genre was on the joys of military leave. This was a privilege hard to come by early in the war: childlike images of reunion and delight touch on a frequent refrain of soldiers' complaints and on a constant preoccupation of their loved ones. Here too was a simple and touching reminder of what the war was all about: the defence of hearth and home.[52]

A fourth theme is more specific, and refers back to the origins of this art form in the popular culture and art of the Vosges. The recovery of Alsace and Lorraine after forty-three years of German occupation was another motif of *imagistes d'Epinal* during and after the war. Two good examples are by the celebrated war artist, Hansi, whose upbringing in German Alsace did little to dampen his Gallic enthusiasm. Jean-Jacques Waltz (alias Hansi) developed a distinctive style of naive art, with a bit too much wit and satire to fit in comfortably with the *imagiste* tradition. His French patriotism made him a positive nuisance to the German authorities in pre-war Strasburg, and for his 'treasonable' activities in art, he was sentenced on 11 July 1914 to one year in prison. Before his incarceration, he managed to make his way to Switzerland and then to France, where he served both as an interpreter to the French High Command and as a popular war artist.[53]

Both of these posters present Hansi's wartime *images d'Epinal* at their best. The first is of a French soldier giving a French lesson in Alsace to children finally free from the yoke of the German language. The second is of a miraculous event. Following the Armistice, as legend had it, the graveyards of Alsace flowered unnaturally in November, and tricolours or ribbons of red, white, and blue spontaneously appeared on the graves, announcing to the dead that Alsace was once again free, happy, and French. Hansi himself lived long enough to celebrate in poster form the re-liberation of his beloved Alsace in 1945. The theme of rebirth and rejuvenation after defeat was drawn directly from the post-1815 tradition of *images d'Epinal*.[54]

Most of this genre projected universal and readily understood messages. The sweetheart pining for her beloved; the images of panache and élan which come straight out of children's books; the delicate counterpoint of white sisters presenting red flowers and fruit to black invalids; the avuncular face of a spy and of the men presumably taking him off to be shot; in these examples (and in thousands more)[55] we see all the components of this form of art: a childlike innocence; an appeal to a heroic, martial past; a comic-strip simplification of war to the level of eternal verities.

But this preference for the allegorical and the naive should not delude us into concluding that this work is in any way unsophisticated or unthinking. On the contrary, it is an attempt to return to a stylized past at a time when the present was perhaps too unpalatable to face directly.

Other forms of escapist art were, of course, available in abundance. Schoolboy eroticism parading as patriotic bravado appeared in numerous forms.[56] This kind of commercial vulgarity was repeated by the score in wartime postcards, many of which touched soldiers' sense of isolation and loneliness by peddling traditional views of women as the *repos du guerrier*. What *images d'Epinal* offered were cleaned-up and time-honoured versions of these icons of comfort and peace. They were a legitimate and respectable carrier of messages which came in many other (and more salacious) forms.

Popular culture and the avant-garde in wartime

Images d'Epinal served another purpose. They provided a language of popular culture which some of the most prominent avant-garde artists exploited during the war. Dufy, Braque, Léger, and Picasso all drew *images d'Epinal* during the war. Perhaps the most celebrated example of this wartime mix of the forward-looking and backward-looking elements in art is the work of Jean Cocteau. After the outbreak of war in 1914, Cocteau led a crusade against the exotic, dangerous, and (what he took to be) Germanic influences in modern art. In his journal *Le Mot*, he presented many illustrations of the virtues of the Mediterranean versus the Nordic, the Gallic versus the Teutonic, the poetic versus the prosaic, or in other words, the French cause versus the German. Somehow he got it into his head that cubism was a German development, until an encounter with Picasso convinced him he was wrong.[57]

The art of *Le Mot* had much in common with *images d'Epinal*, including the search for an historical context in which to place the war. After Italy had joined the Allies in 1915, Cocteau celebrated the event by elaborating on the traditional profile cameo of Dante, and announcing to the world that 'Dante is with us.'[58] The same mixture of childlike art with patriotism may be seen in another avant-garde journal *L'Elan*, to which Picasso was a contributor. One cartoon in this journal had the United States hovering in the background in a vision of nations at war conceived of as a children's dance.

For evidence that wartime currents in art were both experimental and traditional we may observe one of the most remarkable cultural collaborations of the war, between Cocteau and Picasso on the ballet *Parade*. This work was performed first in a Parisian benefit evening for *mutilés de guerre*. In May 1917, there was an astonishing reworking of the language of French folk art – slapstick, the circus, the music hall. Among the sources used by Cocteau were the *Cris de Paris*, a children's primer listing alphabetically and illustrating the various street-vendors of Paris in the characteristic manner of *images d'Epinal*. Here Cocteau found the figures chosen for the ballet. The dancers wore masks – 'ambulant pieces of cubist art' – designed by Picasso. In *Parade*, cubism met the childlike art of the *images d'Epinal*.[59]

Imagining war: from *images d'Epinal* to films and back again

Images d'Epinal provided a medium finely suited for the creation of an imaginary war, either after the defeat of 1815 or after the victory of 1918. During the war itself, and in the years since the Armistice, that imaginary war was refought time and again in the visual arts.

Images d'Epinal were powerful vehicles for the mobilization of the imagination in wartime and for the rewriting of history – even while it was happening – in a form considered by artists and commercial distributors (and their audience) to be suitable for popular consumption.

This kind of historical mystification reached its height not through poster art but rather through the cinema industry, which came into its own as a focus of popular culture and entertainment in the period of the Great War. My argument here is that films continued what *images d'Epinal* had begun: the sanitization of the worst features of war and its presentation as a mythical or romantic adventure.

Of course there were films which attempted the opposite. For example, Lewis Milestone's film *All quiet on the Western Front* (1930) aimed at a different, pacifist, message, proclaimed in a self-consciously

American accent designed to break down the national barriers between former enemies. There were many British, French, and German films which offered an ambiguous account of trench warfare. G.W. Pabst's *Westfront 1918* (1930) abjured romanticism. *Journey's end* (1931), directed by James Whale, and starring Colin Clive in the tragic role of Lieutenant Stanhope, emphasized the tensions and hardships as much as the heroism; so did the 1937 French film of Dorgelès' novel *Les croix de bois*, directed by Raymond Bernard, and Léon Poirier's *Verdun. Vision d'histoire* (1932). But for all their power, these films are exceptions. A decade of conventional film imagery preceded these more enduring treatments of war, which appeared during the general reassessment of the conflict at the end of the 1920s. Most films which recreated the 1914–18 war did so in a mythical or mundane manner, carrying on the tradition of *images d'Epinal*.[60]

Gance's *J'accuse* and the search for aesthetic redemption

This is the context in which we must set Abel Gance's *J'accuse* and his reveries on the return of the dead. Gance was the romantic film-maker *par excellence*. In *J'accuse* there is both a realistic element and a visionary rejection of realism. His soldiers fight in real trenches, the contours of which were surveyed for Gance by Blaise Cendrars. As I have noted already, Cendrars was a pre-war veteran of the Foreign Legion, and later an avant-garde poet. During the war Cendrars saw some of the fiercest fighting on the Somme. In one encounter, he lost his arm.[61] *J'accuse* was a propaganda film, commissioned by the French army, but Gance's febrile imagination made it get somewhat out of hand. There is no other Great War propaganda film like it, a denunciation of German atrocities and responsibility for the carnage, to be sure, but also a unique blend of messages about the martial virtues *and* about the cruelties and costs of war.

Like many other early film-makers, Gance's primary interest was in imagery and poetry rather than in doctrine and politics. His theatricality reflected the origins of his career in the cinema. He was born in 1889 in Paris, and began to make a name for himself in the theatre world of pre-war Paris. A play, *The victory of Samothrace*, interested Sarah Bernhardt until the war intervened. Rejected by the army on grounds of ill-health, Gance sold film scripts to the major French companies, Gaumont and Pathé, and started to work as an actor and director in 1914–16. He was fascinated by distorting mirrors and lenses, which produced images he later called 'subjective vision'. As I have already noted in chapter 1, the film *J'accuse* was financed partly by Pathé and received the blessing of the French army's cinematographic service, where Gance worked from 1917.[62]

The title *J'accuse* itself indicated its usefulness in reviving flagging spirits among civilians and soldiers after 1917, following the long, bitter years of fighting and after war weariness clearly had set in.[63] The film was completed and shown for the first time a few days after the Armistice to an inter-Allied audience at the Hôtel Dufayel on the Champs Elysées. Its public opening was at the Gaumont Palace in March 1919. The London première was in May 1920; in New York, a year later, in May 1921, Gance dedicated the film to President Harding. He made the acquaintance of D.W. Griffith, through whom the film was acquired by United Artists. Its commercial success surpassed all expectations.[64]

J'accuse elided patriotic reveries with dreams of the Day of Judgment. The passage from the conventional to the eternal is worth sketching in some detail, since it establishes the precise points at which Gance, in the manner of *imagistes d'Epinal* grafted older images of the sacred onto an ordinary account of village life and love.

The triangle

I have already presented the rudiments of Gance's story in chapter 1. The setting is a village in the Midi, and a familiar love triangle. The film opens with a 'farandole', a village dance, and then turns to the circle around Edith Laurin (played by Maryse Dauvray), the unhappy wife of François (played by Romuald Joubé), a brute with a taste for dogs, hunting, and blood. The far more refined Jean Diaz, a poet (played by Severin Mars), is drawn to Edith. She finds consolation in Diaz's company and in the grandiloquent lyric poetry he writes. One of his poems is entitled 'Les pacifiques' and paints in heavy brushstrokes the idyllic sentiments stirred in him by nature and by Edith. While reading her these poems, Jean and Edith are spied by François, who carefully aims his gun at a nearby sparrow and kills it. The same brutality is shown by Gance in an unusual scene of marital rape and despairing sexual submission.

War

Then war breaks out, and François is immediately mobilized. Not Jean Diaz, who has a few weeks to go before joining his unit. To protect his honour, François sends his wife away to family in the east, and here, as we noted in chapter 1, is the source of the tragedy. The Germans occupy the village in which Edith is living, and a German soldier rapes her. Here too is the first use of 'J'accuse' as a statement in the film. On hearing of the rape, Jean Diaz hurls at the Germans the epithet 'J'accuse', and immediately joins up. There follows an act of heroism by Diaz and reconciliation with his rival François, serving in the same unit.

On leave, Jean finds his mother on her death-bed. She asks him one more time to read 'Les pacifiques', and Jean Diaz gives her this pleasure one last time. After she dies, Diaz casts the phrase 'J'accuse' this time at the war itself, which kills the old as well as the young.

Angèle
Time passes, and still the war goes on. On a rain-swept evening, Edith returns home. She brings with her a little girl, Angèle, to whom Edith had given birth after the rape. She tells all to Jean Diaz and her father, a patriot of the war of 1870, who is so horrified by the news, that he leaves the village. Only Diaz can protect Edith from her husband's wrath, and the poet agrees to pretend that the child is his cousin, entrusted to him to care for. When François returns home, he smells a rat, and traps Edith into admitting that Angèle is her child. He then accuses the couple of being the parents, and is stopped from violence only by Edith's full admission. This too provokes murderous feelings in François, who is only just stopped at the point of killing the child. He leaves to go back to the front.

Gance's attitude to the war shifts in his treatment of this child. He shows her persecuted by the children of the village, forced to wear a German helmet and enact a mock execution of a French child. The child actor's tears at this cruelty effectively transmit Gance's sense of the brutalization of children during the war, an ominous development not solely limited to crimes committed by the German army.[65]

Revelation
So far, we have all the elements of a maudlin story of an unhappy marriage, unrequited poetic love, and German atrocities: the stuff of second-rate melodrama in wartime. At this point Gance leaves the civilian world, and provides a vision of the war which transcends his own theatricality and romanticism.

At the front, in 1918, François and Diaz serve as brothers. In one remarkable scene, they reminisce about Edith's charms while men are killed around them. One dead man's feet fall on François' shoulders, but that doesn't interrupt their reverie. As the fighting gets more intense, different images appear. Vercingétorix himself stands in the trenches, urging his descendants to greater deeds of heroism. As the danger grows, Diaz pens a score of letters, each dated a month later, and asks a friend to mail them to Edith in case he dies, to shield her from the shock. Then the terrible bombardment takes its toll, and Diaz goes mad. In a total daze, he asks his rival François to mail the letters to Edith; François, ennobled by the camaraderie of the trenches, accepts the letters and ministers to his friend, before he too is mortally wounded. In hospital side by side, like Kuragin and Prince André, they suffer heroically their common fate in war. Laurin dies.

It is at this point that the dream of the return of the dead comes to the mad Jean Diaz. He draws the villagers to Edith's home to hear the third 'J'accuse', directed against their venality and weakness, and meant to shock them into a decent life, worthy of the men bleeding for them. When the dead arise, and come down village lanes, they are reversing the cycle of pilgrimage. The sacred comes to the secular, and visits upon their consciences a judgment that strikes them to the quick.

After the revelation, Jean Diaz is beyond help. Edith cannot reach him. Little Angèle tries to comfort him by putting chalk in his hand as if to teach him how to write. The word he scrawls with her help is 'J'accuse'. This precedes the fourth and final use of that *cri de coeur* by Gance. Totally mad, Diaz finds the poems he wrote before the war, 'Les pacifiques'. He sees their lyrical peacefulness, and tears them up. The soldier has killed the poet, we are told. Then he dies, with a final accusation, this time of the sun for staring down on all this suffering.

Redemption

Notice the transformation of the guilty party in the four episodes when the term 'J'accuse' is used. First it is the Germans, then the war, also a German crime. But once Gance shifts the scene to the trenches, his intention changes and so does his message. The third time the phrase is used, it is against the villagers who steal and cheat while their men are torn to pieces. The fourth time, the phrase indicts nature itself for its indifference to human suffering. Each has sins to account for that suffering to expiate. Taken together the toll of misery at the front is so great that the petty worries, fears, or loves of villagers fade away. Jean Diaz, the author of 'Les pacifiques', becomes Jean Diaz the accuser. This is why the soldiers with whom he served rise from their graves and take up their crosses. Through their suffering, they bring to their families – made up of ordinary, weak people – and to the viewers of 1919 a glimpse of the need for the nature of redemption. That is why Christ on the Cross is the last image before the film finally comes to an end.

In 'The return of the dead', Gance found a visionary surrealism, a romantic language of nightmarish quality. *J'accuse* started out as a standard and unremarkable propaganda film about the nobility of the French war effort and German barbarity. But with the assistance of Blaise Cendrars, a disabled man who had seen war in all its ugliness, a man who had just gone through the surreal experience of Apollinaire's interment, Gance's film ascends to another level of art. It rises from conventional pieties to transcendental ones.

Cendrars said that he was a jack-of-all-trades on the set of *J'accuse*, but we have no record of the precise part he played in shaping this film. I have already noted his personal loss of Apollinaire, a close friend and poet, a soldier who died just as the war was over. Gance too suffered this and many other losses. These were among the thoughts he jotted down in his notebooks in November 1918 while making 'The return of the dead':

The cemeteries refuse corpses every evening. First Act: Ruins. Second Act: Ruins. Last Act: Ruins . . . How all unhappiness is alike . . . And how I wish that all the dead of the war would rise up one night and return to their country into their houses, to discover whether their sacrifices were for anything. War would stop on its own, strangled by the immensity of the horror. Until 1914 I had only suffered for myself. For two years, I have suffered for others, and have forgotten my own despair. I didn't know it could be so terrible . . . To walk nude between two trenches, to make each side hesitate for fear of killing one of their own . . . because what one kills in war is not men, but uniforms, and because God is silent, both in the heavens and in Rome . . . to create for several instants a Truce of Man each night when I shall pass, a spectre of the trenches . . . [66]

The Christology of the end of *J'accuse* is unsubtle, but compelling. It bears the romantic signature of Gance, a man who took monumental risks, who according to one critic wanted to be Victor Hugo, Henri Barbusse – the soldier-pacifist author of *Le feu* – and D.W. Griffith rolled up into one.[67] Add a touch of the New Testament, and it is clear from whence Gance derived the imagery which lifted his message from banality to the mythical realm.

In *J'accuse*, Gance and Cendrars used the camera to move out of the mundane world of pre-war bathos and wartime propaganda – the world of *imagerie d'Epinal* – to another level of film-making. Here Gance's debt to Griffith and *Civilization* (1916) is apparent.[68] Parallels abound with Griffith's *The heart of the world*, filmed in part on Salisbury Plain in 1918, with Erich von Stroheim as Griffith's military advisor.[69] Never one for modesty, Gance put his own mark on the programme notes distributed at the film:

Since the great Red Tragedy has not had its Homer and its Rouget de Lisle, since the tears, the blood, the widespread suffering, the gestures of the heroes and the starry eyes of the dead have not yet found their sculptors and their painters, we have tried humbly to create a lyricism of the eye and to make the images sing.[70]

Such an approach to his art was bound to offend as well as to please. His admirers saw the film as 'the first great cry of protest in cinema' against war.[71] One soldier sent a poem to the *Courrier cinématographique*: 'To Abel Gance, in respectful homage and admiration for his magnificent film *J'accuse*!'[72] Others were less enthusiastic, speaking of his 'defeatism'[73] or his 'foolish pretentiousness'. The contemporary film-maker Louis Delluc scoffed at Gance:

To create something in the admirable chaos of cinema, it isn't enough to evoke Homer, Albrecht Dürer, Rouget de Lisle and to accumulate paradoxically pretty pictures and well-made, perhaps too well-made images. True humanity, above all in cinema, doesn't permit declamations, a theatrical attitude, literature.[74]

137

To another critic, if Gance were the Hugo of the cinema, it was only for a few moments that his vision overpowered his pomposity.[75] To others, the return of the dead wasn't remotely as powerful as Barbusse's novel *Le feu*. Gance may have been inspired by it, but in *J'accuse* 'gushing sentimentality, extreme symbolism takes over, and the human tragedy is seen only through the deforming prism of a melodrama of passion'.[76]

Gance was an acquired taste, but it was one millions cultivated in the early postwar period. *J'accuse* was marketed through sophisticated publicity,[77] and was a commercial success in the United States and Britain. By 1923 it had made a profit seven times the considerable sum of 500,000 francs it had cost to make.[78] Given the variation in ticket prices in different countries, it is difficult to derive a total audience for the film. A conservative estimate would be that between 1 and 2 million people saw it.

The power of the film is both technical and substantive. It mixed styles of camerawork in a way that married the conventional use of shadows and dramatic lighting with unconventional experiments in the presentation of dreamwork. It drew viewers into the mundane world of love and jealousy and then led them into another realm, the magical world of the trenches and the mythic world of the dead.

Interwar films and the return of the dead

Gance was not alone. Other film-makers working in the interwar cinema touched the same deep chord of mass mourning for the 'Lost Generation' of the Great War. The attractions of the silent cinema in this context are apparent. In the dark, to the accompaniment of appropriately spiritual music, millions could half dream of the war, its supernatural aura, and of the men who had fallen. Cinema was a kind of semi-private séance, bringing old images to millions through 'modern' technology. In these theatres, which grew rapidly after the war,[79] mass audiences could dwell quietly on the eternal theme of the return of the dead from the field of battle, a theme which has appeared in films from their earliest days to the present. Most recently, witness one of Akira Kurasawa's *Dreams* (1989), or nightmares, in which a Japanese soldier is pursued by a vicious dog and by the soldiers killed under his command and through his incompetence, all dead, but oblivious of the fact.

From Gance to Kurasawa, films have entered the realm of the mythical, by telling stories about eternal themes, common to all cultures, about death, sacrifice, love, friendship, and resurrection. The very title of one celebrated silent film helps us to see how this was done. *The Four Horsemen of the Apocalypse*, a film based on the Blasco Ibáñez novel, was one of the first great 'blockbusters', reaching an audience in the tens of millions. Directed by Rex Ingram in 1920, it starred Rudolf Valentino in a love story which shifts from Argentina to Paris.

The Four Horsemen of the Apocalypse

A summary of the plot gives little clue to its wide appeal. Clearly Valentino and his co-star Alice Terry brought the film a glamour that attracted huge audiences. The story was less scintillating. An immigrant from Spain made his fortune from cattle. His two daughters married a Frenchman and a German. Their children are rivals, and keep the national characteristics of their motherlands. The boys of German origin march in goose-step; Julio, the son of the Frenchman, played by Valentino, grows up to be a libertine. On the death of the grandfather, the Germans cash in their inheritance and march back to Germany. Julio's family returns to France, and he studies art in Paris.

Valentino (Julio Desnoyers) seduces Marguerite Laurier (played by Alice Terry), the wife of a French senator. But as in *J'accuse* world events overshadow romance. Above the lovers there lives a strange Russian philosopher, Tchernoff. On the eve of the outbreak of war in 1914, this modern Jeremiah tells Valentino: 'It is the beginning of the end – the brand that will set the world ablaze . . . And when the sun rises in a few hours the world will behold the Four Horsemen – enemies of mankind; those who go before the Beast – the Four Horsemen of the Apocalypse.' The doom foretold in the Book of Revelation is about to come to pass, as Tchernoff shows Valentino in a book of St John decorated by Dürer prints. Conquest, War, Pestilence, and Death appear in the sky above the two men.

And indeed, just as the philosopher had foretold, the horrors of battle descend. The German army sweeps forward and arrives on the Marne. The subtitles announce: 'The serpent had uncoiled itself, twining its grey and green body through the fertile valley of the Marne.' There the soldiers act like beasts, and destroy the Desnoyers' house. Julio's father is made to dig his own grave. Spared, he returns to Paris, and tells his son Julio of German atrocities. Julio must fight, his father says, and even if he encounters his cousins on the other side, he must kill them.

The senator enlists too and is blinded. 'At Lourdes in the sacred grotto, victims of the war god's lust find rest and peace from the din of battle.' Laurier and his wife, now a nurse, are among them. 'For four years had war, pestilence and death held sway until the nations of the Old World were torn asunder and lay bleeding, crying out to a just God to free them from the forces of evil.' We see Julio in the trenches, an 'open grave' facing the German trenches, 'another yawning pit of misery'. Julio encounters his German cousin in a shell-hole. They face each other, each about to shoot, when both are killed by a shell.

Death sweeps all before it. But Valentino's soul is ennobled by his heroic death. He appears to his lover in a vision, and instructs her to return to her husband, who was blinded in combat and needs her help. Then we meet the remnants of the family at Julio's grave, in a sea of crosses. Tchernoff is in the background, and is asked by Julio's father if he knew his son. The answer is yes, 'I knew them all', and with arms outstretched, he points to the countless numbers of the dead. The Four Horsemen appear in the sky one last time. The final caption reads: 'Peace has come – but the Four Horsemen will still ravage humanity – stirring unrest in the world until all hatred is dead and only love reigns in the heart of mankind.'[80]

From Napoléon to J'accuse II

The parallels between Gance's first version of J'accuse and The Four Horsemen are striking. The same shift from melodrama to myth takes place, the same move from German atrocities to common suffering. But there was also a wide gulf which lies between Ingram's melodrama and the haunting resonances of the final sequence of Gance's J'accuse. Most of J'accuse, though, bears little resemblance to its final moments, and belongs to the same histrionic world as The Four Horsemen. Ingram used Tchernoff to touch on Biblical themes and the possibility of redemption. But Gance's romantic exploration of the mythical through the scene of 'The return of the dead' is of an entirely different order. It is his filmic genius which elevates J'accuse above most contemporary films set in the war.

Gance returned to J'accuse in the 1930s. But in the mean time he left the theme of the return of the dead from the field of battle to explore other mythic elements of warfare in filmic form. In Napoléon (1927), considered by many to be his masterpiece,[81] Gance avoided sacred and apocalyptic themes and concentrated on nationalist propaganda. The film was backed by the right-wing publisher François Coty.[82] In Napoléon, Gance created a patriotic poster, an image d'Epinal par excellence. In this context, what matters is the way Gance's film reiterated the old legends about Napoleon and the romance of war, and recreated a martial genius directly drawn from the older traditions of French graphic art. But apart from its technical achievements, Napoléon represented a return to older, more conventional views of the soldier-hero and the dignity of arms. By the mid-1920s, without a war cloud in sight, 'J'accuse' had become 'Je crois'. In Napoléon Gance presented war without the shadows, without the nightmares and the haunting images of the fallen to which he was to return when the real possibility of armed conflict recurred in the late 1930s.

Whereas Gance abandoned for a time his angry cinematic accusations against the futility of war, others picked up the theme, and used the image of the fallen to deepen its power. I have already noted the impact of Lewis Milestone's film version of Remarque's *All quiet on the Western Front*, the tone and texture of which are entirely different from those of *J'accuse* or *The Four Horsemen*, and certainly remote from *Napoléon*. The last frames of *All quiet* bring us back to a variant on the theme of the return of the fallen. They show the gathering together of the fallen. The members of Paul Baumer's platoon, all dead, march into the distance, and cast a backward glance at us as they depart.[83]

In the same realist and unheroic tradition was Raymond Bernard's 1932 film version of Dorgelès' novel *Les croix de bois*. This account of the simple pleasures and stoicism of a doomed platoon of French soldiers faithfully follows Dorgelès' story. But at its end we see the central figure, played by Pierre Blanchard, fatally wounded, and beginning to dream a 'Gancian' dream. He sees an army of soldiers of different nations each carrying his own cross *en route* to eternity. We should note that Dorgelès was also the author of a celebrated novel, *Le retour des morts*, which ends with a scene like the last dramatic moments of Gance's *J'accuse*. The dead in Dorgelès' novel return to see if the wrongs and injustices of the world have been righted. But unlike Gance, Dorgelès' shades find that their survivors have learned nothing and forgotten nothing. His image of a horde of angry dead men besieging Paris reverses Gance's motif of aesthetic redemption, and turns a religious dream into a secular nightmare.[84]

Gance couldn't resist the Apocalypse for long. In *La fin du monde* (1931), he avoided all ambiguity by playing Christ himself; and as I have noted above (p. 17), the religious drama of the first *J'accuse* is renewed in his sequel to the story, released in January 1938. The sound version lacks the force of the first, in part because voices diminish the dream-like effect of the sequence of the dead returning.

The force of the second *J'accuse* lies elsewhere, in the context of the interwar movement of French *anciens combattants*. Their moral language, unsuited to the confrontation with Hitler, but redolent of the sufferings of the Great War, appealed to millions.[85] *J'accuse* spoke that language and shares its vices as well as its virtues. Jacques Delahoche, president of the International Conference of Associations of War Wounded and War Veterans (CIAMAC) gave the film his organization's moral blessing as a work of art which embodied the 'profound sentiments of humanity, justice and peace' of all ex-servicemen.[86]

Gance, like virtually every other major film-maker, was not a pacifist. He was a celebrant of Gallic military virtues who drew on a distinctively French tradition in the graphic arts. This fact may help to account for the contrast between his commercial success in France and the relative failure of this film outside France.[87] This intensely French style of militant republican patriotism emerged in the 1830s, took on a new lease of life in the *images d'Epinal* of the 1914–18 war, and provided a filmic language in the years after the Armistice. In other countries, parallel lithographic enterprises existed, but their work appears more derivative than distinctive. Cartoonists worked in every major newspaper in all combatant countries to spread hatred of the enemy and Allied solidarity. Caricatures were usually hastily drawn sketches of icons developed elsewhere. In France, elsewhere initially was Epinal; by 1918 it was everywhere.[88] If the naive and the sentimental were salient features of the visual re-presentation of the 1914–18 war, it is largely because of the force of the cultural traditions from which they emerged.

In France after the war both the Pellerin firm and *imagerie d'Epinal* went into decline. The firm tried to shore up its fortunes by diversifying into advertising and phonograph records in the interwar years and afterwards, but never recaptured the golden days of the 1914–18 war. The Pellerin style outlasted the business. Nothing could capture its nostalgia for its Napoleonic heyday better than what may have been its last great commercial venture: a stylized life of Charles de Gaulle, from St Cyr to Verdun to the wilderness to the Presidency of the Republic. But even this series of images, like much of de Gaulle's own rhetoric, was a gesture to a vanished age.[89]

A few year after Gance had made the second version of *J'accuse*, the theme of life beyond the grave was still of ongoing interest to the cinema-going public. A survey taken by the British newspaper *Sunday Dispatch* in 1940 asked readers what kind of a film ending they preferred and which films offered it. The majority of the 577 people who responded said they like to see the dead heroes and heroines of the story marching off reborn, as it were, and fading into the sunset.[90] Their favourite film of this kind was *Three comrades*, a 1937 film produced by Joseph Mankiewicz for Metro-Goldwyn-Mayer. The screenplay, written by Scott Fitzgerald, was derived from the novel of Erich Maria Remarque, in which one ex-soldier is killed by Fascists in postwar Germany and the lover of another ex-soldier dies of tuberculosis contracted as a child in the war. The last scene does indeed show the three comrades and the lover striding into a celestial future, gathered together again like Paul Baumer's ghostly platoon in *All quiet on the Western Front*.[91] But such a comforting outcome is remote from the extraordinary imagery of both versions of Gance's *J'accuse*.

Conclusion

Films provide many instances of the twentieth-century revival of popular romanticism. While remote from its early nineteenth-century origins, such romanticism was still sufficiently robust to serve as a popular language about suffering and aesthetic redemption in war. Any account of the cultural codes through which mourning was expressed in the period of the Great War must explore this rich area of the history of popular culture.

In effect, the Great War both created myths and made millions seek them out and cling to them. As we have seen in chapter 3, stories about angels on battlefields or other miraculous events proliferated during the conflict. After the war, séances offered a way for the living to approach the dead. Given the appalling casualty lists and the shock of bereavement experienced by virtually every household, it is not surprising that the business of spiritualism prospered in the postwar years.

The cinema is part of that history. Its evolution in the immediate postwar period reflected earlier currents in the history of the graphic arts. But above all, films show well the imprint of the experience of mass death and mass bereavement on the cultural history of early twentieth-century Europe.

In the period of the Great War, the history of the avant-garde cannot be separated from the history of more conventional artists and audiences. Indeed, when set against the backdrop of the 1914–18 conflict, the preoccupations of surrealist artists and other members of the avant-garde appear less esoteric, self-indulgent, and introverted than the surrealists themselves were prepared to admit. Their images of shattered forms and landscapes were all too mundane to millions of ex-soldiers.[92] To see the lingering cruelties of war required only a stroll around the streets of Paris, Berlin, or Vienna, where wounded ex-servicemen eked out a living by selling whatever or whomever they could.

Gance's experiments with the camera were well known in surrealist circles.[93] Antonin Artaud played Marat in *Napoléon*. He wrote that 'The cinema essentially reveals an entire occult world with which it comes into contact.'[94] 'The imaginary is that which tends to become real', wrote André Breton, a surrealist poet and entrepreneur who had served in the war as a stretcher-bearer.[95] Dreams were central to surrealist art, and Gance was a pioneer of their expression on film.[96] On the one hand Gance's romantic religiosity and patriotism described a cast of mind most surrealists abhorred. But in his art there is clear evidence that surrealism followed rather than led the contemporary fascination with dreams, the subconscious, the occult.

Gance was asked in 1965 about the nature of surrealist cinema. He replied that it was iconoclastic, but its tendency to destroy conventional icons had distinguished ancestors. Among them were Swedenborg, Balzac, Hugo, Breughel, Bosch. They shared with Miró, Klee, Schoenberg, Boulez the urge to 'liberate the ordinary from its servitude, by exploring the limits of the imaginable'. Gance himself placed his own work in the company of these pioneers, and with some justification.[97]

Gance's films straddled the divide – more apparent than real – between experimental art and popular culture. He was able to do so because he spoke of universal preoccupations of the postwar years. His original idea in the 1919 version of *J'accuse* was to make one of the heroes who dies in the war return and live with his widow and her new husband in a supernatural *ménage à trois*.[98] Even though he scrapped this idea, it can be seen as symbolizing much of the imaginative world of the postwar decades. All over Europe in the interwar years, people had to live with the shadow of war. The dead were there, in one way or another, living among the living. In their public ceremonies on Armistice Day and in their private thoughts and dreams, the survivors had to live with the fallen. The evidence of films, as much as other facets of the arts to which I now turn, helps us to understand how they did so.

6

The apocalyptic imagination in art: from anticipation to allegory

Eschatology, the science of the last things, flourished during and after the Great War. Among its most powerful and lasting forms were painting and sculpture, produced by both soldiers and civilians. Through an examination of the work of a number of artists, we can appreciate the richness and diversity of the search for older forms and images by means of which enduring visions of the Great War were fashioned.

Most of these works revived aspects of the nineteenth-century romantic tradition. Within the literature of art history, this finding breaks no new ground. Apocalyptic motifs have preoccupied artists of many different schools and periods.[1] But by placing these twentieth-century renderings of a set of ancient themes within the wider cultural history of the war, it may be possible to show how a number of artists drew upon and amplified other currents of cultural expression in the period following the outbreak of war in 1914.

To develop this point may prove useful in another way. It may help to obliterate the outmoded distinction between elite and masses, between avant-garde and rear-guard, between highbrow and middlebrow, which still bifurcates scholarship in cultural history. The art discussed in this chapter was little known at the time of its creation; its dissemination in later years was limited. But the work of Beckmann, Dix, Rouault, Stanley Spencer was neither marginal nor esoteric; they were closer to the centre of their culture than may appear at first sight, and shared much with the peoples among whom they lived and worked. What they had in common above all was a sense that, at a time of universal mourning, their task was not to reject the sacred as a language of expression, but to recast its message. To this end, they created art which took older artistic forms to portray the Apocalypse and other Biblical themes and turned them to new uses.

In chapter 7 I explore some wartime versions of the apocalyptic imagination in prose. Here I pursue the theme of the end of days as a visual motif. Starting in the pre-war years, I then turn to a number of artists who, after 1914, created visions of war which mixed old and new in profound and enduring ways.

Before the Apocalypse: 'theology beyond reason'

In the two decades before the 1914–18 war, artists working in distant parts of Europe shared a surge of interest in apocalyptic themes. A number of commentators have explored the question as to the prophetic character of these images.[2] It is true that in the decade or so before the outbreak of war in 1914, there was much discussion of violent upheavals to come. Apocalypticians rarely agreed among themselves, but the spectrum of calamities they used before the Great War did not extend to the one that actually occurred. However feverish their language, the Somme and Verdun were beyond their wildest dreams. What these artists left us, therefore, was not prophecy but a visual language from which later imaginings of war were formed.

The occult and the revolt against materialism

That pre-war upsurge in apocalyptic reference revived older romantic, religious, and spiritualist motifs.[3] Many were drawn from unconventional sources, and in particular from theosophy. Here was a body of thought which shared some (but not all) of the premises of spiritualism, discussed in chapter 3. Both were havens for Victorian dissenters. On both sides of the Atlantic, throughout Europe, and in India, men and women uncomfortable with sedate Victorian religious teachings and with scientific materialism were drawn to the Theosophical Society, founded in 1875 in New York. Its leading light was Madame Helena Petrova Blavatsky, author of *Isis unveiled* (1877) and a host of other meditations on the one eternal truth, obscured by warring churches and contemporary materialism.[4] She pointed to a clairvoyant future, the foundations for which were being laid by many enquiring minds, including some of the finest scientists of the day. One prominent exponent of this faith was Annie Besant, English freethinker and pioneer in the fight for contraception, and president of the Theosophical Society from 1907.[5] The German branch of the movement broke away in 1913 to form the Anthroposophical Society. Its guiding light was Rudolf Steiner, a prominent Goethe scholar.[6] Many theosophists were humanists; others blended elements of humanism with racialist ideas. Theosophy was a house of many mansions.[7]

This mixture of the occult, Eastern exoticism, and nineteenth-century romantic speculation on the sublime, drawing in particular on Schiller and Goethe, proved attractive to many artists in the pre-war period. Piet Mondrian joined the Theosophical Society in 1909, after a decade of speculation on theosophical themes. The composers Scriabin, Stravinsky, and Arnold Schoenberg were familiar with the work of Blavatsky and Steiner. Many other artists and writers dabbled in this ecumenical movement.[8] Paul Klee emphatically denied that he was a theosophist, though much of his work shows both a familiarity with and an affinity for spiritualist ideas. 'My hand', he wrote,

is wholly the instrument of some remote power. It is not my intellect that runs the show, but something different, something higher, and more distant – somewhere else. I must have great friends there, bright ones, but sombre ones, too.[9]

Kandinsky and Der Blaue Reiter

Ringbom has suggested that the source of Klee's interest in theosophy during his period in Munich before the Great War was his association with Wassily Kandinsky.[10] Indeed the pre-1914 blending of Russian and German idealism in theosophy may be seen most strikingly in Kandinsky's work and reflections. Born in Moscow in 1866, and resident in Munich from 1896, he repeatedly meditated on theosophical themes, and in particular on the universal catastrophe he believed was on the way. In 1912, he wrote of the coming collapse as a cosmic vibration, a resonance (*Klang*), which would both destroy all, but would be 'a detached praise of life, like a hymn of rebirth'.[11]

Kandinsky's Russian Orthodox beliefs, to which he adhered throughout his life,[12] predisposed him to explore the mystical realm. And 'nowhere else in Europe', James Billington tells us, 'was the volume and intensity of apocalyptic literature comparable to that found in Russia' in the last decades of the Romanov dynasty.[13] Echoing strains in popular religion, this apocalypticism took on many forms before 1914. The master of modern ballet Sergei Diaghilev spoke in 1905 of a coming day of judgment, a 'summing-up' prepared by artists but which would sweep them all away. 'The only wish that I, an incorrigible sensualist, can express', he added 'is that the forthcoming struggle should be as beautiful and as illuminating as the resurrection.'[14] Aleksander Blok's poetry spoke of the 'last day' and damned the city as 'a curse of the beast'. Vladimir Maiakovskii liked to wear the mantle of 'the thirteenth Apostle', the man who alone would 'come through the buildings on fire' to see the 'second tidal flood'. To him Apocalyptic images were a form of 'theology beyond reason.'[15]

There were echoes of these themes in Jewish writings and art. Liberated from the Pale of settlement, Jewish writers and artists were caught between two worlds. Not for them the certainties of the past; but neither were they able freely to enter the Christian world. As if a reminder of the dangers that remained were necessary, the great

22. Sketch for *Der Blaue Reiter*, 1911, by Wassily Kandinsky

pogroms of Kishinev in 1903–4 brought home the precariousness of their new-found freedom. This is the world of the writer Isaac Bashevis Singer, a master of mysticism and ambivalence, as well as of the artists Chaim Soutine and Marc Chagall.[16] Whatever their origins, Russian intellectuals and artists presented this dual aspect: the more they 'tried to plunge into the future, the more they tended to drift back into the past'.[17]

In this context, Kandinsky's work takes on precisely the Janus-like character I have identified as central to pre-1914 artistic expression as a whole. In Billington's words, his abstract paintings were like Russian icons, less concerned with the external world, and more an exploration of invisible, spiritual forces.[18]

Between 1903 and 1908, Kandinsky travelled throughout Europe and North Africa, before settling back in Munich. It was there that he founded with the Bavarian artist Franz Marc an artists' circle called Der Blaue Reiter ('the Blue Rider');[19] and it was in this period that much of his apocalyptic art was created.

Two publications show the variety of Kandinsky's artistic interests and his ongoing preoccupations with the occult world of theosophy. The first is the *Blaue Reiter Almanac*, which first appeared in 1912.[20] The second is Kandinsky's essay *Concerning the spiritual in art*, written in 1909, but published finally in 1911 while the almanac was being prepared.[21]

Kandinsky and Marc conceived in June 1911 the idea of producing an almanac, which would describe the dynamic artistic events of the current year. Its reach would be broad, both stylistically and geographically. There would be no boundaries between 'high' and 'low' in this enterprise. It aimed at placing a 'folk print beside a Picasso', 'a Chinese work beside a Rousseau', children's art beside Egyptian images.[22] There is room for peasant art, 'Artistic trends in African secret societies', puppetry, and mystery plays. They solicited a manifesto from the Italian futurists. Kandinsky told Marc: 'Schoenberg *must* write on German music'; Max Pechstein of the Berlin 'New Secession' was asked to produce a Berlin letter. Matisse was approached for a contribution; he gave permission to reproduce his paintings, but declined to write anything. The art dealer Daniel-Henry Kahnweiler sent photographs of paintings by Picasso from Paris;[23] and Russia had to be represented. Kandinsky insisted:

We must show that something is happening *everywhere*. We will include some reports on the Russian religious movement in which *all* classes participate. For this I have engaged my former colleague Professor Bulgakov (Moscow, political economist, one of the greatest experts on religious life). Theosophy must be mentioned briefly and powerfully (statistically, if possible).[24]

The finished product varied from the plan in some important respects. Art, music, theatre were all represented. But there were some omissions and changes. *Imagerie d'Epinal* failed to arrive in time. Pechstein's letter never materialized, and theosophy is not discussed directly. Its shadow is there nonetheless. Marc's friend August Macke produced an essay on 'Masks', full of spiritual lyricism. 'Form is a mystery to us', Macke wrote, 'for it is the expression of mysterious powers. Only through it do we sense the secret powers, the "invisible God".'[25]

Other texts took up similar themes, elaborated by a series of religious paintings from Bavarian churches. Franz Marc bowed before Cézanne and El Greco, as masters in expressing the *'mystical inner construction, which is the great problem of our generation'.*[26] The Russian artist David Burliuk introduced 'The "savages" of Russia', including the poet Andrei Bely, a follower of Rudolf Steiner's theosophy.[27] Kandinsky added an obituary of the Jewish painter Eugen Kahler, who died at the age of thirty in Prague. Gone was Kahler's 'delicate, dreaming, severe soul, with its pure Hebrew cast of unappeasable mystical sadness'.[28] In an appeal to potential subscribers to the *Almanac*, Marc returned explicitly to eschatology:

Today art is moving in a direction of which our fathers would never even have dreamed. We stand before the new pictures as in a dream and we hear the apocalyptic horsemen in the air. There is an artistic tension all over Europe.

There was, Marc concluded, a 'secret connection of all new artistic production',[29] the awareness of which lay behind the idea of Der Blaue Reiter. Its aim was to speak to the yet unknowing world of these spiritual developments.

Though the *Almanac* was to be the first of a series, no subsequent volume appeared before the outbreak of a war which took the lives first of Macke in 1914 and then of Marc, at Verdun in 1916. Without his friend and partner, Kandinsky refused to go on with the project.[30]

Standing like a solitary beacon, Der Blaue Reiter was dominated by the idea of unifying the arts. But its most powerful message stressed its members' unification with wider spiritual movements. This is where Kandinsky's theosophy took on its central importance. In his essay for *Der Blaue Reiter Almanac*, 'On the question of form', Kandinsky set out his views on art and creativity, on the search for 'the positive', for the 'new value that lives within' man. He likened that search to the penetration of a *'white, fertilizing ray'* which leads to evolution, to elevation',[31] to the search for the spiritual, the 'revelation' of which is the 'special task' of each period.[32]

That revelation can be heard: *'The world sounds. It is a cosmos of spiritually effective beings. Even dead matter is living spirit.'*[33] Materialism has no capacity to hear; it must be replaced, Kandinsky argued, by sounds vibrating in the creative arts of the time.[34] 'The *final* goal (knowledge) is reached through delicate vibrations of the human soul', vibrations which echo the 'sounding cosmos'.[35] The *Blaue Reiter almanac* was, for Kandinsky, one of the instruments through which these sounds were registered.

These views are entirely consistent with aspects of the theosophical systems of Steiner and Blavatsky. The overlap between these positions was developed much more elaborately in a book Kandinsky completed while preparing the *Almanac*. *Concerning the spiritual in art* is a romantic essay, full of sacred analogies. Like John the Baptist, the artist

sees and points the way. The power to do this he would sometimes fain lay aside, for it is a bitter cross to bear. But he cannot do so. Scorned and hated, he drags after him over the stones the heavy chariot of a divided humanity, ever forwards and upwards.[36]

This artist is at the pinnacle of a triangle, often alone, often scorned as a 'charlatan or madman. So in his lifetime stood Beethoven, solitary and insulted.'[37] And, Kandinsky could have added, so stood Steiner and his followers, devotees of the symbol of the triangle as the expression of spiritual forces. 'Painting is an art', he noted, 'and art is not vague production, transitory and isolated, but a power which must be directed to the improvement and refinement of the human soul – to, in fact, the raising of the spiritual triangle.'[38]

Sixten Ringbom has pinned down precisely the elements of theosophy from which Kandinsky created his philosophy of art and colour. Theosophists believed that the clairvoyant (like the artist) could see the 'higher matter in which thoughts and feelings form patterns without any resemblance to the objects of the physical plane'. Psychic photography recorded not these thoughts, but the disturbances caused in 'higher matter' by them. When we see them, we are moved. These vibrations were the spiritual music which Kandinsky intended to transform into visual art. 'Colour is the keyboard, the eyes are the hammers, the soul is the piano with many strings. The artist is the hand which plays, touching one key or another, to cause vibrations in the soul.'[39]

His companion Gabriele Münter shared his interest in occult and spiritualist publications.[40] In their library were a number of Kandinsky's marginalia, which show that he was particularly interested in spirit photography. He underlined heavily a 1908 article in the journal *Übersinnliche Welt* ('The supernatural world') on 'Transcendental photographs'.[41] He had a copy of Aksakow's *Animismus und Spiritismus*, in which spirit photography was described.[42] Kandinsky was aware of the experiments of Charcot and of the French physician, Hippolyte Baraduc, author of *Les vibrations de la vitalité humaine*.[43] In their library of the occult was also a German translation of a major theosophical work, Besant and Leadbeater's *Thought-forms*.[44] Art as telepathy, Ringbom concludes, was an approach to his work which Kandinsky formed in part through contact with these theosophical writings.[45]

Kandinsky's explorations of theosophy had a detached quality. In effect, he was a fellow traveller of the theosophist movement. By not joining the German section, he avoided wasting much time in the heated controversies of the pre-war years. Never having signed on, he never had to reject it. He was shrewd enough to take out of theosophy what

23. *Allerheiligen 1*, 1911 by Wassily Kandinsky

appealed to his temperament, and to leave those with an abiding interest in sectarian politics to fight it out by themselves.[46] The result was a theosophical distillate in Kandinsky's theory of art, a unique *mélange* of Goethe, Schiller, and Steiner, whipped up (to use a culinary metaphor) in an anti-materialist soufflé.

This is the philosophical background not only to the Blaue Reiter movement, but also to a number of apocalyptic images Kandinsky painted in the immediate pre-war period. In this period he took up the theme of All Saints, with the dead rising from their graves, as well as the Horsemen of the Apocalypse. In 1913, he and Marc started a project of creating a new illustrated edition of the Bible. Marc explored creation myths, and found expression in 1913–14 for his view 'that there is no great and pure art without religion'.[47] Kandinsky chose as his subject the Book of Revelation. His pre-war Compositions VI and VII are meditations on catastrophe, which he saw as the prelude to a period of rebirth.[48] All these images reflect his philosophical preoccupations, steeped in theosophy and stoked by his admiration for the simplicity and clarity of Bavarian religious folk art.[49]

Meidner and urban apocalypse

A second expression of the apocalyptic temperament in art before 1914 focused on a very terrestrial environment. This time the upheaval was envisioned in an urban landscape, that of imperial Berlin. Ludwig Meidner was born in Bernstadt in Silesia in 1884. After training in the Königliche Kunstschule (Royal School of Art) in Breslau and a period of study in Paris, where he befriended the Italian artist Modigliani, he returned to Germany and to an impoverished artist's life in Berlin.[50]

The city was one of the most rapidly growing industrial centres in Europe. In the five decades since German unification in 1870, its population had quadrupled. Growth in Paris and London was roughly half as rapid. Whereas in 1871 Berlin's population was half that of Paris, by the eve of the Great War the populations were virtually the same.

Meidner was one of millions who migrated to a city which was both a provincial capital and the seat of government of a world power. Berlin was also a massively growing industrial metropolis, with big chemical and electrical enterprises. The giant Siemens firm created its own industrial city of 100,000 people in Siemensstadt in the suburb of Spandau. In two generations the urban landscape had been transformed.[51]

It was this landscape which, in his dreams and nightmares, Ludwig Meidner tore apart. Meidner was a polemicist who delighted in insulting other artists or distancing his work from what he called their 'shabby goods'.[52] But behind the polemics, histrionics, and idiosyncrasies, Meidner's work expressed a second form of the pre-war art of catastrophe. His apocalypticism drew on the international tension surrounding chronic Balkan conflicts, but primarily it presented the coming upheaval as an urban event.

The history of landscape painting in the eighteenth century is replete with doom-ridden anti-urban figuration,[53] as is much nineteenth-century fiction, poetry, and critical writing. For Meidner's generation there was another source of urban apocalypticism. He was not alone in drawing deeply on Nietzsche's writings,[54] and in particular, his Jeremiads in *Thus spake Zarathustra* on the coming destruction of cities, where 'everything infirm, infamous, lustful, dusky, overmusty, pussy, and plotting putrefies together'. Zarathustra prophesies:

Woe unto this great city! And I wish I already saw the pillar of fire in which it will be burned. For such pillars of fire must precede the great noon. But this has its own time and its own destiny.[55]

The 'pillar of fire' – in Hebrew 'Shoah' – reverts back to the original Biblical meaning of holocaust, as a ritual purification or sacrifice.[56]

Meidner's attitude to city life was ambivalent. Though he lived in extreme poverty, his vision of urban life was not wholly negative. Berlin was a city he both loved and hated.[57] In one sense, his subject was the dynamism of the metropolis, 'our real homeland', its shapes, its sounds, its dangers. He celebrated the muscular newness of metropolitan life, while probing the explosive potential of such vast concentrations of people. In 1914 he wrote:

Let's paint what is close to us, our city world! The wild streets, the elegance of iron suspension bridges, gas tanks which hang in white-cloud mountains, the roaring colours of buses and express locomotives, the rushing telephone wires (aren't they like music?), the harlequinade of advertising pillars, and then night . . . big city night.[58]

This was the positive side of his outlook. Not far below the surface was a darker vision; here he spoke of his strolls around Berlin during the heat wave of 1912:

Sometimes when I feel a nocturnal need I venture forth into the city . . . and hustle headlong along the pavements . . . The screams of clouds echo around me, burning bushes, a distant beating of wings, and people shadowy and spitting. The moon burns against my hot temples . . . The city nears. My body crackles. The giggles of the city ignite against my skin. I hear eruptions at the base of my skull. The houses near. Their catastrophes explode from their windows, stairways silently collapse. People laugh beneath the ruins.[59]

The 'ruins' are what he painted, in strokes of feverish anticipation of chaos and the triumph of evil. Cities shelled; women raped; people trapped in a world gone mad; mutilated soldiers: these are his urban citizens. In 1920 he recalled the stiflingly hot summer eight years before, when he began painting this cycle of apocalyptic visions. 'My brain bled dreadful visions. I could see nothing but a thousand skeletons jigging in a row. Many graves and burnt cities writhed across the plains.'[60]

I unloaded my obsessions onto canvas day and night – Judgment days, world's ends, and gibbets of skulls, for in those days the great universal storm was already baring its teeth and casting its glaring yellow shadow across my whimpering brush-hand.[61]

This sense of art as anticipation is more flattering to the artist than it should be. An examination of Meidner's apocalyptic painting leads to an alternative reading. In these works he was responding to urban upheaval and violence invading the cities, both well-worn nineteenth-century themes expressing middle-class fears of crime, revolution, 'degeneration', and rapid urban development.[62] Pre-war painting captured this older mood, deeply imprinted in nineteenth-century cultural life. Meidner was aware of international tensions. But his art didn't anticipate the Great War; he materialized visions of urban chaos which were the commonplace of late-Victorian pessimism.[63]

The iconography of nineteenth-century political violence is most evident in Meidner's oil canvas *Revolution*, painted in 1913. This work is also known as *The battle of the barricades*. There are clear references to Delacroix's *Liberty leading the people*, painted in the shadow of the French Revolution of 1830. This time, a proletarian figure dominates the painting. His grip on a flag or staff is pronounced, but his expression and cry are ambiguous. Chaos rules on the city streets, and anxiously peering at the scene, at bottom left, is a figure resembling the artist.[64] No triumphant heroism here; only the sense of *domestic* upheaval, festering just beneath the surface of the city.

Those who have seen anticipations of war in Meidner's pre-war work have missed the ominous conflict visible to anyone walking the streets of Berlin. In the year Meidner painted *Revolution* the Social Democratic party, dedicated to the overthrow of the regime and the largest single party in the Reichstag, organized massive demonstrations in the streets of the capital. Equally visible were public celebrations of the Kaiser's birthday. The Kaiser was wont to speculate on how many strikers ought to be shot if they marched on the streets of Berlin.[65] The potential collision between a reactionary Junker elite and a mass proletarian party was part of everyday conjecture. That the headquarters of the German army, the most powerful military force in the world, was in Potsdam, a stone's throw from Berlin, added another dimension to coffee-house conversation on the catastrophe to come. But it was class war and not international conflict which loomed on the horizon in the years when Meidner painted his apocalyptic landscapes.

An exhibition of the works of the Italian futurists in Berlin in the spring of 1912 may have influenced Meidner's sense of composition, through their use of fractured lines and broken images. He was rude about their work, just as he was abrupt in discussing many other contemporaries, but some stylistic affinities are there nonetheless.[66] Both in his political outlook and in this choice of subject-matter, though, Meidner's pessimism obliterated any sense that he was engaged in a common project with the Futurists. Much more evident is his admiration for the German masters, and in particular Albrecht Dürer. Echoes of Hieronymus Bosch appear in some of his drawings, and there are parallels with Delacroix's *Massacres of Scio*.[67]

Meidner's oil painting of 1912 *Die Abgebrannten* (*Heimatlöse*) ('The burnt out or homeless') is a scene which could have been taken from accounts of the devastation of Paris after the destruction of the Commune in 1871. Broken men lie outside demolished housing in a sombre night scene. More violent still is his ink-and-graphite drawing of 1913, *Apokalyptische vision*, adding sexual defilement to urban destruction. Fleeing women pass a rape victim, still prone and exposed. Standing above them is a demonic male figure, not in military uniform. The threat is not from without; violation and torture appear to come from within society.

The tendency of the ordinary to turn into the infernal was a theme Meidner treated in a number of pre-war paintings. There is the dual canvas painted in 1913, on one side of which is a rather benign *Landschaft* ('Landscape'), with houses and trees intact under a clouded sky. On the other side is *Apokalyptische Landschaft*, with explosions in the distance, isolated individuals fleeing, and the painter in the foreground, a witness like a Biblical prophet to the destruction of his city. Another double canvas, with *Burning cities* on both sides, raises the same notion of an urban time-bomb, waiting to go off. The source of the fire is never specified.

It is true that Meidner approached the theme of war victims before 1914. In *Schrecken des Krieges* ('Horrors of war') he shows three mutilated men conversing; the stumps of their arms and legs as well as their nakedness testify to their pitiful state. In 1911, in the same year, he presented a vision of families of refugees in *Die Gestrandeten* ('The stranded ones'). Probably inspired by Georg Heym's pre-war poetry,[68] these tempera-and-ink drawings are distinct from the landscapes, since they are placed outside the urban setting dominating the apocalyptic cycle.

In one tempera-and-ink drawing of 1913, *Shelling of a city*, Meidner brought together these two dimensions of his pre-war vision. Officers confer as a battery fires directly into Berlin. Isolated individuals flee, and a figure like the Angel of Death hovers nearby. The uniforms of the soldiers are stylized; it is unclear whether the German army or another force is wreaking havoc on the city.

After the outbreak of war, Meidner continued to explore the apocalypse. In two *Apokalyptische Landschaften*, of 1915 and 1916, the red or ochre sky defines the infernal moment. And in *The last day* (1916), huddled, frightened figures are scattered over a ruined world. This, the last of his apocalyptic paintings, presaged his return to traditional Judaism. In the war years, he began exploring religious themes, and had found, apparently, a modicum of peace. 'My years of struggle', he recalled in later years, 'were over.'[69]

Between 1910 and 1916 Meidner was an artist fascinated, at times obsessed, by the apocalyptic idea. The subject seemed to suit his highly strung temperament. But what he saw was neither entirely idiosyncratic nor a premonition of the future. These images are shocking today, but they were the common currency of other artists and writers in pre-war Berlin.[70] The same doomed men and women of the metropolis inhabited the verse of the poets in Meidner's Berlin circle. Georg Heym wrote in 1912:

> The people on the streets draw up and stare,
> While overhead huge portents cross the sky;
> Round fanglike towers threatening comets flare,
> Death-bearing, fiery snouted where they fly.[71]

24. *Bombardement einer Stadt* by Ludwig Meidner

Meidner's friend Jakob van Hoddis announced the 'End of the world' in a poem of that title ('Weltende') written in 1911:

> The bourgeois' hat flies off his pointed head,
> the air re-echoes with a screaming sound.
> Tilers plunge from roofs and hit the ground,
> and seas are rising round the coasts (you read).
>
> The storm is here, crushed dams no longer hold,
> the savage seas come inland with a hop.
> The greater part of people have a cold.
> Off bridges everywhere the railroads drop.[72]

Meidner's apocalyptic landscapes are more than the febrile excursions of an isolated artist. They reflect a wider preoccupation with apocalyptic images among pre-war artists and writers. In Meidner's art there is little of the celebration of violence, machinery, and speed of the Italian Futurists.[73] Instead, there is a sense that destruction was imminent, that it was 'a necessary and cathartic evil', in Carol Eliel's phrase, but an evil nonetheless.[74]

What better way of capturing both the mood of pre-war social conflict within the German Empire and the anguish and exhilaration of the revolutionary upheaval which socialists announced time and again would be an inevitable outcome of the capitalist system? It is true that international tensions were frequently in the news. But the central conflict on the agenda in 1911–14 was the potential for class war, not the gigantic clash of European arms. For decades the Cassandras had spoken of the explosive mixture of poverty, deprivation, and anger in these gigantic cities. Berlin was teeming with tenements, or human barracks – *Mietkasernen* in German.[75] Meidner lived among them, in the belly of the whale. Here is a neglected source of his apocalyptic visions, one remote from the battlefields soon to engulf the whole of the European continent.[76]

Instead of perpetuating the romantic myth of the artist as 'seer', so dear to Kandinsky and so many of his contemporaries,[77] and proclaiming his work and that of Meidner as intimations of the Great War, historians would be better advised to recognize that the environment of domestic political conflict, and in particular class conflict, was sufficiently overheated to supply these artists with more than enough ominous material for their eschatological explorations. That material was there on the streets of Berlin, for anyone with eyes to see it.[78]

Equally it would be a mistake to reduce Meidner's art (or Kandinsky's) to a mere reflection of political tensions. Much more was involved than that. I have shown two forms of pre-war apocalyptic art. On the one hand, there were the cosmic speculations of Kandinsky and his excursions into theosophy. On the other hand, Ludwig Meidner drew visions from the daily realities of urban dynamism and political tensions. Both created a visual grammar for those who, after the outbreak of war in 1914, brooded on the future and put their minds to the task of imagining the Apocalypse.

Apocalyptic images: from anticipation to allegory

It is not my intention to provide a broad or representative survey of wartime art or of postwar visual meditations on trench warfare.[79] Nor is it possible to offer more than a glimpse of the vast range of religious reference in the art of all combatant countries.[80] My purpose is more modest: it is simply to demonstrate the gap which separates the pre-war apocalyptic tradition in painting from a number of later explorations of the genre.

The outbreak of war abruptly ended one phase of apocalyptic art, the art of anticipation. Instead, apocalyptic motifs became the core of a series of visual allegories about war. The use of allegory, a device of indirection, of the interposition of a narrative form between artists and audience,[81] was important for many artists after 1914. Allegory was there for those unwilling or unable to resort to abstract or realistic descriptive techniques in their approach to imagining the war. For sources of such allegorical art, many painters turned back to the old masters, and in particular the art of the sixteenth century. The shadows of Holbein and Grünewald, among others, fell over this work, and provide another link between old and new in the complex attempts made after 1914 to imagine the catastrophe of war.

Otto Dix, the trenches and the Flood

When it came, the Apocalypse was neither urban nor cosmic. The war experienced by soldiers and imagined by those in and out of uniform after 1914 was located in a different kind of landscape from that envisioned by Kandinsky or Meidner. The scene of war was essentially rural, but with such marks of carnage and devastation as to resemble a desert covered in mud, twisted metal, and putrefaction. Above all, it was an infernal landscape. The German artist Otto Dix put it this way: 'Lice, rats, barbed wire, fleas, shells, bombs, underground caves, corpses, blood, liquor, mice, cats, artillery, filth, bullets, mortars, fire, steel: that is what war is. It is the work of the devil.'[82]

No one could capture directly what the war was really like; those who tried usually trivialized the subject. 'What we soldiers have experienced out here in the past few months', wrote Franz Marc in early 1915, 'is beyond belief.'[83] War, he told his mother, 'is more frightful than I could ever have dreamed'.[84] He was dead ten months later, killed on horseback near Verdun. Instead of resorting to the visual clichés of propaganda, so remote from the soldier's war, or adopting the naive approach of *imagerie d'Epinal*, a number of artists both during and after the conflict chose the language of allegory to express their amazement and their horror about the war.

Dix is the first of the apocalypticians·in uniform I discuss in this chapter on the war in the visual arts. In 1914 he was a 24-year-old amateur painter in Dresden.[85] His early work on *Night in the city* and *Sunrise 1913* shows both his affinities with the strong lines of Van Gogh, whose work was exhibited in Dresden in 1912, and with Meidner's (and the Futurists') fascination with urban landscapes.[86] We see here too evidence of Dix's engagement with the writings of Nietzsche, whose head he sculpted in plaster in 1912, and whose shadow was cast over so much of the art of the first decades of the twentieth century.[87]

A number of Dix's drawings and paintings at this time express a set of interests which would preoccupy him in later years. He explored religious symbols in *The nun* (1914), mythical themes in *Dying warrior* (1913), and outcast sexuality in *The prostitute* (1913). Although never a conventionally religious man, he was thoroughly conversant with the

25 *Streichholzhändler* by Otto Dix (1920)

Bible, and was drawn to deviants as those who were, in a way, closer to God than were conventional people.[88]

Dix volunteered in 1914. He shared the naive view of many young soldiers that the war would bring them into contact with a range of 'tremendous' experiences inaccessible in civilian life.[89] It is said that he carried in his soldier's pack both the Bible and Nietzsche,[90] and his self-portrait in 1914, as a bald warrior, attests to his embrace of the excitement of the war in its early phase.[91]

In another 1914 painting, *Self-portrait as Mars*, we see Dix's taste for allegory. Here the collage of shapes, colours, and animal forms recalls pre-war apocalyptic images. Only this time, the Apocalypse suggests older motifs; after 1914, in a sense, classical mythology, mediated by Nietzsche, had come alive. In his later drawings from the front, Dix followed this mythical perspective, so powerfully captured by another Nietzschean in uniform, Ernst Jünger.[92]

Many of his wartime drawings capture the uncanny, surreal landscape of the trenches. Many were drawn on the back of postcards sent back to a friend in Dresden, Helena Jakob. Partly to counteract boredom, Dix tried to fix in his mind some of the images of the four years he spent in uniform, as an artilleryman and machine-gunner in Champagne, on the Somme, in Russia. But underlying this descriptive approach was the beginning of a revulsion about the war which became more pronounced after the Armistice. With Jeremiah, he wrote in his diary at the Somme front, 'Cursed be the day on which I was born; the day on which my mother gave birth must have been unblessed.'[93] Later it was this darker side of apocalyptic art which Dix would make his own, but during the war he still retained some elements of pre-war apocalypticism. Witness his painting *Awakening* (1918), which mixes forms, colours, and horses in a manner reminiscent of Kandinsky, and Marc's pre-war work.[94]

How different in style and content were his postwar meditations on trench warfare. From the early 1920s, Dix dropped any element of celebration of the warrior or neutrality about the nobility of his calling. Back in Dresden in 1920, he painted grotesque images of prostitutes and German soldiers, for instance in his *Memories of the mirrored rooms in Brussels* and mutilated veterans on *Pragerstrasse*, the *Match-seller*, and in *Skat players*. In Düsseldorf in 1923, he painted *The trench*, the first of a series of epic works which borrowed heavily from Grünewald and German Renaissance art.[95]

In the following year, Dix created a cycle of fifty etchings, simply entitled *Der Krieg*. They are among the most searing works on war in any artistic tradition. To depict the dehumanization of soldiers in war, Dix went back to photographs of the devastation of the trenches. We know of his interest in Goya in this period,[96] but there is also much here to indicate his growing exploration of the hideous images of Grünewald and Cranach.

These etchings were completed in the same year that a pacifist activist, Ernst Friedrich, published a two-volume set of photographs of mutilated bodies, hanging prisoners-of-war, and disfigured veterans. *War against war* is almost unbearable to look at, and that may have limited the impact of the photographs displayed in his Anti-Kriegs-museum in Berlin.[97]

It was Dix who showed how to capture the infernal character of the Great War, for in this task allegory was far more powerful than photographic realism. Allegory was a form Dix explored in many other paintings,[98] but for our purposes there are two which firmly establish the character of his postwar apocalypticism.

The first is the triptych with predella which he painted in 1932 entitled *War*; the second is entitled *Flanders* (after Henri Barbusse's *Under fire*), painted four years later, in 1936. The triptych's left panel shows a column of marching soldiers. Initially accompanied by a dog in an early sketch, these men pass a wheel in the final version. The central panel is dominated by an impaled figure, suspended on a tree above

26. *Der Krieg* (*War* triptych, 1929/1932) by Otto Dix

the battle, a dead man whose hand points to the carnage below. The echoes of Grünewald's Isenheim altarpiece in Dix's early drawings are unmistakable, especially in the pock-marked legs of one soldier buried upside down in the mud. In the right-hand panel, one soldier (with Dix's own features)[99] is dragging a wounded comrade from the trench; another is crawling away alone. As if to parallel the left-hand panel, these human, dignified responses of ordinary soldiers in an inhuman, undignified landscape, bracket the Crucifixion in the centre. A similar counterpoint is in the predella, where soldiers hang their food from the ceiling to keep the rats from devouring it. Their living quarters are surrounded by skulls and bones, buried in the walls of the trench system itself. In form, the predella recalls the bleak horizontal lines of Holbein's *Christ in the Tomb* of 1521.

The religious iconography is clear: from the road to Calvary, to Crucifixion, to Descent from the Cross, to entombment. But the presence of images of decency does not imply the presence of God or salvation. Indeed, the reference to Holbein's extraordinary painting of *Christ in the tomb* is (from a Christian point of view) unnerving. There, in Holbein's masterpiece of 1521, an entirely realistic Christ is laid out in the tomb in such a way as to suggest that though the Crucifixion has happened, that is the end of the story. There is no sign whatsoever of the Resurrection. The sheer horizontality of Holbein's masterpiece challenges conventional Christian faith. As we have seen in our discussion of war memorials, pure horizontality is too austere for most artists, who wish to provide a message of hope. It was not for them to dwell on the doubt that Holbein's painting created in the mind of Dostoyevsky's Prince Mishkin, who said that it *almost* made him lose his faith.[100] Dix's painting goes one step further: the 'almost' is gone. Human decency is affirmed, but faith in God is absent.

The retention of a humanist faith, and its expression in allegory, is even more directly evident in Dix's painting of 1936, entitled *Flanders*. The subject is a celebrated scene in Henri Barbusse's novel *Under fire*. As we shall see in chapter 7, Barbusse ended his novel allegorically, through the depiction of a modern version of the legend of the Flood. This scene describes the moment when soldiers from both sides awake from a night of infernal rain. Mud-encrusted soldiers become part of the landscape, growing out of trees and branches as if inhabiting one of Dante's *Bolgias*. The sign of the crown of thorns is visible in the centre of the painting. But resurrection is near. Soldiers awaken from the infernal night and, in Barbusse's book, they rise to cry out against war as an abomination which must never happen again.[101] Thus the hopeful 'dawn' of Barbusse's *Under fire*, published in 1917 and available in German in 1918, is present in Dix's painting, through a golden, though cloud-covered sunrise on the left and a blue sky, with the setting moon clearly visible on the right of the painting.

Barbusse had written an introduction to a book promoting Dix's 1924 cycle of headings on the war.[102] The prominence of Barbusse in left-wing veterans' politics meant that anything to do with his work would be anathema to the Nazis. Dix's painting of 1936 is an act of defiance.

For our purposes, what is most important is that the allegory he has chosen is Noah and the Flood, a Biblical landscape in which those like Dix and Barbusse, who had been through the worst of the war as enemy soldiers, cry out together against its repetition. Here the Apocalypse is reconfigured as an allegory of hope, just as Barbusse had intended twenty years before. Seven years later, in the midst of the Second World War, Dix painted his first *Resurrection*, once more returning to the German Renaissance, and to Grünewald's final, luminous vision of eternal glory.[103]

Beckmann's 'Resurrection'

After the outbreak of the Great War, there are striking similarities between the apocalyptic art of Dix and that of his German contemporary Max Beckmann. Beckmann was thirty in 1914, six years older than Dix, and already an established artist in Berlin, a recognized member of the Berlin Secession, with powerful works to his credit, such as *The destruction of Messina* (1909) and *The sinking of the Titanic* (1912).[104]

Like Dix, Beckmann initially supported the German war effort, though his reactions captured the turbulence of the period and the complexity of emotions stirred by these disturbing days. Witness the dry-point print entitled *Declaration of war 1914*. It shows a group of people in Berlin trying to get a glimpse of a newspaper with the latest war news. Their faces show a range of reactions, from shock to concern to apparent detachment.[105]

Like Dix, Beckmann volunteered, though exempted from military service in 1903 on medical grounds. Beckmann (like Dix) carried Nietzsche in his military gear. Like Dix, he saw the human wreckage of battle, this time in East Prussia in 1914 and near Ypres in Belgium in 1915, when gas warfare began. Unlike Dix, Beckmann saw no combat, but served as a hopsital orderly, regularly attending to men with gruesome wounds and caring for them after they were operated on.[106]

Like Dix, he saw on the Western Front a landscape which gave the word 'fantastic' a new and heightened meaning. He passed 'strangely unreal cities like lunar mountains, cities of the dead, both the newly massacred and the long-since buried, hurled into the air time and again like a mockery of the Resurrection.[107] He described one scene to his first wife Minna:

Yesterday we came through a cemetery which was completely ruined by grenade fire. The tombs were ripped open, and the coffins lay around in uncomfortable positions. The indiscreet grenades had exposed the ladies and gentlemen to the light – bones, hair, clothing peeked out from the coffins.[108]

It was the resurrection, among other religious motifs, which he painted in 1916–18, after a breakdown occasioned by the strain of work as a medical orderly led to his being invalided out of the army.

In his wartime work, Beckmann developed a style both romantic and ironic, disclosed by his jibe to a friend that instead of serving in Belgium, he wished he could read Jean Paul on Mars.[109] Here Beckmann is referring to the author of dream visions, including *Speech of the dead Christ*.[110] Irony and bitterness had replaced the artist's curiosity in his approach to the war. Now the 'inexpressible absurdity of life', its character as a 'paradoxical joke' bore heavily on him.[111] By mid-1915, he likened torn-up streets to the scene of the Day of Judgment; he repeatedly dreamed of the 'destruction of the world'. 'Everything is foundering', he told his wife, 'and I keep thinking only of how I will paint the head of the resurrected one against the red stars in the sky of the Final Judgment.'[112] In 1916 he wrote to a friend: 'if you cannot find a way out of this mess you are the biggest fool in the world'.[113] There were millions of such fools, whose madness at war Beckmann approached through the apocalyptic vision *Resurrection*.

Beckmann's *Resurrection* bears little resemblance to the work of the Blaue Reiter school.[114] Before the war, Beckmann had distanced himself from Marc and Kandinsky's apocalypticism, describing it acidly as empty mysticism;[115] and Beckmann quickly turned his back on those who felt gratitude for the war as a purifying force. On 26 September 1914 (as it happened, the day August Macke was killed), Franz Marc asked Kandinsky the rhetorical question: 'is there a single man who wishes the war had never occurred?'[116] There were many such men; after an initial period of reflection, Beckmann was one of them.

By the end of the war, Beckmann was even more emphatic in what kind of spiritual art he rejected and what kind he intended to create:

Through four long years now we have gazed into the grimace of horror. Perhaps some of us have, thereby, gained a deeper understanding. We have got rid of much which was taken for granted. From a thoughtless imitation of the visible, from a weak archaism of empty decoration and from a falsely sentimental mysticism we may now proceed to a transcendental objective.

Among the guides he sought out to help him in this new enterprise, this attempt to build 'a new church' in which men could 'cry out their fury and despair, all their poor optimism, joy and wild longings' were Grünewald, Brueghel, Cézanne, and Van Gogh.[117]

Dominating the unfinished *Resurrection* of 1916–18 are an exploding

27. *Auferstehung* by Max Beckmann

sun and a dark moon on the horizon. Houses are ripped open. In one of them, Beckmann, his wife, his son, and friends are standing passively, gazing at a corpse hovering nearby. Above them is a recently revived figure, facing away from the viewer, head bowed and apparently still rubbing his eyes. Complex groups of people stand awaiting judgment to the left and right of this central section.[118]

Beckmann had addressed this theme in his oil painting *Resurrection* of 1909, but in an entirely orderly and conventional manner. His wartime study is in another realm entirely. What sets apart the later painting is its enrichment by his experience of the chaos of war and by the studies he made of the wounded soldiers he cared for and of those beyond help. His resurrected men are his wartime companions, emerging from the long night of war into an uncertain day, lit by a dying sun.

Beckmann's wartime *Resurrection* is emphatically non-triumphal. Its theme suggests hope, but in both the unfinished painting and in a dry-point sketch of 1918 that hope is literally disembodied. This detached point of view may point towards Beckmann's struggle with the problem of theodicy. As Sarah O'Brien-Twohig has observed:

Unable to reconcile the idea of a loving, benign God with the appalling suffering he witnessed as a voluntary medical orderly, he was 'filled with rage at God for having made us so we cannot love each other'. To find an explanation for such evil he turned to the mystical doctrines of Gnosticism, Buddhism and the Cabbala, and to the pessimistic philosophy of Schopenhauer.[119]

The gnostic idea that 'the world was created by an evil demiurge as a prison for souls which must struggle to return to their original state in the realm of Good or Light beyond material creation'[120] has always been heretical within the Christian tradition. Beckmann's reference to the Resurrection in this painting is therefore a questioning of conventional beliefs through the exploration of the conventional setting of the Apocalypse. This gnostic pessimism, this sense of despair over the ugliness of the war and the suffering it entailed, marked this phase of Beckmann's art, created in the wake of his breakdown in Flanders in 1915. It is this brooding melancholy, this *soleil noir* (in Julia Kristeva's phrase),[121] which dominates Beckmann's *Resurrection* of 1916–18.

Beckmann claimed that he was totally uninterested in politics.[122] Though he created lasting monuments to the violence accompanying the German revolution of 1919 in his masterpiece *Night* and in other works,[123] it is in the non-political realm that we should locate his apocalyptic painting.

After the war some saw links between Beckmann's visions of war and the anti-war writings of Henri Barbusse. I have already noted the same parallel with reference to Otto Dix's war paintings.[124] The critic Eduard Bendemann wrote in the *Frankfurter Zeitung* on 7 June 1919 that Beckmann's graphic works were 'perhaps the only images with which the pictorial arts might compete with Henri Barbusse's representation of the war: they even seem like illustrations to Barbusse's book'.[125] A more critical line was taken by Paul Westheim, editor of the radical journal *Das Kunstblatt*. In 1923 he accused Beckmann of a lingering romanticism, in which radical political change mattered less than the exploration of mythical themes.[126] Both Bendemann and Westheim were right. Beckmann's apocalyptic works share the revulsion of Barbusse as to the waste, the suffering, the pointlessness of the war. But the cold, exploding sun of Beckmann's *Resurrection* is not that of the Biblical dawn and the new covenant which Barbusse and other political activists announced. Beckmann's is a harsher, more pessimistic, vision, brooding on the disaster rather than on the better days to come.

English Apocalypse: Stanley Spencer of Cookham

It would be a mistake to believe that the apocalyptic temperament was (or is) exclusively German. While it is true that many German artists meditated on the end of days in this period, other artists in Britain and France, with very different points of view, joined them in this search for a visual language appropriate to a catastrophe on the scale of the Great War. One such artist was Stanley Spencer. Born and raised in the Berkshire village of Cookham, Spencer studied at the Slade School of Art, exhibited in Roger Fry's second post-impressionist exhibition in 1912, and in 1915, at the age of twenty-four, joined the Royal Army Medical Corps.

He was one of those soldiers in the British army that never got into war literature: the men who also served, as orderlies, porters, cleaners, launderers, and the like. No glory here. Spencer, like thousands of other forgotten men, inhabited the vast underbelly of the British army, and did so in very unheroic settings. The first was Beaufort War Hospital in Bristol, where the sick and wounded were cared for alongside civilian lunatics. The second was Macedonia, where he was attached to the 7th Royal Berkshire Regiment, a unit that had turned him down as physically unfit (too small) when he had tried to enlist in 1914.

After demobilization, Spencer returned to Cookham, and to religious art, but of a very unconventional kind. His was a spiritualism with marked similarities to that of Blake, albeit on a less powerful and certainly less beautiful plane. Nevertheless, Spencer followed Blake into the figurative world of the everydayness and the normality of the spiritual life. The war did not create this interest, but it gave him the material and memories to extend it in striking ways.

Spencer spent the early postwar years on many different projects, but among the most important were a series of paintings on the Passion of Christ, begun in 1920 and continued intermittently throughout his life. These paintings show how Spencer's pre-war fascination with both the Pre-Raphaelites and with Gauguin's rounded portraits developed after the war. The painting of Christ carrying the Cross (now in the Tate Gallery) was executed in 1921 while Spencer was living at Sir Henry Slessor's home in Bourne End, near Cookham. In this work, the obscurity of the Christ figure, masked and hidden by the local people of Cookham, echoes Breughel's compositions, and shares a positively Flemish taste for the particularism of local settings.[127] Between 1924 and 1926, Spencer worked on a *Resurrection*, located in the Cookham churchyard. In the centre, at the entrance to the church, is a seated figure, carrying a book, whose form anticipates the Christ of his *Resurrection of the Soldiers*, designed in the early 1920s and executed at Burghclere between 1928 and 1932.

This cycle of frescoes realized in a specially constructed chapel in Burghclere, near Newbury in Berkshire, is more original than any of these previous works. Spencer's benefactors, Mr and Mrs J.L. Behrend, gave him the chance to realize his vision, and then dedicated the chapel to the memory of Mrs Behrend's brother, who had died of illness contracted while on military service in Macedonia during the Great War.[128]

Again, the traditional character of the project is clear. The form of the enterprise recalls Giotto's frescoes in the Arena Chapel in Padua, or more likely, John Ruskin's description of them. But both in its evocation of the entirely ordinary and unheroic world of military life, at home and abroad, and in its treatment of the resurrection, Spencer's work is unique in war art. A series of side panels takes us through scenes of Spencer's war, in the drab and dreary corridors of Beaufort War Hospital, to the brown and dusty hillsides of Macedonia. In these paintings, nobody fights, no one kills, no one dies. There are some wounded men portrayed, one being painted with iodine, and one whose apparently frostbitten legs we see protected from contact with his sheets. But there is no pain in them. Nor is there any joy in the faces of the soldiers carrying on their mundane lives. It is as if they are all in a trance, stuck in a dreamworld of onerous tasks, avoided where possible, or simply endured. There is only one officer, sitting astride a blanket which only after careful scrutiny we discover is actually covering a horse. He is either trying to teach his men map-reading or simply telling them where they are. In either case, none of his men appears to take the slightest interest. In its unromantic, unmilitary, unofficered normality, Spencer's war memorial is like no other in Britain or (to the best of my knowledge) on the Continent.[129]

The most remarkable feature of Spencer's chapel is the central panel portraying the Resurrection. Just as in his painting of Christ carrying the Cross, here the Saviour is hard to find. He is near the top of the wall above the altar, seated, receiving from a group of risen soldiers the crosses which presumably marked their graves. This Christ resembles, though in complex ways, the seated figure in the earlier *Resurrection at Cookham*. The centre of the Burghclere work is dominated by two horses, who have fallen down, craning their necks around to see why the cart they had carried had collapsed. Above them and below the Christ is a young soldier, staring at the wooden Christ figure on a Cross he held in his hands, seemingly oblivious of the risen Christ by his side.

All this takes place on a Macedonian hillside, where animals graze, soldiers sleep, then rise from their graves in fur jackets, polish epaulets, unwind their puttees, cut the wire fallen on another soldier's head and body, and generally go about their business. As Spencer later recalled, the painting is Resurrection as Armistice, when soldiers rise and hand in their crosses as they would hand in their guns when the need for them ended.[130] There are soldierly handshakes in one corner of the painting, but absolutely no joy.[131]

Most of the men in Spencer's frescoes share the same dark features, rounded heads, and stubby figures. Either in menial tasks or in military routine, their bearing and manner have none of the marks of the cubist features of Nevinson's war art or of the individual portraiture of

28. *The Resurrection of the Soldiers* (1928–32) by Stanley Spencer, Burghclere Memorial Chapel

Muirhead Bone. Spencer evidently chose his own way, remote from both the avant-garde and the rear-guard of British art, in the exploration of spiritual realities.

The image of the rising of the dead of the Great War which graces the Burghclere war memorial fresco was in no sense simply a reflection of

Spencer's eccentric religiosity. He spoke a spiritual language many contemporaries used and adapted to their particular circumstances. Protestant iconography in England was more restrained than the reservoir of German Renaissance painting from which Dix and Beckmann drew their inspiration, but both Blake and the Pre-Raphaelites provided ample artistic material for Spencer. When he came to paint his frescoes at Burghclere between 1928 and 1932, he testified both to the robustness of the English mystical tradition and to the capacity of the apocalyptic temperament to see transcendence even in the carnage of war. None of this needed the war to establish it; it was all there for those, like Stanley Spencer, who believed in the incontrovertible imminence of the spiritual life,[132] and who maintained that belief in the decades following 1914–18.

Rouault and resistance to the apocalyptic temptation

Allegorical imagery has played a central role in Catholic devotion, and in the work of the French painter Georges Rouault there are many examples of the art of allegory as a means of placing the disaster of the Great War in a transcendental and religious framework. But here the use of allegory departs from that of Dix, Beckmann, and many other painters. For Rouault, allegory serves the purpose of affirming, rather than questioning, denying, or transforming, the central tenets of Christian faith.

We can understand much about the temptation to succumb to nihilism, to give in to despair about human nature in the shadow of the Great War, to renounce religious beliefs, conventional or otherwise, by introducing the work of a man who refused to do so. The apocalyptic imagination speaks in a language halfway between hope and despair. While despair was never far from the work of Georges Rouault, it is the hope, indeed the certainty, of mercy and salvation, which places his painting outside the apocalyptic tradition.

In this sense, Rouault's art was conservative. He placed his trust in the Resurrection and not in the Apocalypse, in the risen Christ and not directly in the transformation of this world. As we shall see below, socialists like Henri Barbusse nurtured a different kind of apocalyptic hope, one far removed from the way of the cross imagined by Rouault. Both saw meaning in the suffering of the war, but understood it in very different ways.[133]

The struggle to express Catholic hope in art is evident in much of Rouault's painting, and in particular in his war cycle, *Miserere*, painted from 1916 to 1928, and exhibited and published only after the Second World War.[134] Completed just before Spencer and Dix began their work on the Burghclere Chapel and the War Triptych, this set of meditations on war and suffering takes as its text the first verse of the 51st Psalm: 'Have mercy upon me, O God, according to thy loving-kindness.'

The aim of this work is, therefore, acceptance of the will of God. It provides a form of aesthetic redemption which fulfils the function of 'religious discourse' described by Julia Kristeva. She holds that, alongside 'aesthetic and particularly literary creation',

religious discourse in its imaginary fictional essence, set[s] forth a device whose prosodic economy, interaction of characters, and implicit symbolism constitute a very faithful semiological representation of the subject's battle with symbolic collapse.

These symbols themselves are resurrected through art, and retain a power for healing, the effectiveness of which, in her view, lies in their being 'closer to catharsis than to elaboration'.[135] It was Rouault's aim in *Miserere* to resurrect through art the symbolic universe of French Catholicism, and thereby help heal the wounds of the Great War.

Born in war-torn Paris on 27 May 1871, the day before the last resistance of the Paris Commune was snuffed out among the tombstones of the cemetery of Père Lachaise, Rouault was too infirm for military service in 1914. Already a celebrated painter, a pupil of Gustave Moreau alongside Matisse, and a fellow 'Fauve',[136] Rouault was a fervent Catholic, who came to his mature beliefs after the turn of the century. He had attended Protestant schools as a child, but after an early apprenticeship in a stained-glass workshop Rouault developed a life-long affinity for the anonymous popular art of the medieval cathedrals. After the death of his teacher, Moreau, he went through a personal crisis, from which he emerged a profoundly religious man, no longer weighed down by a conflict between his art and his religion.[137]

In part his convictions were formed through his association with the novelist Léon Bloy, who celebrated medieval piety and castigated the vulgar art of the modern secular world.[138] As one of his characters affirms in his novel *La femme pauvre*, 'If art does not go on its knees . . . it must necessarily go on its back or its belly.'[139] Rouault's search for Christ in his work was unmistakable, but the earthiness of his paintings of prostitutes and criminals went too far for Bloy. In 1907, he wrote to Rouault, that he was 'a lost friend . . . if you were a man of prayer, a eucharist, an obedient soul, you could not paint these horrible canvasses'.[140] Their association survived this rift, and the social vision and compassion of Bloy's Catholicism remained important for Rouault.[141]

Bloy died in 1917. By then Rouault had embarked on a project in religious art unparalleled in his generation. When war broke out, Rouault's heart went out to the people of France, to their 'resignation', their faith.[142] Through the sponsorship of the art-dealer and publisher Ambroise Vollard, he was able to embark three years later on a

29. *Miserere* by Rouault

Herculean task: the creation of one hundred etchings to illustrate a book, in either one or two volumes, on the sufferings of the war. The project took ten years to complete. In the end it constituted 'only' fifty-eight etchings, published in 1948 after years of litigation between Rouault and Vollard's family.[143]

The working title of the book was initially *Guerre et Miserere*, but was then reduced by Rouault to *Miserere*, both out of preference for the Latin and out of a belief that the single word suited the design of the first print.[144] As a whole, it is a war memorial of a kind not produced before or since. As one Catholic writer, Abbé Morel, put it:

This was precisely the time when every town in France was commissioning stone, marble, or bronze monuments to the memory of the victims of the recent slaughter. Many such monuments were erected on the roads of France and the rest of Europe. But I know none other that attains, not the immensity, but the grandeur, the inwardness, and thus the effectiveness and spiritual power achieved by Rouault in this work.

Following Goya, Rouault had found a way

to participate in the battle by rebuilding what the battle had destroyed in man. And there were a lot of things to fight against, as the war left great ruins in its aftermath – illusions, spiritual blindness, and despair.[145]

This was a war memorial that no one saw until after two decades of wrangling over property rights. Essentially, it constituted a materialized prayer, a 'sort of last communion', in Abbé Morel's words, first drawn, then photographed onto copper, then painstakingly etched, then produced in the simplicity of black-and-white prints.[146]

Miserere has no clear-cut sequence or division into narrative sections. Print 1 looks like the frontispiece of a book. Christ's bowed head is below an angel. The same profile of Christ's submission appears in prints 2 and 3, but thereafter, Rouault presents the wretched of the earth: the vagabond (4), the outcast (5, 11), the prostitute (14, 15), the condemned (18). Print 27 introduces a non-Christian element, that of Orpheus searching hell for Eurydice. Thereafter, at approximately the mid-point of the cycle, the presence of death and the hope of resurrection become more prevalent. Print 28 is of skulls in a charnel house, awaiting resurrection, prefigured in print 29, entitled *Sing Matins, a new day is born*. Print 31 (with the legend 'That ye love one another') is of Christ on the Cross. It is followed (32) by an image of Emmaus, of the proof of Christ's victory over death, registered as well in the face on Veronica's veil (33).

It is at this point that Rouault turned explicitly to the theme of war. The same bookish frame of print 1, *Miserere*, appears in print 34, entitled *Guerre*. Here the bowed head of the dead soldier replaces the Christ of the first print, now suspended above the fallen man. The soldiers' way of the cross begins with a son in uniform embracing his father, with the hollow words of reassurance, 'this will be the last time', as death awaits his departure. *Homo homini lupus* (37), death with a soldier's cap, is followed by images of civilian culpability: a Chinaman as inventor of

30. *Guerre* by Rouault

gunpowder (38); smiling civilians, captioned 'Nous sommes fous' (39); war factories (44). Anxious women (41–3) await the worst. In print 46, angels lift a fallen soldier. The caption reads: 'The just, like sandalwood, perfume the axe that strikes them.' He awaits burial in the next two prints (47–8).

Here the obvious development is to resurrection, but instead Rouault

175

breaks the sequence, and turns to stylized images of the war: a stiff-necked Kaiser Wilhelm (49), a stoical France (50), the Archbishop of Rheims (51), the long-suffering 'poilu' (52), and 'The Virgin of seven swords' (53), possibly the mourning mothers of France.

Print 54 is of a wartime legend, *Debout les morts*, to which I return in chapter 8 (see below, pp. 205–7). It shows death calling forth fallen soldiers to carry on the battle, a theme popularized by many Catholic writers in wartime, including Léon Bloy.[147] Rouault's print is entirely unsympathetic to Bloy's celebration of a trench miracle. Indeed, this sentiment of romantic Catholicism, celebrated by Barrès and a host of lesser writers, is described as a travesty of the Resurrection, a misuse of Catholic faith for patriotic purposes.

The series ends with Christ on the Cross, 'obedient until death' (57), and with the injunction (58) taken from Isaiah 53:5 that it is 'through his stripes that we are healed'. Healing is the last word of the cycle, and the one word which captures its aim and direction.

One observer likened these prints, with their message about 'Miserere' and 'Guerre', to 'the arched doorway of a Cathedral', a 'dual entrance' to the House of God.[148] To another, the original engravings produced a book 'whose weight is over twenty-one kilogrammes' and which 'resembles a tombstone'.[149] Both have captured Rouault's intent. He sought and found a visual language of mourning, in part after the death of his own father in 1912,[150] in part in the aftermath of the death of his spiritual mentor Léon Bloy in 1917, in part after the death of over 1 million Frenchmen in the Great War.

Rouault's art encapsulates a visual language of mourning, one which stops short of the mystical or the apocalyptic. There are no inscriptions taken from the Book of Revelation, from Daniel or Ezekiel, the traditional sources of apocalyptic art. His was not a theology of impatience, but of resignation. His art was intended to heal, but only through the one true hope: submission to the will of the Lord and an abiding faith in the truth of the Resurrection. 'You talk of [my] fervour', he replied to one observer of his work. 'Yes, it is my only possession, like the women at the sepulchre, with continuing love I await the resurrection.'[151]

Visions of war, the sacred, and the language of healing

Apocalypticians can't wait. They see the end of time rushing towards them. Before the war, some of their visions, and the beliefs embedded in them, were hopeful. Following the crash would come rebirth and renewal. After 1914, the art of anticipation turned to allegory, the allegory of catastrophic disaster.

In the wake of the Great War, apocalyptic art took on new forms, appropriate to an age of mass bereavement. The artists who explored this terrain sought inspiration from a variety of spiritual sources, from the Bible, theosophy, and the occult, and from the work of Blake, Goya, Grünewald, and Holbein, in the effort to imagine the war and its human costs.

Rouault, it is true, was one who stopped short of the apocalyptic tradition. At times he came close to it, but ultimately stayed within the borders of the church. He clung to faith in the Resurrection, and not in the Apocalypse.[152] His case is a useful one to describe the boundary conditions of what is as much a temperament as a theological position.

Yet even across the yawning gap of doctrinal orthodoxy, these artists spoke a common language. After 1914, most sought in the Biblical tradition a range of signs and symbols through which to imagine the war and the loss of life entailed in it. The art they produced was intended to help to heal, perhaps in precisely the way Kristeva has suggested, through 'catharsis', not 'elaboration'. Here is one essential point to which the sacred returned in the period of the Great War: as a vocabulary of mourning, and as a code through which artists expressed in enduring ways the enormity of the war and the suffering left in its wake.

7

The apocalyptic imagination in war literature

The history of spiritualism and the visual arts suggested some of the ways in which the Great War, however modern in the way it was fought, also triggered an avalanche of the 'unmodern'. This is clear too in much of the literature produced both by soldiers and non-combatants during the war and in its aftermath. Fiction, memoirs, short stories, and plays reveal a wealth of evidence as to the war's mobilization of motifs and images derived from the classical, romantic, and religious traditions of European literature. One of the most salient instances of the backward-looking character of this body of writing is its use of apocalyptic images. The varied and rich appeal to a traditional eschatology, to a sense of the world coming to an end, shows precisely the opposite. The Great War was, in cultural terms, the last nineteenth-century war, in that it provoked an outpouring of literature touching on an ancient set of beliefs about revelation, divine justice, and the nature of catastrophe.[1]

I centre the discussion on three apocalyptic visions, three Jeremiads, written at almost exactly the same time, during the slaughter of 1916–17 on the Western Front. These texts, as much as others written after the Armistice, show how writers drew deeply on older cultural traditions to express their anguish and their compassion.

The Flood: Barbusse's *Le feu*

Already an established novelist before the war, Henri Barbusse is well known as the Zola of the trenches, the man who conveyed the character of trench warfare in terms which directly echo those of Zola's account of the catastrophe of a pit disaster in *Germinal*.[2] What they shared was an apocalyptic imagination, a disposition to see the outline of a new covenant, a new future, in the dawn following the catastrophe.

Barbusse joined up on the outbreak of the war, and, after a brief period of preparation in the 39th Territorial Regiment, at his own request he was transferred to the 231st Infantry Regiment, and went into the line as a common soldier in the 55th Division.[3] His attitude to the war was at first unequivocal. This was a moral crusade against

178

Germany, a struggle against a nefarious power which (so he told his wife on 4 August) could not win the war and would sue for peace before being crushed.[4] A few days later he wrote a letter to the editor of *L'Humanité*, the socialist daily, outlining his view on the war:

far from giving up the ideas I have always defended, I intend to serve them by taking up arms. This war is a social war which will advance our cause, perhaps definitively. It is directed against our old infamous time-honoured enemies: militarism and imperialism, the Sabre, the Boot, and, I add, the Crown. Our victory will be the annihilation of the central lair of the kaisers, the crown princes, the lords and their henchmen who imprison a people and would imprison others. The world will be emancipated only by opposing them. If I sacrifice my life and if I go to war with joy, it is not only as a Frenchman, but above all as a human being.[5]

Here is the characteristic Republican nationalism of the late nineteenth century. Barbusse fought for France, and by doing so fought for humanity.

In 1914 Barbusse was forty-one years old. He had been exempted from military service on grounds of health when conscripted with his 'class' in 1893, but twenty years later Barbusse retained some memories of the trappings of military life. He noted the same habits, the same jokes, the same smells. This time 'the only difference is that discipline is easier and beds are absent'.[6]

The real war hit Barbusse in the first week of 1915, when he went into the trenches first near Soissons, and later in Artois.[7] He celebrated the new year near Crouy on the front to the northeast of Paris, soaked to the bone:

What a life. Mud, earth, rain. We are saturated, dyed, kneaded. One finds dirt everywhere, in pockets, in handkerchiefs, in clothes, in food. It is a haunting memory, a nightmare of earth and mud, and you have no idea what a weird-looking fellow I am. My gun has the air of being sculpted in clay.[8]

German troops opposite sang their national anthem; Barbusse thought he heard the Austrian national anthem as well on the other side of the line,[9] a reflection probably of drink and bonhomie.

And then came the shelling and the killing. Between 9 and 13 January 1915, about half of Barbusse's unit was killed. Still the rain poured down, through his supposedly rainproof cape, and there was little to eat. He didn't change his clothes in two weeks.[10]

Throughout the chaos and confusion, Barbusse kept a record. On 11 January 1915 he told his wife: 'I took notes to digest all this in detail, I will make sense of it when quiet returns . . . Quelle existence!'[11] Two weeks later he tried to describe what a bombardment was like: 'It's terrible; it is a vision of horror of which one can know only after one has been under shrapnel and shellfire.'[12]

179

In these letters home we can see the emergence of Barbusse's apocalyptic language about the war. In May 1915 he told his wife of one encounter, 'a deafening fracas, a really terrible apotheosis of supernatural power'.[13] Afterwards came the removal of the corpses.

What impressions I have, my child, and really only on a battlefield like this can one have a precise idea of the horror of these great massacres. The trenches are an extraordinary topsy-turvy world, a chaos of weapons, bullets, grenades, fuses, equipment mixed with bodies.

Among the German corpses, Barbusse found touching family letters as well as religious literature.[14]

He helped bring in from no man's land some wounded French soldiers, for which effort he was awarded the Croix de guerre.[15] He found the time to read both Virgil and Goethe, preferring Latin lucidity to Germanic *fumisme* (airy phrases).[16] He also shared with his wife some of the common outrage about the inequalities of risk faced by common soldiers and staff officers. 'It is always thus, the glory goes not to the poor men in the line of fire', but to the 'shirkers' behind the desks, the ' "arrivistes", who multiply'.[17]

Later in 1915, he was cited for bravery again, this time for setting up a first-aid post in a particularly dangerous part of no man's land during an artillery bombardment. After seventeen months on active service, suffering from pulmonary damage, exhaustion, and dysentery, he was invalided out of the front lines, and, after hospital treatment, posted to a reserve unit.[18]

By early 1916, Barbusse found himself behind a desk, as a secretary in the office of recruitment of the high command. He had landed in the belly of the whale, and the relative peace and quiet of bureaucratic life provided him with the environment in which his novel about the war, *Le feu*, begun in hospital, was completed. By March 1916 he told his wife:

My book on the war is not new, oh no. I try to describe a squad of soldiers through different phases and movements of a company. It isn't easy to do it properly. I copy passages and I scavenge everything from my work as a secretary for my work as a novelist.[19]

Barbusse decided to publish his book in two forms, first serially in a monthly literary journal, *L'Oeuvre*, and then as a book. This was a nineteenth-century convention, which gave to the journal's editor the chance to avoid military censorship and do the job himself. Such minor changes as took place annoyed Barbusse terribly. Some of his language was cleaned up ('Nom d'un chien' in place of 'Nom de Dieu'), but as it happened, the editor probably did him a favour. His act of self-censorship partially bypassed army scrutiny, which might have taken a more caustic view of many of Barbusse's scenes.[20]

The articles in *L'Oeuvre* appeared in August 1916. The book itself was completed in November. Its publication in early 1917 was a literary event. It sold rapidly and was greeted with critical acclaim.[21] The turbulence of 1917 helped to provide echoes of his apocalyptic message. The Russian Revolution added 'proof' that Barbusse was right: the old world was in the crucible. This was one reason why a German translation of *Le feu* was banned in Germany and Austria.[22] In France, the strikes of 1917 and the mutinies on the Chemin des Dames added weight to the general mood of uncertainty about the future. The old shibboleths – such as *la guerre à l'outrance* (war to the bitter end) – no longer held. A new vision was needed, and in *Le feu* Barbusse provided one. Winner of the foremost French prize for fiction, the Prix Goncourt, *Le feu* became a best-seller. By July 1918, 200,000 copies had been sold.[23]

Barbusse was now a celebrity, and was determined to use his position to speak out against war, both this war and all wars. Here was the origin of his work in veterans' politics, through the Association Républicaine des Anciens Combattants (ARAC).[24] His moral stance was that of a modern Noah, who had been through the Flood, and demanded a new covenant, a new order, an order without war.

Le feu offered a message of hope. This is what helped to give his book its massive appeal and power. It spoke to the bereaved as much as to the soldiers with whom Barbusse had served. One teacher from the Ardèche, aged twenty, had lost her husband in the war. She wrote to Barbusse to thank him for his book and for his message of hope. She 'took courage to think that those who died did not die in vain – if the present cataclysm produces a modification of human destiny'. 'One can't remake life', Barbusse mused, 'but one can avoid death' in future.[25] It was this task, the avoidance of the calamity of war, which Barbusse was to make his life's work.

In that effort, he relied on *Le feu* as evidence of his bond with the common soldier. He, Barbusse, had broken through the circle of nationalist lies and distortions, and had told the truth the *poilus* had known all along. In September 1917, he appealed directly to soldiers in a new edition of his book. 'You have liked my book', he began:

because it is a book of truth. You have found in it your hardships and your suffering, you found in it the great war as you fought it . . . You are dignified when we hide from the world none of the pain you have borne. Shady journalists have dared to write that you must be misled and lied to in order to be better led; that readers in the rear cover their faces modestly and block their ears why one reveals to them all that man is capable of undergoing to save the idea of justice; . . . you know me, I have known that only the truth is worthy of you.[26]

This element of truth-telling while the war was going on separated Barbusse's fiction from most of the other prose I shall discuss. The urgent need to explain to soldiers why they suffer, why the wounded cry out in pain, the necessity of giving 'an answer in the face of the silent and demanding dead' were matters not of memory but of solidarity with the men still undergoing the ordeal of the war.[27] 'Certainly I have not taught you anything, brothers who have taught me so much', Barbusse affirmed. 'At least – you have told me and I believe you – I will help you in retelling what you have been. I will help you to guard the hell that haunts you.'[28]

But that infernal experience was not an end in itself. It started men thinking:

The old man buried in his trench, in the limitless expanse of the night, the man of the people, with a simple heart, a man of purity, of the right and the good, starts to think, behind the small immediate causes of the war, what are the great causes, and beyond the dark night which falls or the feeble morning which follows, what are the days and years to come . . . He sees the war as it is, in its entrails. He asks the vast question which always follows, sooner or later, from the sensibility, the dignity, the liberty of men: why?

The choices were clear. On the one hand, the road to a better future, 'The destruction of mad militarism, everywhere and for always, equality of citizenship, no more disorderly despotism.'[29] On the other hand, a rampant nationalism, callously invoking the name of the dead to serve reactionary political ends.

This dance of the dead revolted Barbusse. This 'comedy of the resurrection of cadavers', he felt, was an abomination 'when it consists of dressing them up in cheap finery and when they are made to speak falsely against the common interest'. 'Only those', he noted in June 1919,

whom chance has saved in the war will have the right to invoke without lies the witness and the example of those dead whom they brushed against, whom they touched; but we prefer to stand back from this moving invocation.

The only acceptable attitude, in our view, to bring to their tombs, as one comrade put it, is 'impeccable silence'. At least, if we do not speak in their name, no one else should dare to do so. A father has no moral right to use the heroic death of his son to add bluster to his personal prestige, to draw admiration to himself, . . . [or] to support a politico-commercial doctrine which, consciously or not, would provoke new massacres and lead humanity into the abyss.[30]

Moral outrage and hope: in Barbusse's writing, they are inseparable. Here is the source of the optimism in his work which others writing in the apocalyptic mode during and after the war did not share.

Always Barbusse held up the beacon of a better future. The language he used to do so was almost always romantic, but occasionally it was tinged as well with sacred or ritual reference. 'I will prevent the forgetting of the light of moral beauty and *the perfect holocaust which burned in you* during the monstrous and disgusting horror of the war', he wrote in his September 1917 preface 'aux anciens combattants'.[31] Here he used the term 'holocaust' in its original Greek sense as a ritual sacrifice wholly consumed by fire. Now, the connotation of the word 'Holocaust' has been irrevocably changed by its popular misapplication to the entirely unritualistic and unredeemable crimes of the Nazi concentration camps. Before the Nazis, the word meant what Barbusse intended it to mean: a purification by fire, a preparation through voluntary sacrifice of a better life to come. Holocaust was a form of aesthetic redemption: it gave meaning to the pain, the suffering, the loss of life in the war.

Barbusse's anti-clerical credentials were unambiguous. The redemption he saw on the horizon was entirely secular. 'A universal brightness (*clarté*) dawns. The people are cleaning out the old regimes which lived off them and corrupted them.'[32] In their place they will establish a moral order superior to that of religion. Primitive religion may have been pure, but in their institutional forms, the churches took on 'specific social propaganda', always in support of the 'reactionary bloc', because 'religion embodies authority and not enlightenment' and defends the privileges of the few against 'the liberation of the multitude'.[33]

A French officer in the United States took it upon himself to refute some of Barbusse's anti-clerical observations. Barbusse had said that priests did not share the same hardships as front-line soldiers. They served as stretcher-bearers and orderlies, but not as infantrymen. His critics denied this as a slur against the clergy, who had shed their blood alongside fellow soldiers. Barbusse stood his ground. He had been there; he knew:

I was 23 months at the front as a simple foot soldier. And I did so voluntarily: exempt from military service before the war, I volunteered on the day war was declared, departed as a volunteer, stayed in the line as a volunteer, as one of my citations notes. These citations have been published often. The last states that I always volunteered for dangerous missions. I was evacuated three times for conditions contracted during the war. I will not be lectured to by anyone on the subject of my stance during the war.[34]

This was an essential feature of Barbusse's moral stature: he spoke – and had earned the right to speak – as an Old Testament prophet, who had seen things most men fortunately never see. His stance in the special category of soldier as witness protected him during the war from patriotic calumnies against his treatment of the war or his patriotism. How could anyone doubt his credentials?

But Barbusse's message was more than just love of country. His firm belief was that the fire of war had to consume all the ugly forms of primitive nationalism, so widespread during the conflict. It was obvious, he noted, that the French soldier in the trenches fought against

German nationalism. But if his sacrifices were to be justified, he had to fight as hard against the French variant, equally 'ferocious, disastrous, imprisoning, hypocritical, gathering to itself all prejudice and all the "Big Words"'. His call to French soldiers in July 1917 was to reject both 'Deutschland über alles', and 'France before all'. 'Love France as you love your mother . . . but don't place her before justice and morality.'[35]

Le feu was indeed the Jeremiad of the trenches. Its aim was the truth, but more in the character of a prophetic account than a documentary treatment. This non-realistic, at times surrealistic, tone exasperated one prominent critic, Norton Cru, who argued that Barbusse's book was a total distortion of the war the soldiers knew. Barbusse wrote of sectors and engagements he could not possibly have known about. The book begins in the winter of 1915, after 500 days of war, but the winter of Barbusse's war was a year earlier. More trenchantly, Cru argues that Barbusse had no sense of the psychology of the front-line soldier; his errors of description of military topography and organization were gross and repeated. His monstrosities were fantastic, not real. 'He deformed the dead', who are shown in many postures they could not have held, 'as he deformed everything else, because despite his repeated claims, he had no idea what the infantryman's war was really like'.[36]

This indictment is both valid and irrelevant. The 'truth' Barbusse wanted to establish was that war was ugly; that soldiers stank; that bodies putrefied; that it was an abomination, which must never happen again. The literary technique he adopted was a kind of heightened realism, very much in the tradition of Zola, where the rudiments of the story came out of his own experience, but the story itself transcended it. By claiming to be a truth-teller above all, Barbusse invited the calumnies of Norton Cru and his other critics. But they missed the point. His tale was Biblical, not factual.

The best evidence for this reading of Barbusse's *Le feu* is in the book's final chapter, 'Dawn'. I have already noted Otto Dix's rendering of this scene in his painting *Flanders* of 1932.[37] The expressionism of the scene is overwhelming, and its Biblical reference unmistakable. The relentless rain has stopped:

Where are the trenches?

We see lakes, and between the lakes there are lines of milky and motionless water. There is more water even than we had thought. It has taken everything and spread everywhere, and the prophecy of the men in the night [that the trenches were disappearing] has come true. There are no more trenches; these canals are the trenches enshrouded. It is a universal flood. The battlefield is not sleeping; it is dead.[38]

The mud-encrusted men don't speak or move, in 'this fantastic paralysis of the world'.[39] Some corpses float in the mire, an arm protrudes from the morass; the German trenches suffer the same devastation, their inhabitants indistinguishable from the French, indeed unidentifiable as human beings at all.

It is the end of all. For the moment it is the prodigious finish, the epic cessation of the war.

I once used to think that the worst hell in war was the flame of shells; and then for long I thought it was the suffocation of the caverns which eternally confine us. But it is neither of these. Hell is water.[40]

The survivors of the deluge 'pursued by an unspeakable evil which exhausts and bewilders them' begin to stir.[41] They see two mud-covered men sleeping upright, supporting each other in oblivion, a 'double monument of human woe'. Some German soldiers stagger towards them to surrender; they 'sleep all jumbled together in the common grave'.[42] When the narrator awakes with his friend Paradis, they look out over the 'calamitous plain' and grunt simply, 'That's war.' More than the terror of battle,

War is frightful and unnatural weariness, water up to the belly, mud and dung and infamous filth. It is befouled faces and tattered flesh, it is the corpses that are no longer like corpses, floating on the ravenous earth.[43]

Their vision was not of a tiny corner of this man-made hell. The war would start again, and spread its hold over 3,000 kilometres. Only a madman could imagine it all.

It will be no good telling about it, eh? They wouldn't believe you; not out of malice or through liking to pull your leg, but because they couldn't . . . No one can know it. Only us.[44]

But even soldiers had to forget what they had seen. If they did remember, another man added, 'there wouldn't be any more war'.[45]

Here is where the vision emerges; where despair turns to hope. Another sodden, wind-chilled survivor cries out: 'There must be no more war after this!' His call was picked up by others: 'It's too stupid – it's too stupid.' Men need to live, not as beasts but as men. The narrator looks out on the world:

I shall never forget the look of those limitless lands wherefrom the water had corroded all colour and form, whose contours crumbled on all sides under the assault of the liquid putrescence that flowed across the broken bones of stakes and wire and framing; nor, rising above those things amid the sullen Stygian immensity, can I ever forget the vision of the thrill of reason, logic and simplicity that suddenly shook these men like a fit of madness.[46]

Someone cried 'there will be no more war when there is no more Germany'.[47] Others went further; they had to abolish war itself.

This discussion took place among distorted and dislocated corpses who, Barbusse remarked, seemed to join in the discussion. They aren't heroes, one soldier remarks, only murderers, accomplished at their trade.[48] The men whose real interests are served by war are far from the stench of the battlefield. Their spectres are there though, spirits at which the soldiers hurl abuse. Equality and only equality will banish them forever. One man adds: 'If the present war has advanced progress by one step, its miseries and slaughter will count for little.' At the remark, 'a tranquil gleam emerges; and that line of light, so black-edged and beset, brings even so its proof that the sun is there'.[49]

The egalitarian covenant these men affirm out of their mud-soaked misery is the redeeming feature of their suffering. Here we see the point of the apocalyptic tale Barbusse has told. Only after the Flood, when devastation is universal, can men turn away from the abominations of war and of the societies that made it.

There are echoes of Dante here. The icy last *Bolgia* of hell, in which Judas and Brutus are frozen together, is recalled at the end of *Under fire*. But closer to Barbusse's style was that of the prophetic texts in the Old Testament. To use them enabled him to sidestep the issue of Christian redemption, of soldiers resembling Christ, a theme found in much Great War prose.[50] The muscular indictments of Isaiah and Jeremiah and the language of Genesis about the Flood are his true literary sources, providing him, as it had utopian socialists before him, with an apocalyptic language in which he could locate his yearning for a world without war.

Nemesis: Karl Kraus' *The last days of mankind*

If Barbusse spoke with the direct voice of French socialist romanticism, on the other side of the line the apocalyptic imagination spoke in a much more ambiguous, dialectical voice. The greatest literary exploration of the apocalyptic genre in the period of the Great War was the mammoth play *The last days of mankind*, written between 1915 and 1922 by the Austrian satirist Karl Kraus, editor of the journal *Die Fackel* (*The Torch*), founded in 1899.[51]

Kraus was a year younger than Barbusse, born in Moravia in 1874. Raised in Vienna, he fled the law for a career first as an actor and then as a writer, with a special love for the theatre. He was a man of many parts: a Jewish convert to Catholicism, a man with conservative sympathies increasingly drawn to radical political positions.[52]

Kraus' attitude to the outbreak of war was remote from that of Barbusse. He was shocked, disgusted, dismayed by the cult of the heroic proclaimed from virtually every quarter in the summer of 1914, but he still retained a lingering sympathy for some of the values of his own society. On 19 November 1914 he read in public an article published the following month under the title 'In these great times' (*In dieser grossen Zeit*).[53] It is a splendid evisceration of the romantic glow of the early months of the war among those incapable of seeing that being enthusiastic for war is like shouting hurrah for bubonic plague. Language itself was mobilized in 1914, and indeed the responsibility of writers and in particular journalists in preparing the public for the war was a theme to which Kraus returned throughout the following years. Those who speak sense about the war, he 'who has something to say', Kraus wrote, 'come forward and be silent'.[54]

The god of commerce reigns in the war, Kraus said, a god with a human face:

the Jewish plutocrat, the man who sits at the cash register of world history collects victories and daily records the turnover in blood. The tenor of his couplings and headlines which shriek with greed for profit is such that he claims the number of dead and wounded and prisoners as assets; sometimes he confuses mine and thine with mines and tines (*mein und dein und Stein und Bein*).

This not-so-veiled reference to Moriz Benedikt, the editor of the *Neue Freie Presse*, dignified by Kraus as being 'the Lord of the hyenas',[55] located Kraus within a conservative tradition bordering on anti-Semitism. His diatribe also reflected a populist campaign shared by both left and right during the war.[56]

More controversially, Kraus refuses to follow Romain Rolland and other dissidents in their condemnation of the German shelling of Rheims Cathedral in the early months of the war.[57] Kraus' ironic voice makes it impossible to fix his position on this and other issues. He writes: 'I know full well that cathedrals are rightfully bombarded by people if they are rightfully used by people as military posts. "No offence i' the world", says Hamlet.' But then, he adds, when will 'the war of cathedrals against people' begin, in the same way that the war of markets has spilled over onto the battlefields?[58] The quick shift of metaphor glides over the fact that Kraus aired the German justification for the shelling of Rheims Cathedral, that its roof was an observation post. Even if his purpose were entirely satirical, the doubt remains as to his own position. His stance appears to be 'a plague on both your houses': all are guilty in war. There are no moral distinctions between targets; Rheims Cathedral was hit because that is the way of war. As he wrote to William Heinemann, he couldn't stomach 'all this halfpenny newspaper rubbish about Rheims . . . If I were a military officer defending Rheims I should have to put an observation post on the cathedral roof; and if I were his opponent I should have to fire on it.'[59] Anti-German or anti-Austrian certainties appear to be out of bounds for Kraus, at least at this stage of the conflict.

Later in the same essay, Kraus poses the question: is the war 'a redemption or only the end?'[60] The reference not only to prophetic texts but to Shakespeare is characteristic of Kraus, and provided him with a resource from which he created his gigantic apocalyptic satire, begun the following year, *The last days of mankind*.

The evolution of the project is a complex story, told authoritatively by Edward Timms in his study of Kraus and Habsburg Vienna.[61] Timms points out that in the pre-war period the apocalyptic motif recurs in Kraus' writings. Eight days after the Austrian annexation of Bosnia and Herzegovina, on 13 October 1908, Kraus published 'Apokalypse', a vision in which the airship corresponded to the war in heaven foreseen in the Book of Revelation, chapter 9. Nature had warned mankind that 'it is not only machines that exist, but also storms!' The 'great dragon' was cast out of the earth, 'neither was his place found any more in heaven . . . A cosmic dissatisfaction manifests itself on all sides.'[62] Timms notes the links between Kraus' use of the Book of Revelation and his public reading of the *Traumdichtungen*, the prophetic writing of the German romantic, Jean Paul.[63] Equally important is the way he drew on Shakespeare, not just Hamlet but in particular the demonic, jocular, whimsical, vicious judgments voiced by Lear's Fool, Caliban, and Timon of Athens.

Both literary and Biblical sources provided Kraus with a resource from which he could progressively distance himself from his society, and the nationalist frenzy of the war. This was the appeal of the apocalyptic mode: it suited the monumental scale of the war as well as bypassing the pointless discussion of who made what mistake at what moment to bring on the catastrophe. Apocalypse is a judgment on a civilization as a whole, not on one or two incompetent leaders.

There are certain surface parallels between *Under fire* and *The last days of mankind*. Both use documentary material for imaginative purposes. Both lift the reader's gaze to metaphysical questions, but do so against the backdrop of realistic material. Both excoriate the hypocrisy and inhumanity of the war. Both offer an uncompromisingly pacifist message. Kraus had read *Under fire* by October 1917.[64] Just as Barbusse had returned to French literary sources, and especially to Zola, to frame his indictment of the war, so Kraus drew out of German and English letters, and particularly the theatre of Büchner and Shakespeare, the poetry from which his 'tragic operetta' of the war was framed.

For our purposes, the most important motif in the play is the apocalypse described in scene 54. The vision is told by 'the grumbler', a Shakespearean seer in constant dialectical debate with 'the optimist', the conventional wartime observer. It is important not to fall into the trap of seeing 'the grumbler' as Kraus. By concentrating on the apocalyptic scenes, we can appreciate how the prophetic voice enables him to offer judgment of his society without using the self-righteous and morally superior tones so many pacifists like Bertrand Russell, for example, adopted during the war.

The scene begins with a news report of the conversion of trees, 'on whose branches the birds had sung their songs', into wood pulp and then into the newspapers printing lies about the war – all in a day. A newshawker is selling the paper, crying 'Extra'. It is then that 'the Grumbler announces that he has heard 'the echo of my blood-haunted madness'. He attends to

this one sound, out of which ten millions who are dying accuse me of still being alive, I who had eyes so to see the world, and whose stare struck it in such a fashion that it became as I saw it. If heaven was just in letting this come about, then it was unjust in not having annihilated me . . . Why was I not given the mental power to force an outcry out of desecrated mankind? Why is my shout of protest not stronger than this tinny command that has dominion over the souls of a whole globe?[65]

The Grumbler says he has documents to prove all his charges, for a time after the war. But his purpose is other since that time will never come:

I have written a tragedy, whose perishing hero is mankind, whose tragic conflict, the conflict between the world and nature, has a fatal ending. Alas, because this drama has no actor other than all mankind, it has no audience![66]

Then the bill of indictment is read. First fallen soldiers stand accused:

why did you have to pass into the beyond? I saw you on the day when you marched out. The rain and the mud of this fatherland and its infamous music were the farewell, as they herded you into the cattle car! I see your pale face in this orgy of filth and lies in this frightful farewell at a freight station, from which the human material is dispatched.

. . . And you, noble poet's heart, who between the voices of the mortars and the murderers, attended to the secret of a vowel – have you spent four years of your springtime beneath the earth in order to test your future abode? What had you to seek there? Lice for the fatherland?

All this you had to suffer because 'madness and profiteering had not vented on you enough of their cowardly spite'.[67]

Then come 'the ringleaders of this world crime, the ringleaders who always survive'. 'What, you scoundrels', the Grumbler went on:

you did not know, you have no idea, that among the millions of possibilities of horror and shame, the consequences of a declaration of war, . . . the misery of one hour of a captivity that was to last for many years? Of one sigh of longing and of sullied, torn, murdered love? Were you not even capable of imagining what hells are opened up by one tortured minute of a mother's hearkening into the distance, through nights and days of this years-long waiting for a hero's death? And you did not notice how the tragedy became a farce, became through the simultaneousness of a new and hateful nuisance and a mania for fossilized forms, an operetta, one of those loathsome modern operettas, whose libretto is an indignity and whose music is torture?

What, and you there, you who have been murdered, you did not rise up against this order?[68]

Politician and soldier, criminal and victim, each shares the blame for the disaster. The leaders' sin was the worst, since far from following their 'duty, to curb mankind's bestial impulse – they have unleashed it!'[69]

After the indictment, the judgment, in full prophetic tones:

And from the lascivious wine of its debauchery all peoples have drunk, and the kings of the earth have fornicated with the press. And the horseman of the apocalypse drank to it, he whom I saw galloping through the German Reich, long before he actually did so . . . He is rushing at full speed in all the streets. His moustache stretches from sunrise to sunset and from south to north. 'And power was given to him that sat thereon to take peace from the earth, and that they should kill one another.' And I saw him as the beast with the ten horns and the seven heads and a mouth like the mouth of a lion. 'They worshipped the best saying, Who is like under the beast? Who is able to make war with him? And there was given unto him a mouth speaking great things.' And we fell through him and through the whore of Babylon, who, in all tongues of the world, persuaded us that we were each other's enemy, and there should be war![70]

. . . you who were sacrificed did not rise up against this scheme? . . . You did not repent . . . You did not spit this glory to their faces? . . . You did not break out, did not desert for a holy war, to liberate us at home from the archenemy who daily bombarded our brains with lies? . . . you the dead, do not rise up out of your trenches to take these vipers to account, to appear to them in their sleep with the twisted countenances that you wore in your dying hour, with the lustreless eyes of your heroic waiting, with the unforgettable masks to which your youth was condemned by this regime of madness![71]

The Shakespearean echoes here are palpable: Macbeth and Richard III, pursued by their victims, have come to the trenches. So has Henry V, listening to common soldiers during the night before Agincourt, dwelling on the eternal question, what if the cause not be just and the severed limbs of soldiers return to confront him who dismembered them? And as in Gance's *J'accuse*, and in much of the poetry discussed below in chapter 8, the apocalypse begins with the invocation, the imploring of the dead to return as accusing spiritis:

So, rise up and confront them as the personification of a hero's death, so that the cowardice of the living, empowered to command, might finally come to know death's features and look death in the eye for the rest of their lives. Wake their sleep with your death cry![72]

They, the dead, are the agents of vengeance and of redemption. 'Save us from them', from contact with the killers, the Grumbler begs:

As sure as there is a God, without a miracle there can be no salvation! Come back! Ask them what they have done with you! What they did, as you suffered through them, before you died through them! . . . Arms-bearing corpses . . . step forth, you beloved believer in the spirit, and demand your precious head back from them! . . . It is not your dying, but what you have lived through that I want to avenge.[73]

The Grumbler has preserved the truth of the crime, and of the need for vengeance, and through vengeance, redemption, just as Horatio and Fortinbras preserved the truth of Hamlet's life and death and cleansed the kingdom by their remembrance, by explaining 'to the yet unknowing world / How these things came about'. *Hamlet* showed redemption in this world, but the Grumbler adds, 'should the times hear no more', 'a being above them' surely would hear about a tragedy 'of mankind breaking down'. This

Spirit, which has compassion for the victims, would hear it, even had he renounced for all future time any connection with a human ear. May he receive this era's fundamental tone, the echo of my madness haunted by blood through which I too am guilty of these sounds. May he accept it as redemption.[74]

Here ends the apocalyptic diatribe, and, as befits an operetta, its heightened tone is echoed but reduced immediately in the following scene. There Austrian and German officers are feasting on a suckling pig, while a band plays the tune 'Good Old Noah Knew it Well'.[75]

But the apparitions do come, just as the Grumbler said they would, presenting horrifying 'apparitions' of the war's victims, men, women, children. The last word is that of an unborn syphilitic child, begging to be aborted: 'To these realms you must not drag us. / Offspring are we but of corpses. / Here the air is noxious-foul.' The stage directions announce the final destruction of the world: 'Total darkness. Then, on the horizon, the wall of flames leaps high. Death cries off stage.'[76]

It is hard to imagine a more vivid representation of apocalyptic theatre. The anger of the Prophets is evident; so is the nightmarish pursuit of guilt in Shakespeare's tragedies and histories. Despite the extremes of imagery which grow in awfulness as the play approaches its culmination, there is still a moral order at work. The evil world is destroyed; Sodom and Gomorrah are consumed in flames; a divinity is invoked and his wrath descends. While Kraus' prose and poetry have nihilistic elements, his writing stops short of abandoning the sacred, even when it is drowning in the blood of the innocent.

English apocalypse: Shaw's *Heartbreak House*

The Irish-born English playwright and Fabian socialist, George Bernard Shaw, was fifty-seven at the time of the outbreak of the Great War. His play *Pygmalion* had just opened to favourable reviews, and was a relief in its gentle ironies to many offended by his harsher indictments of the hypocrisy of English polite society. One of his early plays, *Mrs Warren's profession*, written in 1892, is about brothel-keeping and gentility; it was banned from performance and kept off the English stage until 1925.

Shaw, in short, was no stranger to controversy. He advocated a form of evolutionary socialism which would come about when the educated administrative classes of England learned the simple truth that poverty was vice and its elimination virtue. Like the other two members of the Fabian triumvirate, Sidney and Beatrice Webb, Shaw had little interest in foreign affairs until they forced themselves on him in 1914.[77]

His stance in the early months of the war was characteristic: whenever Englishmen spoke of moral issues, the stench of hypocrisy was soon to arise. The invasion of Belgium by Germany was a crime, he argued in *Commonsense about the war*.[78] But if Britain was really concerned about defenceless Belgians, she would have urged Belgium to grant the German army passage across her borders and then protest; thereby countless lives would have been saved. Instead, the morality of British intervention was really a cloak for imperial rivalries, which were well developed before the war.[79]

To add insult to injury Shaw annoyed the patriotic by denouncing their horror over the sinking of the Lusitania in 1915 as humbug. They showed, he snorted, far less interest in the victims of the British disasters at Festubert and Gallipoli. This passage, included in the introduction to *Heartbreak House*, written in 1919 after the play was completed, as well as his defence of German civilization against the mindless charge that it was intrinsically barbaric,[80] show how important it was for Shaw to combat what George Orwell later called the 'moral pollution' of the war.

In *Heartbreak House*, Shaw expressed in a dreamlike, disjointed, surrealistic series of sketches his despair about the war and the incapacity of civilians to comprehend the nature of the catastrophe that had descended on them. Though Shaw wrote that he had begun the play before the war, there is overwhelming evidence that whatever had been germinating in his mind took written form between March 1916 and May 1917.[81] In effect, his apocalyptic play was composed virtually simultaneously with Barbusse's *Under fire* and while Kraus was at work on his *Last days of mankind*. The recourse to apocalyptic language in literary responses to the war was, therefore, an international phenomenon. All three wrote under the shadow of the great slaughter at Verdun and on the Somme.

Shaw and the Webbs spent much of June 1916 together in Sussex. Virginia and Leonard Woolf joined the company of elegant, witty, and irreverent middle-class people in a house named Wyndham Croft. The house provided some features of the play's set, and the guests, some of the characters. In the garden, Shaw drafted the early scenes. He recalled hearing the low rumble of the guns in France, preparing for the offensive on the Somme, then two weeks away.[82]

Adding to the play's drama was another event of 1916. On 1 October, a German Zeppelin, the L-31, was shot down over north London. The day after, Shaw went to see the downed airship. Shaw had the honesty to admit that the whole incident had fascinated him. To the Webbs he confessed:

What is hardly credible, but true, is that the sound of the Zepp's engines was so fine, and its voyage through the stars so enchanting, that I positively caught myself hoping next night that there would be another raid. I grieve to add that after seeing the Zepp fall like a burning newspaper, with its human contents roasting for some minutes (it was frightfully slow) I went to bed and was comfortably asleep in ten minutes. One is so pleased at having seen the show that the destruction of a dozen people or so in hideous terror and torment does not count. 'I didn't half cheer, I tell you', said a damsel at the wreck. Pretty lot of animals we are.[83]

The rumble of the artillery and the hum of the engines: these are the sounds out of which Shaw created his apocalyptic drama.

As in all Shavian enterprises, we must never take any of his introspective statements at face value; he was too much of a satirist for directness. Furthermore, we have the problem that many of Shaw's plays are twins, and non-identical ones at that. He frequently wrote a separate preface and published it independently of the play. In the case of *Heartbreak House*, the preface was composed in June 1919, after the play was written, but before it was first performed in New York in November 1920.[84]

The preface is as angry and despairing as the play, though in different ways. The bleak, rancorous, mean-spirited months separating the Armistice of November 1918 and the Peace Treaty of Paris signed on 28 June 1919 are the period when the preface was written. Shaw was intensely aware of the thickening of spirit associated with the perpetuation, despite the Armistice, of the Allied blockade of Germany and Austria. In effect the war was continuing only against civilians, and at a time of the worst influenza epidemic in history.[85] The madness of beggaring Germany (which inevitably would mean beggaring Britain), was a viewpoint expressed with anger by another Bloomsbury figure of the time, John Maynard Keynes.[86]

To Shaw this cruelty was but a symptom of a deeper malaise, a 'heartbreak', or (in his idiosyncratic idiom) a chronic impoverishment of the spirit. This disease had spread widely before the war, and had been rendered into unforgettable theatre by many authors, but above all by Chekhov. This is the unavoidable reference in the subtitle of the play: 'A fantasia in the Russian manner on English themes.'

But polite society in England had webs of self-delusion of their own particular kind, woven out of the strands of imperial safety:

To British centenarians who died in their beds in 1914, any dread of having to hide underground in London from the shells of an enemy seemed more remote and fantastic than a dread of the appearance of a colony of cobras and rattlesnakes in Kensington Gardens.[87]

But through a wilful ignorance of political science, and a failure to find out how war could be avoided, this period of innocence had abruptly come to an end. Nemesis struck

and when she struck at last she struck with a vengeance. For four years she smote our first-born and heaped on us plagues of which Egypt never dreamed. They were all as preventable as the great Plague of London, and came solely because they had not been prevented. They were not undone by winning the war. The earth is still bursting with the dead bodies of the victors.[88]

'Solely because they had not been prevented': there's the rub. Ignorance lay behind collective guilt. Darwinism became Social Darwinism which fuelled the brutality of what Shaw calls the 'Prussian religion' taught to Prussia by Britain.[89] The educated classes failed to see the combustible nature of these views, and instead wandered off into the esoteric and dark corners of spiritualism, to cure the hypochrondria of *Heartbreak House*. If séances failed, the illusions of love and marriage were available. In short all the chimeras of bourgeois life testified to the failure of British society to work out how to live. Instead after 1914 they showed their predilection for dying. 'Thus were the first-born of Heartbreak House smitten; and the young, the innocent, the hopeful expiated the folly and worthlessness of their elders';[90] and this from a man nearing sixty years old. Shaw does not indicate what guilt he bore for his lamentable state of affairs, though he had little doubt as to the rottenness of the world he had helped build.

That rottenness was exposed by a panoply of public hysteria, intolerance, and cruelty which attended the unfolding of the war of attrition in Britain. The 'war delirium', this 'moral pestilence',[91] led to injustice, persecution, and mindless hatred of anything German. All of it was mobilized to justify the losses multiplying cruelly as the months went by. Sacrifices in defence of liberty, some said; but to Shaw they were a kind of expiation, and a vain expiation at that, of 'the heedlessness and folly of their fathers'.[92] Even the survivors who came back unscathed had paid a price. They had left 'creative work to drudge at destruction'; some grew to relish it; others 'hated it to the end'.[93]

Moral decay before the war; a moral desert in wartime. What made it worse was the theatricality of it all for civilians. We should recall Shaw's account of his own vision of the falling Zeppelin, when we read his indictment of England, a place where: 'There was a frivolous exultation in death for its own sake, which was at bottom an inability to realize that the deaths were real deaths and not stage ones.' This 'cinematic' reduction of human suffering to the status of a performance was perhaps unavoidable. No one could grasp the dimensions of the disaster; hence it was turned into a romance or merely imagined as a series of familiar individual misfortunes, a railway accident, a shipwreck, that is, the stuff of cinema.[94] This trivialization was necessary; otherwise recruiting would have been impossible. The parallels with some of Kraus' invective are apparent.

Shaw tried to explain in the preface why he had kept his play off the stage before the Armistice. Here some exaggerated sense of decorum is visible, a sense of not wanting to offend which was alien to both Kraus and Barbusse. Shaw wrote in 1919:

When men are heroically dying for their country, it is not the time to show their lovers and wives and fathers and mothers how they are being sacrificed to the blunders of boobies, the cupidity of capitalists, the ambition of conquerors, the electioneering of demagogues, the Pharisaism of patriots, the lusts and lies and rancours and bloodthirsts that love war because it opens their prison doors, and sets them in the thrones of power and popularity.[95]

This tendency to pull his punches – for comedy to be 'loyally silent'[96] – may reflect some of the limits within which British, as opposed to Continental, polemics were conducted. British writers in general, and Shaw in particular, were less at war with the values of their society than were many of their European colleagues; hence the absence in Britain of what is called, following Herzen, an intelligentsia.[97] This truth is captured in the following exchange in Kraus' *Last days of mankind*:

The Grumbler   There is no English satirist.
The Optimist   Bernard Shaw.
The Grumbler   Precisely.[98]

Despite sharp differences in national styles and political cultures, many writers during and after the Great War, among them Shaw, turned back to the ancient tradition of apocalyptic drama to express their anger, their pain, their despair.

As I noted above, Shavian drama and Shavian polemics should not be equated. Though the play itself is far more dreamlike and disjointed than the preface, nevertheless it illustrates many of the points I have noted above: the tendency for the comfortable classes to mistake romantic literature for life,[99] the emptiness of conventional marriages, the crassness of commercial life, the pointlessness of it all.

In the midst of the drawing-room comedy about his two grown-up daughters and a third younger woman contemplating marriage to a businessman clearly (and unflatteringly) modelled on the Food Controller, Lord Devonport, and a burglar desperate to be caught, stands a mad seafaring man, Captain Shotover. He is Shaw's Lear figure, attempting to find a higher truth, a seer at the end of his life, longing to blow up the whole, diseased structure of English society, this 'Soul's prison we call England'. In another metaphor, closer to his profession, Shotover predicts that the ship of state 'will strike and sink and split'.

Instead nemesis comes from the air. In Act One, we are told that Shotover stores dynamite in a cave near the house, in order 'To blow up the human race if it goes too far.'[100] He carts dynamite around the house from time to time. But unexpectedly, his world is threatened by aerial bombardment. In Act Three, 'a dull explosion is heard'. The lights go out. Further explosions follow. 'The judgment has come', shouts Shotover, turning on all the lights in his house. The profiteer and the burglar hide in the cave, where a bomb lands and kills them. The rest are spared, and (as did Shaw) admit to having found bombardment a 'glorious experience'. The Captain announces the end of the crisis: 'Turn in, all hands. The ship is safe', and falls asleep to the tune of 'Keep the home fires burning.'

Crisis in Greek means judgment, and so it is in Shavian drama. Here the bitter anger of the middle years of the war produced one of his darkest and most difficult dramas. To express his despair, and his sense of shared responsibility of the disaster, Shaw, one of the elders, turned to specifically British literary sources. We have seen how the preface dwelled upon plague metaphors. But the play is more British than Biblical in character. The metaphor of the ship of state foundering on the rocks was derived from Carlyle.[101] The visionary turning away from his corrupt world suggests a Blakean inheritance too.

Above all, it is Shakespeare who provided Shaw with the dramatic materials from which he fashioned his sombre play. The links with King Lear are apparent: three daughters (two cynical kin; and one innocent, who comes to love Shotover), no mother and an old father, foolish in his ways. Who could miss the analogy?[102] The storm in Lear shows the heavens breaking, sending forth their wrath as the airships do in Shaw's play.

The ending of *Heartbreak House* – its stay of execution, as it were – suggests that Shaw's despair made him deny his England even the dignity of tragedy. The worst penalty for the inhabitants of *Heartbreak House* was to go on living their meaningless lives for ever. There is an appeal voiced by the Captain that the English can still learn 'navigation' and live, or 'leave it and be damned'.[103] But it is a feeble call, drowned by the intoxication bred by the excitement of bombing. 'A pretty lot of animals we are', as Shaw berated himself after the Zeppelin raid he had witnessed. Tragedy had been replaced by farce.

Implications and variations

In earlier chapters of this book, I have shown how eschatological motifs proliferated in wartime and postwar films, the graphic arts, painting, and sculpture. In the penultimate chapter I shall deal with similar themes in poetry. Here my intention is to supplement the discussion with reference to literary texts, both fiction and plays, which use apocalyptic images and motifs.

Variations on a theme

These texts are rich and varied, created by a range of writers from those usually deemed 'modernist' to those totally entrenched in nineteenth-century conventions. Yet again, this spectrum suggests the need to revise our understanding of the cultural history of this period. The gulf between the romanticism of Barbusse, the expressionism of Kraus, the iconoclasm of Shaw, and the apocalyptic images of many 'modernist' writers, may not be as great as first appears. Modernists reconfigured conventions; they didn't discard them.

One such reconfiguration was with respect to apocalyptic motifs, so powerfully evocative of romantic flights of the imagination in earlier periods. The precedents were there. The work of Blake was a frequent point of reference,[104] though many took canonical texts about the end of time as sources of inspiration and invective. German expressionist theatre and poetry was full of such Scriptural reference.[105] So was French literature, particularly (though not only) of Catholic inspiration.[106]

Jean Giono

The invocation of apocalyptic motifs in wartime and postwar literature is far more widespread than those discussed here. In French literature, the most powerful expression of the apocalyptic temperament was Jean Giono's novel *Le grand troupeau* (1931). It was to be the first of a series he intended to call 'Apocalypse'.[107] The lyrical qualities of *Le grand troupeau* transcend those of the three texts I have examined above. The novel tells the story of a small Provençal town, its shepherds and its flocks torn apart by the war. The Biblical reference is both rich and subtle. There is also the powerful treatment of civilians and soldiers alike, of a woman notified that her husband is dead, of the village wake, in which his neighbours place salt on the table to recall the dead man as the salt of the earth, of the comfort given to a dying soldier by his companions. *Le grand troupeau* is a striking work of poetic fiction, vividly coloured with prophetic vision. A glimpse of the final passage in the book should give some idea of the gentle language of hope with which Giono concludes his revelation. The shepherd offers a blessing to the child of a soldier back from the war. His ram is by his side, and approaches the child to greet him as a newborn lamb. 'Leave him,' said the shepherd. It's a good sign when animals are present at the birth of a child. One more animal on the earth.' For the child, the shepherd offers this prayer:

Child, said the shepherd, all my life I have been a herdsman. You, little one, by the grace of your father, I have come to seek you at the edge of the flock, at the moment when you are going to enter the great flock of men to realize your dreams.

First, I say to you: here is the night, there are the trees, there are the animals; soon you will see the day. Now you know all.

And more, if God hears me, he will give to you the gift of loving slowly, slowly in all your loves, as the farmer grips the plough and furrows more deeply every day . . .

You will find your way on the strength of your own shoulders.

The great gift will be yours to bear frequently the burden of others, to be for them like a fountain on the side of the road.

And you will love the stars . . .

Holding the child above his head, the ram bellows, and a star, the shepherd's star, the star of St John, rises in the night.[108]

For Giono, the Apocalypse was not a literary form, but a living reality. He was one of seven writers who contributed in 1960 to a remarkable project: the creation of a unique book of the Apocalypse of St John. The book was specially prepared. It weighed 400 pounds, cost 1 million dollars, and was decorated with a bejewelled cover made by Salvador Dali. Among the other contributors were Jean Cocteau and (as we shall see below) Ernst Jünger.[109]

In his essay, Giono recalled how in 1905 his father had taken him to the roof of their cowshed to tell him of the Apocalypse, the seeds of which were 'in me, in your mother, and in you yourself'.[110] It was the business of the living to assist in this 'great theatrical' event, his father affirmed.[111] Since we are all invited, and since men can't leave a spectacle without spectators, the Apocalypse doesn't destroy life; it preserves it;[112] and it does so outside of time. The Apocalypse is a spectacle 'in which the actors are perhaps dead thousands of years and who, if they are not dead, are, most probably, about to enact a scene today which will be staged thousands of years from now'.[113]

Giono's father was also a man of this world, a cobbler, with the story-telling ability of a craft at the heart of village gossip and wisdom.[114] He was also an anarchist, convinced that 'the mountains of iniquity are not geographic'. St John of Patmos was to him 'a fortune-teller of ministers' doings' and he could read the future in the cups the powerful hold in their hands.[115] When he went off to war in 1914, Jean told his father of the fantastic war he endured, and of the surreal images and landscapes he had glimpsed. When he returned, his father, soon to die, reiterated the message, 'Remember the Apocalypse.'[116] Giono did, unforgettably, in *Le grand troupeau*, a unique moment in the history of twentieth-century literature.

Ernst Jünger

The romantic nature of this apocalypticism is evident in the writing of another contributor to *L'apocalypse*. Ernst Jünger was also a veteran of the Great War, repeatedly wounded and decorated with the highest award for bravery, Pour le Mérite. His attitude to the war was complex, but bore not a trace of pacifism. His memoir *In Stahlgewittern* ('Storm of steel'), published initially in 1920 and later in six revised editions, is an enduring literary treatment of trench warfare.[117] As in much war literature, Jünger adopted a factual manner, but also referred to the war as a cosmic event, a beast showing its claws, producing storms and tempests, the sounds of which evoked in him 'incredible awe'.[118]

Forty years later, Jünger returned to this theme. In his contribution to *L'apocalypse*, his emphasis is less on the Vision than on the Visionary, the Seer. 'Seers are the eyes of the people', Jünger affirms, 'they are, simply, the eyes of Man. What they see on the watery shores, the splendour and fall of Babylon, the struggle of angels and animals, the beginning and the end of all things, is an image of human destiny.' In their minds, 'Babylon will always stand and always will be in decline.'[119]

They possess a gift – eyes which contemplate the gods and which are observed by other eyes. Ezekiel, the St John of the Old Testament, sees on the shores of the river Kebar the eternal pathway towards a dazzling four-tiered crown, and St John sees on the shore of Patmos the fur and plumage of the Apocalyptic Beasts.[120]

Seers speak in their language of origin, but the quest for the apocalyptic is common to all. 'To place God in his setting, that is the great theme of man',[121] Jünger writes, but that setting is and must be anthropomorphic. Echoing Giono, he continues, 'In each mortal, the world is born anew, and it disappears in each one of us.'[122] All we can do is imagine God in our own likeness. 'The Revelation is perceived as a voice and contemplated in an image.' The seer

sees with human eyes and hears with human ears, he perceives the words in the language of his people. As high as the earth reaches, God must bend down to him. Man's setting for God is as a man in his own likeness, as another man who struggles with him in the obscure valley, at the edge of the waters, in the earthly night. Man struggles with Him until dawn, and even if man emerges victorious, he must withdraw before having seen God's face.[123]

Yet again, the theatrical character of the Apocalypse is emphasized. At centre stage is the Seer, for whom and through whom the drama unfolds. The romantic voice here is unmistakable.

Apocalyptic echoes

Many other writers explored this cultural form, without sharing Jünger's political outlook or Giono's poetry or religious convictions. Karl Kraus' contemporary, Stefan Zweig, wrote a play entitled *Jeremias* in 1915; it 'celebrated defeat and renunciation', and was staged first in Switzerland in February 1918 and then in Germany (appropriately enough) in October 1918.[124] Zweig's friend Franz Werfel also explored the life of Jeremiah and other apocalyptic themes in *Höret die Stimme* ('Hearken to the voice'), written in 1937, when the Spanish village of Guernica was destroyed from the air.[125]

D.H. Lawrence's *Women in love*, written during the war and published in 1921, reflected his wartime apocalyptic mood. Gerald Crich, the master of industry, freezes to death in the snow. There are also similarities between Lawrence's *Kangaroo* (1926), set in Australia but expressing Lawrence's views on English society in wartime, and Shaw's *Heartbreak House*. In both, the Zeppelin symbolizes the precariousness of civilian life and the doom it so richly deserves. In *Kangaroo*, Lawrence wrote of the Zeppelin as 'high, high, high, tiny, pale, as one might imagine the Holy Ghost'.[126] It is worth recalling too that one of Lawrence's posthumously published works incorporates his reflections on the Book of Revelation. The book is entitled *Apocalypse*.[127] Even a glance at the vast literature surrounding the well-known cadences of T.S. Eliot's 'The wasteland' and W.B. Yeats' 'The Second Coming' remind us that apocalyptic images were inextricably part of literary responses to the Great War and its aftermath.[128]

Apocalyptic language had many uses. First it helped to resolve the literary problem as to how to present the monumental scale of the war, a conflict of dimensions so vast as to defy realistic description. Apocalyptic motifs provided a solution. Furthermore, apocalyptic narrative offered an alternative to historical narrative. The stylized endings of the plays of Kraus and Shaw, as much as the new covenant in Barbusse's 'The dawn', precluded treating the war as having a beginning, a middle and an end. Some British writers, Robert Graves for example, used irony to expose the inadequacies of a conventional narrative applied to the chaos of the Great War.[129] Apocalyptic time is patently other than historical time; to go back to the apocalypse is to bypass realistic representation.

Secondly, it shifted the level of discussion of the war away from the individual and the ephemeral to the collective and the timeless. There is no pilot in Shaw's vision of the Zeppelin depositing its bombs on 'Heartbreak House'. The failure to 'master' the times is generalized; all are guilty and all must suffer the consequences. Barbusse blamed the Germans for the war at first, but by the time he wrote *Under fire*, he indicted nationalism as a whole. The stakes had risen. For Kraus the wholly shabby structure of capitalist depravity lay behind the conflagration. To writers who wanted to shift the register of the discussion upward, to raise general (indeed eternal) issues, apocalyptic language had much to offer.

Apocalypse and protest

Apocalypse was also useful for opponents of the war with no illusions as to the unpopularity of pacifist statements. Barbusse was in a class of his own here; his status as a combatant gave him the moral authority to speak out against the war while it was still going on. Civilians could not do so with impunity, except in allegory or metaphor. Apocalyptic language traditionally provided both. According to one literary scholar, apocalyptic writing encompasses a 'subversive vision', an affirmation both of doom and of divine justice.[130]

After the Russian Revolution of February 1917, it was easier to voice views about the way the war was turning the world upside down. Men with impeccable conservative credentials, like Lord Lansdowne in Britain, began to worry that by the time the war was over, everything for which it had been fought would have been sacrificed in the effort.[131] This generalized malaise of the third year of the war is reflected in the three works examined in detail above. But even after the war had ended, this mood of uncertainty and fear for the future brought back the relevance of many older texts about the Day of Judgment and the folly of man.

The Apocalypse and the end of the nineteenth century

Here Apocalypse meant the end of the nineteenth-century bourgeois world, its smugness, its conviction in the inevitability of progress. Whatever businessmen thought, many writers were not at all sure that bourgeois Europe could or should be 'recast', in the phrase of one influential historical account.[132] But even if old ways were restored, it was apparent that the war had consumed much of the decency and idealism of the societies that had waged it.

The use of apocalyptic imagery here ironically confirmed older traditions by announcing their demise. Consider the treatment of what the war had 'exploded' in a widely read novel of the 1920s, F. Scott Fitzgerald's *Tender is the night* (1926). One of Fitzgerald's themes is that the Great War was the last nineteenth-century war, which in its early days had brought to the surface a degree of loyalty to community and nation, a commitment to defend what was, that could not have been created overnight. It took years, perhaps generations, to secure these bonds. Once mobilized, once sacrificed in the mud of the trenches, in years of deadly attrition, this cultural capital could hardly be reclaimed. Once spent, it was gone. This sentiment lies behind the outburst of Fitzgerald's ex-soldier Dick Diver, on a postwar tour of the battlefields of the Somme. 'This western-front business', Diver said, couldn't be done again, not for a long time. The young men think they could do it but they couldn't. They could fight the first Marne again but not this. This took religion and years of plenty and tremendous sureties and the exact relation that existed between the classes . . . You had to remember Christmas, and postcards of the Crown Prince and his fiancée, and little cafés in Valence and beer gardens in Unter den Linden and weddings at the mairie, and going to the Derby, and your grandfather's whiskers . . . This kind of battle was invented by Lewis Carroll and Jules Verne and whoever wrote *Undine*, and country deacons bowling and marraines in Marseilles and girls seduced in the back lanes of Wurttemberg and Westphalia . . . This was the last love battle . . . All my beautiful lovely safe world blew itself up here with a great gust of high explosive love.[133]

The same sense of the end of an older (and better) world, of the unravelling of human ties, of decencies now out of place, is treated with subtlety and complexity in Ford Madox Ford's war tetralogy *Parade's end* (1924–7). Ford's Christopher Tietjens is a seventeenth-century York-shireman adrift in time, accidentally parachuted into the twentieth century and into the trenches.[134]

The Apocalypse and collective madness
The notion of a world gone mad, filled with abominations, is common both to fiction denouncing the war and to more equivocal statements about the nature of the conflict. Here the weirdness of the battlefield, the mundane presence of the grotesque and sickening inevitably evoked what Kermode calls 'canonical' apocalyptic writing,[135] and in particular references to the Biblical texts of Ezekiel, Daniel, and Revelation. Erich Maria Remarque was only one of many writers who presented surrealistic images of halves of human bodies impaled on trees, of dismembered limbs scattered around emplacements, of the uncanny company of the dead in the trenches.[136] These images were used regardless of the point of view of the writer about the war. Here is Ernst Jünger's description of the contents of a recently captured French trench in Les Eparges, east of Verdun:

My attention was caught by a sickly smell and a bundle hanging on the wire. Jumping out of the trench in the early morning mist, I found myself in front of a huddled-up corpse, a Frenchman. The putrid flesh, like the flesh of fishes, gleamed greenish-white through the rents in the uniform. I turned away and then started back in horror: close to me a figure cowered beside a tree. It wore the shining straps and belt of the French, and high upon its back there was still the loaded pack, crowned with a round cooking utensil. Empty eye sockets and the few wisps of hair on the black and weathered skull told me that this was no living man. Another sat with the upper part of the body clapped down over the legs as though broken through the middle. All round lay dozens of corpses, putrefied, calcined, mummified, fixed in a ghastly dance of death. The French must have carried on for months without burying their fallen comrades.[137]

Otto Dix's series of prints 'Der Krieg', as we saw in chapter 6, captured in visceral form this oft-repeated fictional imagery.

Many war memoirs in fictional form return to these nightmarish images. They invite us to ask with Kent in *King Lear* 'Is this the promised end?' Much war literature posed that question. So did much art. Partly this work grew out of the prior 'spiritualization' of the conflict, its portrayal in popular propaganda as a war of the sons of light against the sons of darkness, in which supernatural forces were mobilized in many conventional and unconventional forms early in the war.[138]

This conceit was viciously satirized in an entirely different kind of war literature, through the iconoclastic crudities of Céline, in his *Voyage au bout de la nuit* (1932). But Céline's inversion of the normal order of the universe, his celebration of perversity and malevolence, reads more like a version of Milton's *Paradise lost* written from the point of view of Satan than a rejection of the divine order.[139]

Conclusion

The reiteration and proliferation of apocalyptic images and metaphors in Great War literature show how the conflict expanded the literary space occupied by an older set of icons carrying messages about the end of time, the collapse of order, the final judgment. The implication of recourse to this body of work was paradoxical. In describing images of the end of time, these writers helped turn the clock back. Apocalyptic echoes linked the 1914–18 war with an earlier time when chiliastic notions were part of ordinary language.

This set of apocalyptic references and metaphors, like a nova, grew in intensity in literature just as it was about to fade away. At the end of the Second World War, when, after Hiroshima, the real possibility of universal annihilation emerged, and when Auschwitz opened up new avenues of horror, this older literary language did not fully revive in Europe[140] as it had done twenty-five years before. Some echoes could be heard; witness the volume on the Apocalypse to which Jean Giono, as well as Ernst Jünger and Jean Cocteau contributed in 1960.[141] But in literature (though not in films or postmodern philosophy) these were voices from the past.[142] Their literary imagery had grown out of date, or had become unusable. Apocalypse is predicated on divine justice; where was justice after the gas chambers? The literary metaphor of the Apocalypse could accommodate virtually every human catastrophe except the ultimate one. The archaic quality of this language was a link with the past; it drew the mind back to older visions and older certainties. After 1945 those visions, these literary sites of memory, seemed to fade away, leaving abstraction and silence in their wake.[143]

8

War poetry, romanticism, and the return of the sacred

Both during the war years and afterwards, the dead returned to the living in prose and poetry. In Britain, France, and Germany, many writers used verse to keep the voices of the fallen alive, by speaking for them, to them, about them. Soldiers developed their own form of this genre. Their soliloquies were sad, evocative, often moving, and rarely either simply patriotic or straightforwardly pacifist. Much of this verse was written by men who continued to serve even when they knew the madness of doing so.

In one sense, therefore, war poetry is a set of meditations on the dead and their passing. To privilege this facet of war poetry is to highlight its fusion of the 'old' and the 'new'. Some poems were experimental; others were written in conventional forms. Much of it arose out of the perceived need not to reject out of hand traditional languages about the dead, but rather to reformulate and reinvigorate older tropes about loss of life in wartime.

Much war poetry was reactive. What many soldier-poets could not stomach were the loftier versions of civilian romance about war. Those too old to fight had created an imaginary war, filled with medieval knights, noble warriors, and sacred moments of sacrifice. Such writing in poetry and prose, the 'high diction' of the patriots,[1] was worse than banal; it was obscene. In its place, war poets set before our eyes the faces, words, and gestures of once-living men. Some were those with whom they had served; others, their erstwhile enemies. The dead were their companions and entered their verse as companions were wont to do.

Some went further still. True, they protested at civilian lies and self-deceptions. But they also went on to recast older romantic traditions to express at one and the same time the dignity of the men who had fought and the degradation to which they had been subjected. More than a few war poets thereby found a language half way between lyricism, on the one hand; and realism, bitterness, and anger, on the other.

War poets have become both the psalmists and the prophets of our century. It is no accident that Benjamin Britten turned to Wilfred Owen's 'Anthem for doomed youth' as the sacred text around which he framed his *War requiem*, written after the Second World War but as much a meditation on the Great War. The music captures the dialectical relationship of the old and the new in war poetry, and its quest for the sacred, even in the midst of war.

This chapter makes no pretence of being a general history of war poetry. Its purpose is simply to explore one theme which war poets explored alongside those who worked in other languages in the arts, in films, painting, sculpture, prose, as well as in conventional and unconventional religious forms. That theme is the return of the dead from the field of battle.

The structure of this chapter is in three parts. First I point to the civilian motif of the mobilization of the 'glorious dead'. Secondly, I discuss some soldier-poets' reactions against this conceit. Thirdly, I describe the ways the resurrection of the dead in poetry opened up a sacred space for meditation on the war, and on those who died in it. Here traditional elements of romanticism were redefined and reaffirmed.

Patriotic myth: 'Debout, les morts!'

An insignificant encounter on the Western Front in 1915 occasioned one of the most widely disseminated patriotic myths of the early years of the war. It is a story of magic and mystery, found in many forms. Perhaps the best known is that of Maurice Barrès. His version was given to him first-hand, by an obscure Lieutenant Péricard. He told of a clash at Bois-Brûlé, during which French soldiers had suffered terrible losses. The death of one 'hero' opens the narrative:

We had fought for three days; all that were left in the trench were a few harassed men, completely isolated, with a shower of grenades falling on our heads. If the Boches only knew how few we were! Their artillery thundered. A lieutenant (his name escapes me), who came to reinforce the position, smoking his cigarette and laughing at the bombs, was hit in the temple. He was propped up in the parapet, his two hands behind his back, his head slightly tilted. Blood spurted from his wound, in an arc, like wine squirting out of a cask. His head tilted more and more, then his body slid, and suddenly fell.

The men in this unit were isolated, exhausted, and terrified. One man, Bonnot, 'took no notice', and 'continued to fight like a lion, alone against how many?' This example helped to restore Péricard's will to resist. He surveyed the position, realizing that they were in a desperate situation. He walked down the line of trenches, which were

full of French bodies. Blood everywhere. At first, I walked hesitantly, alone among all the dead . . . Then little by little I got my courage back. I dared to look at the corpses, and it seemed to me that they were looking at me.

Péricard's men thought he was mad. Then the Germans renewed their attack:

Their grenades flooded down like an avalanche. I retreated among the outstretched bodies. I thought, 'Well, is their sacrifice going to be for nothing? They fell in vain? And the Boches will come back? And they will steal our dead? . . .' I got angry. I don't remember precisely my words or actions. I only recall that I cried out something along these lines: 'Arise! Why are you flung on the ground? Get up and let's throw the pigs out!'

Here was the moment of the miracle:

Dead men arise! A touch of madness? No. *Because the dead answered me.* They said, 'We follow you.' And rising at my call, their souls mixed with my soul and stoked a mass of fire, a large river of fused metal. Nothing was able to astonish or to stop me. I had the faith that moves mountains. My voice had got hoarse shouting orders during these two days and that night; but now it came back, clear and strong.

. . . I don't know what happened after that. There is a gap in my memory; action devoured memory. I have simply the vague idea of a disorderly battle, in which, in the front line as always, Bonnot got separated. One of the men in my section wounded in the arm, continued to throw grenades covered with his own blood on the enemy position. I had the impression that my own body had become the body of a giant, with endless energy, a clarity of thought that gave me the power to see on ten sides at once, to shout an order to one, while giving another order by hand, to shoot and at the same time duck a grenade.

The dead provided arms as well as inspiration:

Twice we ran out of grenades, and twice we found at our feet sacks of grenades, mixed with sacks of earth. All day long, we had passed by without seeing them. But had it been the dead who had placed them there?

In case we had missed the point, the tale makes explicit the religious character of the episode. Péricard told Barrès that

All through the night and for several days thereafter, I kept the religious emotion which had taken me over the moment I had recalled the dead. I sensed something similar after holy communion. I knew I had lived hours which I would never know again, during which my head, having broken through the low ceiling, had come up against a mystery of the invisible world of heroes and gods.

The miracle was not an individual experience. It was the expression of the 'soul' of France, the fusion of the living and the dead so beloved of romantic patriots like Barrès. Here is the way Péricard ended his story:

At that moment, certainly, I had gone beyond myself . . . I know that I am not a hero. I shake with fear each time I have to go over the top . . . It was the living who had provided the example and the dead who had led me by the hand. The cry had not come from the mouth of a man, but from the heart of all those who lay there, the living and the dead. A single man couldn't find that tone of voice. There had to be the collaboration of several souls, raised by the circumstances, several of whom had already soared into eternity . . .

It would be a lie to say that I pretended to monopolize the glory of our regiment that day. The cry was not mine, but it was of us all. The more you place me in the mass, the closer you come to the truth. I was only a tool in the hands of superior powers.[2]

'Voilà les faits', Barrès concluded, in retelling the story (in French) to the British Academy in 1916.[3] His subject was 'The ancient heraldry of France, or its eternal traits displayed in the present war and in old epics.' The song of Roland and other medieval texts were placed alongside this modern tale of heroism, and presented a seamless web of Gallic nobility, rooted (as he wrote time and again) in the soil and blood of France.[4]

Poetic reactions

The same story was told by dozens of journalists, hack poets, politicians, and graphic artists. It was enshrined in a 'best-selling' *image d'Epinal*,[5] and developed in pamphlets and orations throughout the war.

It also occasioned a passionate outburst by one serving soldier who did not survive the war. Marc de Larreguy de Civrieux was a young Catholic, who passed through the ranks of French conservatism and royalism, via Action Française, before joining the army in 1914. His military service led him to reject violently the patriotic shibboleths of Barrès. To those who echoed the cry 'Debout, les morts!', Larreguy replied:

> Let them sleep in peace,
> The dead! After all, what harm have they done you
> That you pursue them into their gloomy refuge?
> After having carried the load
> Of so many evils and so many heinous crimes
> After being damned for your civilian hatreds,
> Having sacrificed their youth and their blood,
> Don't they have the right that the passer-by,
> Sympathising with their sins,
> Lets them finally to decay in tranquillity.
>
> Let them sleep in peace,
> Beneath the frozen earth and the thick grass,
> In the happy oblivion of their supreme pose!
> So that they will never feel
> The worm feasting on them
> And through which their flesh decomposes!
> So that never again will they open their eyes,
> And forget this stinking world,

> For the compassionate and eternal nothingness
> In which their corpses rest![6]

Barrès came in for abuse in another piece of his poetic invective, entitled 'Epistle from a monkey in the trenches to a parrot in Paris'. There he fumed against Barrès' 'eye-wash' in the *Echo de Paris,* and decried his disgraceful ardour for war. In another fiercely angry poem, 'To those for whom life is "dear" and who hold the life of "others" so cheap', he is the unnamed target, Marianne's pet parrot, whose cries were heard in the slaughter-house where she swung her cleaver 'dripping with blood fresh tapped'. Larreguy could accept none of Barrès' certainties about why the war had to be fought. Instead, as he wrote in what could have been his epitaph, 'The Soldier's soliloquies':

> Better for me to just keep mum
> And, when it's my own turn to die
> Depart this life for kingdom come
> But never know the reason why.

He was killed near Verdun in November 1916.[7]

Luckier was the French poet René Arcos, who was older than Larreguy, and a prominent figure in the group around Jules Romains and the journal *La nouvelle revue française.*[8] He survived the war and worked alongside Romain Rolland in the propagation of the European idea.[9] His anger was as marked as that of Larreguy. In his collection of essays published in 1920, *Pays du soir,* he reiterated the attack on the Barrèsian vision of the mobilization of the dead:

After having pursued with zeal and method the extermination of obscure living people, our leaders invented the mobilization of the dead. The dead were their property, . . . their imperial guard.

'The dead must be served', 'we must not ignore the voice of the dead', became catch phrases in the effort to sell whatever politicians wanted to sell. The dead became a 'silent army' needed 'to guard their banks, parliaments, racing stables, and their prostitutes' diamonds'. They voted 'en masse for the government'. At every turn, the dead were invoked to legitimate the status quo. Was it really true, he asked rhetorically in *Pays du Soir,* that by 1920 the dead of Flanders and Artois, who had given their lives freely, had become 'our enemies'?[10] No, the dead were beyond nation and beyond class:

> Leaning one against another
> The dead, without hatred and without a flag
> Hair matted with dried blood,
> The dead are all on the same side.[11]

There is an uncanny resemblance between these sentiments and those of an English poet equally distant from the heroic illusions of civilian journalism.[12] Charles Hamilton Sorley was born in the same year as Larreguy, in 1895. His immunization from virulent nationalism may have come as a result of a visit to Germany in 1914. Early in the war, he expressed unease at Rupert Brooke's war poetry for turning duty into high sentimental melodrama. Brooke was the English equivalent of Barrès, though at least he had served. Sorley too knew of what he wrote. After he was killed in October 1915, this poem was found in his papers:

> When you see millions of the mouthless dead
> Across your dreams in pale battalions go,
> Say not soft things as other men have said,
> That you'll remember. For you need not so.
> Give them not praise. For, deaf, how should they know
> It is not curses heaped on each gashed head?
> Nor tears. Their blind eyes are not your tears flow.
> Not honour. It is easy to be dead.
> Say only this, 'They are dead.' Then add thereto,
> 'Yet many a better one has died before.'
> Then, scanning all the o'ercrowded mass, should you
> Perceive one face that you loved heretofore,
> It is a spook. None wears the face you knew.
> Great death has made all his for evermore.[13]

In 'Two Sonnets', Sorley describes death as 'no triumph, no defeat: / Only an empty pail, a slate rubbed clear, / a merciful putting away of what has been'.[14] Just as in the work of Larreguy, here is a poetic plea for rest, not resurrection.

A fourth, younger poet who was too young to fight, picked up the theme of the mobilization of the dead in a much more sardonic manner. Bertolt Brecht's early poetry was closer to René Arcos' biting wit than to Sorley's quiet manner, but the theme was the same. In his 'Legend of the dead soldier', written in 1920, Brecht brought the rhythms of music hall to the demolition of the Barrèsian school of thought:

> And when the war reached its final spring
> With no hint of a pause for breath
> The soldier did the logical thing
> And died a hero's death.
>
> The war however was far from done
> And the Kaiser thought it a crime
> That his soldier should be dead and gone
> Before the proper time.

So a medical board dug up what was left of him, passed him fit for service, as a man who 'merely lost his nerve', 'filled him up with a fiery schnapps', 'shoved two nurses into his arms / And a half-naked tart', hid his stench by a priest's incense, and marched him back to war, so that for a second time he could go off 'to a hero's death / Just like the manual said'.[15]

The poem is a raucous rendition of a theme treated by Georg Grosz in a cartoon showing a German medical board passing a skeleton for military service.[16] This is probably the most vicious caricature of the theme of the mobilization of the dead, though it was mirrored by the notorious 'trial' of Barrès by the surrealists for 'crimes against the safety of the mind' in May 1921. The poet Benjamin Péret marched around as the German unknown soldier, spouting meaningless verse, thereby spreading the accusation across the Rhine.[17] This form of politics as theatre succinctly captured the revulsion felt by radical poets and artists at the nationalist mysticism of 'Debout, les morts'.

Conversations with the dead

Most poets who wrote about the dead were not politically active people. Their verse was not placed in the service of a political cause, though most preserved some vestiges of the loyalty to nation or community which impelled them into the army in the first place. What they try to offer is compassion in place of political commitment. Ambivalent about the war, they retained their loyalty to their former comrades who, in many cases, lay by their side. Their evocation of the fallen frequently took the form of giving the dead the capacity to speak or see or go home again.

Consider the work of the German poet Heinrich Lersch. He had volunteered in August 1914, very much the patriot, but he was turned down initially on grounds of ill health. He finally got into the army, served in Champagne, where in May 1915 he was buried alive during an artillery bombardment. That ended his spell of front-line service, and tempered his ardent patriotism.

Lersch's poem 'Wenn es Abend wird' ('When night falls') is characteristic of one form of this romantic vision, the return of the dead to their homes:

> When the last shadows of the setting sun slip across the
> battlefield,
> From graves in woodlands and glens, the dead arise,
> From graves in woodlands and glens,
> From graves in heath and dune,
> They stand beside their knolls praying,
> Facing home, on foreign soil.
>
> A bird sings in the night.
>
> Then they fall out, rise up, glide homewards,
> Over ruined towns, over fields laid waste,

Over armies still fighting,
Past shimmering rivers, away, away to their homeland.

The image is one familiar to the spiritualist community (see pp. 54–77). Wartime photography and memoirs also present many such instances of military units at prayer, before or after battle. But instead of thanking God in their hour of victory, as Hindenburg had done after Tannenberg, or rejoicing in their safe return from the battlefield, these men are dead. What they want is to go home:

There when night begins to fall,
Shadows draw near from the frontiers of the Fatherland,
From mountains and oceans,
Like shadows, clouds, red at sunset, sinking like larks
    into their nests.

Everywhere.

Over there, at the edge of the wood,
Where between ripening cornfields a footpath,
Bordered by poppies and cornflowers,
Winds upwards.
There are figures; happy gestures of outstretched arms;
Blessing hands touching nodding ears of corn,
Bowed necks lower eyes full of pained joy
Into the sea of stems, and raise to their pale lips
The bright red and blue of wild flowers.
Kneel, arms stretched out towards the golden riches of life,
In the flowering clover.[18]

This poem is in two parts. The first touches on soldiers at prayer and the sacred; the second descends to the sentimental. It is as if their sacred status is compromised the closer to home they come, and instead of building up to a crescendo the poem disintegrates into conventional verse about pastoral pleasures. It is an attempt to move away from patriotic certainties, but a failed attempt, because the poet can't quite escape from the natural beauty and call of the Fatherland.

Anton Schnack could. He explored the same motifs as Lersch, but brought to them a more powerful sense of compassion. He was a veteran of Verdun and the great battles of 1918, and brought to his verse the need to explore 'whatever mourns in man'.[19]

One of his poems, 'Der Tote' ('The dead soldier') revives the dead of the Great War, but imagines the unfulfilled promise of their lives in a more indirect way than did Lersch. He observes a dead German soldier, 'Head still full of memories of the other side of the Rhine':

That mouth had many things left to say;
Maybe about gardens strolled through in autumn,

211

> Maybe about ochre-coloured cattle,
> Maybe about the poverty of his grey old mother
> Or that ear, pale, small, still full of thunderstorms,
> Of deep waves of sound,
> Enjoying hearing again the blackbirds
> In the pear-tree of spring,
> The shouting of the city children out in the country;
> In his eye this:
> A net full of white fish, bluish-looking stars;
> Was not a Gothic doorway overgrown with ivy,
> Gleaming in the dark, once reflected in it?[20]

The romantic repertoire of images is here, but it serves to highlight what the dead soldier could no longer do, not how beautiful the Fatherland was. Who killed him? Someone with the same local sympathies and rhythm of life. Now, Schnack observes, his dead comrade

is just a dark shape, a death, a thing, a stone, destroyed beyond measure, filling the night with its outrage at man's cruelty.[21]

That cruelty was the poet's responsibility too, one which he did not shrug off. This is what makes Schnack's verse so similar to that of Wilfred Owen. Both understood what soldiering meant, and knew that they were killers as well as victims. Consider Owen's 'Strange Meeting' in the context of this international theme of the poetic resurrection of the dead of the Great War:

> It seemed that out of battle I escaped
> Down some profound dull tunnel, long since scooped
> Through granites which titanic wars had groined.
>
> Yet also there encumbered sleepers groaned,
> Too fast in thought or death to be bestirred.
> Then, as I probed them, one sprang up, and stared
> With piteous recognition in fixed eyes,
> Lifting distressful hands, as if to bless.
> And by his smile, I knew that sullen hall, –
> By his dead smile I knew we stood in Hell.

The setting is battle itself, and in place of a bucolic reverie, Owen presents a descent into hell, this time with an unusual guide. His Virgil was a German soldier he, the poet, had killed.

> 'Strange friend,' I said, 'here is no cause to mourn.'
> 'None,' said the other, 'save the undone years,
> The hopelessness.'

'Whatever hope is yours, / Was my life also', says the ghost, and then lists, as Schnack did, the catalogue of pleasures lost, laughter not heard, courage and wisdom thrown away.

> 'I would have poured my spirit without stint
> But not through wounds; not on the cess of war.'

But he was ripped from life by the poet, the man by chance he met in hell:

> 'I am the enemy you killed, my friend.
> I knew you in this dark: for so you frowned
> Yesterday through me as you jabbed and killed
> I parried; but my hands were loath and cold.
> Let us sleep now . . .'[22]

How far we have travelled from the poetic forms of romantic love of the Fatherland. None of Lersch's sentimentality here, though the affinities with Schnack's harder verse are apparent.

There is also a striking similarity to a poem written by Siegfried Sassoon, 'Enemies', about a dead English soldier, confronting dead Germans, killed by the poet. He took their lives in anger, enraged like Achilles after the death of Patroclus. Here the poet looks on at the scene of the dead on both sides trying to understand what had happened to them.[23]

These men in their own ways faced their responsibility for killing, for filling the 'cess of war'. Through images of the dead (in a sense) living 'normal' lives, or having still-human sensibilities, they acknowledged their own sense of guilt at their complicity in the monstrous crimes of war.

The poetic motif of the dead among the living was used in other ways. One of the most prominent is the absorption, the ingestion of the dead by those still alive. The living are half dead, and the dead half alive; both in a liminal world, full of images most of us fortunately never manage to see.

One war poet who suffered from a surfeit of such memories was Ivor Gurney. In 'Ballad of the three spectres' he captured the nightmarish quality of these visitations of the dead, and the likelihood of joining them:

> As I went up by Ovillers
>   In mud and water cold to the knee,
> There went three jeering, fleering spectres,
>   That walked abreast and talked of me.

One predicted he, the poet, would get a 'nice Blighty' wound; the second said no such luck, 'he'll freeze in mud to the marrow'; but the third, the worst of all 'spat venomously' and prophesied:

> 'He'll stay untouched till the war's last dawning
>   Then live one hour of agony.'

The poet called the first two 'liars': he wasn't lightly wounded, and still unfrozen, but awaited the day before deciding whether the third spoke

213

the truth.[24] This poem is a rare example of malice or jealousy among the dead for the living. It is an example of what Robert Jay Lifton, in another context, has called 'the guilt of the survivor'.[25] The dead in Gurney's poem are sardonic and positively hope for his demise. And why shouldn't they? After all, he had been spared.

In the hands of other poets, this theme was treated without Gurney's biting morbidity. The Italian war poet Giuseppi Ungaretti wrote of the 'barely heard whispering' of the dead, 'No more than the increase of grass, / Happy where no man passes.' No biting asides here, or indeed in most other invocations of the voices of the dead.[26]

Some even adopted a kind of fond playfulness with this set of images. One powerful example is the poetry of Guillaume Apollinaire, whose military and literary career I have already considered in chapter 1. Consider his poem, 'Bleuet' ('Cornflower'). The cornflower (already evoked by Lersch) is again the equivalent of the English 'poppy'; the flower appropriate for wreaths and commemoration.

Young man
You are joyous and your memory is bloodied
Your soul is also red
With joy
You have absorbed the life of those who died close to you
You have decision in you
It is 5 o'clock and you would know
How to die
If not better than your elders
At least more piously
For you know death better than life
O sweetness of other times
Immemorial slowness[27]

As in all the verse of Apollinaire, this poem expresses an ambivalence, a strong undercurrent of irony, a powerful dialectical sense of contradiction.[28] Not for him the heaviness of Gothic imagery, the solemnity of Owen. But the terrain is the same, the invocation of piety, and so is the bitter-sweet memory of the men who had already died and those soon to join them. They, like the flowers, absorb the living matter in the soil, flourish, and then fade away. This is the language of evanescence, echoing Biblical passages, but with Apollinaire's lightness of touch.

Mourning for the dead, whom the poet bears like a cloak on his shoulders, is treated even more directly in 'Ombre' ('Shadow'):

Here you are near me once more
Memories of my comrades dead in battle
Olive of time
Memories composing now a single memory

As a hundred furs make only one coat
As those thousands of wounds make only one newspaper article
Impalpable dark appearance you have assumed
The changing form of my shadow
An Indian hiding in wait throughout eternity
Shadow you creep near me
But you no longer hear me
You will no longer know the divine poems I sing
But I hear you I see you still
Destinies
Multiple shadow may the sun watch over you
You who love me so much you will never leave me
You who dance in the sun without stirring the dust
Shadow solar ink
Handwriting of my light
Caisson of regrets
A god humbling himself[29]

This poem, written in 1917, brings the fallen to life, and within his poetry they are seen as part of the 'changing form' of his shadow.[30]

Much of Apollinaire's poetry has a disarming panache, which, however, does not fully obscure his intention both to explore the sacred and to resist the elevated tone other poets adopted in its presence. Consider the poems 'Voici le cercueil' ('Here is the coffin') and 'Vive la France', characteristic calligrams, or image-poems:

> Here is
> the   cof
> fin in which
> He rested
> rotting
> and p
> ale

> Long   live   France!
> He sleeps in his li
> ttle   soldier's   bed
> My   resuscitated
> P o   e t

[31]

Where is the emphasis in this poem: on the 'resuscitated poet', 'rotting and pale' or on 'his little soldier's bed' or even on the patriot's salute? Apollinaire offers us all of them, and in the mocking form of a drawing of a casket on a bier. The gallows' humour of the soldier tempers the seriousness of the subject.

Not so in 'Endurçis-toi, vieux coeur . . .' ('Harden, old heart'), where he loses his jaunty manner and listens

> to the piercing cries
> that the wounded in agony utter a long way off
> O men lice of the earth O tenacious vermin[32]

Or in his earlier poem about the outbreak of war 'La petite auto' ('The little car'), where he imagines sardonically that 'Nations were rushing together to know each other / through and through', only to bring us up with a Gothic start in the very next line, which tells us that 'The dead were trembling with fear in their dark dwellings.'[33] *Eros* and *thanatos*, erotic associations and images of death, are liberally blended in Apollinaire's poetry. The jarring mix of opposites is also apparent in a mid-war poem 'Exercice':

> All four Class of 1916
> Reminiscing not prophesying
> Prolonging the ascetic life
> Of those who exercise the art of dying.[34]

Here is the voice of the soldiers' songs, the barrack ballads that caught the emotion and swagger of the men at the front. Apollinaire captured the mixed mood of these men, not far from the dead, yet clinging defiantly to life.

Apollinaire was an iconoclast with a flare for tradition. Romantic elements abound in his work. Paradox was his *métier*, and his stance halfway between the modern and the conventional gives an added dimension to his war poetry.[35] He never questioned his patriotism, wore his uniform with dash, but did not ignore the ugliness of the war. His experiments in form provided a visual component to his delight in contradictions, to the mix of metaphors of love and war, of horses' flanks and women's thighs, of the profane in the midst of the sacred. He aimed to mediate between opposites and antagonists, as in his well-known poem 'La jolie rousse' ('The pretty redhead'):

> Here I stand before everyone a man full of sense . . .
> Who has seen war both in the Artillery and the Infantry
> One who has been wounded in the head and trepanned under
> chloroform
> One who has lost his best friends in the terrible slaughter
> I know as much about what is old and what is new as a single person
> could know
> And without troubling now about this war
> Between ourselves and for our own sakes my friends
> I sit in judgment on this long quarrel between tradition and invention
> Between order and adventure[36]

The modernists were not the enemies of 'order', but exuberant *bons vivants* who 'want to bequeath to you vast and strange domains'. He asked his shocked elders for pity, the last thing in the world one would expect from a modernist:

> Pity on us who are always fighting on the frontiers
> Of limitlessness and the future
> Pity our mistakes pity our sins[37]

How much of this was mocking, how much straight is impossible to tell. But the force of his verse served as a bridge between the old and the new, between the sacred and the profane, between the patriot and the man of the world. His friend André Billy described Apollinaire as 'the man best qualified to represent the Baroque in modern times',[38] full of rich styles, moods, and images. His poetic resuscitation of the fallen shows one way in which he breathed life into ancient metaphors about the return of the fallen in wartime.

War poetry and the Bible

Naturally, images of the Passion of Christ abounded in war poetry. Pre-war verse prepared the way. Consider 'Mankind', by the Austrian poet Georg Trakl:

> Round gorges deep with fire arrayed, mankind;
> A roll of drums, dark brows of warriors marching;
> Footsteps through fog of blood, black metals grind;
> Sad night of human thought, despair high-arching;
> Here fall's Eve's shadows, hunt, red coin consigned.
> Cloud, pierced by light, and the Last Supper's end;
> This bread, this wine, soft silence have in keeping.
> The Twelve in number here assembled stand;
> Cry out at night, under branched olives sleeping.
> Into the wound Saint Thomas dips his hand.[39]

This poem was written in 1911–12, in anticipation of violence.[40] Trakl committed suicide early in the war, after a painful period of service as an officer in Galicia with the Austrian Medical Corps. His verse is full of romantic images, as in 'Grodek', where 'the night embraces / Dying warriors' and 'The sister's shade now sways through the silent copse / To greet the ghosts of the heroes', or 'Im Osten' ('Eastern Front') where 'Ghosts of the fallen are sighing.' Here spiritualism and a dark spirituality merge in a familiar and gloomy romantic haze.[41] The same dark glow illuminated the verse and prose in *Der Wanderer zwischen beiden Welten* (*A wanderer between two worlds*), written by Walter Flex, who was killed in October 1917.[42]

At the early stages of the war, French soldier-poets made similar gestures towards the sanctification of the trenches. This was the signature of Charles Péguy, killed in late August 1914, as well as that of Jean-Marc Bernard, a neo-classical poet, killed in 1915. Bernard dedicated 'Nos Clochers' ('Our church spires') to Barrès, and in 'De Profundis' he proclaimed that dead soldiers lie 'Clothed in their sacramental blood'.[43] Mystical Christian verse in Breton was among Jean-Pierre Calloc'h's contribution to the war effort. 'I know that You will come. I know that you are near. I believe in the mystery of Grief', he wrote in 1915, while serving in the infantry. He died on the Western Front two years later.[44] These poets were not alone in the world of French literature in spiritualizing the war and the comradeship of suffering in the trenches.[45] Their advantage over civilians like Barrès was obvious: they had the moral authority to say quietly what he shouted from the rooftops of Paris, far from the killing fields.

English war poets employ other kinds of romantic rhetoric. Some are embittered; others, straightforwardly lyrical. Most do not escape from a spiritual framework which, with qualifications, their poems reaffirm. Siegfried Sassoon's poetry is a case in point. It is a mistake to interpret his war service as a time when he escaped from romanticism and spiritual simplicities after a spell in the trenches. In November 1915 he drafted a poem 'The Redeemer'. Christ appears in the trenches not with a 'thorny crown' but only the 'woollen cap' of 'an English soldier, white and strong'. He joins men struggling along a ditch. The original ending was maudlin and conventional:

> But in my heart I knew that I had seen
> The suffering spirit of a world washed clean

By March 1916 this had been transformed into:

> And someone pitched his burden in the muck
> Muttering, 'O Christ Almighty, *now* I'm stuck!'[46]

The second couplet is, of course, better poetry, but its existence does not constitute proof that the poet had moved into a different, demystified, register. For example, in March 1917, a full year later, Sassoon wrote 'In the Church of St Ouen'. It is quintessentially romantic:

> Time makes me be a soldier. But I know
> That had I lived six hundred years ago
> I might have tried to build within my heart
> A church like this, where I could dwell apart
> With chanting peace. My spirit longs for prayer,
> And, lost to God, I seek him everywhere.[47]

No irony here, though it can be found in abundance elsewhere in his writing.

The same refashioning of romanticism in religious form marks much of Wilfred Owen's poetry. Consider his 'Soldier's dream', begun at Craiglockhart in October 1917, and reworked through the next year:

> I dreamed kind Jesus fouled the big-gun gears;
> And caused a permanent stoppage in all bolts;
> And buckled with a smile Mausers and Colts;
> And rusted every bayonet with His tears.

Alas, the miraculous disarmament is foiled, because 'God was vexed' who 'gave all power to Michael', content to put the instruments of death into working order.[48] Owen's meditation on Christianity is a complex theme, well beyond the limits of this chapter.[49] But this poem, among others, points to the persistence of romantic traditions in war poetry as a whole.

The split is between Old Testament and New Testament motifs in war-poets' writing. While the Old Testament theme of sacrifice was challenged and reshaped, New Testament parables and images still retained their force. Even Isaac Rosenberg, the one Jewish soldier-poet among those whose verse has lasted, adopted this motif. In an early war poem, 'On receiving news of the war', he writes:

> Red fangs have torn His face.
> God's blood is shed.
> He mourns from His lone place
> His children dead.[50]

Hardly consonant with Jewish teaching, this sentiment was echoed in much other christological verse produced during the war. In contrast, Rosenberg's style was entirely different when he meditated on Moses the killer and on King Saul, who died in battle after consorting with the witch of En-Dor.[51] For what Owen called 'the pity of war', poets turned to New Testament images, though there is much in the Psalms, Lamentations, and the Prophets on which they could have drawn for the theme.

Some exceptions should be noted. The divine order was not accepted uncritically, and some flirted with angry, iconoclastic images. Ivor Gurney's 'amazed heart', confronted by a world of pain, 'cries angrily out on God'.[52] And Herbert Read went well beyond the sensibilities of most of his fellow-poets in 'The crucifix':

> His body is smashed
> through the belly and chest

> the head hangs lopsided
> from one nail'd hand.
>
> Emblem of agony
> we have smashed you![53]

The exclamation at the end of the poem removes the possibility of a sad reading of the first stanza. It is an accusation, a cry of anger at the emptiness of the religious framework so many other poets accepted.

A similar anger is active in Richard Aldington's poems, but its echoes are almost all Old Testament in character. Here his work was symptomatic of a broader sensibility at work among English soldier-poets. The accusation that the young had died while the old stood back was a commonplace during and after the war.[54] Aldington voiced it in 'The blood of the young men', where he presents soldiers

> Crying for our brothers, the men we fought with,
> Crying out, mourning them, alone with our dead ones;

who point an accusing finger at the 'old men' who 'will grow stronger and healthier' feasting on the 'Blood of the young, dear flesh of the young men'.[55]

The image of human sacrifice is unmistakably that of the 'Akedah', the legend of Abraham and Isaac. Three well-known war poems transformed the story. The first is 'The parable of the old man and the young', written by Wilfred Owen at Scarborough in July 1918. The preparation of the sacrifice is made, following Genesis. Then the 'Ram of pride' is offered in place of Isaac.

> But the old man would not so, but slew his son,
> And half the seed of Europe, one by one.[56]

The second is Osbert Sitwell's 'The modern Abraham', also written in 1918. It tells of the pride of the patriarch who 'Loves his country in the elder way' and sent ten sons to be killed in the war. In Sitwell's 'The next war', written in November 1918, the Akedah is similarly transformed, this time as a repeated human sacrifice, in which the sons of the fallen are sacrificed in their turn.[57]

We have few poems which speak of the fathers' reaction to this accusation. One of the most disturbing, and most elusive, is a simple couplet 'The common form', by Rudyard Kipling, whose son was killed at Loos in 1915:

> If any question why we died,
> Tell them, because our fathers lied.[58]

It is one of Kipling's 'Epitaphs of the War (1914–18)', and can be read in two ways. The phrase 'because our fathers lied' can be seen as the answer to the question in the first line of the couplet. But it is also possible that Kipling is suggesting that the answer to the question 'why did they die?' lay in the mind of the reader. Only he or she can do better than the lies told by the fathers.[59] In either case, the old are indicted, and someone else must speak the truth.

In reworking the legend in Genesis about the sacrifice of Isaac, English poets challenged religious conventions and an entire idiom of praise of the 'noble dead'. But we see here the recasting of older themes, not their supersession. At this point Kipling, the poet of Empire – and the man who chose the emblem from Ecclesiasticus, placed on Lutyens' 'great stone' in British and Imperial war cemeteries: 'Their name liveth forevermore' – joined Käthe Kollwitz, who sculpted the enduring war memorial of herself and her husband on their knees in front of the grave of their son in Belgium. They, the elders, had failed to stop the sacrifice, and their sons had paid the price.

Conclusion

This exploration of one – and only one – aspect of Great War poetry lends weight to the view that far from ushering in modernism, the Great War reinforced romantic tendencies in poetic expression about war. For most, it was not the romanticism of Barrès, to be sure; his posture had been discredited by its own excesses. But what took its place was a different kind of romanticism, a refashioned set of ideas and images derived from a range of older traditions.

The soldier-poet was in the end a romantic figure. He was the upholder of moral values, the truth-teller *par excellence*, the man who faced fear and death and spoke about them to the yet unknowing world. He ventured into the domain of the sacred, the no man's land between the living and the dead, and acted as interlocutor between communities in mourning: soldiers and civilians, men and women, young and old. It was (and remains) his voice which reaffirmed the values of the men who fought, their loyalty to one another, their compassion for those who suffered on both sides, their stoical acceptance of fate. At times, he expressed outrage at the injustice at the young being slaughtered while the old looked on. But most of this body of verse was an affirmation, even when cataloguing the awfulness of war.

A complex process of re-sacralization marks the poetry of the war.[60] Over time, many romantic celebrations of sacrifice were indeed rejected. But war poets did not turn away from the sacred. Theirs is not the poetry of 'demystification'. Many sought to reach the sacred through the metaphor of resurrection. What better means of evoking feeling for the brotherhood of the living and the dead than by hearing them speak again?

Admittedly, this kind of poetic spiritualism was disturbing rather than reassuring. Most writers who engaged in this dialogue with the dead offered no solutions to the moral problems posed by the war. Indeed, their ambivalence is perhaps their most striking common characteristic. Soldier-pacifists, militant bearers of a message of peace, patriots of more than one country, Christian free-thinkers, their mixed messages puzzle as much as they move the reader. As in the poetry of Apollinaire, dialectical, rather than directly patriotic or pacifist statement, was their strength. Their poetry ministered; it didn't preach. Their 'modernism' was the product of a recasting of traditional language, not its rejection. They are the first in a long line of twentieth-century romantics, who walk backwards into the future, struggling to understand the chaotic history of this century.[61]

9
Conclusion

The Great War and the persistence of tradition

In his ninth 'Thesis on the philosophy of history', Walter Benjamin addresses an issue crucial to this study: the dialectical relationship between old and new, between 'traditional' and 'modern' in twentieth-century cultural history. Benjamin recalls:

A Klee painting named 'Angelus Novus' shows an angel looking as though he is about to move away from something he is fixedly contemplating. His eyes are staring, his mouth is open, his wings are spread. This is how one pictures the angel of history. His face is turned towards the past. Where we perceive a chain of events, he sees one single catastrophe which keeps piling wreckage upon wreckage and hurls it in front of his feet. The angel would like to stay, awaken the dead, and make whole what has been smashed. But a storm is blowing from Paradise; it has got caught in his wings with such violence that the angel can no longer close them. This storm irresistibly propels him into the future to which his back is turned, while the pile of debris before him grows skyward. This storm is what we call progress.[1]

No image does more to capture the subtle and contradictory elements embedded in European cultural history in the period of the Great War. Benjamin's 'angel of history' did indeed float into the future with his gaze fixed firmly on the past. His back was turned on us, those who have come after; the onward march towards 'modernism' did not concern him. Instead his eyes were directed towards the 'wreckage' strewn at his feet, the 'pile of debris' left by the 'storm' we call the Great War.[2]

It is the central contention of this book that the backward gaze of so many writers, artists, politicians, soldiers, and everyday families in this period reflected the universality of grief and mourning in Europe from 1914. A complex traditional vocabulary of mourning, derived from classical, romantic, or religious forms, flourished, largely because it helped mediate bereavement. The 'sites of memory', like Benjamin's *Angelus Novus*, faced the past, not the future.[3]

The search for 'meaning' in the wake of war

The aims of this study are limited: to describe only one aspect of the cultural history of the Great War and to do so primarily with respect to three major combatant countries, Britain, France, and Germany. These findings are, therefore, tentative, but they suggest a set of questions which may be used to explore the cultural history of other nations in this period. We have seen how symbols were retrieved from the past to help people mourn. These symbols framed contemporary searches for some vestiges of 'meaning' in the war and in the appalling losses it entailed. I have tried to show in a number of ways how that search was conducted, and in what forms it was expressed.

I have built on the foundations of a rich historical literature, much of which concerns the political dimension of the search for 'meaning' during and after the war. I have exploited too an imposing array of studies of commemorative forms as expressions of artistic and architectural styles and configurations. Both bodies of learning offer insights on the problem of 'meaning' which complement the approach adopted here.

I have tried to add to this body of knowledge by concentrating on the universal problem of grief and its social expression. However powerful the aesthetic or political messages available to those in mourning, there was another level on which they lived the 'meaning' of the war. That level was private, sometimes solitary, frequently hidden from view, but no one can doubt it was there. It involved timeless questions about the truncation of millions of lives, about promise unfulfilled, about the evanescence of hope.

Anyone approaching the cultural history of the war who misses this third level leaves out what sadly was at the heart of the experience of war for millions. Their war was imprinted with the wrenching experience of loss, the 'meaning' of which was sought at least as much in the existential as in the artistic or political spheres. It is true that the Great War introduced political issues to every dimension of social life, but some issues in wartime were both political and more than political. The experience of mass bereavement was one such issue.

Human reactions to war are infinitely complicated and delicately coded. Grief, I believe, is a state of mind; bereavement a condition. Both are mediated by mourning, a set of acts and gestures through which survivors express grief and pass through stages of bereavement. That process of separation from the dead, of forgetting as much as remembering, is central to this book.

Cultural codes and the language of mourning: the visual, the verbal, the social

There are three ways in which this human catastrophe was encoded culturally in Europe in this period. The first was visually, through images of the dead and of their return, a set of metaphors which frequently shifted into meditations on apocalyptic themes. The second was in prose and poetry, evidencing the same tendency to 'see' the dead among the living. Here too sacred icons and images proliferated. Sacred languages in the visual arts were not rejected; they were reconfigured. The powerful current of spiritualism in wartime testified to the same search for the sacred, albeit in unconventional forms.

The third form of cultural encoding was social; that is to say, it was expressed through social action. This was organized usually on the local level, though the grand ceremonies of Armistice Day registered the same impulse. Most (but not all) of these measures were small-scale, with the human dimensions of Klee's *Angelus Novus*.[4] They offered mutual assistance, support, and commemorative rites, shared by men and women in family circles, by those gathered in forms of religious worship, and in larger groups, in widows' organizations, in commemorative meetings in universities and colleges, in reunions of comrades in arms, at the unveiling of local war memorials, and finally, by the ceremonies conducted on behalf of the 'imagined community' of the nation itself. Here the distinctions between and among the political and the existential fade, for the question as to how to remember the 'Lost Generation' all too often had disturbing personal, communal and political repercussions.

Mourning and tradition

In a host of ways, these varied cultural forms carried messages about mourning which were highly traditional in character. Why was this so? Some clues may be found in an interpretive framework developed by Julia Kristeva. Using a vocabulary derived from psychoanalysis, she has explored the power of what we have termed 'traditional' structures of thought to express the anguish and hope of men and women in mourning. In our discussion of Rouault's war cycle *Miserere* in chapter 6, we introduced her approach to what may be termed forms of aesthetic redemption. Her argument has profound implications for the whole of our study. Kristeva suggested that 'religious discourse' alongside 'aesthetic and particularly literary creation',

set[s] forth a device whose prosodic economy, interaction of characters, and implicit symbolism constitute a very faithful semiological representation of the subject's battle with symbolic collapse.

225

31. *Angelus Novus*, 1920, by Paul Klee

'Symbolic collapse' threatened all those who tried to understand the meaning of loss of life in the Great War. Art and ceremony helped shore up these symbols, through which grief was expressed and bereavement experienced. Following Kristeva, we can see how it was not only individuals, therefore, but also the symbols of meaning which were 'resurrected' during and after the war. Through their elaboration, expression and revival, these images and icons were shared by millions in mourning. What we have called traditional languages of loss, in the visual arts, in prose and poetry, and inscribed in social forms of mourning, thereby contributed to the process of healing, perhaps, as Kristeva suggests, more through 'catharsis' than 'elaboration'.[5] Such an approach clarifies much about the cultural aftermath of the Great War, and the flowering in its wake of an older set of languages about suffering and loss.

The commonality of cultural history

To approach the cultural history of the war from this angle has other merits. It discloses fully the European character of the war. This is a story with fewer national boundaries than is to be found in most histories of the period. To bring these diverse cultures together in the aftermath of this murderous war is to place less emphasis than others do on the facts of victory and defeat. They mattered; but all too often victory had a taste of ashes. It could not be otherwise in a war in which 9 million men died throughout the world; about half of this ghastly total was registered in these three countries alone. Recalling this aspect of the war also helps to cast further doubt on the outmoded idea that Germany went through a special path, a *Sonderweg* in the nineteenth and twentieth century. As we have now seen, all major combatants went through a 'special' path, the path of collective slaughter.

The cultural history of the Great War was a common history in another way too. The weight of evidence presented here supports the view that we must eliminate once and for all the tendency surgically to bifurcate cultural history into elite and popular compartments, into two registers, high and low, 'cultivated' and 'uncultivated', elevated and vulgar, elevating and clichéd. Some distinctions between cultural forms persist, to be sure. The Great War made a pure distinction between 'high' and 'low' much more difficult to uphold.[6] When the issues are universal, so are the responses evoked to them. Popular films, poster art, avant-garde painting, as much as poetry and prose registered a set of meditations on the sacred, of different levels of profundity to be sure, but which were reflections of the wrenching loss suffered by millions in wartime. Gestures matched words. Bereavement was understood and lived both privately and at the collective level, in families, associations, and in communities first constructing and then gathering in front of war memorials, prominent and obscure, to remember the fallen. Whatever form it took, this invocation of the dead is an unmistakable sign of the commonality of European cultural life in this period. Here class or rank mattered less than the simple distinction between those who lost someone and those who did not. Among the many legacies of the Great War, this bond of bereavement was one of the most prominent and the most enduring.

1914 and 1945

Continuities proliferate in this area, but in one important respect, the cultural history of the Great War was unique. The process of breathing life into the symbolic language of romantic, classical, and religious reference, so visible after 1914, was much more problematic after 1945. In effect, the search for 'meaning' after the Somme and Verdun was hard enough; but after Auschwitz and Hiroshima that search became infinitely more difficult.

This notion is part of what Adorno meant when he made his now celebrated pronouncement that 'to write lyric poetry after Auschwitz is barbaric'. He went on to add that 'literature must resist this verdict'. Herein lies the paradox not only of poetry but of art itself in our century: 'The abundance of real suffering tolerates no forgetting'; this suffering, in Hegel's terms, this 'consciousness of adversity . . . demands the continued existence of art while it prohibits it; it is now virtually in art alone that suffering can still find its own voice, consolation, without immediately being betrayed by it'. In effect, after 1945 poetry is an act of defiance, a quixotic refusal to descend into silence.[7]

After the Second World War, the same flaring up of older languages appropriate to a period of mass mourning did not take place. We have noted the profusion of apocalyptic images after 1914; after 1945, a few echoes are heard, but the rest is silence. Other voices emerged, and other cultural forms appeared. Many of them were abstract, and thereby both more liberated from specific cultural and political reference and less accessible to a mass audience. Their austere simplicity is powerful and compelling, and points to 1945 as the real caesura in European cultural life. Whether or not these abstract images have the same power to heal as did older symbolic forms is a difficult question; the answer is probably not.[8]

In another respect the Second World War is more of a divide than the first. After 1945, older forms of the language of the sacred[9] faded, and so had the optimism, the faith in human nature on which it rested. The warm exuberance of Apollinaire's verse is a case in point. In his poem, 'La jolie rousse', he simply refused to choose between the 'old and the new'. All he asked for was understanding and pity; pity for those of

> Us who are always fighting on the frontiers
> Of limitlessness and the future
> Pity our mistakes pity our sins[10]

After 1945, such humane compassion seemed strangely out of place, and so did the rhetoric of 'limitlessness and the future', resting so securely on a belief in human decency and progress. 'What those monstrous and painful sights' of the 1939–45 conflict 'did damage to', Kristeva tells us:

> are our systems of perception and representation. As if overtaxed or destroyed by too powerful a breaker, our symbolic means find themselves hollowed out, nearly wiped out, paralyzed. On the edge of silence the word 'nothing' emerges, a discreet defense in the face of so much disorder, both internal and external, incommensurable. Never has a cataclysm been more apocalyptically outrageous; never has its representations been assumed by so few symbolic means.[11]

It was the vision of Walter Benjamin, a victim of the Second World War, and not that of Apollinaire, who died at the end of the Great War, which accurately described the future; a future where angels are paralysed in flight or buried under a 'pile of debris' entirely filling the sky.

Notes

Introduction

1 For full casualty figures, see J.M. Winter, *The Great War and the British people* (London, Macmillan, 1985), ch. 3.

2 Paul Fussell, *The Great War and modern memory* (Oxford, Oxford University Press, 1975).

3 The best formulation of this position is by Samuel Hynes in his remarkable book *A war imagined. The Great War and English culture* (London, Bodley Head, 1991). It subtly develops and goes beyond the earlier, seminal work of Fussell.

4 Hynes, *A war imagined*.

5 See Fussell, *The Great War and modern memory*, and T.W. Bogacz, ' "A tyranny of words": language, poetry, and antimodernism in England in the First World War', *Journal of Modern History*, 58 (1986), pp. 643–68.

6 For a similar argument, see Rosa Bracco, *Merchants of hope. Middlebrow writers of the First World War* (Oxford, Berg, 1993).

7 See the stimulating remarks in Modris Eksteins, *Rites of spring. The modern in cultural history* (New York, Bantam Books, 1989), and in Clement Greenberg, 'Beginnings of modernism', in Monique Chefdor, Ricardo Quinones, and Albert Wachtel (eds.), *Modernism. Challenges and perspectives* (Urbana, University of Illinois Press, 1986), pp. 17–24.

8 In the visual arts, the best statement of this position is Ken Silver's *Esprit de corps. The art of the Parisian avant-garde and the First World War, 1914–1925* (London, Thames & Hudson, 1989). A similarly sensitive approach is adopted in R. Wohl, 'The generation of 1914 and modernism', in Chefdor, Quinones, and Wachtel (eds.), *Modernism*, pp. 66–78.

9 The literature on this subject is mountainous. One could do worse than start with Clement Greenberg's seminal remarks in his 'Modernist painting', in Geoffrey Battock (ed.), *The new art: a critical anthology* (New York, E.P. Dutton, 1966); see also the essays in Greenberg's *Art and culture* (London: Thames & Hudson, 1973). For an earlier and even more trenchant exposition of the modernist revolution, see R.H. Wilenski, *The modern movement in art* (New York, Frederick A. Stokes, 1927).

10 D.W. Fokkema, *Literary history, modernism and postmodernism* (Amsterdam, John Benyaminus Publishing Co., 1984); René Wellek, 'The term and concept of symbolism in literary history', in *Discriminations: further concepts of*

criticism (New Haven, CT, Yale University Press, 1970), esp. pp. 90–120; M. Stark, ' "The murder of modernism": some observations on research into expressionism and the post-modernism debate', in R. Sheppard (ed.), *Expressionism in focus* (Blairgowrie, Scotland, Lochee Publications Ltd, 1987), pp. 27–46; Paul de Man, *Blindness and insight. Essays in the rhetoric of contemporary criticism* (Minneapolis, University of Minnesota Press, 1983), chapters 8–9.

11 Peter Faulkner, *Modernism* (London, Methuen, 1977), pp. 1, 14.

12 H.N. Schneidau, *Waking giants. The presence of the past in modernism* (Oxford, Oxford University Press, 1991), p. 20.

13 Brian A. Rowley, 'Anticipations of modernism in the age of romanticism', in Janet Garton, *Facets of European modernism. Essays in honour of James McFarland presented to him on his 65th birthday, 12 December 1985* (Norwich, University of East Anglia, 1985), p. 17.

14 Ezra Pound, 'Hugh Selwyn Mauberley', in *Collected shorter poems* (London, Faber and Faber, 1952), p. 191.

15 Astradur Eysteinsson, *The concept of modernism* (Ithaca, NY, Cornell University Press, 1990), p. 8.

16 Once again, the literature in this field is vast. Two key essays on the notion are Harry Levin, 'What was modernism?', in his *Refractions: essays in contemporary literature* (New York, Oxford University Press, 1966) and Raymond Williams, 'When was modernism?', in his *The politics of modernism. Against the new conformists* (London, Verso, 1989). For some other recent explorations, see: M. Calinescu, *Five faces of modernity: modernism, avant-garde, decadence, kitsch, postmodernism* (Durham, NC, Duke University Press, 1987); Frederick Karl, *Modern and modernism: the sovereignty of the artist, 1885–1925* (New York, Atheneum, 1985); Andreas Huyssens, *After the great divide: modernism, mass culture, postmodernism* (Bloomington, IN, Indiana University Press, 1986); Michael H. Levenson, *A Genealogy of modernism: a study of English literary doctrine, 1908–1922* (Cambridge, Cambridge University Press, 1984); Suzanne Clark, *Sentimental modernism. Women writers and the revolution of the word* (Bloomington, IN, Indiana University Press, 1991).

17 T.S. Eliot, 'Ulysses, order and myth', in Frank Kermode (ed.), *Selected prose of T.S. Eliot* (New York, Harcourt Brace Jovanovich, 1975), p. 177; as cited in Eysteinson, *The concept of modernism*, p. 9.

18 M. Bradbury and J. McFarlane, 'The name and nature of modernism', in Bradbury and McFarlane (eds.), *Modernism 1890–1930* (Harmondsworth, Penguin Books, 1976), pp. 27, 29.

19 Eysteinson, *The concept of modernism*, p. 16.

20 In its extreme form, the argument states that 'today modernism negates the notion of tradition itself'. See T.W. Adorno, *Aesthetic theory*, trans. C. Lenhardt (London, Routledge & Kegan Paul, 1984), p. 31. For a neat demolition of this position, see Edward Shils, *Tradition* (Chicago, University of Chicago Press, 1981), pp. 160ff.

21 Wilenski, *The modern movement in art*, p. 165n.

22 David Cannadine, 'War and death, grief and mourning in modern Britain', in J. Whaley (ed.), *Mirrors of mortality. Studies in the social history of death* (London, Europa Publications, 1981), pp. 187–219.

23 For a discussion of melancholy and mourning in the context of postmodernism, see Martin Jay, *Force fields. Between intellectual history and cultural critique* (London, Routledge, 1993), pp. 84–97.

24 For the *locus classicus*, see Benedict Anderson, *Imagined communities. Reflections on the origin and spread of nationalism* (London, Verso, 1983); for some doubts on the usefulness of national boundaries in the study of social history see J.M. Winter, 'Premisses', in J.L. Robert and J.M. Winter, *Paris, London, Berlin. Capital cities at war, 1914–1919* (Cambridge, Cambridge University Press, forthcoming).

25 For the 'brutalizing' effects of the war, see George Mosse, *Fallen soldiers. Reshaping the memory of the world wars* (New York, Oxford University Press, 1990).

26 For a beginning, see J.-J. Becker, Annette Becker, Stéphane Audoin-Rouzeau (eds.), *Guerres et cultures. Vers une histoire comparée de la grande guerre* (Paris, Armand Colin, 1994).

27 Although it is time to put to rest some of the more sweeping judgments of Philippe Ariès, in his *The hour of our death*, trans. H. Weaver (New York, Oxford University Press, 1990), and *Western attitudes towards death*, trans. P.M. Ranum (Baltimore, Johns Hopkins University Press, 1974).

28 See the thoughtful remarks of Antoine Prost, 'Les représentations de la guerre dans la culture française de l'entre-deux-guerres', *Vingtième siècle*, 41 (1994), pp. 23–31.

29 I am grateful to Elisabeth Domansky for discussions on this point.

30 I return to this point in chapter 9, pp. 228–9. For an introduction to the vast literature on Holocaust commemoration, see James E. Young, *The texture of memory. Holocaust memorials and meaning* (New Haven, Yale University Press, 1993); E. Domansky, 'Die gespaltene Erinnerung', in M. Koppen (ed.), *Kunst und Literatur nach Auschwitz* (Berlin, Erich Schmidt Verlag, 1993), pp. 178–96. See also the thoughtful comments in G. Steiner, *Language and silence* (Harmondsworth, Penguin Books, 1979 edn).

31 See the discussion in chapter 9, and Julia Kristeva, *Black sun. Depression and melancholia*, trans. L.S. Roudiez (New York, Columbia University Press, 1989), p. 223.

32 Pierre Nora (ed.), *Les lieux de mémoire* (7 vols., Gallimard, 1984–92).

33 Northrop Frye, *The anatomy of criticism* (Princeton, Princeton University Press, 1957); *Spiritus mundi. Essays on literature, myth and society* (Bloomington, Indiana University Press, 1976), and many other works.

34 See the discussion in chapter 9, pp. 223–6.

1. Homecomings: the return of the dead

1 Bibliothèque de l'Arsenal. Fonds Rondel, A. Gance, 'J'accuse'. See also the book of the film, which appeared three years after its release. A. Gance, *J'accuse. D'après le film* (Paris, La Lampe Merveilleuse, 1922).

2 See Blaise Cendrars, *La main coupée* (Paris, Denoël, 1946), which appeared in English and in abridged form under the unlikely title of *Lice*, trans. by Nina Rootes (London, Peter Owen, 1973). See also Raymond Warnier, 'Blaise Cendrars, voyageur et prophète: évocation de l'ère cubiste', *Marginales*, 16,

78 (1961), pp. 47–50, and Jay Bochner, *Blaise Cendrars: discovery and re-creation* (Toronto, University of Toronto Press, 1978), p. 58.

3 For the same image, see Jean Cocteau, *Thomas l'imposteur* (Paris, Gallimard, 1923), p. 150. Thomas is shot, but says: 'Je suis perdu, si je ne fais pas semblant d'être mort.' The narrator adds: 'Mais, en lui, la fiction et la réalité ne formaient qu'un. Guillaume Thomas était mort.'

4 Oliver Barnard (ed.), *Apollinaire. Selected poems* (London, Anvil Press Poetry, 1986), p. 127.

5 Blaise Cendrars, *Oeuvres complètes* (8 vols., Paris, Denoel, 1964), vol. VIII, pp. 665–71.

6 See chapter 8 for a discussion of Apollinaire's poem 'Ombres', to which Cendrars is clearly referring.

7 Cendrars, *Oeuvres complètes*, vol. VIII, pp. 662–3.

8 Ibid. pp. 663–4.

9 Ibid. p. 664.

10 Ibid. pp. 664–5.

11 Ibid. p. 172.

12 See the painting by J. Galtier-Boissière, *Procession des mutilés de guerre, 14 juillet 1919*, reproduced on the jacket of A. Prost, *Les anciens combattants et la société française 1914–1939* (Paris, Gallimard, 1985).

13 See the wonderful evocation of this issue by Sebastian Japrisot in his recent novel *Une long dimanche de fiançailles* (Paris, Folio, 1993). See also the discussion below in chapter 7.

14 On pilgrimage, see the discussion in chapter 7 below, and David Lloyd, 'Tourism, pilgrimage and the commemoration of the Great War in Great Britain, Australia and Canada, 1919–1939', PhD dissertation, University of Cambridge, 1995.

15 Archives Nationales (AN), F2/2125, Law No. 1588, dated 17 December 1915. See the discussion of this issue in Yves Porcher, *Les jours de guerre. La vie des Français au jour le jour entre 1914 et 1918* (Paris, Plon, 1994), and in Y. Porcher, 'La fouille des champs d'honneur. La sépulture et des soldats de 14–18', *Terrain. Carnets du patrimoine ethnologique*, 20 (1993), pp. 37–56. I am grateful to Yani Sinanoglou for drawing this reference to my attention.

16 AN F2/2125, letter of Fabian Ware, 24.8.16.

17 The return of the unknown soldier reiterated this point about those who were left on the Continent. See the archives of the Commonwealth War Graves Commission, a checklist of which recently has been prepared by Alex King.

18 AN F2/2125 letters of 20 April 1915, 20 July 1915, 3 November 1915 on the difficulties this chapter of civil–military relations caused.

19 AN F2/2125, letters of 6 February and 14 February 1915.

20 AN F2/2125, letter of 21 July 1919, Mayor of Compalay to Prefect of Seine et Marne; see also Report of National Commission on War Cemeteries, p. 2.

21 AN, F2/2125, copy of J. Challarel, 'La question des sépultures militaires', *La Française*, 10 April 1919.

22 'Deux conceptions', *L'art funéraire et commémoratif*, 2 (July 1919). (This journal is cited hereafter as *AFC*.)

23 Anon. 'Echos', *AFC*, 8 (December 1919).

24 As cited in *Bulletin mensuel des veuves et orphelins de la Grande Guerre*, 2

(November–December 1920), p. 2.

25 AN F2/2125, J. Challarel, 'La question des sépultures militaires'; and letter of a group of mothers and widows of Allies to Ministry of Interior, 25 February 1919.

26 AN F2/2125, 31 May 1919 meeting.

27 Octave Aubert, *Louis Barthou* (Paris, Librairie Aristide Quillet 1935).

28 AN F2/2125, meeting of 31 May 1919.

29 AN F2/2125, instruction of 18 June 1919.

30 AN F2/2125, instruction of 10 September 1919.

31 Anon., 'Deux conceptions', *AFC*, 2 (July 1919).

32 Anon., 'Les morts de la guerre', *AFC*, 8 (December 1919).

33 'Atavisme', *AFC*, 8 (December 1919).

34 *Souvenirs et fraternité*, 4 (May 1920).

35 See the *Bulletin de l'union des pères et des mères dont les fils sont morts pour la patrie*, especially 5 (December 1918).

36 J. Gaillardin, 'Le transfert des corps de combattants', *AFC*, 3 (July 1919); Les marchands de la mort', *AFC*, 5 (August 1919).

37 Anon., 'Après 18 mois d'efforts', *AFC*, 20 (December 1920), p. 1; Ministère des pensions, des primes et des allocations de guerre, *Rapport au President de la République Française*, in *Journal officiel*, 2 October 1920, pp. 14644–7.

38 AN F2/2125, letter of Maginot to Ministry of Interior, authorizing the transfer of bodies, 25 May 1921; and 'Organization of the service for the return of bodies', Ministry of Pensions instructions, 1921.

39 Anon., 'Pour les victimes glorieuses de la grande guerre', *AFC*, 33 (January 1922). In 1921, 39,000 bodies were transferred; in 1922, 265,425 applications were made. It is unclear how many actual transfers took place, but 300,000 is a plausible approximation.

40 Anon., 'Le scandale des exhumations', *AFC*, 33 (January 1922).

41 Chillingly recounted in a later setting in the recent French novel of Jean Rovaud, *Champ d'honneur* (Paris, Les Editions de Minuit, 1990), which won the Prix Goncourt in the year of its publication.

42 'Allocution du Général Président', *Souvenir français*, 30 (June 1923), p. 87.

43 George Mosse, *Fallen soldiers* (New York, Oxford University Press, 1990).

44 I am grateful to Ken Inglis for advice on this point. See P. Longworth, *The unending vigil* (London, Constable, 1967); and James M. Mayo, *War memorials as political landscape: the American experience and beyond* (New York, Praeger, 1984).

45 Mosse, *Fallen soldiers*, pp. 94–8; Cannadine, 'War and death, grief and mourning in modern Britain', p. 214.

46 Prost, *Les anciens combattants*.

47 Ken Inglis, 'Entombing unknown soldiers: from London and Paris to Baghdad', *History and Memory*, 5 (1993), pp. 7–31. Inglis' work in this field is indispensable.

48 On the Australian War Memorial, see Ken Inglis, 'A sacred place: the making of the Australian War Memorial', *War & Society*, 3, 2 (1985), pp. 99–125. On the 1993 ceremony, see Ken Inglis, 'The rite stuff', *Eureka Street*, 4 (1994), pp. 23–7.

49 Not only in Germany. How to mark the spot where the last of the Paris

Communards were lined up and shot at the end of the suppression of the Paris Commune has raised the same kinds of problem. See M. Reberioux, 'La commune', in Pierra Nora (ed.), *Les lieux de mémoire* (Paris, Gallimard, 1984), pp. 614–49. The literature on the contested commemoration of the Vietnam war is growing rapidly. See J.C. Scruggs and J.L. Swerdlow, *To heal a nation. The Vietnam Veterans' Memorial* (New York, Praeger, 1985), and V. Scully, *Architecture: the natural and the man-made* (New York, St Martin's Press, 1991).

50 Mosse, *Fallen soldiers*, chapter 4; Inglis, 'Entombing unknown soldiers'; R. Kosseleck, 'Bilderverbot. Welches Totengedenken?', *Frankfurter Allgemeine Zeitung*, 8 April 1993.

2. Communities in mourning

1 I am grateful to Ken Inglis for discussions on this point. The literature on this subject is vast. For a start, see the classics: Sigmund Freud, 'Mourning and melancholia', in *Collected papers*, trans. by Joan Riviere (London, Hogarth Press, 1950), vol. IV, pp. 152–70; M. Klein, 'Mourning and its relationship to manic-depressive states', *International Journal of Psychoanalysis*, 21 (1940), pp. 125–53; J. Bowlby, 'Processes of mourning', *International Journal of Psychoanalysis*, 42 (1961), pp. 317–40; J. Bowlby, 'Pathological mourning and childhood mourning', *Journal of the American Psychoanalytic Association*, 11 (1963), pp. 500–41. For syntheses see C.M. Parkes, *Bereavement. Studies of grief in adult life* (London, Tavistock Publications, 1972); C.M. Parkes and R.S. Weiss, *Recovery from bereavement* (New York, Basic Books, 1983); G. Gorer, *Death, grief and mourning in contemporary Britain* (London, Cresset, 1965); B. Schoenberg, I. Gruber, A. Wiener, and A.H. Kutscher (eds.), *Bereavement: its psychosocial aspects* (New York, Columbia University Press, 1975); Mardi J. Horowitz, 'A model of mourning: change in schemas of self and other', *Journal of the American Psychoanalytic Association*, 38, 2 (1990), pp. 297–324.

2 Meyer Fortes, *Kinship and the social order. The legacy of Lewis Henry Morgan* (Chicago, Aldine, 1969), pp. 241, 251, 110, 123, 239. For the distinction between blood kinship, fictive kinship, and figurative kinship, see Julian Pitt-Rivers, 'The kith and the kin', in J. Goody (ed.), *The character of kinship* (Cambridge, Cambridge University Press, 1973). For other approaches to the subject, see Ernest Gellner, 'Ideal language and kinship structure', *Philosophy of Science*, 24 (1957), pp. 235–41; Rodney Needham, 'Descent systems and ideal language', *Philosophy of Science*, 27 (1960), pp. 96–101; Gellner, 'The concept of kinship', *Philosophy of Science*, 27 (1960), pp. 187–204; Maurice Bloch, 'The moral and tactical meaning of kinship terms', *Man*, 6 (1971), pp. 79–87. I am grateful to Barbara Bodenhorn for drawing my attention to these references.

3 Jacques Garmier, *Hommage à mon ombre* (Macon, Protat Frères, 1916), pp. 11, 21.

4 Jane Catulle-Mendès, *La prière sur l'enfant mort*, as cited in Françoise Thébaud, 'La guerre et le deuil chez les femmes françaises', in J.-J. Becker, A. Becker, and S. Audoin-Rouzeau (eds.), *Guerre et cultures* (Paris, Armand Colin, 1994), pp. 103–11, esp. p. 108.

5 Pierre-Jakez Helias, *Le cheval d'orgueil. Mémoires d'un Breton du pays bigoudin* (Paris, Plon, 1975), pp. 8–9. See also the reference to the sad announcement in J. Giono, *Le grand troupeau* (Paris, Gallimard, 1931), discussed in chapter 7.

6 Harold Owen, *Journey from obscurity* (Oxford, Oxford University Press, 1968), pp. 232–4.

7 Imperial War Museum, Wakeman Papers 67/305/1 (hereafter WP), Malcolm Wakeman to Captain E.F. Falkner, recruiting officer, Town Hall, Manchester, 2.3.17.

8 WP, Malcolm Wakeman to parents, 24.7.18; 10.8.18; 17.8.18.

9 WP, Malcolm Wakeman to parents, 1.10.18.

10 WP, cables dated 6.10.18 and 7.10.18; the time of receipt identified from Miss Waken to Mrs Pierce, 8.10.18.

11 WP, Wakeman to G. Hickling, 22.10.18.

12 WP, Wakeman to Mrs Pierce, 10.10.18.

13 WP, cable, Wakeman to family 'Malcolm cheerful. Home tomorrow. Wakeman.'

14 WP, Mrs Wakeman to Wakeman, 17.10.18 and 18.10.18.

15 WP, Wakeman to F.W. Anthony, 22.10.18; Wakeman to Marion Kate Winser, 23.10.18.

16 WP, cable 1.10.18.

17 WP, Wakeman to Couther, 22.10.18.

18 WP, Chaplain Beadle to Wakeman, 21.10.18.

19 WP, letter of Wakeman to Air Ministry 29.10.18, 5.11.18, 4.12.18, 29.12.18.

20 WP, Wakeman to Air Ministry, 16.12.18, 31.12.18; Air Ministry to Wakeman, 30.12.18, 27.1.19.

21 WP, Mrs Pierce to Wakeman, 7.11.18; Mrs Helen Eright to Wakeman, 19.10.18; Hilda Trotter to Wakeman, 23.10.18.

22 WP, Wakeman to Private W.R. Osborn, 29.10.18.

23 WP, Sister Alice Collinge to Wakeman, 21.11.18.

24 Imperial War Museum, A.S. Lloyd papers, R. Julian Yeatman to Mrs Lloyd, 10.8.16.

25 For full information, see the data-base prepared by Peter Dennis and Jeff Grey of the Australian Defence Forces Academy, Canberra.

26 This was not the case in Britain, where the cable came unadorned. I am grateful to Michael McKernan of the Australian War Memorial for help on this point.

27 The examples are legion in both the Imperial War Museum and Australian War Memorial collections.

28 For further support in the French case for the argument that front and home front were closely linked, see Stéphane Audoin-Rouzeau, *Men at war. Trench journalism and national sentiment in France 1914–1918*, trans. H. McPhail (Oxford, Berg, 1992).

29 Mortlock Library of South Australia, Adelaide. Red Cross papers (hereafter RCPA), SRG 76/32, Papers on establishment of Australian Red Cross Society Information Bureau, suggestion of Mr Hackett, n.d.

30 On the earlier history of the Red Cross, see R. Durand and J. Meurant (eds.), *Préludes et pionniers. Les précurseurs de la Croix-Rouge 1840–1860* (Geneva, Société Henry Dunant, 1991). I am grateful to F.B. Smith for drawing my

attention to this collection. See also P. Boissier, *Histoire du Comité international de la Croix-Rouge. Vol. I: De Solférino à Tsoushima* (Paris, Plon, 1963); André Durand, *Histoire du Comité international de la Croix-Rouge. Vol. II: De Sarajevo à Hiroshima* (Geneva, Institut Henry-Dunant, 1978); Geoffrey Best, *Humanity in warfare* (London, Hutchinson, 1980).

31 Australian War Memorial, Canberra. Red Cross papers (hereafter RCPC) 1 DRL/428, Report of the work of the Australian Red Cross, January 1917, p. 19.

32 RCPC, 1 DRL/428, Miss L.A. Whybrow to the editor, *British Australasian*, 23.4.19.

33 RCPC, 1 DRL/428, Australian Wounded and Missing Inquiry Bureau, Report, 1–21 November 1916.

34 RCPC, 1 DRL/428, Report for 1916–17.

35 RCPC, 1 DRL/428, Deakin to Lieutenant Colonel Scott, 56th Bn AIF, 9.8.17.

36 RCPC, 1 DRL/428, Major Brambury to Deakin, 15.9.16.

37 RCPC, 1 DRL/428, Deakin to Miss Schofield, sister in charge, 20th Casualty Clearing Station, BEF, 25.7.18.

38 RCPC, 1 DRL/427, Mrs G. Marriott to Miss Whybrow, 29.4.19.

39 RCPC, 1 DRL/428, L. Owen to Vera Deakin, 23.11.17.

40 RCPC, 1 DRL/428, file on Corporal C.T. Owen, 1916.

41 RCPA, Call to the legal profession, 26.10.15.

42 RCPC, 53/6, files of missing men, J.A. Briggs.

43 RCPC, 53/6, files of missing soldiers, S.C. Allen and R.B. Allen, letter of Stephen Allen to mother, 8.7.16.

44 RCPC, 53/6, file on Allen brothers, Captain Wills to Mrs Allen, 1.3.17.

45 RCPC, 53/6, file on Allen brothers, Will Hale, Wogga Wogga, to Miss Allen, 16.6.17.

46 RCPC, 53/6 file on Allen brothers, Sergeant Assenheim to Mrs Allen, 28.6.17.

47 RCPC, 53/6, file on Allen brothers, Charles Fry to Miss Allen, 5.2.18.

48 RCPA, SRG 76/1/2432, file on Corporal K.C. Moore.

49 RCPA, SRG 76/1/6776, file on F.L. Donnelly.

50 RCPA, SRG 76/1/36–9, file on L. Marks.

51 RCPA, SRG 76/1/36–9, file on J.R. Skinner.

52 RCPA, SRG 76/1/36–9 file on D. James.

53 RCPC, 53/6, file on E.S. Brown, cable of 17.8.15 to Revd Newmark.

54 RCPC, 53/6, file on E.S. Brown, Major Gallagher to Mrs Brown, 21.8.15.

55 RCPC, 53/6, file on E.S. Brown, Gerald Campbell to Mrs Brown, 24.9.15.

56 RCPC, 53/6, file on Lieutenant Colonel E.S. Brown. Clippings and letters collected by E.N. Watter.

57 A pine tree exists next to the Australian War Memorial in Canberra, grown from the seeds of a cone sent home to his mother by a soldier at Gallipoli.

58 RCPA, SRG 76/32, Papers of South Australian Red Cross, letter of Agnes Rigney to Sir Josiah Symon, 28.9.15.

59 RCPA, SRG 76/32, letters of Mrs Snell to Symon, 4.12.15; 19.4.16; Agnes Rigney to Symon, 28.9.15; Mrs Donaldson to Symon, 27.11.17.

60 RCPA, 76/1/4797, file on Frederick William Dumont.

61 RCPC, 55/4, prisoner-of-war files, files on E.H. Dowd. This file is typical of thousands of others in this invaluable collection.

62 RCPC, 55/4, prisoner-of-war files, file on E.H. Dowd.

63 RCPC, 55/4, prisoner-of-war files, file on T.H. Dowell, Dowell to Chomley, 2.3.17.

64 RCPC, 55/4, prisoner-of-war files, file on T.H. Dowell, Amy McFarlane to Australian Red Cross, 20.6.18.

65 RCPC, 55/4, prisoner-of-war files, file on T.H. Dowell, Chomley to Private P. O'Connor.

66 RCPC, 55/4, prisoner-of-war files, file on T.H. Dowell, Chomley to Dowell, 25.4.18.

67 RCPC, 55/4, prisoner-of-war files, file on T.H. Dowell, Chomley to (brother) F.E. Dowell, 16.12.18.

68 RCPC, 55/4, prisoner-of-war files, files on A.C. Down, died of wounds 9.10.18.

69 RCPC, 55/4, prisoner-of-war files, file on C.P. Down.

70 See note 2 on p. 235.

71 AWM 164, Roll of Honour forms, obituary of Charles Berg.

72 AWM 164, form on Robert Rae, letter of Elizabeth Grace to Hayes, 28.9.40, addressed: 54a Kennington Rd, Lambeth.

73 First and foremost, in a magisterial manner, by Prost, *Les anciens combattants*; R. Whalen, *Bitter wounds. German victims of the Great War 1914–1939* (Ithaca, NY, Cornell University Press, 1984); Graham Wootton, *The politics of influence. British ex-servicemen, Cabinet decisions and cultural change (1917–57)* (London, Routledge, 1963); G. Wootton, *The official history of the British Legion* (London, Macdonald & Evans, 1956); Charles Kimbell, 'The ex-service movement in England and Wales, 1916–1930', PhD thesis, Stanford University, 1990.

74 AN, Paris, F7/13243, files on Associations des mutilés et victimes de guerre.

75 Sophie Delaporte, 'Les blessés de la face de la grande guerre', MA thesis, Jules Verne Université de Picardie, 1992.

76 See the rhetoric presented and analysed by A. Prost in *In the wake of war. Anciens combattants and French society 1914–1940*, trans. H. MacPhail (Oxford, Berg, 1992).

77 See the file on Vidal in AN, F7/13243, and report of lecture at Marseilles, 18 May 1919.

78 AN, F7, 13243, Vidal, 'Pour les veuves de guerre', *Le Pays*, 1.6.19.

79 AN, F7, 13243, report of meeting in Nancy 21.4.16.

80 See the discussion in chapter 1.

81 AN, F7, 13243, figures from *Liberté*, 31.7.23.

82 Calculations based on Winter, *The Great War and the British people*, chapter 8.

83 AWM 164, form for K.S. Williams.

84 IWM, papers of J. Bennett, 83/14/1, note of Mrs Estelle Perrett, 1.2.88.

85 D. Thompson, 'The poor law and the elderly in England, 1850–1900', PhD dissertation, University of Cambridge, 1980.

86 Susan Pedersen, 'Social policy and the reconstruction of the family in Britain and France, 1900–1945', PhD dissertation, Harvard University, 1989.

87 See Harriet Jackson, 'Widows and pensions in France 1870–1940', PhD thesis, New York University, forthcoming. See also Theda Skocpol, *Protecting soldiers and mothers: the political origins of social policy in the United States* (Cambridge, MA, Harvard University Press, 1992) for comments on the earlier impact of the US civil war on subsequent welfare measures.

88 Jeffrey Lerner, 'The public and private management of death in Britain,

1890–1930', PhD dissertation, Columbia University, 1981, tables 2–3, pp. 233, 235.

89 Whalen, *Bitter wounds*, p. 76.

90 Ibid. p. 131.

91 J. Cole, 'Demobilization', in Robert and Winter, *Paris, London, Berlin*, chapter 7.

92 IWM, Claydon papers, note of Len Wade on father-in-law Private Albert Claydon.

93 See the forthcoming University of Cambridge MLitt dissertation of Ingrid James, 'Widows and widows' pensions in Britain during and after the First World War'.

94 T. Bonzon, 'Transfer payments', in Robert and Winter, *Paris, London, Berlin*, ch. 10.

95 Thébaud, 'La guerre et le deuil', p. 10.

96 Whalen, *Bitter wounds*, p. 77.

97 E. Hilmer Smith, *History of the Legacy Club of Sydney* (Sydney, Waite and Bull, 1944), p. xi.

98 Mark Lyons, *Legacy. The first fifty years* (Clayton, VI, Lothian, 1978), pp. 14–15.

99 Bean, in Smith, *Legacy Club of Sydney*, p. xiii.

100 Smith, *Legacy Club of Sydney*, 'Year 1926–7', pp. 6–15.

101 Ibid. pp. 25, 35.

102 Lyons, *Legacy*, p. xiv; see also M.H. Ellis, *The torch. A picture of legacy* (Sydney, Angus and Robertson, 1957).

103 AWM 164, letter of Mrs Rebecca Hinds to Hayes, 22.10.41.

104 AWM 164, form of Harry Richard Aiken, letter of Mrs Aiken to Hayes, 6.3.40.

105 See the Wakeman papers in the IWM for details on this point.

106 IWM, A.S. Lloyd papers, Manning poem, July/August 1917; Manning to Mrs Lloyd 23.11.18.

107 IWM, Wakeman papers 67/305/1, The St Barnabas Hostels, *How to reach 'the Hallowed Areas' in France and Belgium*, 1923.

108 Wakeman papers, *How to reach 'the Hallowed Areas'*, pp. 4–11.

109 Lloyd, 'Tourism, pilgrimage and the commemoration of the Great War'.

110 AWM archives, Longstaff clippings, 'Great War picture', *Hobart Mercury*, 20 November 1929, and Will Longstaff, *The Menin Gate at Midnight* (n.d.), text in AWM, Canberra. I am grateful to Marie Wood for her help in tracing these references.

111 On Desvallières, see Jean-Philippe Rey, 'Desvallières et la guerre de 1914–1918', *Bulletin de la société historique de l'art français* (1988), pp. 197–211. Found, through the kindness of Annette Becker, in the library of the Centre Georges Pompidou in Paris.

112 I am grateful to Annette Becker for drawing this work to my attention. It is discussed in her *La guerre et la foi* (Paris, Armand Colin, 1994), pp. 128ff.

3. Spiritualism and the 'Lost Generation'

1 On Britain see: A. Wilkinson, *The Church of England and the First World War* (London, SPCK, 1978); S. Mews, 'Religion and English society in the First World War', PhD dissertation, University of Cambridge, 1973; A. Marrin,

The Church of England in the First World War (Raleigh, NC, 1974); K.W. Clements, 'Baptists and the outbreak of the First World War', *Baptist Quarterly* (April 1975). On France, see N.-J. Chaline (ed.), *Chrétiens dans la première guerre mondiale* (Paris, Cerf, 1993); J. Fontana, *Les catholiques français pendant la grande guerre* (Paris, Les éditions du Cerf, 1990); G. Cholvy and Y.-M. Hilaire, *Histoire religieuse de la France contemporaine 1880/1930* (Paris, Privat, 1986); J. Le Goff and R. Rémond (eds.), *Histoire de la France religieuse*, vol. IV (Paris, Seuil, 1993); J.-M. Mayeur, 'Le catholicisme français et la première guerre mondiale', and D. Robert, 'Les Protestants français et la guerre de 1914–1918', both in *Francia* (1974). On Germany, see J.A. Moses, 'State, war, revolution and the German Evangelical Church, 1914–18', *Journal of Religious Studies*, 17 (1992), pp. 47–59); J. Jenkins, 'War, theology, 1914 and Germany's *Sonderweg*: Luther's heirs and patriotism', *Journal of Religious History*, 16 (June 1989), pp. 292–310; D.R. Borg, *The Old Prussian Church and the Weimar Republic: a study in political adjustment, 1917–1927* (Hanover, NH, University Press of New England, 1984); Karl Hammer, 'Der deutsche Protestantismus und der Erste Weltkrieg', *Francia*, 2 (1974), pp. 398–414; and Richard van Dülmen, 'Der deutsche Katholizismus und der Erste Weltkrieg', *Francia*, 2 (1974), pp. 347–76.

2 This gap has been filled recently for France. See Annette Becker, *La guerre et la foi* and Chaline (ed.), *Chrétiens dans la première guerre mondiale*.

3 See Nicole Edelman, 'L'histoire du spiritisme en France 1850–1914', State thesis, Université de Paris-VII (1992); and Alex Owen, *The darkened room. Women, power and spiritualism in late nineteenth century England* (Cambridge, Cambridge University Press, 1989).

4 L. Barrow, *Independent spirits. Spiritualism and English plebeians, 1850–1910* (London, Routledge, 1986).

5 N. Edelman, 'Les tables tournantes arrivent en France', *L'Histoire*, 75 (1985), pp. 16–23; and N. Edelman, 'Allan Kardec, prophète du spiritisme', *L'Histoire*, 98 (1987), pp. 62–9.

6 Marion Aubrée and François Laplantine, *La table, le livre et les esprits* (Paris, J.C. Lattes, 1990), pp. 87–8.

7 J. Pierrot, *The decadent imagination 1880–1900*, trans. D. Koltman (Chicago, University of Chicago Press, 1981).

8 Aubrée and Laplantine, *La table*, pp. 47–8.

9 *Revue spirite* (January 1913), p. 6.

10 Ibid. pp. 2–6.

11 On provincial spiritualism, see the forthcoming PhD theses of Lynn Sharp (University of California, Irvine) on France and of Jenny Hazlegrove (University of Melbourne) on Britain.

12 See Barrow, *Independent spirits*.

13 R. Haynes, *The society for psychical research 1882–1982. A history* (London, Macdonald, 1982), pp. 183–94; J. Oppenheim, *The other world. Spiritualism and psychical research in England, 1850–1914* (Cambridge, Cambridge University Press, 1984).

14 I.V. Hull, *The entourage of Kaiser Wilhelm II, 1888–1918* (Cambridge, Cambridge University Press, 1982); J.C.G. Röhl and N. Sombart (eds.), *Kaiser Wilhelm II. New interpretations* (Cambridge, Cambridge University Press, 1982).

15 On European spiritualism and theosophy, see the discussion in chapter 6, pp. 146–53, and S. Ringbom, *The sounding cosmos. A study of the spiritualism of Kandinsky and the genesis of abstract painting*. Acta academiae Aboensis, Series A, Humaniora, vol. 38, no. 2 (Abo, Abo Akademi, 1970), pp. 50–3.

16 T. Mann, *The magic mountain*, trans. H.T. Lowe-Porter (New York, Alfred Knopf, 1980 edn), pp. 653–81, citations at pp. 709, 715.

17 D. Cannadine, 'War and death, grief and mourning in modern Britain', in J. Whaley (ed.), *Mirrors of mortality* (London, Europa Publications, 1981), p. 227.

18 L. Lambert, 'Les mystères d'Outre-Tombe', *Art funéraire et commémoratif*, 12 (April 1920); see also Aubre and Laplantine, *La table*, p. 274.

19 Kevin, I. Jones, *Conan Doyle and the spirits. The spiritualist career of Sir Arthur Conan Doyle* (Wellingborough, Aquarium, 1989), pp. 109, 129, 131.

20 Ibid. p. 111.

21 Ibid. p. 114.

22 Ibid. p. 131.

23 Ibid. p. 131.

24 Ibid. p. 122.

25 A. Conan Doyle, *The history of spiritualism* (London, Cassell, 1926), vol. I, p. 226.

26 A. Conan Doyle, *The new revelation and the vital message* (London, Hodder & Stoughton, 1919), preface and pp. 77–8.

27 K.I. Jones, *Conan Doyle*, p. 117.

28 Ibid. p. 117.

29 R. Brandon, *The spiritualists. The passion for the occult in the nineteenth and twentieth centuries* (London, Weidenfeld & Nicolson, 1983), pp. 168–9. I am grateful to Ken Inglis for telling me about his Australian tour, some echoes of which are to be found in the archives of the Australian War Memorial in Canberra.

30 J. Arthur Hill (ed.), *Letters from Sir Oliver Lodge. Psychical, religious, scientific, personal* (London, Cassell, 1932), letter of 31 August 1923, p. 181.

31 For this episode, see the clippings in the Australian War Memorial archives, Canberra, on Longstaff. The exchange between Longstaff and Conan Doyle was noted in 'A strange picture', *Sydney Morning Herald*, 3 November 1928; 'Art and the occult', *Melbourne Age*, 13 February 1929.

32 I am grateful to David Lloyd for drawing this point to my attention.

33 'Will Longstaff', *Hobart Mail*, 11 September 1929. See also Anna Gray, 'Will Longstaff's *Menin Gate at Midnight*', *Journal of the Australian War Memorial*, 12 (1988), pp. 64–78.

34 Oliver J. Lodge, *Past years. An autobiography* (London, Hodder & Stoughton, 1931), p. 187.

35 For example, his two articles 'Personal appearances of the departed' and 'Effects of light on long ether waves and other processes', *Journal of the Society for Psychical Research*, 18 (February–March 1918), pp. 32–4 and 213–20.

36 R. Blatchford, 'My testimony', in Sir James Marchant (ed.), *Life after death according to Christianity and spiritualism* (London, Cassell, 1925), p. 118.

37 Oliver J. Lodge, *Raymond or life and death. With examples of the evidence for survival of memory and affection after death* (London, Methuen, 1916), p. 128 (for Mrs Leonard).

38 *Raymond*, p. 85.

39 Ibid. p. 99; Eustace Miles, 'Britain beyond the grave', *Occult Review*, 23, 1 (January 1918), p. 39, as cited in D. Jarrett, *The sleep of reason. Fantasy and reality from the Victorian age to the First World War* (London, Weidenfeld & Nicolson, 1988), p. 196.

40 C. Richet, *Thirty years of psychical research. Being a treatise on metaphysics*, trans. by S. de Brath (London, W. Collins Sons, 1923), pp. 216, 610.

41 Charles A. Mercier, *Spiritualism and Sir Oliver Lodge* (London, Mental Culture Enterprise, 1917), pp. 4, 5, 6, 10.

42 Viscount Halifax, *'Raymond'. Some criticisms* (London, A.R. Mowbray, 1917), pp. 7, 11, 12, 39, 41.

43 K.I. Jones, *Conan Doyle*, p. 132.

44 J.N. Figgis, *Hopes for English religion* (London, Longman, Green & Co., 1919), pp. 181–2, 183.

45 See chapter 5, pp. 119–22.

46 See Yves Villeneuve, 'Marraines de guerre', *Frères d'armes* (1 July, 15 July, 1 August, 15 October 1917). This series of articles was later published as a book. See also the same author's 'Vivons pour nos morts de la guerre', *Frères d'armes* (15 November 1919).

47 Lucien Roure, 'Superstitions du front de guerre', *Etudes*, 153 (1917), p. 727.

48 W.D. Geare, *Letters of an army chaplain* (London, W. Gardner, 1918), p. 84; D. MacFadyen, *Our mess: mess table talks in France* (London, W. Westall & Co., 1920), pp. 124–6. I am grateful to Laurinda Stryker for drawing these references to my attention.

49 F.W. Worlsey, *Letters to Mr Britling* (London, R. Scott, 1917), p. 69.

50 G.K.A. Studdard Kennedy, *The hardest part* (London, Hodder & Stoughton, 1918), pp. 185–7.

51 B. Mathews (ed.), *Christ: and the world at war* (London, James Clarke & Co., 1917), p. 42.

52 T.W. Pym and G. Gordon, *Papers from Picardy by two chaplains* (London, Constable, 1917), pp. 188, 201, 202.

53 All citations from W. Deonna, 'La recrudescence des superstitions en temps de guerre et les statues à clous', *L'anthropologie*, 27 (1916), pp. 243–68.

54 Roure, 'Superstitions', p. 719.

55 The Département de la Somme has some splendid examples in its collection for the Historial de la grande guerre. In France, the business of providing plastic Virgin Marys, ivory coloured, gold or silver-leafed, flourished during the war. See for example advertisements in the *Almanach de la propagation des Trois 'Ave Maria'* (1918).

56 I am grateful to Joanna Bourke for bringing this point (and some splendid examples) to my attention. On Continental Catholic popular piety, see chapter 5 above and David Blackbourn, *Populists and patricians. Essays in modern German history* (London, Allen & Unwin, 1987), esp. chapter 9.

57 See Annette Becker, *La guerre et la foi*; G. Krumeich, *Jeanne d'Arc à travers l'histoire* (Paris, Albin Michel, 1993), and in general, S. Wilson (ed.), *Saints and their cults. Studies in religious sociology, folklore and history* (Cambridge, Cambridge University Press, 1983).

58 *Almanach de la propagation des Trois 'Ave Maria'* (1917), pp. 73, 85.

59 C. Richet, 'Les evénéments psychiques de la guerre. Un appel de M. Charles

Richet aux soldats. '"Avez-vous des pressentiments?"', *Annales des sciences psychiques* (October, November, December 1916), pp. 185–92; and C. Richet, 'L'enquête du prof. Richet sur les faits psychiques de la guerre', *Annales des Sciences Psychiques* (January 1917), p. 21.

60 Richet, 'L'enquête', pp. 18ff.

61 Hereward Carrington, *Psychical phenomena and the war* (New York, Dodd, Mead & Co., 1919), pp. 175ff.

62 Carrington, *Psychical phenomena*, pp. 245–6. See also the tale of a mother informed by the spirit of her dead son that he 'was being well looked after' in a hospital where people spoke a different language from his own. The wounded man couldn't write, but got the message through just the same. M. Maeterlinck, *The wrack of the storm*, trans. by A. Teixeira de Mattos (London, Methuen, 1916), pp. 180ff. For similar messages of hope, see F.B. Bond, *The hill of vision* (Boston, Marshall Jones, 1919) and his *Love beyond the veil. An echo of the Great War* (London, Cassell, 1924).

63 Léon Denis, 'A Père Lachaise', *Revue spirite* (April 1918). The link between the living and the dead was made apparent by the note in the July 1918 issue of the same journal that a spiritualist crèche had been established in Paris. Léon Denis, 'Sursum, corda', *Revue spirite* (July 1918).

64 Eric J. Leed, *No man's land. Combat and identity in World War I* (Cambridge, Cambridge University Press, 1979).

65 Arthur Machen, *The bowmen and other legends of the war* (New York, G.P. Putnam's Sons, 1915), pp. 11–12, 66.

66 Harold Begbie, *On the side of the angels. The story of the angel at Mons. An answer to 'The Bowmen'* (London, Hodder & Stoughton, 1915), pp. 21–44.

67 Anon., 'Notes of the month', *Occult Review*, 22, 1 (July 1915), pp. 7–10.

68 Phyllis Campbell, *Back of the front* (London, George Newnes, 1916), pp. 31–2, 84–5, 94, 98, 100, 112–13, 119. See also her article 'The angelic leaders', *Occult Review*, 22, 2 (August 1915), pp. 76–82. For a similar French view of 'invisible forces' helping the Allies, see anon., 'La justice dans la guerre actuelle', *Revue Spirite* (August–September 1915), p. 450.

69 Ford Madox Ford, 'Arms and the mind', *Esquire*, 94 (December 1980), p. 80, as cited in Hynes, *A war imagined*, p. 106.

70 Lieutenant George Goddard, 'Orthodoxy and the war', *Occult Review*, 27, 2 (February 1918), p. 84.

71 For two examples among many, see J.S.M. Ward, *Gone west* (London, W. Rider & Son, 1919), and his *A subaltern in spirit land. A sequel to 'Gone west'* (London, W. Rider & Son, 1920). Another well-known example is the appearance of the ghost of Wilfred Owen to his brother in November 1918. See D. Hibberd, *Wilfred Owen: the last year, 1917–1918* (London, Constable, 1992), p. 123. (See p. 31 above.)

72 Léon Denis, 'L'avenir du spiritisme', *Revue spirite* (November 1918), p. 324.

73 Julian Laroche, 'Le retour des vainqueurs', *Revue spirite* (February 1919), p. 62.

74 See pp. 133 ff.

75 E.H. Jones, *The road to En-dor, being an account of how two prisoners of war at Yozgad in Turkey won their way to freedom* (London, Bodley Head, 1919), p. 288. I am grateful to Professor Malcolm Lyons for drawing this book to my attention.

76 Ibid. p. 139n.

77 Ibid. pp. x–xi.
78 Ibid. p. 44.
79 Ibid. pp. 87, 90.
80 Ibid. p. 270.
81 Ibid. p. 206.
82 Ibid. p. 285n.
83 Mosse, *Fallen soldiers*.
84 On Kipling and the war, see Frank Field, *British and French writers of the First World War. Comparative studies in cultural history* (Cambridge, Cambridge University Press, 1991), pp. 153–76.
85 The two stories may be found in C. Raine's edition of *Kipling's prose* (London, Faber, 1987), pp. 369–81, and 404–12.
86 See the strikingly similar story of a woman's ghost coming to fetch a soldier about to be killed in Elliott O'Donnell, 'Hauntings in Belgium', *Occult Review*, 21, 4 (April 1915), pp. 223–31.
87 J.M. Winter, *The Great War and the British people*, chapter 9.
88 Fussell, *The Great War and modern memory*.
89 See chapter 6, p. 151, and anon., 'The Ghost in the machine', *Observer*, 6 February 1989.
90 British Library, Barlow Collection, Cup. 407.a.1, E.J. Dingwall, 'Psychic photography', introduction, p. 6; and E. Stead, 'Faces of the living dead', exhibition catalogue. I am grateful to Joanna Bourke for telling me of this valuable collection.
91 Air Marshal Lord Dowding was one of them, claiming to have spoken with fallen pilots during and after the Battle of Britain. See Louis Pauwels and Guy Breton, *Nouvelles histoires extraordinaires* (Paris, Albin Michel, 1982), pp. 111–30. In more recent years, Arthur Koestler and the Cambridge Nobel prize-winner Brian Josephson have helped to keep the tradition alive.
92 *André Breton. La beauté convulsive* (Paris, Centre Georges Pompidou, 1991, exhibition catalogue); and S. Stich, *Anxious visions. Surrealist art* (Berkeley, University of California Press, 1991).
93 Stich, *Anxious visions*, p. 236.
94 See Sarah O'Brien-Twohig, *Max Beckmann's carnival* (The Tate Gallery, Liverpool, 1991).
95 See especially Kiefer's remarkable installation 'The creation of the universe', in the St Louis Museum of Art.

4. War memorials and the mourning process

1 Antoine Prost, 'Les monuments aux morts', in P. Nora (ed.), *Les lieux de mémoire*. Vol. I. *La République* (Paris, Gallimard, 1984), pp. 195–225.
2 Mosse, *Fallen soldiers*.
3 J. Gildea, *For remembrance and in honour of those who lost their lives in the South African War 1899–1902* (London, Eyre & Spottiswode, 1911).
4 G. Mosse, *The nationalization of the masses* (New York: Howard Fertig, 1985).
5 M. Ignatieff, 'Soviet war memorials', *History Workshop*, 17 (1984), pp. 157–63.
6 K. Inglis, 'World War One memorials in Australia', *Guerres mondiales et*

Conflits Contemporains, 167 (1992), pp. 51–8.

7 A. Borg, *War memorials from antiquity to the present* (London: Leo Cooper, 1991). See also the forthcoming PhD dissertation of Catherine Moriarty (University of Sussex) and the 1993 PhD disseration of Alex King (University College, London).

8 Imperial War Museum, clippings on local war memorials in Poplar and Stepney. See in particular the *East London Observer*, 25 August 1917 for the discussion of one such shrine on Prescillar Road. I am grateful to Catherine Moriarty for drawing these records to my attention.

9 Modris Eksteins, *Rites of spring* (New York, Bantam Books, 1989) is full of insights on this and many other points.

10 A. Wilkinson, *The Church of England and the First World War* (London, SPCK, 1978), p. 178. Whether or not churchmen were claiming credit for something begun by their parishioners is a moot point. I am grateful to Ken Inglis for drawing this reference to my attention.

11 Inglis, 'World War One memorials in Australia'.

12 Gaynor Kavanagh, 'Museum as memorial: the origins of the Imperial War Museum', *Journal of Contemporary History*, 23 (1988), pp. 77–97; Borg, *War memorials*, p. 140; Charles Ffoulkes, *Arms and the tower* (London, John Murray, 1939).

13 'Un musée de la guerre', *Tacatacteufteuf*, 5 (1 June 1917).

14 *Aussie*, 16 February 1918, as cited in Ken Inglis, 'A sacred place: the making of the Australian War Memorial', *War & Society*, 3, 2 (1985), p. 100.

15 R. Frank, 'Eine bitte', *Mitteilungen von Ihrer Firma und Ihren Kollegen* (Stuttgart, n.p., 13 November 1915). I am grateful for the help of Irina Rens on this and many other points.

16 Detlef Hoffman, 'Die Weltkriegssammlung des Historischen Museums Frankfurt', in *Ein Krieg wird ausgestellt. Die Weltkriegssammlung des Historischen Museums (1914–1918). Themen einer Ausstellung. Inventarkatalog* (Frankfurt, Dezernat für Kultur und Freizeit, 1976). See the forthcoming PhD dissertation of Susanna Brandt of the University of Düsseldorf on this subject.

17 This collection is now available on microfilm from Adam Matthew Publications, Marlborough, Wiltshire.

18 See Audoin-Rouzeau, *Men at war*; John Fuller, *Troop morale and popular culture in the British and Dominion armies, 1914–1918* (Oxford, Oxford University Press, 1990).

19 Ernst Friedrich, *War against war!* (Seattle, The Real Comet Press, 1987).

20 Again, I am grateful to Ken Inglis for his advice on this point.

21 The Bibliothek für Zeitgeschichte has a splendid collection of photographs of these artefacts.

22 Benno Stitzte and Paul Matzdorf, *Eiserne Kreuz-Nagelungen zum Besten der Kriegshilfe und zur Schaffung von Kriegswahrzeichen* (Leipzig, Strauss, 1916).

23 Ibid. p. 10.

24 See, for example, the ornate plaques made in Graz in this manner. From a photograph in the rich collection of the Bibliothek für Zeitgeschichte.

25 I am grateful for the advice of David Blackbourn on this and many other points. See also Roger Chickering, *We who feel most German. A study of the Pan-German League* (London, Allen & Unwin, 1984). It is worth noting the

importance of the cult of the Virgin among French Catholic soldiers, on which see Annette Becker, 'Les dévotions des soldats', in Chaline (ed.), *Chaétiens*.

26 *Eiserne Kreuz-Nagelungen*, p. 5.

27 Ibid. pp. 6ff.

28 Photographs of the lists are in the Bibliothek für Zeitgeschichte.

29 Paul von Hindenburg, *Out of my life*, F.A. Holt (London, John Murray, 1920), p. 99.

30 See the records of the Ministry of Fine Arts in Paris, AN F22/4770, file 2i, for example. For a full discussion of this problem, see Daniel J. Sherman, 'The discourse of art and the business of memory: monuments in interwar France', in John Gillis (ed.), *Commemoration: the politics of national identity* (Princeton, Princeton University Press, 1994). On the British side, see 'The Royal Academy War Memorials Committee', *Architectural Review*, 45 (January 1919), p. 20, and the discussion of the Civic Arts Association in C. Moriarty, 'Christian iconography and First World War memorials', *Imperial War Museum Review*, 6 (1991), pp. 63–75. For a German view, see *Merkblatt für Kriegerehrungen. Herausgegeben am 1.Juli 1915 vom Landesverein Sächsischer Heimatschutz* (Dresden, Bauamtmann Kurt Hager, 1917).

31 Ken Inglis, 'The homecoming: the war memorial movement in Cambridge, England', *Journal of Contemporary History*, 27, 4 (1992), pp. 583–606.

32 Annette Becker, *Les monuments aux morts*, pp. 24–5.

33 *Le monument aux morts de Mulhouse* (Mulhouse, 1927).

34 P. Poirrier, 'Pouvoir municipal et commémoration: l'exemple du monument aux morts de Dijon', *Annales de Bourgogne*, 61 (1989), pp. 141–54.

35 Archives départementales des Vosges, Epinal. Monuments aux morts aux communes, for Arches, Aumontny, Autigny la Tour, Aystoilles, La Baffe, Bain les Bains, Barville, Belvaincourt, Bruyères, Bult, Bussang, Butrimontier, La Chapelle aux Bois, Châtel sur Moselle, Chaumonsey.

36 Jean Giroud, *Les monuments aux morts dans le Vaucluse* (L'Isle sur Sorgue, Editions Scriba, 1991), annexe III.

37 I am grateful to Ken Inglis for pointing out this feature of the local war memorial. His work has been of seminal importance to all in this field.

38 See the 1994 Cambridge University MLitt dissertation of Catherine Jamet on the war memorials of Oxford and Cambridge.

39 *Architectural Review*, 45 (November 1919), p. xxviii. Many similar advertisements can be found in the French journal *L'art funéraire et commémoratif*.

40 Dan Sherman, 'Les inaugurations et la politique', in P. Rivé, A. Becker, O. Pelletier, *et al.*, (eds.), *Monuments de mémoire. Les monuments aux morts de la première guerre mondiale* (Paris, Mission permanente aux commémorations et à l'information historique, 1991), pp. 277–83.

41 James Stevens Curl, *A celebration of death* (London, Constable, 1980), chs. 7–10.

42 Volker G. Probst, *Bilder vom Tode. Eine Studie zum deutschen Kriegerdenkmal in der Weimarer Republik am Beispiel des Pietà-Motives und seiner profanierten Varianten* (Hamburg, Wayasbah, 1986), pp. 132, 347. The sculpture was destroyed by bombing in 1943.

43 Ibid. pp. 158, 366.

44 Ibid. pp. 138–9, 353.

45 Ibid. pp. 169–71, 373.
46 Ibid. pp. 120–1, 339.
47 Ibid. pp. 160–2, 368.
48 Ibid. pp. 126, 344.
49 Ibid. pp. 153, 363.
50 Ibid. pp. 159, 367. The sculpture is by Aloys Joser and was constructed before 1930.
51 I am grateful to Annette Becker for drawing my attention to this expression of Christian art.
52 M. Wintrebert, *Le vitrail dans le Pas-de-Calais* (Arras, Archives du Pas-de-Calais, Imprimerie Centrale de l'Artois, 1989), p. 26. The glass was the work of Chigot, executed in 1943, and paid for by local parishioners and by the central fund for war damage.
53 *Le vitrail*, p. 41. The glass at Bertincourt is by the Belgian glazier Desmet-Vancaillie, using fifteenth-century art as his model.
54 Ibid. p. 45. For angels transporting a dead soldier's soul to heaven, see the glass in the Eglise Saint-Quentin at Ecourt-Saint-Quentin. It is by J. Dreptin, and was completed in 1928–9.
55 For one of a host of examples, see the glass in the church of Swaffham Prior near Cambridge.
56 Once again, I am grateful to Catherine Moriarty for drawing this example to my attention.
57 Probst, *Bilder vom Tode*, pp. 183, 384.
58 Keith Jeffery, 'The Great War in modern Irish memory', paper delivered to the XXth conference of Irish historians, 6 June 1991, p. 10. Celtic crosses are less prevalent in Northern Ireland, a point made to me by Ken Inglis.
59 Moriarty, 'Christian iconography and First World War memorials'.
60 Gavin Stamp, *Silent cities* (London, Royal Institute of British Architects, 1977), p. 10.
61 Maria Tippett, *Art at the service of war. Canada, art and the Great War* (Toronto, University of Toronto Press, 1984), pp. 81–7.
62 Bobo von Dewitz and Detlef Hoffman, 'Christus in aktualisierter Gestalt. Über ein Motiv der Kriegsfotografie von 1914 bis 1954', *Fotogeschichte. Beiträge zur Geschichte und Asthetik der Fotografie*, 2 (1981), pp. 45–58. Once more thanks are due to Irina Rens for drawing this article to my attention.
63 Anne Stieglitz, 'The reproduction of agony: towards a reception-history of Grünewald's Isenheim altar after the First World War', *Oxford Art Journal*, 12, 2 (1989), pp. 87ff.
64 George Rouault, *Miserere* (Paris, Editions Le Léopard d'or, 1989).
65 J.P. Stern, 'Expressionism', in *Expression and engagement. German painting from the collection* (Liverpool, Tate Gallery, 1990), pp. 9–10.
66 'Otto Dix', symposium of 8 May 1992, Tate Gallery, London. I am grateful for Sarah O'Brien-Twohig for her comments on this point.
67 See the remarkable essay on 'Holbein's Dead Christ' in Kristeva, *Black sun*, pp. 105–38.
68 Mosse, *Fallen soldiers*, chapter 5. See also Berdt Huppauf, 'War and death: the experience of the First World War', in M. Crouch and B. Huppauf (eds.), *Essays on mortality* (Sydney, University of New South Wales, 1985), pp. 65–86.

69 Patricia Dogliani, 'Les monuments aux morts de la grande guerre en Italie', *Guerres mondiales et conflits contemporains*, 167 (1992), pp. 87–94.

70 James M. Mayo, *War memorials as political landscape. The American experience and beyond* (New York, Praeger, 1984).

71 Yves Helias, *Les monuments aux morts. Essai de sémiologie du politique* (Rennes, Mémoire pour le Diplôme d'Etudes Approfondies d'Etudes Politiques, 1977), pp. 104, 132, 134–9, 156, 184, 186.

72 Annette Becker, *Les monuments aux morts*, pp. 76, 88.

73 Prost, 'Les monuments aux morts', pp. 211–12; 217–18.

74 Annette Becker, *Les monuments aux morts*, pp. 75–6, 112, 81, 26.

75 I am grateful for Antoine Prost's advice on this point.

76 Imperial War Museum, clippings on war memorials, *Hertfordshire and Cambridge Reporter*, 31 March 1922.

77 Once again, Ken Inglis was kind enough to help by reminding me of this extraordinary design.

78 Imperial War Museum, clippings on war memorials, 'The war memorial', *Macclesfield Courier and Herald*, 24 September 1921.

79 Imperial War Museum, clippings on war memorials, *Dartford Herald*, 21 February 1921.

80 Prost, *Les anciens combattants*, vol. III, esp. part 2.

81 Prost, 'Les monuments aux morts', pp. 217–19.

82 For example, see the description of the dedication of the *monument aux morts* at Rouen in 1921, 'Le culte de l'UNC pour nos camarades morts', *La voix du combattant*, 13 November 1921.

83 See the journal *Crocodile*, 10 and 25 August 1917, for but one example.

84 For an exposition of the utilitarian case, see Arnold Whittick, *War memorials* (London, Country Life Ltd, 1954); and more generally, Bernard Barber, 'Place, symbol and utilitarian function in war memorials', *Social Forces*, 28 (1949), pp. 64–8. Both of these studies address the problem of Second World War commemoration. For the problem of utility in the context of the Great War, see A. Borg, *War memorials*, pp. 136–42.

85 Richard Knowledge, 'Tale of an "Arabian Knight": the T.E. Lawrence effigy', *Church Monuments*, 6 (1991), pp. 68–76.

86 Ken Inglis and Jock Phillips, 'War memorials in Australia and New Zealand: a comparative survey', in J. Rickard and P. Spearritt (eds.), *Packaging the past? Public histories*, special issue of *Australian Historical Studies* (April 1991), p. 186.

87 See the wealth of detail in *Monuments de mémoire. Monuments aux morts de la grande guerre* (Paris, Mission permanente aux commémorations et à l'information historique, 1991).

88 Remi Roques, 'Monuments aux morts du sud-est de la France', *Provence Historique*, 21 (1981), pp. 262ff. 'Le monument cristallise les deuils d'une société . . .'.

89 Antoine Prost, 'D'une guerre mondiale à l'autre', in M. Ozouf (ed.), *La Mémoire des Français. Quarante ans de commémorations de la seconde guerre mondiale* (Paris, Editions du CNRS, 1984), pp. 26–9.

90 Antoine Prost, 'Verdun', in P. Nora (ed.), *Les lieux de mémoire. 2. La nation* (Paris, Gallimard, 1986), pp. 188–233.

91 Prost, 'Verdun', pp. 188–233.

92 Hoover Institution, Rand Papers, *Marine Trust News*, February 1920.
93 Hoover Institution, Rand Papers, Box 7, '"Bayonet Trench" will be preserved', *Mercury Herald*, 27 September 1920.
94 Hoover Institution, Rand papers, Box 7.
95 Hoover Institution, Rand Papers, Box 7.
96 Hoover Institution, Rand Papers, Box 7.
97 Hoover Institution, Rand Papers, Box 7, 'Simplicity marks dedication today of Rand monument', *Buffalo Courier*, 8 December 1920. Annette Becker has kindly pointed out the similarity with Breton block memorials, which also have this highly neolithic signature. The reference to such forms in the Trench of the Bayonets was probably intentional.
98 I am grateful to Antoine Prost for advice on this point.
99 Eric Homberger, 'The story of the Cenotaph', *The Times Literary Supplement*, 12 November 1976, pp. 1429–30; D. Cannadine, 'War and death, grief and mourning in modern Britain', in J. Whaley (ed.), *Mirrors of mortality. Studies in the social history of death* (London, Europe, 1981), pp. 219ff.
100 C. Hussey, *The life of Sir Edwin Lutyens* (London, Antique Collectors' Club, 1950), on theosophy: pp. 85, 172, 252, 255; on India, pp. 238ff; A. Lutyens, *Sir Edwin Lutyens. An appreciation in perspective* (London: Country Life Ltd, 1942), p. 72.
101 Royal Institute of British Architects, Lutyens Papers, LuE 14/6/13 (i–), Lutyens to Emily, 12 September 1914.
102 Kenneth E. Silver, *Esprit de corps*, p. 224.
103 See Lutyens' draft letter to Alfred Mond on his wish to keep the Cenotaph where it had been put initially, 29 July 1919, LuE 32/23/1, and Lady Emily's letter to her recently knighted husband, LuE 29/2/33 (i), 11 December 1919.
104 On the issue of Lutyens and traditional Christianity, see Lutyens Papers, LuE 29/4/16, Lady Emily to Lutyens, 18 July 1921.
105 *Imperial War Graves Commission*, 6th Report, 1926.
106 On which see Lloyd, 'Tourism, pilgrimage and the commemoration of the Great War'.
107 Vincent Scully, 'The terrible art of designing a war memorial', *New York Times*, 14 July 1991, Arts & Leisure, p. 28. Scully makes Lutyens' vision at Thiepval more pacifist than it was.
108 Scully, 'The terrible art of designing a war memorial', p. 28.
109 Lutyens papers, LuE 14/5/3, letter to Emily, 5 August 1914; and LuE 16/10/5 ii, letter to Emily, 31 May 1918, for evidence of his views on the war.
110 Lutyens Papers, LuE 10/4/2 (i–), letter of 12 July 1917. Reproduced in Clayre Percy and Jane Ridley (eds.), *The Letters of Edwin Lutyens to his wife Lady Emily* (London, Collins, 1985), pp. 349–50. There is a slightly different wording of this letter in Hussey, *Lutyens*, p. 373.
111 Lutyens Papers, LuE 10/6/9 (ii), letter to Emily of 14 September 1917, and LuE 16/12/5 (i), letter to Emily 23 August 1918, on the 'great stone'.
112 Lutyens Papers, LuE 16/7/1, letter to Emily, 14 October 1917.
113 Lutyens Papers, LuE 29/4/16, Lady Emily to Lutyens, 18 July 1921, on his failure to design the RAF memorial. She reminded him that he never lost 'a chance of attacking the Church and all its ministers', not the wisest course of action 'if you want to get things out of church men!' On his work and that

of his colleagues for the Imperial War Graves Commission, see Philip Longworth, *The unending vigil* (London, Leo Cooper, 1985). The archives of the Commonwealth War Graves Commission have records of Lutyens' work. It is hoped that a list of these holdings will be available in the near future.

114 *Lutyens. The Work of the English Architect Sir Edwin Lutyens (1869–1944)* (London, Arts Council, 1981). This catalogue of an exhibition on Lutyens included many designs for his war memorial art. Some of his abstract drawings are in the Lutyens papers, LuE 16/2/12 (i), letter to Emily, 29 August 1918.

115 Lutyens papers, LuE 17/4/2 (i), letter to Lady Emily, 4 August 1919.

116 Lutyens papers, LuE 17/4/2 (iib), letter to Lady Emily, 4 August 1919.

117 Lutyens papers, LuE 17/4/2 (iib), letter to Lady Emily, 4 August 1919.

118 Hans Kollwitz (ed.), *The diary and letters of Kaethe Kollwitz*, trans. by R. and C. Winston (Evanston, IL, Northwestern University Press, 1955), Diary entry of 23 July 1932. (Hereafter referred to as *Diary*.)

119 Alessandra Comini, 'Kollwitz in context', in Elizabeth Prelinger, *Käthe Kollwitz* (New Haven, Yale University Press, 1992), pp. 89–108; Fritz Schmalenback, *Käthe Kollwitz* (Berlin, J.F. Steinkopf, 1990); Catherine Krahmer, *Käthe Kollwitz – in Selbstzeugnissen und Bilddokumenten* (Hamburg, Rowohlt, 1981).

120 Jutta Bohnke-Kollwitz (ed.), *Die Tagebücher* (Berlin, Siedler Verlag, 1989), p. 62, diary entry of 30 November 1909. (The German edition has been used only to refer to excerpts or entries unavailable in the English edition of her diaries and letters.)

121 Karl Unruh, *Langemarck. Legende und Wirklichkeit* (Koblenz, Bernard & Graefe, 1986).

122 Letter to Hans Kollwitz, 21 February 1915, recalling her earlier views, *Diary*, p. 146.

123 *Diary*, entry for 11 October 1916, p. 74.

124 *Diary*, entry for February 1917, p. 78.

125 *Diary*, entry for 1 August 1919, p. 93.

126 *Diary*, entry for 15 July 1915, pp. 64–5.

127 *Diary*, 4 February 1917, p. 77.

128 *Diary*, entry for July 1917, pp. 82–3.

129 *Diary*, entry for 6 November 1917, p. 85.

130 *Diary*, entry for 25 June 1919, p. 92.

131 *Diary*, entry for 11 January 1924, pp. 106–7.

132 *Diary*, June 1926, as cited in Martha Kearns, *Käthe Kollwitz: woman and artist* (New York, The Feminist Press, 1976), p. 191.

133 *Diary*, entry for 22 April 1931, p. 119.

134 *Diary*, entries for 1 June, 4 June, 23 July and 14 August 1932, pp. 120–2.

135 See above, chapter 3.

136 Letter to Hans Kollwitz, 16 January 1916, *Diary*, p. 147.

137 *Diary*, entry for 13 October 1916, p. 76.

138 *Diary*, 22 October 1929, p. 117.

139 Letter to Hans Kollwitz, 21 February 1915, recalling her earlier views, *Diary*, p. 146.

140 *Diary*, entry for 11 October 1916, p. 74.

141 *Diary*, entry for 1 February 1917, p. 78.
142 *Diary*, entry for 1 August 1919, p. 93.
143 *Diary*, entry for 11 October 1916, p. 74.
144 *Diary*, entry for 19 March 1918, p. 87–8.
145 *Diary*, entry for 14 August 1932, p. 122.
146 Elizabeth Prelinger, 'Kollwitz reconsidered', in her *Kollwitz*, pp. 26–7.
147 Prelinger, 'Kollwitz in context', in her *Kollwitz*, p. 40.
148 Ibid. p. 45.
149 Ibid. pp. 53, 173.
150 Prelinger, *Kollwitz*, pp. 167–8.
151 *Diary*, entry for 14 August 1932, p. 122.
152 J.M. Winter, *The experience of World War I* (London, Macmillan, 1988), p. 206, for but one such example of a woman in Munich touching a name on a war memorial.
153 Sigmund Freud, 'Mourning and melancholia', in *Collected papers*, trans. by Joan Riviere (London, Hogarth Press, 1950), vol. IV, pp. 152–70.
154 See the compelling remarks of Julia Kristeva on this point, in her essay on Duras, in *Black sun*, pp. 221ff.

5. Mythologies of war: films, popular religion, and the business of the sacred

1 Elizabeth Eisenstein, *The printing press as an agent of change* (2 vols., Cambridge, Cambridge University Press, 1979), vol. I, pp. 130ff.
2 For a survey, see D. Blackbourn, 'The Catholic Church in Europe since the French Revolution: a review article', *Comparative Studies in Society and History*, 23 (1991), pp. 778–90.
3 Eugen Weber, *Peasants into Frenchmen. The modernization of rural France* (Stanford, Stanford University Press, 1976), pp. 456–7.
4 H. McLeod, *Religion and the people of Western Europe 1789–1970* (Oxford, Oxford University Press, 1981), pp. 28–35.
5 David Blackbourn, *Marpingen. Apparitions of the Virgin Mary in Bismarckian Germany* (Oxford, Clarendon Press, 1993), pp. 46, 164. See also Thomas A. Kselman, *Miracles & prophecies in nineteenth-century France* (New Brunswick, Rutgers University Press, 1983), pp. 54–9.
6 Gérard Cholvy, 'Réalités de la religion populaire dans la France contemporaine', in Bernard Ploneron (ed.), *La religion populaire dans l'occident chrétien* (Paris, Bibliothèque Beauchesne, 1976), pp. 155–6.
7 E. Berenson, *Populist religion and left-wing politics in France, 1830–1852* (Princeton, Princeton University Press, 1984), p. 56.
8 Gérard Cholvy, 'Expressions et évolution du sentiment religieux populaire dans la France du xixè siècle au temps de la Restauration Catholique (1801–60)', *Actes du 99è congrès national des sociétés savantes* (1976), vol. I, pp. 289–320.
9 For one splendid example, see Gérard Cholvy, 'Un saint populaire? La lente renaissance du culte de Saint-Roch dans le diocèse de Montpellier durant la première moitié du xixè siècle', in G. Cholvy (ed.), *Béziers et le Biterrois*

(Montpellier, Faculté des lettres de Montpellier, 1971). See also Berenson, *Populist religion*, p. 62; Judith Devlin, *The superstitious mind. French peasants and the supernatural in the nineteenth century* (New Haven, Yale University Press, 1987); and Blackbourn, *Marpingen*, pp. 179ff.

10 Kselman, *Miracles & prophecies*, p. 92. For the mélange of religious and radical ideas in the 1830s and 1840s see also J. Hecht, 'Utopian socialism and population', in M.S. Teitelbaum and J.M. Winter (eds.), *Population and resources in Western intellectual traditions* (Cambridge, Cambridge University Press, 1988).

11 Geneviève Bollème, 'Littérature populaire et littérature de colportage au xviiiè siècle', in F. Furet (ed.), *Livre et société* (Paris, Mouton, 1965), pp. 61–92; G. Bollème, *La bibliothèque bleue. Littérature populaire en France du xviiè au xixè siècles* (Paris, Julliard, 1971); G. Bollème, *Les almanachs populaires aux vxiiè et xviiiè siècles* (Paris, Mouton, 1971). See also Berenson, *Populist religion*, pp. 70–1.

12 Alain Corbin, *Archaïsme et modernité en Limousin au xixè siècle 1845–1880* (Paris, Rivière, 1975), vol. I, p. 185.

13 Kselman, *Miracles & prophecies*, pp. 32ff.

14 J.D. Delaney (ed.), *A woman clothed with the sun: eight great apparitions of Our Lady in modern times* (New York, Doubleday, 1960).

15 Blackbourn, *Marpingen*, pp. 186ff; Michael Marrus, 'Culture on the move: pilgrims and pilgrimages in nineteenth-century France', *Stanford French Review*, 1 (1977), pp. 206–12.

16 Barbara Corrado Pope, 'Immaculate and powerful: the Marian revival in the nineteenth century', in Clarissa W. Atkinson, Constance H. Buchanan, and Margaret R. Miles (eds.), *Immaculate and powerful. The female in sacred image and social reality* (Wellingborough, Crucible, 1987), p. 173.

17 B.C. Pope, 'Immaculate and powerful', p. 180; René Laurentin and Albert Durand, *Pontmain. Histoire authentique* (3 vols., Paris, Apostolat des Editions, Lethiellex, 1970), vol. I, *Un signe dans le ciel*.

18 Kselman, *Miracles & prophecies*, p. 116.

19 Blackbourn, *Marpingen*, p. 53.

20 Ibid. pp. 123ff; Kselman, *Miracles & prophecies*, pp. 54–9.

21 John McManners, *Church and state in France 1870–1914* (London, SPCK, 1972); J. Sperber, *Popular catholicism in nineteenth-century Germany* (Princeton, Princeton University Press, 1984).

22 Blackbourn, *Marpingen*, p. 54.

23 Kselman, *Miracles & prophecies*, pp. 170–1; Blackbourn, *Marpingen*, pp. 189ff.

24 Blackbourn, *Marpingen*, *passim*.

25 David Blackbourn, *Class, religion and local politics in Wilhelmine Germany. The Centre party in Württemberg before 1914* (London, 1980).

26 For similar instances, see N. Perry and L. Echeverria, *Under the heel of Mary* (London, Routledge, 1988); and W.A. Christian, 'Tapping and defining new power: the first months of visions at Ezquioga, July 1931', *American Ethnologist*, 14 (1987), pp. 140–66.

27 Odile Frossard, *Fonds de l'imagerie d'Epinal. 48J* (Epinal, Archives départementales des Vosges (ADV), 1988), p. 2. See also: J. Mistler, *Epinal et l'imagerie populaire* (Paris, Hachette, 1961); R. Joulet, *Epinal. Images de mille ans d'histoire* (Epinal, 1950).

28 Weber, *Peasants into Frenchmen*, p. 457.
29 Bibliothèque nationale (BN), Salle des estampes, 'Images d'Epinal', Li 59, T.XIII, n.d.
30 Barbara Ann Day, 'Napoleonic art (1830–1835): from the religious image to a new secular reality', PhD dissertation, University of California, Irvine, 1986.
31 BN, Images d'Epinal, Li 59, T.XIII.
32 M.J. Trullard, *La Résurrection de Napoléon. Statue érigée par MM Noisot, grenadier de l'Ile d'Elbe et Rude, statuaire à Fixin (Côte-d'Or)* (Dijon, Guasco-Jobard, 1847), p. 38; as cited in Day, 'Napoleonic art', p. 235.
33 ADV, Publicité, 1910.
34 ADV, Fonds de l'imagerie d'Epinal, 48J, Service d'études, letter of 13 February 1902, Jean Lyon to P. Pelham.
35 'La journée du prolétaire', Bibliothèque nationale, 'Images d'Epinal', Li 59, T.XIII, 1900–5.
36 'Ce qui a fait l'administration communale libérale bruxelloise', BN, Li 59, T.XIII, 1900–5.
37 BN, Images d'Epinal, Li 59, T.XIII, 1881–9.
38 ADV, correspondance, 1912–51.
39 ADV, Services commerciaux, 1910.
40 BN, Images d'Epinal, Li 59, T.XIII, 1881–9.
41 ADV, 48J, Approvisionnement. Balance et inventaire, 1913, for net return; séries commerciales, and correspondance, 1912–51, for details of per-unit and transaction costs. These business records are disordered. A very conservative estimate of production of items must take into account operating costs, amortization, salaries, profits. The following calculation yields a figure of 3.6 million items sold each year. The figure is derived as follows:
   1. Receipts: 1.2 million francs
   2. Transaction costs: 40 per cent
   3. Net receipts: 720,000 francs
   4. Receipts from sale of bundles of 1,000 items: 20 francs
   5. Bundles of 1,000 items sold (720,000/20): 36,000
   6. Annual sales: 3,600,000.
   The margin for error in these calculations is substantial, as the firm's accountants probably intended. But to provide an order of magnitude of sales on the eve of the 1914–18 war, the figure appears reasonable.
42 Kenneth E. Silver, *Esprit de corps: the Parisian avant-garde and the First World War, 1914–1925* (London, Thames & Hudson, 1989), p. 38.
43 ADV, correspondance, 1912–51.
44 Stéphane Audoin-Rouzeau, *La guerre des enfants, 1914–1918* (Paris, Armand Colin, 1993).
45 Some exceptions are Marjorie Beales, 'Advertising in France, 1900–1940', PhD thesis, University of California at Berkeley, 1991; Regina Sweeney, 'The Parisian theater during the First World War', PhD dissertation, University of California at Berkeley, 1992; and Ross Collins, 'Propaganda and control of the press in France during World War I', PhD dissertation, University of Cambridge, 1990.
46 On which see D. Pope, 'French advertising men and the American

"Promised Land" ', *Historical Reflections*, 5, 1 (1978), pp. 117–39.

47 Marie-Monique Huss, 'The popular postcard and French pronatalism in the First World War', in R. Wall and J.M. Winter (eds.), *The upheaval of war. Family, work and welfare in Europe 1914–1918* (Cambridge, Cambridge University Press, 1988).

48 Ken Silver, 'Jean Cocteau and the *Image d'Epinal*: an essay on realism and naiveté', in Arthur King Peters (ed.), *Jean Cocteau and the French scene* (New York, Adam Press, 1984).

49 Jean-Jacques Becker, *1914. Comment les Français sont entrés dans la guerre* (Paris, Presses Universitaires de France, 1977).

50 Kenneth E. Silver, *Esprit de Corps*, pp. 40ff; Ken Silver, 'Jean Cocteau and the *Image d'Epinal*.

51 On the 'théâtre aux armées', see Annabelle Melzer, 'Guerre et spectacle', unpublished paper delivered to the inaugural conference of Historial de la grande guerre, July 1992.

52 Audoin-Rouzeau, *Men at war*; John Fuller, *Troop morale and popular culture in the British and Dominion armies in the First World War, 1914–1918* (Oxford, Oxford University Press, 1990).

53 Henri George, 'Hansi et l'imagerie d'Epinal', *Le Papier Ancien* (1953), pp. 14–16.

54 I am grateful to Cécile Coutin of the Bibliothèque de l'Arsenal, Paris, for drawing this sketch to my attention.

55 The finest collection of *images d'Epinal* produced during the war is held in the Bibliothèque de documentation internationale contemporaine (BDIC) in the Hôtel des Invalides in Paris. My initial steps in this collection were guided with great kindness by Cécile Coutin.

56 There is a rich collection of art work of all kinds in the Imperial War Museum. Thanks are due to Angela Wight for introducing me to it.

57 Kenneth E. Silver, *Esprit de corps*, p. 118.

58 *Le Mot*, 1 July 1915, copy in BDIC, Hôtel des Invalides, Paris.

59 R.H. Axsom, '*Parade*'. *Cubism as theatre* (New York, Garland, 1979); Kenneth E. Silver, *Esprit de corps*, pp. 115ff.

60 Joseph Daniel, *Guerre et cinéma. Grandes illusions et petits soldats 1895–1971* (Paris, Armand Colin, 1972); Paul Monaco, *Cinema and society: France and Germany in the twenties* (New York, Elsevier, 1976); Kevin Brownlow, *The war, the west and the wilderness* (London, Secker and Warburg, 1979).

61 See chapter 1, p. 15.

62 René Jeanne and Charles Ford, *Abel Gance* (Paris, Editions Seghers, 1963), p. 20.

63 Jean Mitry, *Histoire du cinéma. Art et industrie. Vol. II. 1915–1925* (Paris, Editions universitaires, 1969), pp. 254–9.

64 Jeanne and Ford, *Abel Gance*, pp. 26n, 28n.

65 On this theme, see Stéphane Audoin-Rouzeau, *La guerre des enfants, 1914–1918* (Paris, Armand Colin, 1993).

66 A. Gance, *Prisme* (Paris, Editions de la N.R.F., Gallimard, 1930), pp. 158–9, as cited in Jeanne and Ford, *Abel Gance*, pp. 108–9.

67 Georges Sadoul, *Histoire du cinéma mondial. Des origines à nos jours* (Paris, Flammarion, 1949), p. 167.

68 Mitry, *Histoire du cinéma*, vol. II, p. 257.

69 Paul Virilio, *War and cinema. The logistics of perception*, trans. by Patrick

Camiller (London, Verso, 1989), p. 15.

70 Mitry, *Histoire du cinéma*, vol. II, pp. 257–8.

71 H. Fescourt, *La foi et les montagnes* (Paris, Paul Montel, 1959), p. 172.

72 R. Hervouin, 'A Monsieur Abel Gance', *Le Courrier cinématographique*, 10 May 1919, p. 10, as cited in Daniel, *Guerre et cinéma*, pp. 67–8.

73 V. d'Anvers, 'Parlementarisme et cinéma', *La cinématographie française*, 27 December 1919, pp. 16, 25, as cited in Daniel, *Guerre et cinéma*, p. 68.

74 Mitry, *Histoire du cinéma*, vol. II, p. 259.

75 Charles Pornon, *L'écran merveilleux. Le rêve et le fantastique dans le cinéma français* (Paris, La nef de Paris, n.d.), p. 40.

76 Mitry, *Histoire du cinéma*, vol. II, p. 258.

77 Daniel, *Guerre et cinéma*, pp. 64f.

78 Georges Sadoul, *Dictionnaire des films* (Paris, Editions du Seuil, 1968), p. 121.

79 Paul Monaco, *Cinema and society: France and Germany during the twenties* (New York, Elsevier, 1976); Brownlow, *The war, the west and the wilderness*.

80 Rex Ingram, *The four horsemen of the Apocalypse* (London, Pathé, 1922).

81 Kevin Brownlow, *Abel Gance's Napoleon* (London, British Film Institute, 1980).

82 Daniel, *Guerre et cinéma*, pp. 72–3.

83 I am grateful for discussions with David Lloyd on this point.

84 R. Dorgelès, *Le retour des morts* (Paris, Michel Albin, 1926).

85 See Prost, *In the wake of war*.

86 *La cinématographie française*, 14 January 1938, p. 16, as cited in Daniel, *Guerre et cinéma*, pp. 146–7.

87 Bibliothéque de l'Arsenal, Fonds Rondel.

88 The best general collection of wartime images is in the Hoover Institution, Stanford, California. I am grateful to Elena Danielson for her help in guiding me around this wonderful collection. On the subject, see also Eberhard Demm, 'Propaganda and caricature in the First World War', *Journal of Contemporary History*, 28 (1993), pp. 163–92.

89 ADV, Fonds Pellerin, correspondence, 1912–51. The series of images of de Gaulle are still on sale in Epinal. They were included in a recent study, *Paris par image d'Epinal* (Paris, Musée Carnavalet, 1990).

90 Mass-Observation, *Puzzled people. A study in popular attitudes to religion, ethics, progress and politics in a London borough* (London, Victor Gollancz, 1947), pp. 35–8.

91 F. Scott Fitzgerald, *F. Scott Fitzgerald's screenplay for Three Comrades by Erich Maria Remarque*, ed. M.J. Bruccoli (Carbondale, Southern Illinois University Press, 1978).

92 Stich, *Anxious visions*.

93 Ado Kyrou, *Le surréalisme au cinéma* (Paris, Le Terrain Vague, 1963), pp. 28–30.

94 Antonin Artaud, *Oeuvres complètes* (Paris, Gallimard, 1961), iii, p. 80, as cited in C. Blot and A. Laberrère, 'Dimension spéciale du cinéma surréaliste', *Etudes cinématographiques*, 40–2 (1965), p. 263.

95 Taken from *Le revolver à cheveux blancs*, as cited in P. Mazars, 'Surréalisme et cinéma contemporain: prolongements et convergences', *Etudes Cinématographiques*, 40–2 (1965), p. 177. See also the catalogue of an exhibition at the Centre Pompidou in 1991 on *André Breton. La beauté convulsive* (Paris, Centre national Georges Pompidou, 1991).

96 Jean-Marie Mabire, 'Entretien avec Philippe Soupault', *Etudes cinémato-*

graphiques, 38–9 (1965), p. 29.

97 'Témoignages: Abel Gance', *Etudes Cinématographiques*, 38–9 (1965), pp. 36–40.

98 Bibliothèque de l'Arsenal, Paris. Fonds Rondel, Abel Gance, 'J'accuse', 4/RK/S/395.1.

6. The apocalyptic imagination in art: from anticipation to allegory

1 For a classic survey, see Montague Rhodes James' Schweich lectures of the British Academy for 1927, *The Apocalypse in art* (London, Oxford University Press, 1931). See the catalogue of an exhibition on apocalyptic art held in the Wilhelm-Hack Museum in Ludwigshafen am Rhein in 1985, R.W. Gassen and B. Holeczek (eds.), *Apokalypse: Ein Princzip Hoffnung* (Ludwigshafen, Wilhelm-Hack-Museum, 1985).

2 F. Haskell, 'Art & the apocalypse', *New York Review of Books* (15 July 1993), pp. 25–9.

3 Y.F. Heibel, ' "They danced on volcanoes": Kandinsky's breakthrough to abstraction, the German avant-garde and the eve of the First World War', *Art History*, 12 (1989), p. 357, on the way Kandinsky's painting points 'away from modernity'.

4 C.J. Ryan, *H.P. Blavatsky and the theosophical movement* (Pasadena, CA, Theosophical University Press, 1975); J. Symonds, *Madame Blavatsky* (London, Odhams, 1959); J.O. Fuller, *Blavatsky and her teachers* (London, Theosophical Publishing House, 1988); J.A. Santucci, *Theosophy and the Theosophical Society* (London, Theosophical History Centre, 1985).

5 A. Besant, *An autobiography* (London, Allen & Unwin, 1908); J.A. and Olive Banks, *Feminism and family planning in Victorian England* (Liverpool, University of Liverpool Press, 1964), pp. 88–94.

6 R. Steiner, *Theosophy* (London, Kegan Paul Trench, 1908); see the original: *Theosophie: Einfuhrung in übersinnliche Welterkenntnis und Menschenbestimmung* (Leipzig, Altmann, 1920); *Goethes Weltanschauung* (Weimar, E. Felber, 1897).

7 G.L. Mosse, *Towards the final solution: a history of European racism* (Madison, WI, University of Wisconsin Press, 1985), pp. 95–8.

8 Sixten Ringbom, *The sounding cosmos*, pp. 58–9.

9 Sixten Ringbom, 'Art in "the epoch of the Great Spiritual". Occult elements in the early theory of abstract painting', *Journal of the Warburg and Courtauld Institutes*, 29 (1966), p. 412. The citation is taken from W. Grohmann, *Paul Klee: drawings* (London, Thames & Hudson, 1960), p. 17.

10 Ringbom, 'Art in "the epoch of the Great Spiritual" ', pp. 412–13.

11 Ringbom, *Sounding cosmos*, p. 166.

12 Ibid. p. 176.

13 James Billington, *The icon and the axe. An interpretive history of Russian culture* (London, Weidenfeld & Nicolson, 1966), p. 514.

14 As cited in Billington, *Icon*, p. 504.

15 V. Ehrlich, 'The dead hand of the future: the predicament of Vladimir Mayakovsky', *American Slavic and East European Review* (1962), pp. 433–40.

16 Billington, *Icon*, p. 767. See also Jillian Davidson, 'Le mythe du "vieil homme" et de la "nouvelle génération": relation entre l'émancipation et la

première guerre mondiale dans les oeuvres d'I.B. Singer (1904–1981)', in J.J. Becker, A. Becker, and S. Audoin-Rouzeau (eds.), *Guerre et cultures* (Paris, Armand Colin, 1994), pp. 358–73.

17 Billington, *Icon*, p. 515.
18 Ibid. p. 517.
19 On the name, see K. Lankheit, 'A history of the Almanac', in W. Kandinsky and F. Marc (eds.), *The Blaue Reiter Almanac*, trans. H. Falkenstein (New York, The Viking Press, 1974), pp. 18–19n; on Marc, see F.S. Levine, *The apocalyptic vision. The art of Franz Marc as German expressionism* (New York, Harper & Row, 1979). For another view, see A. Zweite, 'Kandinsky et le Blaue Reiter', in *Figures du moderne. L'expressionnisme en Allemagne, 1905–1914* (Paris, Musée de l'art moderne de la ville de Paris, 1991), pp. 194–206.
20 All references to the text are from W. Kandinsky and F. Marc (eds.), *The Blaue Reiter Almanac*, trans. H. Falkenstein (New York, The Viking Press, 1974). A German edition was published in 1965 by R. Piper, the original publisher.
21 W. Kandinsky, *Concerning the spiritual in art*, trans. M.T.H. Sadler (New York, Dover, 1977). (Hereafter cited as *Concerning the spiritual.*)
22 Lankheit, 'History', pp. 15–16.
23 Lankheit, 'History', pp. 19–21.
24 Letter of Kandinsky to Marc, 1 September 1911, as cited in Lankheit, 'History', p. 17.
25 *Blaue Reiter Almanac*, p. 85.
26 Ibid. p. 59. (Italics in the original.)
27 Ibid. p. 72.
28 Ibid. p. 125.
29 Ibid. p. 252.
30 Lankheit, 'History', p. 35.
31 *Blaue Reiter Almanac*, p. 147. (Italics in the original.)
32 Ibid. p. 151.
33 Ibid. p. 173. (Italics in the original.)
34 Ibid. p. 186.
35 Kandinsky, 'On stage composition', *Blaue Reiter Almanac*, p. 190; Ringbom, *Sounding cosmos*, p. 130.
36 Kandinsky, *Concerning the spiritual*, p. 4.
37 Ibid. p. 6.
38 Ibid. p. 54.
39 Ibid. p. 25.
40 On Munter, see A. Hoberg, 'Gabriele Munter – une artiste du Blaue Reiter', in *Figures du moderne. L'expressionnisme en Allemagne, 1905–1914* (Paris, Musée de l'art moderne de la ville de Paris, 1991), pp. 296–308.
41 Ringbom, *Sounding cosmos*, pp. 52–3.
42 On Kandinsky and Munter's library, see Ringbom, 'Art in "the epoch of the Great Spiritual"', Appendix I, pp. 416–17; for one such photograph, see Ringbom, *Sounding cosmos*, p. 53, and plate 20. The source is A.N. Aksakow, *Animismus und Spiritismus* (Leipzig, A. Mutze, 1890), vol. I, plate 4, p. 16.
43 H. Baraduc, *Les vibrations de la vitalité humaine: méthode biométrique appliquée aux sensitifs et aux névrosés* (Paris, J.B. Baillière, 1904).

44 Ringbom, *Sounding cosmos*, p. 55. The book in question is A. Besant and C.W. Leadbeater, *Thought-forms* (London, Adyar, 1961). The German edition appeared in 1908, under the title *Gedankenformen* (Leipzig, Theosoph. Verlagshaus, 1908). Ringbom reproduces sections of Besant and Leadbeater's discussion of the colour plates of 'thought-forms' in his article 'Art in "the epoch of the Great Spiritual"', pp. 417–18.

45 Ringbom, *Sounding cosmos*, chs. 2–3.

46 Ibid. pp. 64–6.

47 L. Lang, *Expressionist book illustration in Germany 1907–1927*, trans. J. Seligman (London, Thames and Hudson, 1976). On Marc's views, see Ringbom, 'Art in "the epoch of the Great Spiritual"', p. 409, and Levine, *Apocalyptic vision*, ch. 5.

48 Ringbom, *Sounding cosmos*, p. 167.

49 Ibid. pp. 162–3.

50 Carol S. Eliel, *The apocalyptic landscapes of Ludwig Meidner* (Munich, Prestel, 1991), pp. 11–13.

51 J.-L. Robert, 'Paris, London and Berlin in 1914', in Robert and Winter, *Paris, London, Berlin*.

52 L. Meidner, 'Anleitung zum Malen von Grosstadtnildern', *Kunst und Kunstler*, 12 (1914), pp. 312–14, as cited in V.H. Miesel (ed.), *Voices of German expressionism* (Englewood Cliffs, NJ, Prentice-Hall, 1970), p. 114. The reference is to Futurist art. For Meidner's rude remarks about Kandinsky, see Yule F. Heibel, ' "They danced on volcanoes": Kandinsky's breakthrough to abstraction, the German avant-garde and the eve of the First World War', *Art History*, 12 (1989), pp. 342–61.

53 See Simon Schama, *Landscape and Memory* (New York, Knapf, 1995). For the documentation on this 'dark side' of the Enlightenment.

54 T. Grochowiak, *Ludwig Meidner* (Recklinghausen, Aurel Bongers, 1966), p. 25.

55 F. Nietzsche, *Thus spake Zarathustra*, trans. W. Kaufmann (Harmondsworth, Penguin Books, 1978), pp. 176–8.

56 See the discussion in chapter 7, pp. 182–3.

57 C. Brockhaus, 'Die ambivalente Faszination der Grossstadterfahrung in der deutschen Kunst des Expressionismus', in H. Meixner and S. Vietta (eds.), *Expressionismus: sozialer Wandel und künstlerische Erfahrung* (Munich, Wilhelm Fink, 1982).

58 L. Meidner, 'Anleitung zum Malen von Grossstadtbildern', as cited in Miesel (ed.), *Voices of German expressionism*, pp. 111–15.

59 Eliel, *Meidner*, p. 45. The original citation is from L. Meidner, *Im Nacken das Sternemeer* (Leipzig, Kurt Wolff, n.d. [1918]), pp. 26–7.

60 L. Meidner, 'Vision des apokalyptischen Sommers', *Septemberschrei: Hymnen, Gebete, Lästerungen* (Berlin, Paul Cassirer, 1920), p. 8, as cited in E. Roters, 'The painter's nights', in Eliel, *Meidner*, p. 65.

61 Meidner, 'Mein Leben', in L. Brieger, *Ludwig Meidner, Junge Kunst*, vol. IV (Leipzig, Klinkhardt and Biermann, 1919), p. 12, as cited in Roters, 'The painter's nights', p. 65.

62 See for instance, Louis Chevalier, *Labouring classes and dangerous classes in Paris during the first half of the nineteenth century*, trans. F. Jellinek (London, Routledge, 1973); D. Pick, *Faces of degeneration. A European disorder, c. 1848–c.*

1918 (Cambridge, Cambridge University Press, 1989).

63 S. Friedlander, 'Themes of decline and end in nineteenth-century imagination', in S. Friedlander (ed.), *Visions of Apocalypse* (London, Holmes & Meier, 1985), pp. 61–83.

64 D.E. Gordon, *Expressionism. Art and idea* (New Haven, Yale University Press, 1987), p. 137.

65 J.C.G. Röhl and N. Sombart (eds.), *Kaiser Wilhelm II. New interpretations* (Cambridge, Cambridge University Press, 1982), p. 31.

66 Eliel, *Apocalyptic landscapes*, p. 33.

67 Carol S. Eliel, 'Les paysages apocalyptiques de Ludwig Meidner', in *Figures du moderne*, p. 332.

68 Patrick Bridgewater, *Poet of expressionist Berlin. The life and work of Georg Heym* (London, Libris, 1991), p. 218.

69 For his religious paintings, see G. Leistner, *Idee und Wirklichkeit. Gehalt und Bedeutung des urbanen Expressionismus in Deutschland, dargestellt am Werk Ludwig Meidners* (Frankfurt, Peter Lang, 1986), pp. 153–75. For the citation on 'peace', see E. Scheyer, 'Briefe Ludwig Meidners an Franz Landsberger', *Schlesien*, 16 (1971), p. 83, as cited in Eliel, *Apocalyptic landscapes*, p. 59.

70 R.F. Allen, *Literary life in German expressionism and the Berlin circles.* Studies in the fine arts. The avant-garde. No. 25 (Epping, Bowker Publishing Co., 1983); Allen, *German expressionist poetry* (Boston, Twayne Publishers, 1981); C. Waller, *Expressionist poetry and its critics* (London, University of London, 1986).

71 Georg Heym, 'Umbra Vitae', in M. Hamburger and C. Middleton (eds.), *Modern German poetry* (New York, Grove Press, 1964), p. 155, as cited in Eliel, *Meidner*, p. 21.

72 Hamburger and Middleton (eds.), *Modern German poetry*, p. 49.

73 On Italian futurism and German expressionism, see P. Demetz, *Italian futurism and the German literary avant garde* (London, University of London, 1987).

74 Eliel, *Meidner*, p. 40.

75 S. Magri, 'Housing', in Robert and Winter, *Paris, London, Berlin*, chapter 13.

76 For some stimulating remarks on this subject, see R. Marz, 'L'expressionnisme dans la métropole de 1910 à 1914', in *Figures du moderne*, p. 327, and J. Lloyd, 'The painted city as nature and artifice', in Irit Rogoff (ed.), *The divided heritage. Themes and problems in German modernism* (Cambridge, Cambridge University Press, 1992).

77 A. Wiedmann, *Romantic roots in modern art. Romanticism and expressionism: a study in comparative aesthetics* (London, Gresham Books, 1980), pp. 106–16; for Apollinaire's version of this romantic pose, see Julia Fagan-King, 'United on the threshold of the twentieth-century mystical ideal: Marie Laurencin's integral involvement with Guillaume Apollinaire and the inmates of the Bateau Lavoir', *Art History*, 11 (1988), pp. 88–114.

78 E. Roters, 'Big-city expressionism: Berlin and German expressionism', in *Expressionism: a German intuition, 1905–1920* (New York, Guggenheim Museum, 1980).

79 For an introduction to the subject, see: Kenneth E. Silver, *Esprit de corps*; S. Hynes, *A war imagined*; M. Tippett, *Art at the service of war. Canada, art, and*

the Great War (Toronto, University of Toronto Press, 1984); M. Eberle, *World War I and the Weimar artists: Dix, Grosz, Beckmann, Schlemmer*, trans. J. Gabriel (New Haven, Yale University Press, 1985); E.L. Kahn, 'Art and the front, death imagined and the neglected majority', *Art History* (June 1985), pp. 192–208; E.L. Kahn, *The neglected majority, 'Les camoufleurs', art history and World War I* (Langham, MD, University Press of America, 1984); M. and S. Harries, *The war artists. British official war art of the twentieth century* (London, Imperial War Museum, 1980); Axsom, *'Parade': cubism as theater*.

80 I discuss this issue in chapter 4 with respect to war memorials. For more general and particular issues, see Annette Becker, *La guerre et la foi*; on symbolism and war art, see Gustave Adolf Mossa, *L'oeuvre symboliste 1903–1918* (Nice, n.p., 1992); for the use of triptych in war art, see *Polyptyques. Le tableau multiple du moyen âge au vingtième siècle* (Paris, Musée du Louvre, 1990). On the German side, see W. Schmied (ed.), *Zeichen des Glaubens. Geist der Avantgarde: Religiöse Tendenzen in der Kunst des 20. Jahrhunderts* (Stuttgart, Electa/Klett-Cotta, 1980). For religious themes in poster art, there is much of interest in the Hoover Institution poster collection, Stanford University, in the BDIC in the Hôtel des Invalides, in the Imperial War Museum in London, and in the Bibliothek für Zeitgeschichte, Stuttgart.

81 Angus Fletcher, *Allegory* (Ithaca, New York, Cornell University Press, 1964).

82 As cited in E. Karcher, *Otto Dix, 1891–1964. Leben und werk* (Cologne, Benedikt Taschen, 1988), p. 38.

83 F. Marc, 'In war's purifying fire', in Miesel (ed.), *Voices*, p. 160.

84 Levine, *The apocalyptic vision*, p. 161.

85 The fullest treatment of Dix is to be found in F. Löffler, *Otto Dix. Leben un Werk* (Dresden, Verlag der Kunst, 1977).

86 *Otto Dix 1891–1961* (London, Tate Gallery, 1992), pp. 70–1. (Hereafter cited as *Dix*.)

87 We await the study of Sarah O'Brien-Twohig on Nietzsche and painting for the first full account of this subject.

88 I am grateful to Ursus Dix for advice on this point.

89 The word 'tremendous' is from an interview cited in D. Schmidt, *Otto Dix im Selbstbildnis* (Berlin, Henschelverlag, 1978), p. 237. The full citation is: 'The war was a horrible thing, but there was something tremendous about it, too.'

90 *Dix*, p. 73, has him carrying *Zarathustra* in his pack; Eberle, *Weimar artists*, p. 22, has him carrying *The Joyous Science*.

91 Dietrich Schubert, *Otto Dix in Selbstzeugnissen und Bilddokumenten* (Reinbeck bei Hamburg, Rowolt-Taschenbuch Verlag, 1980), p. 24, disputes whether the painting is of Dix himself. This is unconvincing, since it is the mood of the early phase of the war which Dix has captured.

92 See chapter 7, p. 199.

93 As cited in O. Conzelmann, 'Nietzsches Nachklang in den Landschaften', in *Der andere Dix – Sein Bild vom Menschen und vom Kriege* (Stuttgart, Klett-Cotta, 1983), p. 133.

94 *Dix*, p. 83.

95 *Dix*, p. 116.

96 Eberle, *Weimar artists*, p. 39.
97 Friedrich, *War against war!*
98 *Dix*, p. 116.
99 *Dix*, p. 193. The image may have recalled classical motifs of 'Menelaus carrying the body of the dead Patroclus from the battlefield of Troy.'
100 See above, p. 112.
101 See below, pp. 185–6.
102 *Dix*, p. 201.
103 Eberle, *Weimar artists*, pp. 52–3.
104 On his pre-war work, see M. Beckmann, *Leben in Berlin. Tagebuch 1908/09*, ed. H. Kinkel (Munich, Piper, 1966), and E.G. Guse, *Das Frühwerk Max Beckmanns – zur Thematik seiner Bilder aus den Jahren 1904–1914* (Frankfurt, M.P. Lang, 1977); on the Berlin Secession, see P. Paret, *The Berlin Secession: modernism and its enemies in Imperial Berlin* (Cambridge, MA, Harvard University Press, 1980).
105 On the background to this drawing, and other facets of Beckmann's response to the 1914–18 war, see C. Schulz-Hoffmann and J.C. Weiss (eds.), *Max Beckmann retrospective* (Munich and New York, Prestel, 1985), p. 388 and C.W. Haxthausen, 'Beckmann and the First World War' in the same volume, pp. 69–80. See also B.C. Buenger, 'Max Beckmann in the First World War', in R. Rumold and O.K. Werckmeister (eds.), *The ideological crisis of expressionism. The literary and artistic German War Colony in Belgium 1914–1918*, Studies in German Literature, Linguistics and Culture, vol. 51 (Columbia, SC, Camden House, 1990), pp. 237–75.
106 B.C. Buenger, 'Max Beckmann's *Ideologues*: some forgotten faces', *Art Bulletin*, 71, 3 (1989), pp. 464–8.
107 Buenger, 'Max Beckmann', p. 257.
108 S. Lackner, *Max Beckmann* (New York, Abrams, 1991), p. 50.
109 Buenger, 'Max Beckmann', p. 257.
110 W.-D. Dube, 'On the "Resurrection"', Schulz-Hoffmann and Weiss (eds.) *Max Beckmann retrospective*, p. 88.
111 These phrases are taken from letters of Beckmann to his wife of 24 September 1914 and 21 May 1915, as cited in Dube, 'On the "Resurrection"', p. 82.
112 Max Beckmann, letters to his wife, 3 April 1915, 24 April 1915, and 11 May 1915, as cited in Dube, 'On the "Resurrection"', p. 82.
113 Buenger, 'Max Beckmann', p. 265.
114 S. O'Brien-Twohig, 'Max Beckmann', in Christas M. Joachimides, Norman Rosenthal, and Wieland Schmidt (eds.), *German art in the 20th century. Painting and sculpture 1905–1985* (London, Prestel-Verlag, 1985), p. 440.
115 Buenger, 'Max Beckmann', p. 245.
116 As cited in W.-D. Dube, *Expressionists and expressionism*, trans. J. Emmons (Geneva, Skira, 1983), pp. 86–7.
117 Lackner, *Beckmann*, pp. 15–16.
118 The best decoding of the painting is in Dube, 'On the "Resurrection"', pp. 84ff; see also S. von Wiese, *Max Beckmanns zeichnerisches Werk 1903–1925* (Düsseldorf, Droste Verlag, 1978), pp. 100–8.
119 O'Brien-Twohig, 'Max Beckmann', p. 440. The phrase 'filled with rage at

God' is from a conversation between Beckmann and Reinhard Piper in 1917.

120 O'Brien-Twohig, 'Max Beckmann', p. 440.

121 Kristeva, *Black sun*, p. 3.

122 Max Beckmann, 'On my painting', in Max Beckmann, *A small loan retrospective of painting, centring around his visit to London in 1938* (London, Marlborough Gallery, 1987); lecture given at New Burlington Art Galleries, London, 1938 (New York, Buchholz Gallery, Curt Valentin, 1941); see also S. Lackner, 'Max Beckmann's mystical pageant of the world', in Schulz-Hoffmann and Weiss (eds.), *Max Beckmann retrospective*, pp. 39–53.

123 Eberle, *Weimar artists*, chapter 4.

124 See above, p. 163.

125 E. Bendemann, 'Max Beckmann', *Frankfurter Zeitung*, 7 June 1919, as cited in Buenger, 'Max Beckmann in the First World War', p. 267.

126 Paul Westheim, *Für und wider* (Potsdam, G. Klepenheuer, 1923), p. 102, as cited in Buenger, 'Max Beckmann', p. 268.

127 *Stanley Spencer. The passion* (Edinburgh, Scottish National Gallery of Modern Art, 1986).

128 G. Behrend, *Stanley Spencer at Burghclere* (London, Macdonald, 1965), p. 62.

129 See chapter 4, pp. 94 ff.

130 R. Carline, *Stanley Spencer at war* (London, Faber, 1978), p. 184.

131 Samuel Hynes calls the scene 'joyous', an emotion remote from the faces and postures of every single figure in the cycle. See Hynes, *A war imagined*, p. 463.

132 Behrend, *Stanley Spencer at Burghclere*; *Stanley Spencer 1891–1959* (London, Arts Council, 1976); Carline, *Stanley Spencer at war*.

133 See chapter 4, pp. 78–116. I am grateful to Diana Goodrich for discussions on this point.

134 G. Rouault, *Miserere: nouvelle édition augmentée de texte et commentaire*, with commentaries by F. Chapon and C.-R. Marx (Paris, Editions le Léopard d'or, 1991).

135 J. Kristeva, 'Psychoanalysis: a counter-depressant', in *Black sun*, p. 25.

136 S. Whitfield, 'An outrageous lyricism', in F. Hergott and S. Whitfield, *Georges Rouault. The early years 1903–1920* (London, Royal Academy of Arts, 1993), pp. 11–14.

137 Whitfield, 'An outrageous lyricism', p. 16.

138 F. Hergott, 'The early Rouault', in Hergott and Whitfield, *Georges Rouault. The early years*, p. 23.

139 L. Bloy, *La femme pauvre* (Paris, Mercure de France, 1937), p. 171.

140 As cited in L. Venturi, *Georges Rouault* (New York, Wylie, 1940), p. 16.

141 J.T. Soby, *Georges Rouault* (New York, Arno Press, 1972), pp. 10–11.

142 Letter of Rouault to André Saurès, 8 August 1914, in *Georges Rouault – André Saurès correspondance* (Paris, Gallimard, 1960), pp. 106–7.

143 Soby, *Rouault*, pp. 28, 28n.

144 Rouault to Saurès, 2 May 1922, in *Correspondance*, pp. 172–3.

145 'Abbé Morel's presentation', in Rouault, *Miserere*, p. 40.

146 Soby, *Rouault*, p. 22.

147 *Miserere* includes a number of illustrative citations, added by Rouault's daughter to the edition. (See 'Note', p. 35.) Opposite print 54 is a direct

citation of Léon Bloy's 'Au seuil de l'Apocalypse', 18 April 1915, celebrating this incident.

148 F. Chapon, 'This hymn of dolours . . .', in Rouault, *Miserere*, p. 55.
149 C.-R. Marx, 'Rouault's legacy', in Rouault, *Miserere*, p. 53.
150 *Miserere*, p. 59.
151 *Miserere*, p. 62.
152 I am grateful for discussions with Antoine Prost on this point.

7. The apocalyptic imagination in war literature

1 For a discussion of definitions, scriptural sources, and literary forms, see C.A. Patrides and J. Wittreich (eds.), *The Apocalypse in English renaissance thought and literature. Patterns, antecedents and repercussions* (Manchester, Manchester University Press, 1984). See also the introduction to Lois P. Zamora, *Writing the apocalypse. Historical vision in contemporary U.S. and Latin American Fiction* (Cambridge, Cambridge University Press, 1989).
2 F. Field, *Three French writers and the Great War* (Cambridge, Cambridge University Press, 1975), chs. 1–2; P. Paraf, 'Les carnets de guerre d'Henri Barbusse', *Les lettres françaises*, 636–7 (13–19 September 1956, pp. 1, 5); Paraf, 'Avant le feu . . . l'aurore – Henri Barbusse, l'enfant, l'adolescent, le jeune homme, d'après des documents inédits', *Les Lettres Françaises*, 685 (1957); J. Cruickshank, *Variations on catastrophe. Some French responses to the Great War* (Oxford, Oxford University Press, 1982), chapter 5.
3 Jean Norton Cru, *Témoins. Essai d'analyse et de critique des souvenirs de combattants édités en français de 1915 à 1928* (Nancy, Presses Universitaires de Nancy, 1993 edn), pp. 555–6.
4 Henri Barbusse, *Lettres de Henri Barbusse à sa femme 1914–1917* (Paris, Flammarion, 1937), letter of 4.8.14.
5 Henri Barbusse, *Paroles d'un combattant* (Paris, Flammarion, 1920), pp. 7–8.
6 Barbusse, *Lettres à sa femme*, 13.9.14.
7 Annette Vidal, *Henri Barbusse. Soldat de la paix* (Paris, Editions Français Réunis, 1953), pp. 58ff.
8 Barbusse, *Lettres à sa femme*, 1.1.15.
9 Ibid. 1.1.15.
10 Ibid. 15.1.15.
11 Ibid. 15.1.15.
12 Ibid. 26.1.15.
13 Ibid. 13.5.15.
14 Ibid. 16.5.15.
15 Ibid. 20.6.15; Vidal, *Barbusse*, p. 58.
16 Barbusse, *Lettres à sa femme*, 28.7.15.
17 Ibid. 28.7.15.
18 Vidal, *Barbusse*, p. 59.
19 Barbusse, *Lettres à sa femme*, 19.3.16.
20 Ibid. 20.8.16, 13.10.16, 20.10.16.
21 Vidal, *Barbusse*, pp. 53–7.
22 Field, *Three French writers*, p. 59.

23 Barbusse, *Lettres à sa femme*, p. 220n.
24 Vladimir Brett, *Henri Barbusse, sa marche vers la clarté, son mouvement Clarté* (Prague, Editions de l'Académie Tchécoslovaque des sciences, 1963); Annie Kriegel, *Aux origines du communisme français* (Paris, Presses universitaires de France, 1963), D. Caute, *Communism and French intellectuals* (London, Macmillan, 1964).
25 Barbusse, *Lettres à sa femme*, 21.5.17.
26 Barbusse, *Paroles*, pp. 43–4.
27 Barbusse, 'Pourquoi te bats-tu?', *Les Nations*, June 1917, in *Paroles*, pp. 9, 11.
28 September 1917 preface to *Le feu*, in *Paroles*, p. 44.
29 'Résurrection', *La Vérité*, 31.1.18, in *Paroles*, pp. 52–3.
30 'Le silence des morts': à M. Marius Montet, avocat, June 1919, in *Paroles*, pp. 106–7.
31 Barbusse, *Paroles*, pp. 44–5. (My italics.)
32 'Pourquoi te bats-tu?', *Les Nations*, June 1917, in *Paroles*, p. 16.
33 'Pourquoi te bats-tu?', *Les Nations*, June 1917, in *Paroles*, p. 15.
34 'Réponse à mes calomniateurs' June 1918, in *Paroles*, pp. 67–8.
35 'Pourquoi te bats-tu?', *Les Nations*, June 1917, in *Paroles*, pp. 19–20.
36 Cru, *Témoins*, p. 565.
37 See chapter 6, p. 162.
38 Henri Barbusse, *Under fire*, trans. W. Fitzwater Wray (London, Dent, 1988 edn), p. 319.
39 Ibid. p. 320.
40 Ibid. p. 322.
41 Ibid. p. 323.
42 Ibid. pp. 324, 325.
43 Ibid. p. 325.
44 Ibid. p. 327.
45 Ibid. p. 329.
46 Ibid. pp. 329–30.
47 Ibid. p. 331.
48 Ibid. p. 340.
49 Ibid. p. 343.
50 For a German example, see Ludwig Renn *War*, trans. W. and E. Muir (London, Martin Secker, 1929).
51 *Die Fackel* has been reprinted in its entirety (Munich, Kosel-Verlag, 1968–76); *The last days of mankind* is available in a full German edition (Heinrich Fischer (ed.), *Werke, V. Die letzten Tage der Menschheit. Tragödie in fünf akten mit Vorspiel und Epilog* (Munich, Kosel-Verlag, 1957)). In English translation, *The last days of mankind* has appeared in reduced and bowdlerized form. See K. Kraus, *The last days of mankind*, trans. and ed. by F. Ungar (New York, Frederick Ungar Publishing Co., 1974). Some remarks of an anti-Semitic and radical nature have been omitted from the English edition. See Edward Timms, *Karl Kraus. Apocalyptic satirist. Culture and catastrophe in Habsburg Vienna* (New Haven, Yale University Press, 1986), p. 371. The passages cited below have not suffered from such distortion; consequently the English text has been used. On the problem of translating Kraus into English, see H. Zohn, 'Krausiana. 1. Karl Kraus in English translation', *Modern Austrian*

Literature, 3 (1970), pp. 25–35. The critical literature on Kraus is huge. For summaries, see the regular listings in the early volumes of *Modern Austrian Literature*.

52 For different views of these contradictions, see Erich Heller, *The disinherited mind. Essays in modern German literature and thought* (New York, Farrar, Strauss, & Cudahy, 1957), pp. 235–56; R. Wistrich, 'Karl Kraus: Jewish prophet or renegade?', *European Judaism* (1975), pp. 32–8; J.P. Stern, 'Karl Kraus and the idea of literature', *Encounter* (August 1975), pp. 37–48; and H. Zohn, 'Karl Kraus: "Jüdischer Selbsthasser" oder "Erzjude"', *Modern Austrian Literature*, 8 (1975), pp. 1–19.

53 Full English text in H. Zohn (ed.), *In these great times* (Manchester, Carcanet Press, 1984), pp. 70–83.

54 *In these great times*, p. 71. On the general subject of Kraus and the war, see J.D. Halliday, *Karl Kraus, Franz Pfemfert and the First World War* (Passau, Andreas-Haller-Verlag, 1986), esp. Chapter 11.

55 *In these great times*, p. 75.

56 See J.-L. Robert, 'The image of the profiteer', in Robert and Winter, *Paris, London, Berlin*, chapter 4.

57 F. Field, 'Karl Kraus, Bernard Shaw and Romain Rolland as opponents of the First World War', in P. Scheichl and E. Timms (eds.), *Karl Kraus in neuer Sicht* (Munich, Fertigsatz, 1986), pp. 158–73.

58 *In these great times*, p. 73.

59 Stanley Weintraub, *Journey to Heartbreak. The crucible years of Bernard Shaw 1914–1918*, New York, Weybright and Talley, 1971), pp. 58–9.

60 *In these great times*, p. 82.

61 See n. 51.

62 Timms, *Kraus*, p. 220.

63 Ibid. p. 222.

64 Ibid. p. 375.

65 *Last days of mankind*, pp. 194–5.

66 Ibid. p. 195.

67 Ibid. pp. 196–8.

68 Ibid. pp. 198–9.

69 Ibid. p. 199.

70 Ibid. pp. 199–200.

71 Ibid. pp. 201–2.

72 Ibid. p. 202.

73 Ibid. pp. 203–4.

74 Ibid. pp. 204–5.

75 Ibid. p. 205

76 Ibid. p. 237.

77 J.M. Winter, *Socialism and the challenge of war* (London, Routledge, 1974), p. 57.

78 George Bernard Shaw, *What I really wrote about the war* (London, Constable, 1931), pp. 22–110.

79 Field, 'Karl Kraus', pp. 161–2.

80 Bernard Shaw, *Collected plays with their prefaces* (London, The Bodley Head, 1972), vol. V. (All references to *Heartbreak House* and its preface are from this edition.)

81 *Heartbreak House*, p. 10; Weintraub, *Journey to Heartbreak*, p. 163.
82 Michael Holroyd, *Bernard Shaw*. Volume III: *1918–1950. The lure of fantasy* (London, Chatto & Windus, 1991), pp. 16–17; *Heartbreak House*, p. 26.
83 As cited in Weintraub, *Journey*, p. 179.
84 *Heartbreak House*, p. 10.
85 Ibid. p. 41.
86 J.M. Keynes, *The economic consequences of the peace* (London, Macmillan, 1919).
87 *Heartbreak House*, p. 18.
88 Ibid. p. 18.
89 Ibid. p. 19.
90 Ibid. p. 22.
91 Ibid. p. 26.
92 Ibid. p. 30.
93 Ibid. p. 31.
94 Ibid. pp. 32–5.
95 Ibid. p. 57.
96 Ibid. p. 58.
97 See J.M. Winter, 'Bernard Shaw, Bertolt Brecht and the businessman in literature', in N. McKendrick and R.B. Outhwaite (eds.), *Business life and public policy. Essays in honour of D.C. Coleman* (Cambridge, Cambridge University Press, 1986), pp. 185–204.
98 As cited in Heller, *The disinherited mind*, p. 252.
99 *Heartbreak House*, p. 83.
100 Ibid. pp. 95, 99, 102.
101 Weintraub, *Journey*, p. 163.
102 Developed by Weintraub in his appendix to *Journey*.
103 *Heartbreak House*, p. 177.
104 See Northrop Frye, *Fearful symmetry. A study of William Blake* (Princeton, Princeton University Press, 1947); Northrop Frye, *Spiritus mundi. Essays on literature, myth and society* (Bloomington, Indiana University Press, 1976), pp. 228–44.
105 A good survey of recent research is Jill Lloyd, *German expressionism. Primitivism and modernity* (New Haven, Yale University Press, 1991); for an older view, see R. Samuel and R. Hinton Thomas, *Expressionism in German life, literature and the theatre (1910–1924)* (Cambridge, W. Heffer & Son, 1939).
106 See Annette Becker, *La guerre et la foi*.
107 J. Giono, *Le grand troupeau* (Paris, Gallimard, 1931); Léon Riegel, *Guerre et littérature. Le bouleversement des consciences dans la littérature romanesque inspirée par la Grande Guerre: littératures française, anglo-saxonne et allemande 1910–1930* (Paris, Editions Klincksieck, 1978), p. 239n; Norma L. Goodrich, *Giono. Master of fictional modes* (Princeton, Princeton University Press, 1973), chapter 1.
108 Giono, *Le grand troupeau*, pp. 251–2.
109 Norma L. Goodrich, 'Jean Giono's new Apocalypse text: "Le grand théâtre" (1960)', *French Review*, 43 (1966), pp. 116–25.
110 Joseph Foret (ed.), *L'apocalypse* (Paris, J. Foret éditeur, 1961), p. 283. (Hereafter referred to as *L'apocalypse*.) The prose and illustrations accompanying the specially produced text were exhibited at the Musée

Jacquement-André and at the Musée d'art moderne de la Ville de Paris in 1961. Foret also produced a film on the project.

111 *L'apocalypse*, pp. 286–7.

112 Ibid. pp. 287–9.

113 Ibid. p. 293.

114 I owe this point to Eric Hobsbawm, who has offered this reason for the prominence of cobblers as sources of information about popular life. As men who produced goods on which they could not cheat – the customers would feel the pinch immediately – they could be trusted with the riches of folklore and acute local detail.

115 *L'apocalypse*, p. 304.

116 Ibid. p. 306.

117 For the English translation, see E. Jünger, *Storm of steel*, trans. B. Creighton (London, Chatto & Windus, 1929).

118 I owe these remarks to Roger Woods' stimulating discussion of Jünger's work, which is also a useful guide to much of the German critical literature on Jünger. R. Woods, *Ernst Jünger and the nature of political commitment* (Stuttgart, Akademischer Verlag Hans-Dieter Heinz, 1982), pp. 17ff, esp. p. 20.

119 *L'apocalypse*, p. 266.

120 Ibid. p. 264.

121 Ibid. p. 285. The title Jünger chose for his contribution was *Sertissages* (Settings).

122 *L'apocalypse*, p. 267.

123 Ibid. p. 258.

124 Stefan Zweig, *Jeremias. Eine dramatische Dichtung in neun Bildern* (Leipzig, Insel Verlag, 1917); Timms, *Karl Kraus*, p. 298.

125 Franz Werfel, *Jeremias: Höret die Stimme* (Frankfurt, S. Fischer Verlag, 1956); P.S. Jungk, *A life torn by history. Franz Werfel 1890–1945*, trans. A. Hollo (London, Weidenfeld & Nicolson, 1990), pp. 160–2; J.C. Davidhach, 'The novelist as prophet: a new look at Franz Werfel's *Höret die Stimme'*, *Modern Austrian Literature*, 24 (1991), pp. 51–67; on the wartime correspondence of these writers, see D.A. Prater, 'Stefan Zweig and Franz Werfel', *Modern Austrian Literature*, 24 (1991), pp. 85–8; J.B. Berlin and H.-U. Lindler, 'Der unveröffentliche Briefwechsel zwischen Franz Werfel und Stefan Zweig', *Modern Austrian Literature*, 24 (1991), pp. 89–122.

126 D.H. Lawrence, *Kangaroo* (London, William Heinemann, 1923); as cited in F. Kermode, 'Word in the desert', *Critical Quarterly*, 10 (1968), p. 22.

127 F. Kermode, 'Apocalypse and the modern', in S. Friedlander, Gerlad Holton, Loe Marx, *et al.* (eds.), *Visions of Apocalypse. End or rebirth* (London, Holmes & Meier, 1985), pp. 84–106. See also Susan Urang, *Kindled in the flame. The apocalyptic scene in D.H. Lawrence* (Epping, Bowker Publishing Co., 1983).

128 Jeffrey M. Perl, *The tradition of return. The implicit history of modern literature* (Princeton, Princeton University Press, 1984), chapters 7–8 for a useful survey of writing on Pound, Lawrence, Yeats, Joyce, and Eliot.

129 See P. Fussell, *The Great War and modern memory* (Oxford, Oxford University Press, 1975); Hynes, *A war imagined*.

130 Lois Zamora, *Writing the Apocalypse. Historical vision in contemporary U.S. and Latin American fiction* (Cambridge, Cambridge University Press, 1989), p. 2.

131 See M. Ceadel, *Pacifism in Britain 1914–1945. The defining of a faith* (Oxford, Oxford University Press, 1980), p. 57.
132 C. Maier, *Recasting bourgeois Europe* (Princeton, Princeton University Press, 1974).
133 F. Scott Fitzgerald, *Tender is the night* (London, Penguin Books, 1965 edn), pp. 66–7.
134 On Ford Madox Ford, see Alan Judd, *Ford Madox Ford* (London, Collins, 1990) and S.J. Stang (ed.), *The presence of Ford Madox Ford. A memorial volume of essays, poems, and memoirs* (Philadelphia, University of Pennsylvania Press, 1981).
135 Kermode, 'Apocalypse', p. 86.
136 Erich Maria Remarque, *All quiet on the Western Front*, trans. A.W. Wheen (London, G.P. Putnam's Sons, 1929), p. 126, on hands hanging on barbed wire, and p. 227, on half a naked soldier 'squatting in the fork of a tree'.
137 Jünger, *Storm of steel*, pp. 20–1.
138 See chapter 3, especially pp. 66–8; and Chaline (ed.), *Chrétiens dans la première guerre mondiale*; and Audoin-Rouzeau, *La guerre des enfants*.
139 On Céline, see P.S. Day, 'Imagination et parodie dans *Voyage au bout de la nuit*', *Australian Journal of French Studies*, 13 (1976), pp. 55–63; Albert Chesneau, *Essai de psychocritique de Louis-Ferdinand Céline* (Paris, Minard, 1971); Julia Kristeva, *Powers of horror. An essay on abjection*, trans. Leon S. Roudiez (New York, Columbia University Press, 1982), chapters 6–11.
140 Though in Latin America it had a new lease on life. See Zamora, *Writing the Apocalypse*, p. 3.
141 Foret (ed.), *L'apocalypse*. See above, p. 199.
142 See Martin Jay's elegant essay, 'The apocalyptic imagination and the inability to mourn' in his *Force fields. Between intellectual history and cultural critique* (London, Routledge, 1993), pp. 84–98. Other apocalyptic echoes can be heard in the cinematic poetry of Andrei Tarkovsky, in particular his apocalyptic film, *Sacrifice*.
143 There is considerable discussion of silence and the Holocaust. Much of it followed Adorno's remarks on poetry. See the discussion and references in chapter 9.

8. War poetry, romanticism and the return of the sacred

1 Bogacz, ' "A Tyranny of words" '.
2 Maurice Barrès, 'Le blason de la France, ou ses traits éternels dans cette guerre et dans les vieilles épopées', *Proceedings of the British Academy*, 7 (1915–16), pp. 339–58.
3 Barrès, 'Le blason', p. 350. For a more dispassionate view of this incident and its idealization, see Cru, *Témoins*, pp. 378–83.
4 On Barrès, see C. Stewart Doty, *From cultural rebellion to counterrevolution: the politics of Maurice Barrès* (Athens, OH, Ohio University Press, 1976). For another typical reference to 'Debout, les morts!', see his preface to Carlos Larronde (ed.), *Anthologie des écrivains français morts pour la patrie* (Paris, Librairie Larousse, 1916), vol. I, p. 12.

5 Archives départementales des Vosges, Fonds Pellerin, lists of wartime sales.

6 Marc de Larreguy de Civrieux, 'Debout, les morts!', *Les poètes contre la guerre. Anthologie de la poésie française 1914–1919*, with an introduction by Romain Rolland (Geneva, Editions du Sablier, 1920), p. 83.

7 See the interesting discussion and translations by Ian Higgins in Tim Cross (ed.), *The lost voices of World War I* (London, Bloomsbury, 1988), pp. 217–20, and Romain Rolland's introduction to *La Muse de sang* (Paris, Librarie du Travail, 1926).

8 Elizabeth Marsland, *The nation's cause. French, English and German poetry of the First World War* (London, Routledge & Kegan Paul, 1991), p. 185.

9 Wolfgang G. Deppe, Christopher Middleton, and Herbert Schönherr (eds.), *Ohne Hass und Fahne. Kriegsgeschichte des 20. Jahrhunderts* (Hamburg, Rowohlt, 1977), pp. 155–6.

10 René Arcos, *Pays du soir* (Geneva, Editions du Sablier, 1920), pp. 29–32.

11 René Arcos, 'Les morts . . .', in *Poètes contre la guerre*, p. 25.

12 This juxtaposition is noted by Elizabeth Marsland in *The nation's cause*, pp. 152–5.

13 See Jon Stallworthy's discussion in Cross (ed.), *The lost voices* pp. 59–60.

14 Cross (ed.), *Lost voices*, p. 61. On Sorley, see J.M. Wilson, *Charles Hamilton Sorley: a biography* (London, Cecil Woolf, 1985).

15 Bertolt Brecht, 'Legende vom toten Soldaten', in *Gesammelte Werke in acht Bänden* (Berlin, Suhrkamp, 1967), vol. IV, p. 1421.

16 M. Kay Flavell, *George Grosz. A biography* (New Haven, Yale University Press, 1988); Matthias Eberle, *World War I and the Weimar artists* (New Haven, Yale University Press, 1985).

17 Maurice Nadeau, *The history of surrealism*, trans. by R. Howard (Cambridge, MA, Harvard University Press, 1989), pp. 64ff.

18 Patrick Bridgewater, *The German poets of the First World War* (London, Croom Helm, 1985), pp. 130–1.

19 Ibid. p. 96.

20 Anton Schnack, 'The dead', from *Tier rang gewaltig mit Tier* (1920), as cited in Bridgewater, *German poets*, p. 100.

21 Bridgewater, *German poets*, p. 101.

22 J. Stallworthy (ed.), *The complete poems and fragments of Wilfred Owen* (London, Chatto & Windus, 1983), vol. I, p. 23.

23 Siegfried Sassoon, *Collected poems* (London, Faber and Faber, 1947), p. 26.

24 J. Stallworthy (ed.), *The Oxford Book of war poetry* (Oxford, Oxford University Press, 1988), pp. 181–2.

25 Robert Jay Lifton, *Death in life. The survivors of Hiroshima* (New Haven, Yale University Press, 1968).

26 Giuseppi Ungaretti, 'No more crying out', in Jon Silkin (ed.), *The Penguin book of First World War poetry* (London, Allen Lane, 1979), p. 240. For a modern equivalent, see Ted Hughes' poem, 'A masque for three voices', in *Rain-charm for the Duchy and other Laureate poems* (London, Faber and Faber, 1992), pp. 29–41 and his commentary on it, pp. 58–60.

27 Bernard (ed.), *Apollinaire*, p. 131.

28 Gilberte Jacaret, *La dialectique de l'ironie et du lyrisme dans 'Alcools' et 'Calligrammes' de G. Apollinaire* (Paris, A.G. Nizet, 1984).

29 G. Apollinaire, *Calligrammes. Poems of peace and war (1913–1916)*, trans. by Anne Hyde Greet (Berkeley, University of California Press, 1980), pp. 134–7.

30 *Calligrammes*, commentary by Anne Hyde Greet and S.I. Lockerbie, p. 415.

31 Bernard (ed.), *Apollinaire* (London, Anvil Press Poetry, 1986), p. 145.

32 Ibid. p. 147.

33 Ibid. p. 117.

34 Ibid. p. 123.

35 Jacaret, *La dialectique de l'ironie*; R. Little, *Guillaume Apollinaire* (London, The Athlone Press, 1976); R. Couffignal, *L'inspiration biblique dans l'oeuvre de Guillaume Apollinaire* (Paris, Minard, 1966).

36 Bernard (ed.), *Apollinaire*, p. 127.

37 Ibid. p. 127.

38 Ibid. p. 7.

39 Georg Trakl, 'Mankind', *Ohne Hass und Fahne*, p. 28.

40 Bridgewater, *German poets*, p. 37.

41 See the interesting discussion by Michael Hamberger of Trakl in Tim Cross, *Lost voices*, pp. 112–23.

42 Fritz Griessbach (ed.), *Walter Flex. Aus dem Nachlass: eine Dokumentation* (Kiel, Orion-Heimreiter, 1978).

43 See Ian Higgins' discussion in Cross (ed.), *Lost voices*, pp. 242–7.

44 See Ian Higgins' discussion in Cross (ed.), *Lost voices*, pp. 270–5.

45 See Ian Higgins' discussion of André Lafon's poetry, in Cross (ed.), *Lost voices*, pp. 288–91, and Teilhard de Chardin's description of the 'exaltation' he felt in the trenches among the men, as cited by Robert Wohl, in Cross (ed.), *Lost voices*, pp. 380–6.

46 As cited in T.W. Bogacz, ' "Sassoon and Company": Siegfried Sassoon's journey to modernity in the Great War', PhD thesis, University of California at Berkeley, 1982, p. 143.

47 Siegfried Sassoon, *Poet's pilgrimage* (London, Collins, 1973), p. 22.

48 Stallworthy (ed.), *Complete poems of Wilfred Owen*, vol. I, p. 182.

49 For a full discussion, see Laurinda Stryker, 'Languages of sacrifice and suffering in England in the First World War', chapter 6.

50 Stallworthy (ed.), *War poetry*, p. 183.

51 The poems are 'Moses' and 'The amulet'; see J. Silken (ed.), *The Penguin book of First World War poetry* (London, Allen Lane, 1979), pp. 200, 210.

52 'Pain', in P.J. Kavanagh (ed.), *Collected poems of Ivor Gurney* (Oxford, Oxford University Press, 1982), p. 36.

53 Herbert Read, *Collected poems* (London, Faber and Faber, 1966), p. 34.

54 See Samuel Hynes' penetrating discussion in *A war imagined*, pp. 247ff.

55 Richard Aldington, 'Blood of the young men', *New Paths* (May 1918), p. 24.

56 Stallworthy (ed.) *Complete poems of Wilfred Owen*, vol. I, p. 174.

57 Hynes, *A war imagined*, p. 247; I.M. Parsons (ed.), *Men who march away* (London, Chatto & Windus, 1966), pp. 179–80.

58 'Common form', in Silkin (ed.), *Penguin Book of First World War poetry*, p. 131.

59 A point originally made by Christopher Hibbert in a paper on war poetry at Clare Hall, Cambridge, 1991.

60 See the extraordinary study by Alphonse Dupront, *Du sacré. Croisades et pèlerinages. Images et langages* (Paris, Gallimard, 1988). I am grateful to

Annette Becker for drawing this work to my attention.

61 See the use of this imagery by Walter Benjamin in his commentary on Klee's *Angelus Novus*, as discussed in chapter 9.

9. Conclusion

1 Walter Benjamin, *Illuminations*, trans. H. Zohn (New York, Harcourt, Brace & World, 1968), pp. 259–60. On Benjamin's use of this image, see Susan Buck-Morss, *The dialectics of seeing. Walter Benjamin and the Arcades project* (Cambridge, MA, MIT Press, 1991); Stéphane Mosès, *L'ange de l'histoire* (Paris, Seuil, 1992); and O.K. Werckmeister, *The making of Paul Klee's career, 1914–1920* (Chicago, University of Chicago Press, 1989), pp. 241–2.

2 See T.W. Adorno's comments on the painting: 'During the First World War or shortly after, Klee drew cartoons of Kaiser Wilhelm as an inhuman iron eater. Later, in 1920, these became – the development can be shown quite clearly – the *Angelus Novus*, the machine angel, who, though he no longer bears any emblem of caricature or commitment, flies far beyond both. The machine angel's enigmatic eyes face the onlooker to try to decide whether he is announcing the culmination of disaster or salvation hidden with it. But, as Walter Benjamin, who owned the drawing, said, 'he is the angel who does not give but takes'. From T.W. Adorno, 'Commitment', in A. Arato and E. Gebhardt (eds.), *The essential Frankfurt School reader* (New York, Continuum, 1975), p. 318. Werckmeister locates the drawing in the context of Klee's ruminations on aircraft and on the 'flying man' as the new angel. This interpretation sees Klee's drawing as a twentieth-century variant of Leonardo's and Swedenborg's sense of manned flight as angelic. See Werckmeister, *Klee's career*, p. 241. In this reading of the drawing, once again we find the most modern forms transformed into carriers of ancient images of transformation and redemption.

3 As noted in the introduction, the retention of the phrase 'Sites of memory' echoes Pierre Nora's multi-volume collection, *Les lieux de mémoire* (Paris, Gallimard, 1984–92), while departing from its approach to cultural history. The phrase also has a specifically English *double-entendre* in the word 'site', suggesting not only place but also sight and vision. This allusion is particularly apposite in the discussion of the theme of the return and remembrance of the dead.

4 See Buck-Morss, *The dialectics of seeing*, p. 94.

5 Kristeva, 'Psychoanalysis: a counter-depressant', in *Black sun*, p. 25.

6 I am grateful to Martin Jay for discussions on these (and many other) points.

7 T.W. Adorno, 'Commitment', in Arato and Gebhardt (eds.), *The essential Frankfurt school reader*, p. 312. See also the same phrase 'To write poetry after Auschwitz is barbaric' in Adorno's essay 'Cultural criticism and society'. For the citation, see T. Adorno, *Prisms*, trans. by Samuel and Shierry Weber (Cambridge, MA, MIT Press, 1981), p. 34.

8 For a powerful discussion of the contrast between abstract and figurative forms of commemorative art, see Kosseleck, 'Bilderverbot. Welches Totengedenken?'.

9 Throughout I have been indebted to the discussion of Alphonse Dupront in his classic study, *Du sacré*.
10 Bernard (ed.), *Apollinaire*, p. 127.
11 Kristeva, *Black sun*, p. 223.

Bibliography

Unpublished sources

1.1 *Archives nationales*, Paris
F2: files on national war cemeteries
F7: police files
F22: Ministry of Fine Arts
F23: First World War series

1.2 *Bibliothèque de L'Arsenal*, Paris
Fonds Rondel

1.3 *Bibliothèque de documentation internationale contemporaine*, Université de
Paris – X, Nanterre and Hôtel des Invalides
Imagerie d'Epinal
Trench journals

1.4 *Bibliothèque nationale*, Paris
Fonds Apollinaire, Bureau des manuscrits, N.a.Fr.
Fonds Barbusse, Bureau des manuscrits, N.a.Fr.
Fonds Cocteau, Imp. Res. Z. La Mesle
Fonds Pellerin, Bureau des Estampes

1.5 *Archives départementales des Vosges*, Epinal
Fonds Pellerin
Monuments aux morts, files for communes

1.6 *British Library*, London
Barlow Collection

1.7 *Cambridge University Library*
Cambridge War Collection

1.8 *Imperial War Museum*, London
Bennett papers
Claydon papers
Imagerie d'Epinal

Bibliography

A.S. Lloyd papers
War memorial inventory papers
Wakeman papers

1.9 *Public Record Office*, Kew
Public works papers
War Office papers

1.10 *Royal Institute of British Architects*, London
Lutyens papers

1.11 *Commonwealth War Graves Commission archives*, Maidenhead

1.12 *Hoover Institution*, Stanford, California
Hoover papers, American relief effort
Rand Papers
War posters

1.13 *Bibliothek für Zeitgeschichte*, Stuttgart
Photographs and documents related to war memorials

1.14 *Australian War Memorial*, Canberra
Red Cross papers
Roll of Honour forms

1.15 *Mortlock Library of South Australia*, Adelaide
Red Cross papers

Published sources

Contemporary journals, newspapers and reviews
Almanach de la Propagation des Trois 'Ave Marias'
Annales des sciences psychiques
L'anthropologie
Architectural Review
L'art funéraire et commémoratif
*Bulletin de l'union des pères et des mères dont les fils sont morts
  pour la patrie*
Bulletin mensuel des veuves et orphelins de la Grande Guerre
La cinématographie française
Crocodile
Le courrier cinématographique
Dartford Herald
East London Observer
Etudes cinématographiques
Die Fackel
Frankfurter Allgemeine Zeitung
Frères d'armes

Hansard
Journal of the Society for Psychical Research
Journal Officiel
Le Mot
Macclesfield Courier and Herald
Occult Review
Revue spirite
Souvenirs et fraternité
Souvenir français
Tacatacteufteuf
La voix du combattant

Published sources

Books and articles

Adorno, T.W., 'Engagement', in *Noten zur Literatur III* (Frankfurt, Suhrkamp Verlag, 1965), pp. 109–35
   Prisms, trans. by Samuel and Shierry Weber (Cambridge, MA, MIT Press, 1981)
   Aesthetic theory, trans. C. Lenhardt (London, Routledge & Kegan Paul, 1984)
Aksakow, A.N., *Animismus und Spiritismus* (Leipzig, A. Mutze, 1890)
Aldington, R., 'Blood of the young men', *New Paths* (May 1918)
Allen, R.F., *Literary life in German expressionism and the Berlin circles*. Studies in the fine arts. The avant-garde. No. 25 (Epping, Bowker Publishing Co., 1983)
   German expressionist poetry (Boston, Twayne Publishers, 1981)
Anderson, B. *Imagined communities. Reflections on the origin and spread of nationalism* (London, Routledge, Verso, 1983)
André Breton. La beauté convulsive (Paris, Centre national Georges Pompidou, 1991)
Apollinaire, G., *Calligrammes. Poems of peace and war (1913–1916)*, trans. by Anne Hyde Greet (Berkeley, University of California Press, 1980)
Arato, A. and Gebhardt, E. (eds.), *The essential Frankfurt school reader* (New York, Continuum, 1975)
Arcos, René, *Pays du soir* (Geneva, Editions du Sablier, 1920)
Ariès, Philippe, *Western attitudes towards death*, trans. P.M. Ranum (Baltimore, Johns Hopkins University Press, 1974)
   The hour of our death, trans. H. Weaver (New York, Oxford University Press, 1990)
Artaud, Antonin, *Oeuvres complètes* (Paris, Gallimard, 1961)
Atkinson, Clarissa W., Buchanan, Constance H., and Miles, Margaret R. (eds.), *Immaculate and powerful. The female in sacred image and social reality* (Wellingborough, Crucible, 1987)
Aubert, Octave, *Louis Barthou* (Paris, Librairie Aristide Quillet, 1935)
Aubrée, Marion, and Laplantine, François, *La table, le livre et les esprits* (Paris, J.C. Lattes, 1990)
Audoin-Rouzeau, Stéphane, *Men at war. Trench journalism and national sentiment in France 1914–1918*, trans. H. McPhail (Oxford, Berg, 1992)
   La guerre des enfants, 1914–1918 (Paris, Armand Colin, 1993)
Axsom, R.H., *'Parade'. Cubism as theater* (New York, Garland Press, 1979)
Banks, J.A. and Olive, *Feminism and family planning in Victorian England* (Liverpool, University of Liverpool Press, 1964)

Baraduc, H., *Les vibrations de la vitalité humaine: méthode biométrique appliquée aux sensitifs et aux névrosés* (Paris, J.B. Baillière, 1904)

Barber, Bernard, 'Place, symbol and utilitarian function in war memorials', *Social Forces*, 28 (1949), pp. 64–8

Barbusse, Henri, *Paroles d'un combattant* (Paris, Flammarion, 1920)

    Lettres de Henri Barbusse à sa femme 1914–1917 (Paris, Flammarion, 1937)

    Under fire, trans. W. Fitzwater Wray (London, Dent, 1988 edn)

Barrès, Maurice, 'Le blason de la France, ou ses traits éternels dans cette guerre et dans les vieilles épopées', *Proceedings of the British Academy*, 7 (1915–16), pp. 339–58

Barrow, L., *Independent spirits. Spiritualism and English plebeians, 1850–1910* (London, Routledge, 1986)

Battock, Geoffrey (ed.), *The new art: a critical anthology* (New York, E.P. Dutton, 1966)

Beales, Marjorie, 'Advertising in France, 1900–1940', PhD dissertation, University of California at Berkeley, 1991

Becker, Annette, *Les monuments aux morts* (Paris, Errance, 1989)

    'Lés dévotions des soldats', in N.-J. Chaline (ed.), *Chrétiens dans la première guerre mondiale* (Paris, Les Editions du Cerf, 1993)

    La guerre et la foi. De la mort à la mémoire (Paris, Armand Colin, 1994)

Becker, Jean-Jacques, *1914. Comment les Français sont entrés dans la guerre* (Paris, Presses Universitaires de France, 1977)

Becker, Jean-Jacques, Becker, Annette, and Audoin-Rouzeau, Stéphane *et al.* (eds.), *Guerre et cultures: vers une historie culturelle comparée de la première guerre mondiale* (Paris, Armand Colin, 1994)

Beckmann, Max, *Leben in Berlin. Tagebuch 1908/09*, ed. H. Kinkel (Munich, Piper, 1966)

    'On my painting', in Max Beckmann, *A small loan retrospective of painting, centring around his visit to London in 1938* (London, Marlborough Gallery, 1987)

    A small loan retrospective of painting, centring around his visit to London in 1938 (London, Marlborough Gallery, 1987)

Begbie, Harold, *On the side of the angels. The story of the angel at Mons. An answer to 'The Bowmen'* (London, Hodder & Stoughton, 1915)

Behrend, G., *Stanley Spencer at Burghclere; Stanley Spencer 1891–1959* (London, Macdonald, 1965)

Bendemann, Edouard, 'Max Beckmann', *Frankfurter Zeitung*, 7 June 1919

Benjamin, Walter, *Illuminations*, trans. H. Zohn (New York, Harcourt, Brace & World, 1968)

Berenson, E., *Populist religion and left-wing politics in France, 1830–1852* (Princeton, Princeton University Press, 1984), p. 56

Berlin, J.B. and Lindler, H.-U., 'Der unveröffentliche Briefwechsel zwischen Franz Werfel und Stefan Zweig', *Modern Austrian Literature*, 24 (1991), pp. 89–122

Bernard, Oliver (ed.), *Apollinaire. Selected poems* (London, Anvil Press Poetry, 1986)

Besant, A., *An autobiography* (London, Allen & Unwin, 1908)

Besant, A. and Leadbeater, C.W., *Gedankenformen* (Leipzig, Theosoph. Verlagshaus, 1908)

    Thought-forms (London, Adyar, 1961)

Best, Geoffrey, *Humanity in warfare* (London, Hutchinson, 1980)

Billington, James, *The icon and the axe. An interpretive history of Russian culture* (London, Weidenfeld & Nicolson, 1966)

Blackbourn, David, *Class, religion and local politics in Wilhelmine Germany. The Centre party in Württemberg before 1914* (London, 1980)

Populists and patricians. Essays in modern German history (London, Allen & Unwin, 1987)

Marpingen. Apparitions of the Virgin Mary in Bismarckian Germany (Oxford, Clarendon Press, 1993)

'The Catholic Church in Europe since the French Revolution: a review article', *Comparative Studies in Society and History*, 23 (1991), pp. 778–90

Blatchford, R., 'My testimony', in Sir James Marchant (ed.), *Life after death according to Christianity and spiritualism* (London, Cassell, 1925)

Bloch, Maurice, 'The moral and tactical meaning of kinship terms', *Man*, 6 (1971), pp. 79–87

Blot, C. and Laberrère, A., 'Dimension spéciale du cinéma surréaliste', *Etudes Cinématographiques*, 40–2 (1965), p. 263

Bloy, Léon, *La femme pauvre* (Paris, Mercure de France, 1937)

Bochner, Jay, *Blaise Cendrars: discovery and re-creation* (Toronto, University of Toronto Press, 1978)

Bogacz, T.W., '"Sassoon and Company": Siegfried Sassoon's journey to modernity in the Great War', PhD thesis, University of California at Berkeley, 1982

'"A Tyranny of words": language, poetry, and antimodernism in England in the First World War', *Journal of Modern History*, 58 (1986), pp. 643–68

Bohnke-Kollwitz, Jutta (ed.), *Die Tagebücher* (Berlin, Siedler Verlag, 1989)

Boissier, P., *Histoire du Comité international de la Croix-Rouge*. Vol. I: *De Solférino à Tsoushima* (Paris, Plon, 1963)

Bollème, G., *Les almanachs populaires aux xviiè et xviiiè siècles* (Paris, Mouton, 1971)

La bibliothèque bleue. Littérature populaire en France du xviiè au xixè siècles (Paris, Julliard, 1971)

'Littérature populaire et littérature de colportage au xviiiè siècle', in F. Furet (ed.), *Livre et société* (Paris, Mouton, 1965), pp. 61–92

Bond, F.B., *The hill of vision* (Boston, Marshall Jones, 1919)

Love beyond the veil. An echo of the Great War (London, Cassell, 1924)

Bonzon, T., 'Transfer payments', in J.L. Robert and J.M. Winter, *Paris, London, Berlin. Capital cities at war, 1914–1919* (Cambridge, Cambridge University Press, forthcoming), chapter 10

Borg, A., *War memorials from antiquity to the present* (London, Leo Cooper, 1991)

Borg, D.R., *The Old Prussian Church and the Weimar Republic: a study in political adjustment, 1917–1927* (Hanover, NH, University Press of New England, 1984)

Bowlby, J., 'Processes of mourning', *International Journal of Psychoanalysis*, 42 (1961), pp. 317–40

'Pathological mourning and childhood mourning', *Journal of the American Psychoanalytic Association*, 11 (1963), pp. 500–41

Bracco, Rosa, *Merchants of hope. Middlebrow writers of the First World War* (Oxford, Berg, 1993)

Bradbury M. and McFarlane, J., 'The name and nature of modernism', in M. Bradbury and J. McFarlane (eds.), *Modernism 1890–1930* (Harmondsworth, Penguin Books, 1976)

Brandon, R., *The spiritualists. The passion for the occult in the nineteenth and twentieth centuries* (London, Weidenfeld & Nicolson, 1983)

Brecht, Bertolt, *Gesammelte Werke in acht Bänden* vol. IV (Frankfurt, Suhrkamp, 1967)

Brett, Vladimir, *Henri Barbusse, sa marche vers la clarté, son mouvement Clarté* (Prague, Editions de l'Académie Tchécoslovaque des sciences, 1963)

Bridgewater, Patrick, *The German poets of the First World War* (London, Croom Helm, 1985)

Poet of expressionist Berlin. The life and work of Georg Heym (London, Libris, 1991)

Brieger, L., *Ludwig Meidner, Junge Kunst*, vol. IV (Leipzig, Klinkhardt and Biermann, 1919)

Brockhaus, C., 'Die ambivalente Faszination der Grossstadterfahrung in der deutschen Kunst des Expressionismus', in H. Meixner and S. Vietta (eds.), *Expressionismus: sozialer Wandel und kunstlerische Erfahrung* (Munich, Wilhelm Fink, 1982)

Brownlow, Kevin, *The war, the west and the wilderness* (New York, Secker and Warburg, 1979)

Abel Gance's Napoleon (London, British Film Institute, 1980)

Buck-Morss, Susan, *The dialectics of seeing. Walter Benjamin and the Arcades project* (Cambridge, MA, MIT Press, 1991)

Buenger, B.C., 'Max Beckmann's *Ideologues*: some forgotten faces', *Art Bulletin*, 71, 3 (1989), pp. 464–8

'Max Beckmann in the First World War', in R. Rumold and O.K. Werckmeister a(eds.), *The ideological crisis of expressionism. The literary and artistic German War Colony in Belgium 1914–1918*, Studies in German Literature, Linguistics and Culture, vol. 51 (Columbia, SC, Camden House, 1990), pp. 237–75

Bushaway, Bob, 'Name upon name: the Great War and remembrance', in Roy Porter (ed.), *Myths of the English* (Cambridge, Polity Press, 1992), pp. 136–67

Calinescu, M., *Five faces of modernity: modernism, avant-garde, decadence, kitsch, postmodernism* (Durham, NC, Duke University Press, 1987)

Campbell, Phyllis, 'The angelic leaders', *Occult Review*, 22, 2 (August 1915), pp. 76–82

Back of the Front (London, George Newnes, 1916)

Cannadine, David, 'War and death, grief and mourning in modern Britain', in J. Whaley (ed.), *Mirrors of mortality. Studies in the social history of death* (London, Europa Publications, 1981), pp. 187–219

Carline, R., *Stanley Spencer at war* (London, Faber, 1978)

Carrington, Hereward, *Psychical phenomena and the war* (New York, Dodd, Mead & Co, 1918)

Caute, D., *Communism and French intellectuals* (London, Macmillan, 1964)

Ceadel, M., *Pacifism in Britain 1914–1945. The defining of a faith* (Oxford, Oxford University Press, 1980)

Cendrars, Blaise, *La main coupée* (Paris, Denoël, 1946)

Oeuvres complètes (8 vols., Paris, Denoël, 1964)

Lice, trans. by Nina Rootes (London, Peter Owen, 1973)

Chaline, N.-J. (ed.), *Chrétiens dans la première guerre mondiale* (Paris, Les Editions du Cerf, 1993)

Chefdor, M., Quinones, R., and Wachtel, A. (eds.), *Modernism. Challenges and perspectives* (Urbana, University of Illinois Press, 1986)

Chesneau, Albert, *Essai de psychocritique de Louis-Ferdinand Céline* (Paris, Minard, 1971)

Chevalier, Louis, *Labouring classes and dangerous classes in Paris during the first half of the nineteenth century*, trans. F. Jellinek (London, Routledge, 1973)

Chickering, Roger, *We who feel most German. A study of the Pan-German League* (London, Allen & Unwin, 1984)

Cholvy, Gérard, 'Un saint populaire? La lente renaissance du culte de Saint-Roch dans le diocèse de Montpellier durant la première moitié du xixè siècle', in G. Cholvy (ed.), *Béziers et le Biterrois* (Montpellier, Faculté des lettres de Montpellier, 1971)

(ed.), *Béziers et le Biterrois* (Montpellier, Faculté des lettres de Montpellier, 1971)

'Expressions et évolution du sentiment religieux populaire dans la France du xixè siècle au temps de la Restauration Catholique (1801–60)', *Actes du 99è congrès national des sociétés savantes* (1976), vol. I, pp. 289–320

'Réalités de la religion populaire dans la France contemporaine', in Bernard Ploneron (ed.), *La religion populaire dans l'occident chrétien* (Paris, Bibliothèque Beauchesne, 1976), pp. 155–6

Cholvy, Gérard and Hilaire, Yves-Marie, *Histoire religieuse de la France contemporaine 1880/1930* (Paris, Privat, 1986)

Christian, W.A., 'Tapping and defining new power: the first months of visions at Ezquioga, July 1931', *American Ethnologist*, 14 (1987), pp. 140–66

Clark, Suzanne, *Sentimental modernism. Women writers and the revolution of the word* (Bloomington, IN, Indiana University Press, 1991)

Clements, K.W., 'Baptists and the outbreak of the First World War', *Baptist Quarterly* (April 1975)

Cocteau, Jean, *Thomas l'imposteur* (Paris, Gallimard, 1923)

Cole, J., 'Demobilization', in J.L. Robert and J.M. Winter, *Paris, London, Berlin. Capital cities at war, 1914–1919* (Cambridge, Cambridge University Press, forthcoming) chapter 7

Collins, Ross, 'Propaganda and control of the press in France during World War I', PhD dissertation, University of Cambridge, 1990

Comini, Alessandra, 'Kollwitz in context', in Elizabeth Prelinger, *Käthe Kollwitz* (New Haven, Yale University Press, 1992), pp. 89–108

Conzelmann, Otto, *Der andere Dix – Sein Bild vom Menschen und vom Kriege* (Stuttgart, Klett-Cotta, 1983)

Corbin, Alain, *Archaïsme et modernité en Limousin au xixè siècle 1845–1880* (Paris, Rivière, 1975), vol. I, p. 185

Couffignal, R., *L'inspiration biblique dans l'oeuvre de Guillaume Apollinaire* (Paris, Minard, 1966)

Cross, Tim (ed.), *The lost voices of World War I* (London, Bloomsbury, 1988)

Crouch, M. and Huppauf, B. (eds.), *Essays on mortality* (Sydney, University of New South Wales, 1985)

Cru, Jean Norton, *Témoins. Essai d'analyse et de critique des souvenirs de combattants édités en français de 1915 à 1928* (Nancy, Presses Universitaires de Nancy, 1993 edn)

Cruickshank, J., *Variations on catastrophe. Some French responses to the Great War* (Oxford, Oxford University Press, 1982)

'Le culte de l'UNC pour nos camarades morts', *La Voix du Combattant*, 13 November 1921

Curl, James Stevens, *A celebration of death* (London, Constable, 1980)

Daniel, Joseph, *Guerre et Cinéma. Grandes illusions et petits soldats 1895–1971* (Paris, Armand Colin, 1972)

d'Anvers, V., 'Parlementarisme et cinéma', *La cinématographie française*, 27 December 1919

Davidhach, J.C., 'The novelist as prophet: a new look at Franz Werfel's *Höret die Stimme*', *Modern Austrian Literature*, 24 (1991), pp. 51–67

Davidson, J., 'Le mythe du "vieil homme" et de la "nouvelle génération": relation entre l'émancipation et la première guerre mondiale dans les oeuvres d'I.B. Singer (1904–1981)', in J.J. Becker, *et al.*, *Guerre et cultures* (Paris, Armand Colin, 1994), pp. 358–73

Day, Barbara Ann, 'Napoleonic art (1830–1835): from the religious image to a new secular reality', PhD dissertation, University of California, Irvine, 1986

Day, P.S., 'Imagination et parodie dans *Voyage au bout de la nuit*', *Australian Journal of French Studies*, 13 (1976)

Delaney, J.J. (ed.), *A woman clothed with the sun: eight great apparitions of Our Lady in modern times* (New York, Doubleday, 1960)

Delaporte, Sophie, 'Les blessés de la face de la grande guerre', Maîtrise, Jules Verne Université de Picardie, 1992

de Man, Paul, *Blindness and insight. Essays in the rhetoric of contemporary criticism* (Minneapolis, University of Minnesota Press, 1983)

Demetz, P., *Italian futurism and the German literary avant garde* (London, University of London, 1987)

Demm, Eberhard, 'Propaganda and caricature in the First World War', *Journal of Contemporary History*, 28 (1993), pp. 163–92

'The battle of the cartoonists: German, French and British caricatures in World War I', unpublished paper

Denis, Léon, 'A Père Lachaise', *Revue spirite* (April 1918)

'Sursum, corda', *Revue spirite* (July 1918)

'L'avenir du spiritisme', *Revue spirite* (November 1918)

Deonna, W., 'La recrudescence des superstitions en temps de guerre et les statues à clous', *L'anthropologie*, 27 (1916), pp. 243–68

Deppe, Wolfgang G., Middleton, Christopher, and Schönherr, Herbert (eds.), *Ohne Hass und Fahne: Kriegsgedichte des 20. Jahrhunderts* (Hamburg, Rowohlt, 1977)

Devlin, Judith, *The superstitious mind. French peasants and the supernatural in the nineteenth century* (New Haven, Yale University Press, 1987)

Dogliani, Patricia, 'Les monuments aux morts de la grande guerre en Italie', *Guerres mondiales et conflits contemporains*, 167 (1992), pp. 87–94

Domansky, E., 'Der Erste Weltkrieg', in Lutz Niethammer *et al.*, *Bürgerliche Gesellschaft in Deutschland. Historische Einblicke, Fragen, Perspektiven* (Frankfurt, Fischer Taschenbuch Verlag, 1990), pp. 285–319

'Die gespaltene Erinnerung', in M. Köppen (ed.), *Kunst und Literatur nach*

Auschwitz (Berlin, Erich Schmidt Verlag, 1993), pp. 178–96

Dorgelès, R., *Le retour des morts* (Paris, Michel Albin, 1926)

Doty, C. Stewart, *From cultural rebellion to counterrevolution: the politics of Maurice Barrès* (Athens, OH, Ohio University Press, 1976)

Doyle, A. Conan, *The new revelation and the vital message* (London, Hodder & Stoughton, 1919)

The history of spiritualism (London, Cassell, 1926)

Dube, W.-D., *Expressionists and expressionism*, trans. J. Emmons (Geneva, Skira, 1983)

'On the "Resurrection"', in C. Schulz-Hoffmann and J.C. Weiss (eds.), *Max Beckmann retrospective* (Munich and New York Prestel, 1984)

Dülmen, Richard van, 'Der deutsche Katholizismus und der Erste Weltkrieg', *Francia*, 2 (1974), pp. 347–76

Dupront, Alphonse, *Du sacré. Croisades et pèlerinages. Images et langages* (Paris, Gallimard, 1988)

Durand, André, *Histoire du Comité international de la Croix-Rouge*. Vol. II: *De Sarajevo à Hiroshima* (Geneva, Institut Henry-Dunant, 1978)

Durand, R., and Meurant, J. (eds.), *Préludes et pionniers. Les précurseurs de la Croix-Rouge 1840–1860* (Geneva, Société Henry Dunant, 1991)

Eberle, M., *World War I and the Weimar artists: Dix, Grosz, Beckmann, Schlemmer*, trans. J. Gabriel (New Haven, Yale University Press, 1985)

Edelman, Nicole, 'Les tables tournantes arrivent en France', *L'Histoire*, 75 (1985), pp. 16–23

'Allan Kardec, prophète du spiritisme', *L'Histoire*, 98 (1987), pp. 62–9

'L'histoire du spiritisme en France 1850–1914', state thesis, Université de Paris-VII (1992)

Ehrlich, V., 'The dead hand of the future: the predicament of Vladimir Mayakovsky', *American Slavic and East European Review* (1962), pp. 433–40

Eisenstein, Elizabeth, *The printing press as an agent of change*, 2 vols. (Cambridge, Cambridge University Press, 1979)

Eksteins, Modris, *Rites of spring. The modern in cultural history* (New York, Bantam Books, 1989)

Eliel, Carol S., *The apocalyptic landscapes of Ludwig Meidner* (Munich, Prestel, 1991)

'Les paysages apocalyptiques de Ludwig Meidner', in *Figures du moderne. L'expressionnisme en Allemagne, 1905–1914* (Paris, Musée de l'art moderne de la ville de Paris, 1991)

Eliot, T.S., 'Ulysses, order and myth', in Frank Kermode (ed.), *Selected prose of T.S. Eliot* (New York, Harcourt Brace Jovanovich, 1975)

Ellis, M.H., *The torch. A picture of legacy* (Sydney, Angus and Robertson, 1957)

Expressionism: a German intuition, 1905–1920 (New York, Guggenheim Museum, 1980)

Expression and engagement. German painting from the collection (Liverpool, Tate Gallery, 1990)

Eysteinsson, Astradur, *The concept of modernism* (Ithaca, NY, Cornell University Press, 1990)

Fagan-King, Julia, 'United on the threshold of the twentieth-century mystical ideal: Marie Laurencin's integral involvement with Guillaume Apollinaire and the inmates of the Bateau Lavoir', *Art History*, 11 (1988), pp. 88–114

Faulkner, Peter, *Modernism* (London, Methuen, 1977)

Fescourt, H., *La foi et les montagnes* (Paris, Paul Montel, 1959)

Ffoulkes, Charles, *Arms and the Tower* (London, John Murray, 1939)

Field, Frank, *Three French writers and the Great War* (Cambridge, Cambridge University Press, 1975)

'Karl Kraus, Bernard Shaw and Romain Rolland as opponents of the First World War', in P. Scheichl and E. Timms (eds.), *Karl Kraus in neuer Sicht* (Munich, Fertigsatz, 1986), pp. 158–73

British and French writers of the First World War. Comparative studies in cultural history (Cambridge, Cambridge University Press, 1991)

Figgis, J.N., *Hopes for English religion* (London, Longman, Green & Co., 1919)

Figures du moderne. L'expressionnisme en Allemagne, 1905–1914 (Paris, Musée de l'art moderne de la ville de Paris, 1991)

Fitzgerald, F. Scott, *Tender is the night* (London, Penguin, 1965 edn)

F. Scott Fitzgerald's screenplay for Three Comrades by Erich Maria Remarque, ed. M.J. Bruccoli (Carbondale, Southern Illinois University Press, 1978)

Flavell, M. Kay, *George Grosz. A biography* (New Haven, Yale University Press, 1988)

Fletcher, Angus, *Allegory* (Ithaca, New York, Cornell University Press, 1964)

Fokkema, D.W., *Literary history, modernism and postmodernism* (Amsterdam, John Benyaminus Publishing Co., 1984)

Fontana, J., *Les catholiques français pendant la grande guerre* (Paris, Les Editions du Cerf, 1990)

Foret, Joseph (ed.), *L'apocalypse* (Paris, J. Foret éditeur, 1961)

Fortes, Meyer, *Kinship and the social order. The legacy of Lewis Henry Morgan* (Chicago, Aldine, 1969)

Frank, R., 'Eine bitte', *Mitteilungen von Ihrer Firma und Ihrer Kollegen* (Stuttgart, n.p., 13 November 1915)

Freud, Sigmund, 'Mourning and melancholia', in *Collected papers*, trans. by Joan Riviere (London, Hogarth Press, 1950), vol. IV, pp. 152–70

Friedlander, S., 'Themes of decline and end in nineteenth-century imagination', in S. Friedlander (ed.), *Visions of apocalypse* (London, Holmes & Meier, 1985), pp. 61–83

Friedlander, S., Holton, G., Marx, L., and Skelnikoff, E. (eds.), *Visions of apocalypse. End or rebirth* (London, Holmes & Meier, 1985)

Friedrich, Ernst, *War against war!* (Seattle, The Real Comet Press, 1987), with an introduction by D. Kellner to a facsimile edition of the original

Frossard, Odile, *Fonds de l'imagerie d'Epinal*. 48J (Epinal, Archives Départementales des Vosges, 1988)

Frye, Northrop, *Fearful symmetry. A study of William Blake* (Princeton, Princeton University Press, 1947)

The anatomy of criticism (Princeton, Princeton University Press, 1957)

Spiritus mundi. Essays on literature, myth and society (Bloomington, Indiana University Press, 1976)

Fuller, John, *Troop morale and popular culture in the British and Dominion armies in the First World War, 1914–1918* (Oxford, Oxford University Press, 1990)

Fuller, J.O., *Blavatsky and her teachers* (London, Theosophical Publishing House, 1988)

Furet, F. (ed.), *Livre et société* (Paris, Mouton, 1965)

Fussell, Paul, *The Great War and modern memory* (Oxford, Oxford University Press, 1975)

Gance, A., *J'accuse. D'après le film* (Paris, La Lampe Merveilleuse, 1922)
    Prisme (Paris, Editions de la N.R.F., Gallimard, 1930)
Garmier, Jacques, *Hommage à mon ombre* (Macon, Protat Frères, 1916)
Garton, Janet, *Facets of European modernism. Essays in honour of James McFarland presented to him on his 65th birthday, 12 December 1985* (Norwich, University of East Anglia, 1985)
Gassen, R.W. and Holeczek, B. (eds.), *Apokalypse: Ein Prinzip Hoffnung?* (Ludwigshafen, Wilhelm-Hack-Museum, 1985)
Geare, W.D., *Letters of an Army Chaplain* (London, W. Gardner, 1918)
Gellner, Ernest, 'Ideal language and kinship structure', *Philosophy of Science*, 24 (1957), pp. 235–41
    'The concept of kinship', *Philosophy of Science*, 27 (1960), pp. 187–204
George, Henri, 'Hansi et l'imagerie d'Epinal', *Le Papier Ancien* (1953), pp. 14–16
    'The Ghost in the machine', *Observer*, 6 February 1989
Gildea, J., *For remembrance and in honour of those who lost their lives in the South African War 1899–1902* (London, Eyre & Spottiswode, 1911)
Gillis, John (ed.), *Commemoration: the politics of national identity* (Princeton, Princeton University Press, 1993)
Giono, Jean, *Le grand troupeau* (Paris, Gallimard, 1931)
Giroud, Jean, *Les monuments aux morts dans le Vaucluse* (L'Isle sur Sorgue, Editions Scriba, 1991)
Goddard, Lieutenant George, 'Orthodoxy and the war', *Occult Review*, 27, 2 (February 1918), p. 84
Goodrich, Norma, L., 'Jean Giono's new Apocalypse text: "Le grand théâtre" (1960)', *French Review*, 43 (1966), pp. 116–25
    Giono. Master of fictional modes (Princeton, Princeton University Press, 1973)
Goody, J. (ed.), *The character of kinship* (Cambridge, Cambridge University Press, 1973)
Gordon, D.E., *Expressionism. Art and idea* (New Haven, Yale University Press, 1987)
Gorer, G., *Death, grief and mourning in contemporary Britain* (London, Cresset, 1965)
Gray, Anna, 'Will Longstaff's *Menin Gate at Midnight*', *Journal of the Australian War Memorial*, 12 (1988), pp. 64–78
Greenberg, Clement, 'Modernist painting', in Geoffrey Battock (ed.), *The new art: a critical anthology* (New York, E.P. Dutton, 1966)
    Art and culture (London, Thames & Hudson, 1973)
    'Beginnings of modernism', in Chefdor, M., Quinones, R., and Wachtel, A. (eds.), *Modernism. Challenges and perspectives* (Urbana, University of Illinois Press, 1986), pp. 17–24
Gregory, Adrian, *The Silence of Memory* (Oxford, Berg, 1994)
Griessbach, Fritz (ed.), *Walter Flex. Aus dem Nachlass: eine Dokumentation* (Kiel, Orion-Heimreiter, 1978)
Grochowiak, T., *Ludwig Meidner* (Recklinghausen, Aurel Bongers, 1966)
Grohmann, W., *Paul Klee: drawings* (London, Thames & Hudson, 1960)
Güse, E.-G., *Das Frühwerk Max Beckmanns – zur Thematik seiner Bilder aus den Jahren 1904–1914* (Frankfurt, M.P. Lang, 1977)
Halifax, Viscount (Wood, C.L.), *'Raymond'. Some criticisms* (London, A.R. Mowbray, 1917)
Halliday, J.D., *Karl Kraus, Franz Pfemfert and the First World War* (Passau,

Andreas-Haller-Verlag, 1986)

Hamburger, M., and Middleton C. (eds.), *Modern German poetry* (New York, Grove Press, 1964)

Hammer, Karl, 'Der deutsche Protestantismus und der Erste Weltkrieg', *Francia*, 2 (1974), pp. 398–414

Harries, M. and S., *The war artists. British official war art of the twentieth century* (London, Imperial War Museum, 1980)

Haskell, F., 'Art & the apocalypse', *New York Review of Books*, 15 July 1993, pp. 25–9

Haxthausen, C.W., 'Beckmann and the First World War', in C. Schulz-Hoffmann and J.C. Weiss (eds.), *Max Beckmann retrospective* (Munich and New York, Prestel, 1985)

Haynes, R., *The Society for Psychical Research 1882–1982. A history* (London, Macdonald, 1982)

Hecht, J., 'Utopian socialism and population', in M.S. Teitelbaum and J.M. Winter (eds.), *Population and resources in Western intellectual traditions* (Cambridge, Cambridge University Press, 1988)

Heibel, Yule F., '"They danced on volcanoes": Kandinsky's breakthrough to abstraction, the German avant-garde and the eve of the First World War', *Art History*, 12 (1989), pp. 342–61

Helias, Pierre-Jakez, *Le cheval d'orgueil. Mémoires d'un Breton du pays bigoudin* (Paris, Plon, 1975)

Helias, Yves, *Les monuments aux morts. Essai de sémiologie du politique* (Rennes, Mémoire pour le Diplôme d'Etudes approfondes d'Etudes Politiques, 1977)

Heller, Erich, *The disinherited mind. Essays in modern German literature and thought* (New York, Farrar, Strauss & Cudahy, 1957)

Hergott, F., 'The early Rouault', in F. Hergott and S. Whitfield, *Georges Rouault. The early years 1903–1920* (London, Royal Academy of Arts, 1993)

Hergott, F. and Whitfield, S., *Georges Rouault. The early years 1903–1920* (London, Royal Academy of Arts, 1993)

Hervouin, R., 'A Monsieur Abel Gance', *Le Courrier Cinématographique*, 10 May 1919, p. 10

Hibberd, D., *Wilfred Owen: the last year, 1917–1918* (London, Constable, 1992)

Hill, J. Arthur (ed.), *Letters from Sir Oliver Lodge. Psychical, religious, scientific, personal* (London, Cassell, 1932)

Hindenburg, Paul von, *Out of my life*, trans. F.A. Holt (London, John Murray, 1920)

Hoberg, A., 'Gabriele Munter – une artiste du Blaue Reiter', in *Figures du moderne. L'expressionnisme en Allemagne, 1905–1914* (Paris, Musée de l'art moderne de la ville de Paris, 1991), pp. 296–308

Hoffmann, Detlef, 'Die Weltkriegssammlung des Historischen Museums Frankfurt', in *Ein Krieg wird ausgestellt. Die Weltkriegssammlung des Historischen Museums (1914–1918). Themen einer Ausstellung. Inventarkatalog* (Frankfurt, Dezernat für Kultur und Freizeit, 1976)

Holroyd, Michael, *Bernard Shaw*. Volume III: *1918–1950. The lure of fantasy* (London, Chatto & Windus, 1991)

Homberger, Eric, 'The story of the Cenotaph', *The Times Literary Supplement*, 12 November 1976, pp. 1429–30

Horowitz, Mardi J., 'A model of mourning: change in schemas of self and other', *Journal of the American Psychoanalytic Association*, 38, 2 (1990), pp. 297–324

Hughes, Ted, *Rain-charm for the Duchy and other Laureate poems* (London, Faber and Faber, 1992)

Hull, I.V., *The entourage of Kaiser Wilhelm II, 1888–1918* (Cambridge, Cambridge University Press, 1982)

Huppauf, Berdt, 'War and death: the experience of the First World War', in M. Crouch and B. Huppauf (eds.), *Essays on mortality* (Sydney, University of New South Wales, 1985), pp. 65–86

Huss, Marie-Monique, 'The popular postcard and French pronatalism in the First World War', in R. Wall and J.M. Winter (eds.), *The upheaval of war. Family, work and welfare in Europe 1914–1918* (Cambridge, Cambridge University Press, 1988)

Hussey, C., *The life of Sir Edwin Lutyens* (London, Antique Collectors' Club, 1950)

Huyssens, Andreas, *After the great divide: modernism, mass culture, postmodernism* (Bloomington, IN, Indiana University Press, 1986)

Hynes, Samuel, *A war imagined. The First World War and English culture* (London, Bodley Head, 1991)

Ignatieff, M., 'Soviet war memorials', *History Workshop*, 17 (1984), pp. 157–63

Imperial War Graves Commission, 6th Report, 1926

Inglis, Ken, 'A sacred place: the making of the Australian War Memorial', *War & Society*, 3, 2 (1985), pp. 99–125

'War memorials: ten questions for historians', *Guerres mondiales et conflits contemporains*, 167 (1992), pp. 5–22

'World War One memorials in Australia', *Guerres mondiales et conflits contemporains*, 167 (1992), pp. 51–8

'The homecoming: the war memorial movement in Cambridge, England', *Journal of Contemporary History*, 27, 4 (1992), pp. 583–606

'Entombing unknown soldiers: from London and Paris to Baghdad', *History and Memory*, 5 (1993), pp. 7–31

'The rite stuff', *Eureka Street*, 4 (1994), pp. 23–7

Inglis, Ken and Phillips, Jock, 'War memorials in Australia and New Zealand: a comparative survey', in J. Rickard and P. Spearritt (eds.), *Packaging the past? Public histories*, special issue of *Australian Historical Studies* (April 1991)

Ingram, Rex, *The four horsemen of the Apocalypse* (London, Pathé, 1922)

Jacaret, Gilberte, *La dialectique de l'ironie et du lyrisme dans 'Alcools' et 'Calligrammes' de G. Apollinaire* (Paris, A.G. Nizet, 1984)

Jackson, Harriet, 'Widows and pensions in France 1870–1940', PhD thesis, New York University, forthcoming

James, Montague Rhodes, *The Apocalypse in art* (London, Oxford University Press, 1931)

Jamet, C., 'Oxford and Cambridge College war memorials', MLitt dissertation, University of Cambridge, 1993

Jarrett, D., *The sleep of reason. Fantasy and reality from the Victorian age to the First World War* (London, Weidenfeld & Nicolson, 1988)

Jay, Martin, *Force fields. Between intellectual history and cultural critique* (London, Routledge, 1991)

Jeanne, René and Ford, Charles, *Abel Gance* (Paris, Editions seghers, 1963)

Jeffery, Keith, 'The Great War in modern Irish memory', paper delivered to the XXth conference of Irish historians, 6 June 1991

Jenkins, J., 'War, theology, 1914 and Germany's *Sonderweg*: Luther's heirs and patriotism', *Journal of Religious History*, 15 (June 1989), pp. 292–310

Joachimides, C.M. (ed.), *German art in the 20th century. Painting and sculpture 1905–1985* (London, Prestel-Verlag, 1985)

Jones, E.H., *The road to En-dor, being an account of how two prisoners of war at Yozgad in Turkey won their way to freedom* (London, Bodley Head, 1919)

Jones, Kevin I., *Conan Doyle and the spirits. The spiritualist career of Sir Arthur Conan Doyle* (Wellingborough, Aquarium, 1989)

Joulet, R., *Epinal. Images de mille ans d'histoire* (Epinal, ADV, 1950)

Judd, Alan, *Ford Madox Ford* (London, Collins, 1990)

Jünger, Ernst, *Storm of steel*, trans. B. Creighton (London, Chatto & Windus, 1929)

Jungk, P.S., *A life torn by history. Franz Werfel 1890–1945*, trans. A. Hollo (London, Weidenfeld & Nicolson, 1990)

Kahn, E.L., *The neglected majority, 'Les camoufleurs', art history and World War I* (Langham, MD, University Press of America, 1984)

'Art and the front, death imagined and the neglected majority', *Art History* (June 1985), pp. 192–208

Kandinsky, W., *Concerning the spiritual in art*, trans. M.T.H. Sadler (New York, Dover, 1977)

Kandinsky, W. and Marc, F. (eds.), *The Blaue Reiter Almanac*, trans. H. Falkenstein (New York, The Viking Press, 1974)

Karcher, E., *Otto Dix, 1891–1964. Leben und Werk* (Cologne, Benedikt Taschen, 1988)

Karl, Frederick, *Modern and modernism: the sovereignty of the artist, 1885–1925* (New York, Atheneum, 1985)

Kavanagh, Gaynor, 'Museum as memorial: the origins of the Imperial War Museum', *Journal of Contemporary History*, 23 (1988), pp. 77–97

Kavanagh, P.J. (ed.), *Collected poems of Ivor Gurney* (Oxford, Oxford University Press, 1982)

Kearns, Martha, *Käthe Kollwitz: woman and artist* (New York, The Feminist Press, 1976)

Kennedy, G.K.A. Studdard, *The hardest part* (London, Hodder & Stoughton, 1918)

Kermode, F., 'Word in the desert', *Critical Quarterly*, 10 (1968), pp. 14–38

'Apocalypse and the modern', in S. Friedlander, Gerald Holton, Leo Marx, *et al.* (eds.), *Visions of Apocalypse. End or rebirth* (London, Holmes & Meier, 1985), pp. 84–106

Keynes, J.M., *The economic consequences of the peace* (London, Macmillan, 1919)

Kimbell, Charles, 'The ex-service movement in England and Wales, 1916–1930', PhD thesis, Stanford University, 1990

King, Alex, 'The politics of meaning in the commemoration of the First World War in Britain', PhD thesis, University College London, 1993

Kipling, R., *Prose selections*, ed. C. Raine (London, Faber, 1987)

Klein, M., 'Mourning and its relationship to manic-depressive states', *International Journal of Psychoanalysis*, 21 (1940), pp. 125–53

Knowledge, Richard, 'Tale of an "Arabian Knight": the T.E. Lawrence effigy', *Church Monuments*, 6 (1991), pp. 68–76

Kollwitz, Hans (ed.), *The diary and letters of Kaethe Kollwitz*, trans. by R. and C. Winston (Evanston, IL, Northwestern University Press, 1955)

Köppen, Manuel (ed.), *Kunst und Literatur nach Auschwitz* (Berlin, Erich Schmidt Verlag, 1993)

Kosseleck, Reinhart, 'Kriegerdenkmale als Identitadtsstiftungen der Uberleben- den', in Odo Marquard and Karlheinz Stierle (eds.), *Identität* (Munich, Wilhelm Fink Verlag, 1979), pp. 237–76

'Der Einfluss der beiden Weltkriege auf das soziale Bewusstsein', in Wolfram Wette (ed.), *Der Krieg des kleinen Mannes. Eine Militärgeschichte von unten* (Munich, Piper, 1992), pp. 324–43

'Bilderverbot. Welches Totengedenken?', *Frankfurter Allgemeine Zeitung*, 8 April 1993

Krahmer, Catherine, *Käthe Kollwitz – in Selbstzeugnissen und Bilddokumenten* (Hamburg, Rowohlt, 1981)

Kraus, K., *Werke, V. Die letzten Tage de Menschheit. Tragodie in funf Akten mit Vorspiel und Epilog*, ed. Heinrich Fischer, (Munich, Kosel-Verlag, 1957)

The last days of mankind, trans. and ed. by F. Ungar (New York, Frederick Ungar Publishing Co., 1974)

In these great times, ed. H. Zohn, (Manchester, Carcanet Press, 1984)

Kriegel, Annie, *Aux origines du communisme français* (Paris, Presses universitaires de France, 1963)

Kristeva, J., *Powers of horror. An essay on abjection*, trans. L.S. Roudiez (New York, Columbia University Press, 1982)

Black sun. Depression and melancholia, trans. L.S. Roudiez (New York, Columbia University Press, 1989)

Krumeich, G., *Jeanne d'Arc à travers l'histoire* (Paris, Albin Michel, 1993)

Kselman, Thomas A., *Miracles & prophecies in nineteenth-century France* (New Brunswick, Rutgers University Press, 1983)

Kyrou, Ado, *Le surréalisme au cinéma* (Paris, Le Terrain Vague, 1963)

Lackner, S., 'Max Beckmann's mystical pageant of the world', in C. Schulz-Hoffmann and J.C. Weiss (eds.), *Max Beckmann Retrospective* (Munich and New York, Prestel, 1985)

Max Beckmann (New York, Abrams, 1991)

Lambert, L., 'Les mystères d'Outre-Tombe', *L'Art funéraire et commémoratif*, 12 (April 1920)

Lang, L., *Expressionist book illustration in Germany 1907–1927*, trans. J. Seligman (London, Thames and Hudson, 1976)

Lankheit, K., 'A history of the Almanac', in W. Kandinsky and F. Marc (eds.), *The Blaue Reiter Almanac*, trans. H. Falkenstein (New York, The Viking Press, 1974)

Laroche, Julian, 'Le retour des vainqueurs', *Revue Spirite* (February 1919), p. 62

Larronde, Carlos (ed.), *Anthologie des écrivains français morts pour la patrie* (Paris, Librairie Larousse, 1916)

Laurentin, René and Durand, Albert, *Pontmain. Histoire authentique* (3 vols., Paris, Apostolat des Editions, Lethiellex, 1970)

Lawrence, D.H., *Kangaroo* (London, William Heinemann, 1923)

Leed, Eric J., *No man's land. Combat and identity in World War I* (Cambridge, Cambridge University Press, 1979)

Le Goff, J. and Rémond, R. (eds.), *Histoire de la France religieuse*, vol. IV (Paris, Seuil, 1993)

Leistner, G., *Idee und Wirklichkeit. Gehalt und Bedeutung des urbanen Expressionismus in Deutschland, dargestellt am Werk Ludwig Meidners* (Frankfurt, Peter Lang, 1986)

Lerner, Jeffrey, 'The public and private management of death in Britain, 1890–1930', PhD thesis, Columbia University, 1981

Levenson, Michael H., *A genealogy of modernism: a study of English literary doctrine, 1908–1922* (Cambridge, Cambridge University Press, 1984)

Levin, Harry, 'What was modernism?', in his *Refractions: essays in contemporary literature* (New York, Oxford University Press, 1966)

Levine, F.S., *The Apocalyptic vision. The art of Franz Marc as German expressionism* (New York, Harper & Row, 1979)

Lifton, Robert Jay, *Death in life. The survivors of Hiroshima* (New Haven, Yale University Press, 1968)

Little, R., *Guillaume Apollinaire* (London, The Athlone Press, 1976)

Lloyd, David, 'Tourism, pilgrimage and the commemoration of the Great War in Great Britain, Australia and Canada, 1919–1939', PhD dissertation, University of Cambridge, 1995

Lloyd, Jill, *German expressionism. Primitivism and modernity* (New Haven, Yale University Press, 1991)

   'The painted city as nature and artifice', in Irit Rogoff (ed.), *The divided heritage. Themes and problems in German modernism* (Cambridge, Cambridge University Press, 1992)

Lodge, Oliver J., *Raymond or life and death. With examples of the evidence for survival of memory and affection after death* (London, Methuen, 1916)

   'Personal appearances of the departed', *Journal of the Society for Psychical Research*, 18 (February–March 1918), pp. 32–4

   'Effects of light on long ether waves and other processes', *Journal of the Society for Psychical Research*, 18 (February–March 1918), pp. 213–20

   Past years. An autobiography (London, Hodder & Stoughton, 1931)

Löffler, F., *Otto Dix. Leben und Werk* (Dresden, Verlag der Kunst, 1977)

Longworth, Philip, *The unending vigil* (London, Constable, 1967)

Lutyens. The work of the English architect Sir Edwin Lutyens (1869–1944) (London, Arts Council, 1981)

Lutyens, A., *Sir Edwin Lutyens. An appreciation in perspective* (London, Country Life Ltd, 1942)

Lyons, Mark, *Legacy. The first fifty years* (Clayton, Victoria, Lothian, 1978)

Mabire, Jean-Marie, 'Entretien avec Philippe Soupault', *Etudes Cinématographiques*, 38–9 (1965), p. 29

MacFadyen, D., *Our mess: mess table talks in France* (London, W. Westall & Co., 1920)

Machen, Arthur, *The Bowmen and other legends of the war* (New York, G.P. Putnams Sons, 1915)

McKendrick, N. and Outhwaite, R.B. (eds.), *Business life and public policy. Essays in honour of D.C. Coleman* (Cambridge, Cambridge University Press, 1986)

McLeod, H., *Religion and the people of Western Europe 1789–1970* (Oxford, Oxford University Press, 1981)

McManners, John, *Church and state in France 1870–1914* (London, SPCK, 1972)

Maeterlinck, M., *The wrack of the storm*, trans. by A. Teixeira de Mattos (London, Methuen, 1916)

Magri, S., 'Housing', in J.-L. Robert and J.M. Winter, *Paris, London, Berlin. Capital cities at war, 1914–1919* (Cambridge, Cambridge University Press, forthcoming)

Maier, C., *Recasting bourgeois Europe* (Princeton, Princeton University Press, 1974)

Mann, T., *The magic mountain*, trans. H.T. Lowe-Porter (New York, Alfred Knopf, 1980 ed.)

Marchant, James (ed.), *Life after death according to Christianity and spiritualism* (London, Cassell, 1925)

Marquard, Odo and Stierle, Karlheinz (eds.), *Identität* (Munich, Wilhelm Fink Verlag, 1979)

Marrin, A., *The Church of England in the First World War* (Raleigh, NC, 1974)

Marrus, Michael, 'Culture on the move: pilgrims and pilgrimages in nineteenth-century France', *Stanford French Review*, 1 (1977), pp. 206–12

Marsland, Elizabeth, *The nation's cause. French, English and German poetry of the First World War* (London, Routledge & Kegan Paul, 1991)

Marz, R., 'L'expressionnisme dans la métropole de 1910 à 1914', in *Figures du moderne. L'expressionnisme en Allemagne, 1905–1914* (Paris, Musée de l'art moderne de la ville de Paris, 1991)

Mass-Observation, *A puzzled people. A study in popular attitudes to religion, ethics, progress and politics in a London borough* (London, Victor Gollancz, 1947)

Mathews, B. (ed.), *Christ: and the world at war* (London, James Clarke & Co., 1917)

Mayeur, J.-M., 'Le catholicisme français et la première guerre mondiale', *Francia*, 2 (1974), pp. 377–97

Mayo, James M., *War memorials as political landscape: the American experience and beyond* (New York, Praeger, 1984)

Mazars, P., 'Surréalisme et cinéma contemporain: prolongements et convergences', *Etudes cinématographiques*, 40–2 (1965), p. 177

Meidner, L., 'Anleitung zum Malen von Grossstadtbildern', *Kunst und Künstler*, 12 (1914), pp. 312–14

Im Nacken das Sternemeer (Leipzig, Kurt Wolff, n.d. [1918]), pp. 26–7

'Vision des apokalyptischen Sommers', *Septemberschrei: Hymnen, Gebete, Lasternungen* (Berlin, Paul Cassirer, 1920)

Meixner, H., and Vietta, S. (eds.), *Expressionismus: sozialer Wandel und kunstlerische Erfahrung* (Munich, Wilhelm Fink, 1982)

Melzer, Annabelle, 'Guerre et spectacle', unpublished paper, Historial de la grande guerre, 1992

Mercier, Charles A., *Spiritualism and Sir Oliver Lodge* (London, Mental Culture Enterprise, 1917)

Merkblatt für Kriegerehrungen. Herausgegeben am 1. Juli 1915 vom Landesverein Sächsischer Heimatschutz (Dresden, Bauamtmann Kurt Hager, 1917)

Mews, S., 'Religion and English society in the First World War', PhD thesis, University of Cambridge, 1973

Miesel, V.H. (ed.), *Voices of German expressionism* (Englewood Cliffs, New Jersey, Prentice-Hall, 1970)

Miles, Eustace, 'Britain beyond the grave', *Occult Review*, 23, 1 (January 1918), p. 39

Mistler, J., *Epinal et l'imagerie populaire* (Paris, Hachette, 1961)

Mitry, Jean, *Histoire du cinéma. Art et industrie*. Vol. II. *1915–1925* (Paris, Editions universitaires, 1969)

Monaco, Paul, *Cinema and society: France and Germany during the twenties* (New York, Elsevier, 1976)

Le monument aux morts de Mulhouse (Mulhouse, 1927)

Moriarty, C., 'Christian iconography and First World War memorials', *Imperial War Museum Review*, 6 (1991), pp. 63–75

Moses, J.A., 'State, war, revolution and the German Evangelical Church, 1914–18', *Journal of Religious Studies*, 17 (1992), pp. 47–59

Mosès, Stéphane, *L'ange de l'histoire* (Paris, Seuil, 1992)

Mossa, Gustave Adolf, *L'oeuvre symboliste 1903–1918* (Nice, n.p., 1992)

Mosse, George, *The nationalization of the masses* (New York, Howard Fertig, 1985)

　Towards the final solution: a history of European racism (Madison, WI, University of Wisconsin Press, 1985)

　Fallen soldiers. Reshaping the memory of the world wars (New York, Oxford University Press, 1990)

La muse de sang (Paris, Librairie du Travail, 1926)

Nadeau, Maurice, *The history of surrealism*, trans. by R. Howard (Cambridge, MA, Harvard University Press, 1989)

Needham, Rodney, 'Descent systems and ideal language', *Philosophy of Science*, 27 (1960), pp. 96–101

Niethammer, Lutz, Frevert, Ute, Medick, Hans, *et al.*, *Bürgerliche Gesellschaft in Deutschland. Historische Einblicke, Fragen, Perspektiven* (Frankfurt, Fischer Taschenbuch Verlag, 1990)

Nietzsche, F., *Thus spake Zarathustra*, trans. W. Kaufmann (Harmondsworth, Penguin Books, 1978)

Nora, Pierre (ed.), *Les lieux de mémoire* (7 vols., Paris, Gallimard, 1984–92)

O'Brien-Twohig, Sarah, 'Max Beckmann', in C.M. Joachimides, N. Rosenthal, and W. Schmidt (eds.), *German art in the 20th century. Painting and sculpture 1905–1985* (London, Prestel-Verlag, 1985)

　Max Beckmann's carnival (The Tate Gallery, Liverpool, 1991)

O'Donnell, Elliott, 'Hauntings in Belgium', *Occult Review*, 21, 4 (April 1915), pp. 223–31

Oppenheim, J., *The other world. Spiritualism and psychical research in England, 1850–1914* (Cambridge, Cambridge University Press, 1984)

Otto Dix 1891–1961 (London, Tate Gallery, 1992)

Owen, Alex, *The darkened room. Women, power and spiritualism in late nineteenth century England* (Cambridge, Cambridge University Press, 1989)

Owen, Harold, *Journey from obscurity* (Oxford, Oxford University Press, 1968)

Paraf, P., 'Les carnets de guerre d'Henri Barbusse, I–II', *Les lettres françaises*, 636–7 (13–19 September 1956), pp. 1, 5, and (20–26 September 1956), pp. 1, 5

　'Avant le feu . . . l'aurore – Henri Barbusse, l'enfant, l'adolescent, le jeune homme, d'après des documents inédits', *Les lettres françaises*, 685 (1957)

Paret, P., *The Berlin Secession: modernism and its enemies in Imperial Berlin* (Cambridge, MA, Harvard University Press, 1980)

Paris par image d'Epinal (Paris, Musée Carnavalet, 1990)

Parkes, C.M., *Bereavement. Studies of grief in adult life* (London, Tavistock Publications, 1972)

Parkes, C.M. and Weiss, R.S., *Recovery from bereavement* (New York, Basic Books, 1983)

Parsons, I.M. (ed.), *Men who march away* (London, Chatto & Windus, 1966)

Patrides, C.A. and Wittreich, J. (eds.), *The Apocalypse in English renaissance thought and literature. Patterns, antecedents and repercussions* (Manchester, Manchester University Press, 1984)

Pauwels, Louis and Breton, Guy, *Nouvelles histoires extraordinaires* (Paris, Albin Michel, 1982)

Pedersen, Susan, 'Social policy and the reconstruction of the family in Britain and France, 1900–1945', PhD thesis, Harvard University, 1989

Family, dependence, and the origins of the welfare state: Britain and France 1914–1945 (Cambridge, Cambridge University Press, 1993)

Percy, Clayre, and Ridley, Jane (eds.), *The letters of Edwin Lutyens to his wife Lady Emily* (London, Collins, 1985)

Perl, Jeffrey M., *The tradition of return. The implicit history of modern literature* (Princeton, Princeton University Press, 1984)

Perry, N. and Echeverria, L., *Under the heel of Mary* (London, Routledge, 1988)

Pick, D., *Faces of degeneration. A European disorder, c.1848–c.1918* (Cambridge, Cambridge University Press, 1989)

Pierrot, J., *The decadent imagination 1880–1900*, trans. D. Koltman (Chicago, University of Chicago Press, 1981)

Pitt-Rivers, Julian, 'The kith and the kin', in J. Goody (ed.), *The character of kinship* (Cambridge, Cambridge University Press, 1973)

Ploneron, Bernard (ed.), *La religion populaire dans l'occident chrétien* (Paris, Bibliothèque Beauchesne, 1976)

Les poètes contre la guerre. Anthologie de la poésie française 1914–1919, with an introduction by Romain Rolland (Geneva, Editions du Sablier, 1920)

Poirrier, P., 'Pouvoir municipal et commémoration: l'exemple du monument aux morts de Dijon', *Annales de Bourgogne*, 61 (1989), pp. 141–54

Polyptyques. Le tableau multiple du moyen âge au vingtième siècle (Paris, Musée du Louvre, 1990)

Pope, Barbara Corrado, 'Immaculate and powerful: the Marian revival in the nineteenth century', in Clarissa W. Atkinson, Constance H. Buchanan, and Margaret R. Miles (eds.), *Immaculate and powerful. The female in sacred image and social reality* (Wellingborough, Crucible, 1987)

Pope, D., 'French advertising men and the American "Promised Land"', *Historical Reflections*, 5, 1 (1978), pp. 117–39

Porcher, Yves, 'La fouille des champs d'honneur. La sépulture et des soldats de 14–18', *Terrain. Carnets du patrimoine ethnologique*, 20 (1993), pp. 37–56

Les jours de guerre. La vie des Français au jour de jour entre 1914 et 1918 (Paris, Plon, 1994)

Pornon, Charles, *L'écran merveilleux. Le rêve et le fantastique dans le cinéma français* (Paris, La nef de Paris, n.d.)

Porter, Roy (ed.), *Myths of the English* (Cambridge, Polity Press, 1992)

Pound, Ezra, 'Hugh Selwyn Mauberley', in *Collected shorter poems* (London, Faber and Faber, 1962)

Prater, D.A., 'Stefan Zweig and Franz Werfel', *Modern Austrian Literature*, 24 (1991), pp. 85–8

Prelinger, Elizabeth, *Käthe Kollwitz* (New Haven, Yale University Press, 1992)

Probst, Volker G., *Bilder vom Tode. Eine Studie zum deutschen Kriegerdenkmal in der*

Weimarer Republik am Beispiel des Pietà-Motives und seiner profanierten Varianten (Hamburg, Wayasbah, 1986)

Prost, Antoine, *Les anciens combattants et la société française 1914–1939* (3 vols., Paris, Fondation nationale des sciences politiques, 1977. One-volume edition published by Gallimard in 1987)

'D'une guerre mondiale à l'autre', in M. Ozouf (ed.), *La mémoire des Français. Quarante ans de commémorations de la seconde guerre mondiale* (Paris, Editions du CNRS, 1984), pp. 26–9

'Les monuments aux morts', in P. Nora (ed.), *Les lieux de mémoire*. Vol I. *La République* (Paris, Gallimard, 1984), pp. 195–225

'Verdun', in P. Nora (ed.), *Les lieux de mémoire*. Vol II. *La nation* (Paris, Gallimard, 1986), pp. 188–233

In the wake of war. Anciens combattants and French society 1914–1940, trans. H. MacPhail (Oxford, Berg, 1992)

'Les représentations de la guerre dans la culture française de l'entre-deux-guerres', *Vingtième siècle*, 41 (1994), pp. 23–31

Pym, T.W. and Gordon, G., *Papers from Picardy by two chaplains* (London, Constable, 1917)

Read, Herbert, *Collected poems* (London, Faber and Faber, 1966)

Rebérioux, M., 'Le mur des Fédérés. Rouge "sang craché"', in P. Nora (ed.), *Les lieux de mémoire* (Paris, Gallimard, 1984), vol. I, pp. 619–49

Remarque, Erich Maria, *All quiet on the Western Front*, trans. A.W. Wheen (London, G.P. Putnam's Sons, 1929)

Renn, Ludwig, *War*, trans. W. and E. Muir (London, Martin Secker, 1929)

Rey, Jean-Philippe, 'Desvallières et la guerre de 1914–1918', *Bulletin de la Société Historique de l'Art Français* (1988), pp. 197–211

Richet, C., 'Les événements psychiques de la guerre. Un appel de M. Charles Richet aux soldats. "Avez-vous des pressentiments?"', *Annales des Sciences Psychiques* (October, November, December 1916), pp. 185–92

'L'enquête du prof. Richet sur les faits psychiques de la guerre', *Annales des sciences psychiques* (January 1917), p. 21

Thirty years of psychical research. Being a treatise on metaphysics, trans. by S. de Brath (London, W. Collins Sons, 1923)

Rickard, J. and Spearritt, P. (eds.), *Packaging the past? Public histories*, special issue of *Australian Historical Studies* (April 1991)

Riegel, Léon, *Guerre et littérature. Le bouleversement des consciences dans la littérature romanesque inspirée par la Grande Guerre (littératures française, anglo-saxonne et allemande 1910–1930* (Paris, Editions Klincksieck, 1978)

Ringbom, Sixten, 'Art in "the epoch of the Great Spiritual". Occult elements in the early theory of abstract painting', *Journal of the Warburg and Courtauld Institutes*, 29 (1966), p. 412

The sounding cosmos. A study of the spiritualism of Kandinsky and the genesis of abstract painting. Acta academiae Aboensis, Series A, Humaniora, vol. 38, no. 2 (Abo, Abo Akademi, 1970), pp. 50–3

Rivé, P., Becker, A., Pelletier, O., *et al.* (eds.) *Monuments de mémoire. Les monuments aux morts de la première guerre mondiale* (Paris, Mission permanente aux commémorations et à l'information historique, 1991)

Robert, D., 'Les Protestants français et la guerre de 1914–1918', *Francia*, 2 (1974), pp. 415–30

Robert, J.-L., 'Paris, London and Berlin in 1914', in J.-L. Robert and J.M. Winter, *Paris, London, Berlin. Capital cities at war, 1914–1919* (Cambridge, Cambridge University Press, forthcoming)

Robert, J.-L. and Winter, J.M., *Paris, London, Berlin. Capital cities at war, 1914–1919* (Cambridge, Cambridge University Press, forthcoming)

Rogoff, Irit (ed.), *The divided heritage. Themes and problems in German modernism* (Cambridge, Cambridge University Press, 1992)

Röhl, J.C.G. and Sombart, N. (eds.), *Kaiser Wilhelm II. New interpretations* (Cambridge, Cambridge University Press, 1982)

Roques, Remi, 'Monuments aux morts du sud-est de la France', *Provence Historique*, 21 (1981), pp. 247–62

Roters, E., 'Big-city expressionism: Berlin and German expressionism', in *Expressionism: A German intuition, 1905–1920* (New York, Guggenheim Museum, 1980)

Rouaud, Jean, *Champ d'honneur* (Paris, Les Editions de Minuit, 1990)

Georges Rouault – André Saurès Correspondance (Paris, Gallimard, 1960)

Rouault, Georges, *Miserere: nouvelle édition augmentée de texte et commentaires*, with commentaries by F. Chapon and C.-R. Marx (Paris, Editions Le Léopard d'or, 1991)

Roure, Lucien, 'Superstitions du front de guerre', *Etudes*, 153 (1917), pp. 720–38

Rowley, Brian A., 'Anticipations of modernism in the age of romanticism', in Janet Garton, *Facets of European modernism. Essays in honour of James McFarland presented to him on his 65th birthday, 12 December 1985* (Norwich, University of East Anglia, 1985)

'The Royal Academy War Memorials Committee', *Architectural Review*, 45 (January 1919), p. 20

Rumold, R. and Werckmeister, O.K. (eds.), *The ideological crisis of expressionism. The literary and artistic German war colony in Belgium 1914–1918*, Studies in German Literature, Linguistics and Culture, vol. 51 (Columbia, SC, Camden House, 1990)

Ryan, C.J., *H.P. Blavatsky and the theosophical movement* (Pasadena, CA, Theosophical University Press, 1975)

Sadoul, Georges, *Histoire du cinéma mondial. Des origines à nos jours* (Paris, Flammarion, 1949)

Dictionnaire des films (Paris, Editions du Seuil, 1968)

Samuel, R. and Thomas, R. Hinton, *Expressionism in German life, literature and the theatre (1910–1924)* (Cambridge, W. Heffer & Son, 1939)

Santucci, J.A., *Theosophy and the Theosophical Society* (London, Theosophical History Centre, 1985)

Sassoon, Siegfried, *Collected poems* (London, Faber and Faber, 1947)

Poet's pilgrimage (London, Collins, 1973)

Schama, Simon, *Landscape and memory* (New York, Knopf, 1995)

Scheichl, P. and Timms, E. (eds.), *Karl Kraus in neuer Sicht* (Munich, Fertigsatz, 1986)

Scheyer, E., 'Briefe Ludwig Meidners an Franz Landsberger', *Schlesien*, 16 (1971)

Schmalenback, Fritz, *Käthe Kollwitz* (Berlin, J.F. Steinkopf, 1990)

Schmidt, D., *Otto Dix im Selbstbildnis* (Berlin, Henschelverlag, 1978)

Schmied, W. (ed.), *Zeichen des Glaubens. Geist der Avantgarde: religiöse Tendenzen in der Kunst des 20. Jahrhunderts* (Stuttgart, Electa/Klett-Cotta, 1980)

Schneidau, H.N., *Waking giants. The presence of the past in modernism* (Oxford, Oxford University Press, 1991)

Schoenberg, B., Gruber, I., Wiener, A., *et al.* (eds.), *Bereavement: its psychosocial aspects* (New York, Columbia University Press, 1975)

Schubert, Dietrich, *Otto Dix in Selbstzeugnissen und Bilddokumenten* (Reinbeck bei Hamburg, Rowolt-Taschenbuch Verlag, 1980)

Schulz-Hoffmann, C. and Weiss, J.C. (eds.), *Max Beckmann retrospective* (Munich and New York, Prestel, 1985)

Scruggs, J.C. and Swerdlow, J.L., *To heal a nation. The Vietnam Veterans' Memorial* (New York, Praeger, 1985)

Scully, Vincent, 'The terrible art of designing a war memorial', *New York Times*, 14 July 1991, Arts & Leisure, p. 28

Architecture: the natural and the man-made (New York, St. Martins Press, 1991)

Shaw, George Bernard, *What I really wrote about the war* (London, Constable, 1931)
Collected plays with their prefaces (London, The Bodley Head, 1972)

Sheppard, R. (ed.), *Expressionism in focus* (Blairgowrie, Scotland, Lochee Publications Ltd, 1987)

Sherman, Daniel J., 'Les inaugurations et la politique', in P. Rivé, .A. Becker, O. Pelletier, *et al.* (eds.), *Monuments de mémoire. Les monuments aux morts de la première guerre mondiale* (Paris, Mission permanente aux commémorations et à l'information historique, 1991), pp. 277–83

'The discourse of art and the business of memory: monuments in interwar France', in John Gillis (ed.), *Commemoration: the politics of national identity* (Princeton, Princeton University Press, 1994)

Shils, Edward, *Tradition* (Chicago, University of Chicago Press, 1981)

Silkin, Jon (ed.), *The Penguin Book of First World War poetry* (London, Allen Lane, 1979)

Silver, Kenneth E., *Esprit de corps. The art of the Parisian avant-garde and the First World War, 1914–1925* (London, Thames & Hudson, 1989)

Silver, Ken, 'Jean Cocteau and the *Image d'Epinal*: an essay on realism and naiveté', in Arthur King Peters (ed.), *Jean Cocteau and the French scene* (New York, Adam Press, 1984)

Skocpol, Theda, *Protecting soldiers and mothers: the political origins of social policy in the United States* (Cambridge, MA, Harvard University Press, 1992)

Smith, E. Hilmer, *History of the Legacy Club of Sydney* (Sydney, Waite and Bull, 1944)

Soby, J.T., *Georges Rouault* (New York, Arno Press, 1972)

Sperber, J., *Popular Catholicism in nineteenth-century Germany* (Princeton, Prince-ton University Press, 1984)

Stallworthy, J. (ed.), *The complete poems and fragments of Wilfred Owen* (London, Chatto & Windus, 1983)

The Oxford book of war poetry (Oxford, Oxford University Press, 1988)

Stanley Spencer 1851–1959 (London, Arts Council, 1976)

Stanley Spencer. The passion. (Edinburgh, Scottish National Gallery of Modern Art, 1986)

Stamp, Gavin, *Silent cities* (London, Royal Institute of British Architects, 1977)

Stang, S.J. (ed.), *The presence of Ford Madox Ford. A memorial volume of essays, poems, and memoirs* (Philadelphia, University of Pennsylvania Press, 1981)

Stark, M., '"The murder of modernism": some observations on research into expressionism and the post-modernism debate', in R. Sheppard, (ed.), *Expressionism in focus* (Blairgowrie, Scotland, Lochee Publications Ltd, 1987), pp. 27–46

Steiner, G., *Language and silence* (Harmondsworth, Penguin Books, 1979 edn)

Steiner, R., *Goethes Weltanschauung* (Weimar, E. Felber, 1897)

   Theosophy (London, Kegan Paul Trench, 1908)

   Theosophie: Einführung in übersinnliche Welterkenntnis und Menschenbestimmung (Leipzig, Altmann, 1920)

Stern, J.P., 'Karl Kraus and the idea of literature', *Encounter* (August 1975), pp. 37–48

   'Expressionism', in *Expression and engagement. German painting from the collection* (Liverpool, Tate Gallery, 1990)

Stieglitz, Anne, 'The reproduction of agony: towards a reception-history of Grünewald's Isenheim altar after the First World War', *Oxford Art Journal*, ·12, 2 (1989), pp. 87–114

Stich, Sidra, *Anxious visions* (Berkeley, CA, University of California Press, 1990)

Stitzte, Benno and Matzdorf, Paul, *Eiserne Kreuz-Nagelungen zum Besten der Kriegshilfe und zur Schaffung von Kriegswahrzeichen* (Leipzig, Strauss, 1916)

Stryker, Laurinda, 'Languages of sacrifice and suffering in England in the First World War', PhD dissertation, University of Cambridge, 1989

Sweeney, Regina, 'The Parisian Theater during the First World War', PhD dissertation, University of California at Berkeley, 1992

Symonds, J., *Madame Blavatsky* (London, Odhams, 1959)

Teitelbaum, M.S., and Winter, J.M. (eds.), *Population and resources in Western intellectual traditions* (Cambridge, Cambridge University Press, 1988)

'Témoignages: Abel Gance', *Etudes Cinématographiques*, 38–9 (1965), pp. 36–40

Thébaud, Françoise, 'La guerre et le deuil chez les femmes françaises', in J.-J. Becker, *et al.* (eds.), *Guerre et cultures: vers une histoire culturelle comparée de la première guerre mondiale* (Paris, Armand Colin, 1994), pp. 103–11

Thompson, D., 'The poor law and the elderly in England, 1850–1900', PhD dissertation, University of Cambridge, 1980

Timms, Edward, *Karl Kraus. Apocalyptic satirist. Culture and catastrophe in Habsburg Vienna* (New Haven, Yale University Press, 1986)

Tippett, Maria, *Art at the service of war: Canada, art and the Great War* (Toronto, University of Toronto Press, 1984)

Trullard, M.J., *La Résurrection de Napoléon. Statue érigée par MM Noisot, grenadier de l'Ile d'Elbe et Rude, statuaire à Fixin (Côte-d'Or)* (Dijon, Guasco-Jobard, 1847)

Unruh, Karl, *Langemarck. Legende und Wirklichkeit* (Koblenz, Bernard & Graefe, 1986)

Urang, Susan, *Kindled in the flame. The apocalyptic scene in D.H. Lawrence* (Epping, Bowker Publishing Co., 1983)

Varnedoe, Kirk and Gopnik, Adam, *High and low. Modern art and popular culture* (New York, Harry N. Abrams, 1991)

Venturi, L., *Georges Rouault* (New York, Wylie, 1940)

Vidal, Annette, *Henri Barbusse. Soldat de la paix* (Paris, Editions Français Réunis, 1953)

Villeneuve, Yves, 'Marraines de guerre', *Frères d'armes* (1 July, 15 July, 1 August, 15 October 1917)

   'Vivons pour nos morts de la guerre', *Frères d'armes* (15 November 1919)

Virilio, Paul, *War and cinema. The logistics of perception*, trans. by Patrick Camiller (London, Verso, 1989)

von Dewitz, Bobo and Hoffman, Detlef, 'Christus in aktualisierter Gestalt. Über ein Motiv der Kriegsfotografie von 1914 bis 1954', *Fotogeschichte. Beiträge zur Geschichte und Asthetik der Fotografie*, 2 (1981), pp. 45–58

von Wiese, S., *Max Beckmanns zeichnerisches Werk 1903–1925* (Düsseldorf, Droste Verlag, 1978)

Wall, R. and Winter, J.M. (eds.), *The upheaval of war. Family, work and welfare in Europe 1914–1918* (Cambridge, Cambridge University Press, 1988)

Waller, C., *Expressionist poetry and its critics* (London, University of London, 1986)

Ward, J.S.M., *Gone west* (London, W. Rider & Son, 1919)

  A subaltern in spirit land. A sequel to 'Gone west' (London, W. Rider & Son, 1920)

Warnier, Raymond, 'Blaise Cendrars, voyageur et prophète: évocation de l'ère cubiste', *Marginales*, 16, 78 (1961), pp. 47–50

Weber, Eugen, *Peasants into Frenchmen. The modernization of rural France* (Stanford, Stanford University Press, 1976)

Weintraub, Stanley, *Journey to Heartbreak. The crucible years of Bernard Shaw 1914–1918* (New York, Weybright and Talley, 1971)

Wellek, René, *Discriminations: further concepts of criticism* (New Haven, Yale University Press, 1970)

Werckmeister, O.K., *The making of Paul Klee's career, 1914–1920* (Chicago, University of Chicago Press, 1989)

Werfel, Franz, *Jeremias: höret die Stimme* (Frankfurt, S. Fischer Verlag, 1956)

Westheim, Paul, *Für und wider: kritische Anmerkungen zur Kunst der Gegenwart* (Potsdam, G. Klepenheuer, 1923)

Wette, Wolfram (ed.), *Der Krieg des kleinen Mannes. Eine Militärgeschichte von unten* (Munich, Piper, 1992)

Whalen, R., *Bitter wounds. German victims of the Great War 1914–1939* (Ithaca, NY, Cornell University Press, 1984)

Whitfield, S., 'An outrageous lyricism', in F. Hergott and S. Whitfield, *Georges Rouault. The early years 1903–1920* (London, Royal Academy of Arts, 1993), pp. 11–14

Whittick, Arnold, *War memorials* (London, Country Life Ltd, 1954)

Wiedmann, A., *Romantic roots in modern art. Romanticism and expressionism: a study in comparative aesthetics* (London, Gresham Books, 1980)

Wilenski, R.H., *The Modern Movement in Art* (New York, Frederick A. Stokes, 1927)

Wilkinson, A., *The Church of England and the First World War* (London, SPCK, 1978)

Williams, Raymond, *The politics of modernism. Against the new conformists* (London, Verso, 1989)

Wilson, J.M., *Charles Hamilton Sorley: a biography* (London, Cecil Woolf, 1985)

Wilson, S. (ed.), *Saints and their cults. Studies in religious sociology, folklore and history* (Cambridge, Cambridge University Press, 1983)

Winter, J.M., *Socialism and the challenge of war* (London, Routledge, 1974)

  The Great War and the British people (London, Macmillan, 1985)

  The experience of World War I (London, Macmillan, 1988)

  'Bernard Shaw, Bertold Brecht and the businessman in literature', in N. McKendrick and R.B. Outhwaite (eds.), *Business life and public policy. Essays in honour of D.C. Coleman* (Cambridge, Cambridge University Press,

1986), pp. 185–204

Wintrebert, M., *Le vitrail dans le Pas-de-Calais* (Arras, Archives du Pas-de-Calais, Imprimerie Centrale de l'Artois, 1989)

Wistrich, R., 'Karl Kraus: Jewish prophet or renegade?', *European Judaism* (1975), pp. 32–8

Wohl, R., 'The generation of 1914 and modernism', in M. Chefdor, R. Quinones, and A. Wachtel (eds.), *Modernism. Challenges and perspectives* (Urbana, University of Illinois Press, 1986), pp. 66–78

Woods, Roger, *Ernst Jünger and the nature of political commitment* (Stuttgart, Akademischer Verlag Hans-Dieter Heinz, 1982)

Wootton, Graham, *The official history of the British Legion* (London, Macdonald & Evans, 1956)

  The politics of influence. British ex-servicemen, Cabinet decisions and cultural change (1917–57) (London, Routledge, 1963)

Worlsey, F.W., *Letters to Mr Britling* (London, R. Scott, 1917)

Young, James E., *The texture of memory. Holocaust memorials and meaning* (New Haven, Yale University Press, 1993)

Zamora, Lois P., *Writing the apocalypse. Historical vision in contemporary U.S. and Latin American fiction* (Cambridge, Cambridge University Press, 1989)

Zohn, H., 'Krausiana. 1. Karl Kraus in English translation', *Modern Austrian Literature*, 3 (1970), pp. 25–35

  'Karl Kraus: "Jüdischer Selbsthasser" oder "Erzjude"', *Modern Austrian Literature*, 8 (1975), pp. 1–19

Zweig, Stefan, *Jeremias. Eine dramatische Dichtung in neun Bildern* (Leipzig, Insel Verlag, 1917)

Zweite, A., 'Kandinsky et le Blaue Reiter', in *Figures du moderne. L'expressionnisme en Allemagne, 1905–1914* (Paris, Musée de l'art moderne de la ville de Paris, 1991), pp. 194–206

Index